Handbook of Mesoamerican Mythology

TITLES IN ABC-CLIO's
Handbooks of World Mythology

Handbook of Arab Mythology, Hasan El-Shamy
Handbook of Celtic Mythology, Joseph F. Nagy
Handbook of Classical Mythology, William Hansen
Handbook of Egyptian Mythology, Geraldine Pinch
Handbook of Norse Mythology, John Lindow

HANDBOOKS OF WORLD MYTHOLOGY

Handbook of Mesoamerican Mythology

Kay Almere Read and Jason J. González

ABC-CLIO
Santa Barbara, California • Denver, Colorado • Oxford, England

Cataloging-in-Publication data is available from the Library of Congress.

ISBN: 0-87436-998-3

06 05 04 03 02 01 00 10 9 8 7 6 5 4 3 2 1

ABC-CLIO, Inc.
130 Cremona Drive, P.O. Box 1911
Santa Barbara, California 93116-1911

This book is printed on acid-free paper ♾.
Manufactured in the United States of America

To Ned and Elizabeth

CONTENTS

PREFACE

Sometime in winter 1997, Kay Read began looking for someone to help her take on this project. Lacking graduate students in her own institution, DePaul University (which focuses on undergraduate teaching), she began inquiring around hoping to find someone somewhere else. One of the people to whom she sent an email message was her own son, Jason González, who, at the time, was finishing up his master's thesis in Maya archaeology at Southern Illinois University (SIU) at Carbondale. Describing the project, she then asked if he knew of a graduate student who might be interested in helping out. A single little line was fired back almost instantly: "I'm a graduate student." And so began a rather fruitful mother-son collaboration, particularly good because, although both of us have traveled extensively and often to Mesoamerica, each of us focuses on different areas.

Kay's training is in art education, history of religions, and ethnohistory, with a special, although not exclusive, focus on the pre-Conquest Mexica (Aztecs). Jason has taught introductory courses at SIU and is trained in the archaeological branch of anthropology, focusing primarily (although again, not exclusively) on the pre-Conquest Maya. We split up the work according to our strengths. Kay has done the bulk of the writing (although certainly not all); Jason has used his computer skills to set up the data, graphic, and long-distance communication programs necessary to the project (because we live six hours apart, and his mother is a computer klutz); and we both have worked on the research. Since that fateful email message, Kay has continued teaching in DePaul's Religious Studies Department; but Jason completed his master's, moved on to the Ph.D. program, and then entered the dissertation stage. We're both really happy this volume is finished, and we have appreciated the chance to delve into mythological topics drawn from such a broad scope of places and times. We also have found working together fun (except for those moments when, as with all families, we drove each other a little nuts). The work, however interesting, has also proven extraordinarily daunting because of its broad scope, covering both a wide geographic area and an enormous time span.

The *Handbook of Mesoamerican Mythology* is meant to serve as a resource introducing teachers, students, and anyone else interested in Mesoamerica to its mythology. The geographic area includes what now is roughly known as Mexico and Central America. In this volume, we have focused primarily on the Mexican Highland and Maya areas, with small forays into Oaxaca and other miscellaneous locations. This was determined partly by the importance of the Mexicans and the Maya to Mesoamerican history, the practical need to limit our scope, and the reality of the kinds of studies available to us. If truth be known, scholars have tended to lavish these two areas (especially the Maya) with a wealth of studies, too often leaving the others underexamined. Our time span begins in the Paleoindian era and moves all the way up to the present—about 25,000 years or more of existence. Our primary focus has been on good stories wherever we could find them: implied in material remains and archaeological artifacts; told on friezes, through sculptures, and in pictures; sung, chanted, related, and expounded in words; retold by travelers, historians, archaeologists, linguists, and ethnographers; or reported by television and newspapers. After all, storytelling constitutes the core activity of myth making.

We have not attempted an exhaustive or deeply analytical study. That would have been both impossible given the project's scope and inappropriate to the readers we hope most to reach. This means we did not make any attempt to delineate conclusively the historical development of the various mythic traditions we address, the diffusion of mythic ideas from one group of people to another, or those mythic traditions that originated in Europe from those exclusively considered native. Such issues are more appropriately addressed in highly detailed, tightly focused studies, which are much better accomplished if they concentrate on a smaller scale and more limited area than that represented by our study.

Instead, our emphasis has been a largely synthetic one, searching for broadly shared themes, loose historical continuities and discontinuities, and that which at least appears mythically similar or distinctive. For this, we are grateful for the hundreds of careful, detailed studies other people have done and upon which we could rely. Of course, not all may agree with the broad strokes with which we paint particular areas and themes. Those may be honest disagreements, representing different but supportable positions, or they may simply be due to our own inadequacies (for which we apologize ahead of time). Moreover, because of the project's breadth, a host of topics have been left unexplored in any depth. Time and time again, we made suggestions or took sides on an issue that could bear more study, including, for example, those mythic continuities and discontinuities that we did happen to at least note. Therefore, we hope the volume serves to encourage more study.

Not the least of other issues that could use more work is the lack of numerous studies outside the Mexican Highlands and Maya areas, both ancient and contemporary. Maya studies, especially, seems to be taking over, and this includes everything from scholarly research to the production of videos and web sites. One might ask why this is so. Is it possible that the field might perhaps be subtly continuing old stereotypes? Until recently, the whole Mesoamerican area was considered "primitive" and therefore incapable of high civilization; it was characterized as nothing more significant than curiously exotic. As late as the third quarter of the twentieth century, scholars argued over whether the Mesoamericans built true cities, a debate that has been brought to a resounding conclusion with the findings that Tenochtitlan held a population of 200,000 or more and that the Maya ceremonial centers also supported high population densities. Moreover, all major centers were structured by highly complex cultural, social, economic, and political patterns. To be on the safe side, we have chosen to use the label "urban-center," but perhaps our definition of "city" needs rethinking. The question we pose is: Does the old primitive label continue to explain the lack of exploration in other, less historically central areas? Do people still think on some level that only the heirs of great centers of civilization deserve deep consideration; that if a community never had any huge pyramids, it's not interesting?

The old primitive label also traditionally split into two contradictory images: either the exotic primitive others were envisioned as brutal and uneducated savages or they were noble folk who retained their inherent human dignity and natural ties to earthly harmony. One might argue that the unfortunate pre-Conquest Mexican Highlanders (especially the Aztecs) received the first image from their interpreters, while the slightly more lucky ancient Maya received the second. Again until the twentieth century's third quarter, it was thought that the Aztecs brutally sacrificed just about everyone in sight, while the peaceful Maya did little else than stare at the sky and create mysterious religious links with all of nature. The Aztecs became hierarchical, urban theocrats, rigidly lording it over all of Mesoamerica, while the Maya were turned into spiritual stargazers, priestly theologians interested only in nature's cycles. Now it is known that this picture simply was not true.

Ancient and contemporary Mexicans and Mayans share more than people used to think. They are both part of a single cultural heritage that has included war and alliance formation; complicated hierarchical and nonhierarchical social relationships; extraordinary sky gazing and scientific and technological developments; complex theologies concerning time and space and the nature of life and death; and deeply embedded sacrificial practices. Yes, the ancient Maya were just as committed as the Aztecs to bloodletting and killing all sorts of plants, animals, and sometimes humans in order to keep the world going properly. This sacrificial tradition reaches back to the Preclassic, predating the Aztecs by a couple of thousand years at least, and forward to the present in well-established but less violent ritual traditions that now often intertwine with Christian sacrificial practices. And examples of large and small ecological disasters can be found among both groups; they (as do humans everywhere) sometimes made and make mistakes where nature is concerned. Does that old rather unfair and unhelpful way of contrasting warlike, savage Aztecs to peaceful, intellectual Maya continue to encourage the currently huge interest in Maya studies, while discouraging a similar interest in the Mexicans? Do we still see the Maya as romantically spiritual and the Mexicans as riddled with rigid religious institutions; have the first become a model for what modern interpreters wish we were, and the second for what we wish we weren't? The authors of this volume hope not.

Another issue that could use more exploration is what some call the "s" word—syncretism. This is the idea that when people mix, their ideas mix. How this clearly common human tendency occurs actually is a highly contested question. We've not attempted to explain how mythic themes move among people, why they change in the ways that they do, or why they retain their continuities with past themes; we've only noted on occasion that these things happen. In some ways, one even could argue that syncretism is an artificial issue. After all, creative, intelligent people all over the world have been exchanging ideas for millennia; ideas rapidly flow among various folk of often enormously different backgrounds, most of whom stubbornly insist on recasting their newly borrowed ideas in their own unique ways and according to their own particular experiences. The sixteenth-century indigenous folk are not really any different on this issue from the Catholic priests who sought their conversion. Each understood the other's tradition from their own perspective, and each altered the other's perspective in significant ways when they re-explained it. Of course, one cannot forget that this was not just a simple encounter between strangers seeking to comprehend each other. One acted to physically and spiritually conquer the other, while the other acted to resist or at least survive both–a hard, usually nasty reality that has continued to shape Mesoamerican mythology for five centuries.

For students of Mesoamerican mythology, this means that we must enter into our studies with a healthy dose of suspicion about those who speak with apparent authority. Everyone's authority (real or assumed) flows at least in part from our own presumptions about a world that others may not share. When a Spaniard explains the Mexica cosmos as layered in thirteen levels reaching up to the source of all existence, one needs to pay close attention to his words that also say the highest deity is like God and the first cause of all, for it sounds suspiciously Christian. Were those thirteen layers really so vertically arranged; was the highest really the first cause? Just because a Nahuatl speaker called the Virgin

Mary "Tonantzin" or "Our Holy Mother" does not mean necessarily that a pre-Christian goddess called Tonantzin existed on the same site before the Virgin; rather the devout simply may have been addressing the new Christian deity in a reverential manner, which continued in part an indigenous form of practice.

The folk or *el Pueblo* have been the greatest contributors to this volume, for we have focused largely on popular mythology. But occasionally, other kinds of myths creep in, those created by intellectuals, scholars, the educated, the well-off, and the powerful. By including such myths, we hope again to break down the dichotomies encouraged by those old primitive categories. All humans make myths, not just those exotics who live a simple spiritual life close to the land; and not all myths are orally related, for many appear first in written form. Much of contemporary mythology about Quetzalcoatl, for example, rests on academic and intellectual written traditions stretching back to the Conquest. And the mythological stories surrounding the historical veracity of the Virgin of Guadalupe have intertwined oral and folk traditions with written, scholarly, and national ones. It would have been both impossible and dishonest to suggest that true mythology appears only in oral form, and never from the mouths of the highly educated. We the authors also have our myths, and we must apologize when, unknowingly, our unexamined ones get in the way of our comprehension of other people's myths. That is the other daunting aspect of this project: how to explain accurately, with some insight and empathy, myths that often seem completely foreign to us.

In the first chapter of this volume we explore myth itself as a general topic, explaining the definition of myth we used to structure the whole project. Since mythology is the topic, it seemed only fair to explain where we're coming from. Throughout this and other chapters, we occasionally provided pronunciation guides to foreign words. These guides do not necessarily use professional linguistic style, which might not be understood by the average lay reader. Moreover, while Kay reads and translates classical Nahuatl and both of us read and speak Spanish, neither of us speaks the hundreds of other indigenous languages of Mesoamerica; this made providing correct pronunciation a challenge and, although we hope not, a mistake or two may have snuck in. The first chapter also offers a quick geographical and historical survey of Mesoamerica from the Paleoindian era to the present and a discussion of some of the challenges and possibilities that structure Mesoamerican studies. In the second chapter we examine history and time itself from a Mesoamerican standpoint, for while the project often assumes a certain historically timed perspective, it is important to realize that numerous Mesoamericans do not share that perspective. We use a very different calendar charting the course of change from the one many, many Mesoamericans have used and continue to use today. The third chapter is an alphabetized collection of selected entries on a variety of ancient and contemporary Mesoamerican deities and other powerful beings. The collection, like the entire project, is not exhaustive. We have tried to include those beings we consider particularly important for one reason or another, but some entries are a bit more idiosyncratic, deities or beings we simply found interesting for some reason. Following these three chapters are an annotated bibliography of selected print and nonprint resources and a glossary, aimed at the uninitiated reader or teacher looking for helpful study aids. Finally, we hope the list of references and the index will help both the uninitiated and initiated to pursue further studies. It was impossible in the encyclopedic format of Chapter 3 to cite every source that helped us structure each entry. Therefore, at the end of each, we list a few key sources that the lay reader will find useful; the rest can be found in the references list.

As always, numerous folk need our thanks for their help in completing this volume, for such projects often take on an air of cooperative teamwork rather than individual accomplishment. Both of us greatly appreciate the friendly services of David Goldstein, without whose excellent research skills this thing might not have been completed. Ceceley Fishman hunted up books and articles, tracked down and reviewed videos (which section she also wrote), sorted through web sites, and cheerfully relieved Kay of such deadly activities as photocopying copious course readings, which gave her a minute or two to actually write. Kay admits that she might have gone quite bananas without both David and Ceceley. Kay also wants to thank her old teacher, Alfredo López Austin, who told her many years ago that she ought to explore more contemporary mythology; his words came instantly to mind when she was asked to do so for this project. Our spouses, Ned Read and Elizabeth Fuller-González, need our thanks for their patience with our unfortunately familiar and probably genetic displays of nerves. We also appreciate Elizabeth for filling in for Jason one spring when he had to take off to Guatemala for an extended period of fieldwork. Grandma Matilda Schwalbach provided support for this "meeting of 'great' minds," and a wonderful quiet hideaway in which to work uninterrupted. Finally, we wish to thank ABC-CLIO for their generous monetary, professional, and overall support of the project, especially Todd Hallman (who has to be the most patient editor we know), Susan McRory (for efficiently handling many last-minute questions and problems), and Liz Kincaid (for helping with our overly enthusiastic reaction toward the illustrations and all resultant problems).

Several excellent resources also need to be noted, both personal and printed. Laura Grillo read and responded helpfully to our definition of myth; Anna Peterson read all of Chapter One and made numerous helpful suggestions especially in the area of contemporary Mesoamerican religious, political, and economic history; and our son-brother Ian Read helped correct and update the final version of the sections on Central American political history. James Halstead kindly read portions, helping us with Church history and technical aspects concerning official Church doctrine. The many excerpts on the Cakchiquel Maya of Panajachel come from an unpublished manuscript, "The World of the Panajachel as Told by its Maya People in 1936 and 1937" by the late Sol Tax. The Native American Educational Services (Chicago) kindly gave us permission to use this absolutely wonderful material. James Brady generously sent us a huge list of sources on caves gathered for his doctoral dissertation, "An Investigation of Maya Ritual Cave Use with Special Reference to Naj Tunich, Peten, Guatemala" (University of California, Los Angeles, 1989). Nicholas Hopkins considerately sent a copy of a paper on Tila, Chiapas, and stories of the Black-Christ that he and Kathryn Josserand presented at the University of Pennsylvania. Andy Hofling generously opened his personal library to us and pointed us in many different directions in our search for various stories. Alan Sandstrom, completely out of the blue, offered us the use of his unpublished but translated transcriptions of contemporary Nahua myths gathered in the course of his own research, asking only to be acknowledged. We can't thank him enough for this rich, invaluable resource. And Max Harris sent us several articles on contemporary folk dances, without which a number of entries would have been far less interesting. Kay would like to thank in particular her Hispanic students in Religions of Native North America (Winter, 1998) who told her some great stories about La Llorona and even gave her a wonderful child's mystery book about La Llorona. Some of the contemporary Nahua cosmological material is drawn partially from Timothy Knab's novel *A War of Witches: A Journey in the Underworld of the Contemporary Aztecs* (HarperCollins, 1995). This material goes unattested in that publication, but is based on his ethnographic work in a Nahua village. A number of delightful conversations Kay held with Tim in Doris Heyden's Mexico City kitchen in summer 1997 confirmed and elaborated on that intricate cosmic vision (the chili rellenos Tim taught Kay to make were darn good too). Doris herself needs to be thanked, for Kay began work on the volume that summer while staying in her middle bedroom, happily raiding her extensive library, and running ideas by this honored grandmother of Mesoamerican mythology.

Kay Read
Jason González
August 2000
"The Bump," Three Lakes, WI

1

INTRODUCTION

Climbing the stairs, I emerged from the bustling, crammed subway station into the subdued light of a summer day in Mexico City's rainy season. The day before at this particular underground stop, a shrine had been dedicated to the Virgencita (Veer´-hen-seeta), the "Little Virgin" (Figure 1). The month before, she had made herself known through a simple water spot that took her shape on the concrete floor of the Hidalgo Metro stop, one of the busiest subway stations in the city's center. But after hundreds of worshipers from all over Mexico so jammed the already crowded station that it became almost impossible to use it for daily travel, the government and the Catholic Church both agreed to create the shrine at a station entrance adjacent to a nearly 500-year-old colonial church. The cement block containing her damp image was removed from the station's floor, placed behind glass, and mounted on the wall of a small arched nook tiled in bright blue, the Virgin's color. Thousands attended the dedication ceremony, ranging from prosperous men and women in business dress to poor folk from Oaxaca (Wa-ha´-ka) dressed in traditional clothing. A government representative spoke at the colorful affair, which was broadcast live on television, and a representative of the Church carefully noted how important the Virgin was to people's faith, without committing either himself or the Church to a genuine miracle. A band even played the appropriate tunes.

As I emerged wondering whether I had found the right entrance, I immediately discovered my way blocked by a long line of quiet worshipers stretching down the street and out of sight. An official stood at the shrine, gently making sure that people took their turn and that no one from the small group crowding around the shrine's front became too pushy. One young man eagerly leaned his camera's telephoto lens as close to the image as he could. Many in the line held an offering of a single rose bought from a woman who had been selling her flowers for years at that same entrance. A couple with two young children waited patiently in the line as it slowly inched toward the shrine. Two peacefully pleased nuns crossed themselves as they left the Virgin's presence.

Figure 1. Shrine of the Virgin of the Metro, Mexico City, 1998 (Kay A. Read)

Known as Guadalupe, the Virgin first appeared here in 1519, enshrined on a banner carried before the small army of Mexico's Spanish conqueror Fernando (Hernán) Cortés. And ever since 1531, when the peasant Juan Diego encountered Guadalupe dressed in her rose-covered blue cape, many Mexicans swear that she has continued to make her presence clear to all those in need whether they be statesmen, warriors, or peasants. In the early twentieth century, Guadalupe led the Mexican revolutionaries (Turner 1974, 105–106, 151–152). And in the summer of 1997, she chose the crowds of a subway station. At the time, the country was floundering in financial crisis. People were suffering, many had failing businesses, and many could not provide an adequate living for themselves or their families. Surely they and the country needed her help as had others many times before in the 500 years since the Conquest.

The Virgin is not the only powerful mythological female in Mesoamerica, for she has sisters in pre-Conquest times who also were mothers, although those maternal figures tended to take somewhat different forms. The Virgin first appeared to a man named Juan Diego on a hill called Tepeyac (Te-pay-yak), which lay just north of Mexico City. The site earlier had been consecrated to an ancient Mexica (Me-shee´-ka) or Aztec[1] deity named Tonantzin (To-nant´-zin), which means "Our Honorable Mother" in Nahuatl (Nah´-wat), the Mexica's language. Thus two honorable mothers, one from the New World and one from the Old, had occupied the same place of worship. Another fifteenth-century Mexica goddess, named Cihuacoatl (See-wa-ko´-wat), or "Snake Woman," was a powerful adviser for mothers-to-be; she also lent her powers to those tilling the land and going to war. Cihuacoatl dressed in the eagle feathers and jaguar blouse of warriors. Both birthing mothers and warriors invoked her presence. Even the second highest political leader in the Mexica domain took Cihuacoatl's name to indicate his advisory power for both agricultural matters and war. He dressed in her garb for high state rituals (*Codex Borbonicus* 1974, fols. 26, 28).

Ancient, pre-Conquest mothers could hold quite a few powers. In the ninth century, the Maya queen, Lady Zak Kuk (Zak-kook´), took office in order to divert the rule of Palenque (Pa-leng´-kay) (a site in today's Chiapas, Mexico) from another genealogical line to her own. Tracing her lineage back to an even older group called the Olmec (Ol´-mek) and to a great goddess archaeologists have fondly named "Lady Beastie," Lady Zak Kuk reigned 60 years before passing the throne to her son Pacal (Pa-kal´). This was a lengthy genealogy, for Lady Beastie was said to have lived at the beginning of time, and the Olmec civilization had died 1,000 years before Lady Zak Kuk and her son even breathed the jungle's air (Schele and Friedel 1990, 221–223).

Although all these potent ladies share motherhood and rely on mythological events for their various extraordinary powers, they have distinctive characters. Lady Zak Kuk and the high political leader who took Cihuacoatl's name were flesh-and-blood figures, whereas others, such as the goddess Cihuacoatl and Guadalupe, are less tangible. For some mythological figures (human or godly), motherhood is the primary power; for others, the ability to bear children is less important than powers in war, state affairs, or agriculture. As evidenced by the commonalities among the goddesses of various Mesoamerican peoples, many myths have been shared throughout time; yet in each era, people also have done things in their own way. Carefully guarded continuity coexists with creative invention in Mesoamerican mythology. And like the myths of these ladies, all Mesoamerican myths combine events that actually happened with events that probably never occurred but that nevertheless are equally important because of their symbolic and metaphorical messages.

This book surveys a wide variety of Mesoamerican myths and mythic beings, primarily focusing on myths of indigenous groups and of the common folk—in other words, those whom Latin Americans refer to as *el pueblo* (el pweb'-lo), "the people." In exploring this rich Mesoamerican world of mythological and metaphorical invention, we first define the nature of myth itself and then discuss the Mesoamericans who made the myths, their worldviews, and their history. This introductory chapter to Mesoamerican mythology is followed by a mythological timeline (Chapter 2) and by an alphabetical presentation of major deities and other powerful beings (Chapter 3). For those wishing further information, Chapter 4 offers an annotated selection of printed resources, and Chapter 5, a selection of films and videos. A glossary can be found at the end of the book. The first time they are introduced, phonetic spellings accompany most foreign names.

MYTHS AND THE REAL WORLD

Like all mythology, Mesoamerican myths cannot be defined simply as false stories, as in "Oh, that's just a myth." When people make such a statement, they usually mean that a particular belief is untrue—for example, the beliefs that toads cause warts, and as Huckleberry Finn thought, that the right incantation said over a dead cat at midnight in a graveyard will get rid of those offending bumps. That definition looks down its nose at old wives' tales, folk stories, and magical rituals because they are not considered either effective or true. But sometimes old wives were smarter than we think, or we hold too narrow a view of truth, or both.

Like myths around the world, Mesoamerican myths are actually true stories, because they describe either explicitly or metaphorically the way people think the actual world really is. But sometimes they describe the actual world in terms that we are not used to, using unusual analogies to model what is true—fantastic creatures doing strange things to impart true messages, or ordinary people acting in extraordinary ways. But in spite of fantastical creatures and extraordinary events, myths are never very far from the actual world. A true story (in that the events really did happen) might illustrate how myth is also true. This story was told in a beginning class in Religious Studies by a student in her first quarter at college.[2]

> When I was very little, I lived on a farm way out in the country. My family was big, so there were always lots of people around, but there were no other children for me to play with, and I got very lonely. So I made up an imaginary friend named Zooma. Zooma was a man who wore a shirt like the repairmen in the TV advertisements for the utility company; it was a grey shirt with two stripes down one side, one yellow and one white. He could climb tall poles just like the repairmen, and was very friendly and helpful. He liked to play every game I wanted to play and he went everywhere with me. At breakfast every day, my Grandfather would ask me, "How is Zooma?" And I would tell him what we had done together.
>
> One day some older cousins came to visit and they made fun of Zooma. They said he wasn't really real and that I was stupid to talk to some imaginary man. I was really hurt at being called a baby, so I killed Zooma. I threw him into the pond. When Grandpa asked how come he hadn't heard about Zooma lately, I told him how I had killed him. Grandpa said that wasn't very nice and he was sorry Zooma was gone. He said, "Why don't you bring him back?" And I said, "You can't bring back someone who's dead!" I felt really sad and guilty then.
>
> Of course, even from the beginning, I knew Zooma wasn't real and that all my play with him was imaginary and my conversations with Grandpa were about something I had made up. It's not that I was stupid. I knew that I hadn't really killed anybody, because I knew he never existed. Still, I really felt like I really had killed him, and I really did feel very guilty and sad about doing that. Zooma was imaginary, but my feelings were not. Besides, he was part of my relationship with my Grandpa, and when I killed him, that part of our relationship was gone, because Grandpa never asked me about Zooma again.

Of course Zooma wasn't real in the sense that this little girl and her grandfather could touch him. But he was real in other ways. First, Zooma came from a true need: the little girl's loneliness and her desire for a friend. Second, he was based on things in the actual world: Television advertisements of utility repairmen who climb poles in grey shirts with two stripes really did exist. Third, Zooma helped build a close relationship between her and a very tangible friend, her grandfather. Fourth, her cousins really had been mean, but they also had spoken some truth. Maybe she hadn't been stupid, but Zooma really was imaginary, and even she knew it. Fifth, the pond really did exist, and someone could drown in it if they fell in—a warning she must have heard a billion times. And finally, the dead really can't be revived—at least, not in the adult world she knew. No wonder she felt real guilt and remorse, not only for her lost friend but for how her world had changed after his death. Even though it was because of him that she had been called a baby, Zooma really did cause her to grow up a little. This true story about an actual little girl's really real imaginary friend points out how myths function metaphorically. Zooma was a mythic being; he was a metaphor, an analogy, an imaginative model for a tangible friend, without being tangible himself. As such, he helped build a tangible friendship between the child and her grandfather, and allowed her to feel actual feelings of guilt and remorse.

Like the personally mythic Zooma, all myths (whether individual or communal) act in and on the tangible world metaphorically. They are at least partially based on actual things without being tangibly real themselves. They express and discuss actual issues and teach real things, even if all the players and events are imaginary. Myths do this because even though actual things happen to us every day of our lives, in order to act at all, we must somehow understand those things and make sense of them. Warts can appear and disappear for no apparent reason, and nocturnal graveyards are scary; little girls on farms really may live in a family with no other children; financial crises hurt both families and individuals; people get conquered; mothers give birth; and pre-Conquest statesmen and rulers run their governments. All that may be tangibly true, but one still needs to understand why and how these things happen and what that means for how one acts now; one must *interpret* events.

The metaphors in myths help us imagine the analogies needed to interpret life's actualities. And by so doing, we can take action to sustain or change them. Young boys can test their courage in graveyards at midnight while trying to get rid of their warts; small girls can gain a little wisdom; people in financial need can find the support to keep going; mothers can gain the courage and knowledge needed to give birth; and statesmen and rulers can devise models for successful rule. Because myths are based on the tangible world, they help us act in that world by allowing us to imaginatively discover the theories by which we can shape our actions.

Mesoamerican myths, like other myths, are true because (a) they describe the tangible world; (b) they explain that tangible world in human terms that make sense to the people telling the stories; (c) by interpreting the tangible world in a humanly meaningful way, they educate, provide guides, offer justification, and give the impetus for real action in the tangible world; and (d) by causing real action, they act back on that tangible world in ways that sometimes confirm the world as it is and at other times transform it by creating new mythic models capable of stimulating new action. Anything that can do these four things is a myth.

Myths come in a wide variety of categories. Zooma was a personal myth, a true story holding special meaning for just one person. But myths also can be communal or social, shared by many people. They can reflect the worldviews of all societal levels, from the privileged to those with fewer advantages. Families have myths, as do clubs, associations, institutions, neighborhoods, cities, and countries. Stories of a school's great football victories are part of its own particular institutional mythology. The legends of George Washington crossing the Potomac River to attack the British and of Father Hidalgo (Ee-dal´-go) crying from his church doors that the Spanish government in Mexico should be overthrown have mythic qualities. They are stories based in fact, which have been embellished by many artists and storytellers because of their heavy symbolic meaning. Often these different categories of myths mesh together in a single context: Medical doctors may find the Virgin of Guadalupe helpful in coping daily with illness and death, tales of a particular medical school's achievements may help its students strive for success in their own lives; and they may learn from the myth of Hidalgo the importance of relieving all human suffering, no matter the sufferer's social class.

Myths also come in many shapes and sizes. Traditionally myths take the form of verbal narratives or stories, tales, and legends. But mythic themes and stories can be imaged, drawn in pictures, carved in stone, embodied by buildings, and "painted" in verse. This is particularly true for Mesoamerica, where stories often have been sung and chanted. In pre-Hispanic times, songsters of myth used books of painted pictures as an integral part of their performances. Many archaeological ruins and ancient sculptures depict mythic themes and stories; the Sun Stone shows among other things the story of the Mexica Five Ages, and ancient temples often show the mythic relationships among the sun, the underworld, and earthly rulers. Mythic themes also can appear in places we don't often think of as mythic, such as theological treatises or the homilies told in church, which refer to beliefs about truth and God. For the thoughts and reasoning therein are based on mythically true stories, such as the sacrifice of Christ, or God's creation of the world. Hence the great Salvadoran martyr Archbishop Oscar Romero moved people to continue resisting oppression, giving them strength in the direst of times with his homilies, because he drew on Biblical myths about the dignity of the downtrodden, liberation, and Christ's own death and resurrection. From the earliest times to the present, Mesoamericans have told myths in many forms and in many styles.

THE MESOAMERICAN MYTHMAKERS

Who Are the Mesoamericans?

The Virgin and her pre-Conquest sisters, Hidalgo, and Archbishop Romero resided (and in some ways still reside) in an area that extends, roughly speaking, from northern Mexico to Nicaragua. In addition to most of Mexico and a part of Nicaragua, this area includes Belize, Guatemala, El Salvador, Honduras, and a bit of Costa Rica (Map 1). Mesoamerican influence also extended to the southwestern

United States at times (Adams 1991, 13–14; Miller and Taube 1993, 9). These boundaries were established by ancient civilizations that predated the Spanish by many thousands of years; in recent times, the independent states have somewhat expanded these territories. Although many different people lived in ancient Mesoamerica, four civilizations were particularly important (Miller and Taube 1993, 10): the Olmec (ca. 1500–1 B.C.), Oaxaca (ca. 600 B.C.–A.D. 521), the Maya (ca. 1500 B.C.–A.D. 1521, and the Central Mexicans (ca. 900 B.C.–A.D. 1521) (see Map 2). The Olmec occupied the Gulf region—today's Veracruz and Tabasco. On Mesoamerica's southern border, near the Pacific coast, lies the mountain valley of Oaxaca. The ancient Maya built their villages and cities primarily in what are now the southern Mexican states of Tabasco, Campeche, Yucatán, Quintana Roo, and Chiapas and the countries of Belize, Guatemala, El Salvador, Honduras, Nicaragua, and Costa Rica. Central Mexicans resided in the high plateaus in and around modern Mexico City. The Mexica (ca. 1350–1521) now are the best known group, although the people living before them in the great city of Teotihuacan (Tay-oh-tee-wa´-kan) (ca. 200 B.C.–650 or A.D. 750) held the farthest-reaching power of anyone in all of pre-Hispanic Mesoamerica; their influence extended all the way from northern Mexico to Guatemala.

Mesoamerica has an extraordinarily diverse geography and climate, ranging from deserts and semiarid zones to mountainous and tropical regions (Map 3). A rugged mountain chain runs along the Pacific side, from Baja California to Nicaragua; another chain borders the eastern, Gulf side. The mountains along the Pacific coast and in the central areas are punctuated by volcanoes, some of which are still active. In the year before the appearance of the Virgin of the Metro, for example, the volcano Popocatepetl (Po-po-ka-te´-pet) was smoking and occasionally blowing ashes over Mexico City. The people living in the village nearest the summit regularly performed rituals to calm the volcano. Earthquakes are also a reality of life in the region. Major temblors have occurred here (most recently, in 1985), and minor shocks are commonplace.

Traveling from the north of Mesoamerica to the southeast, one first encounters a formidable desert lying between the Pacific and the Gulf mountain ranges. From early times until only recently, this desert prevented the growth of complex civilizations in the area; for this reason, it is not a site of Mesoamerican culture, although the mountains bordering it are. Below this desert, large, snowcapped mountains and volcanoes surround the semiarid Basin of Mexico, where Mexico City lies at an altitude of about 8,000 feet. Descending and moving southward from there, one passes through a variety of ecological niches at various altitudes; the thermometer rises as one drops lower. The central and southern coastal areas of both the Gulf and the Pacific Ocean enjoy a tropical climate. In the north of southern Mexico lies the flat Yucatán Peninsula. Its limestone base is clothed in

Map 1 - Modern Nations of Mesoamerica

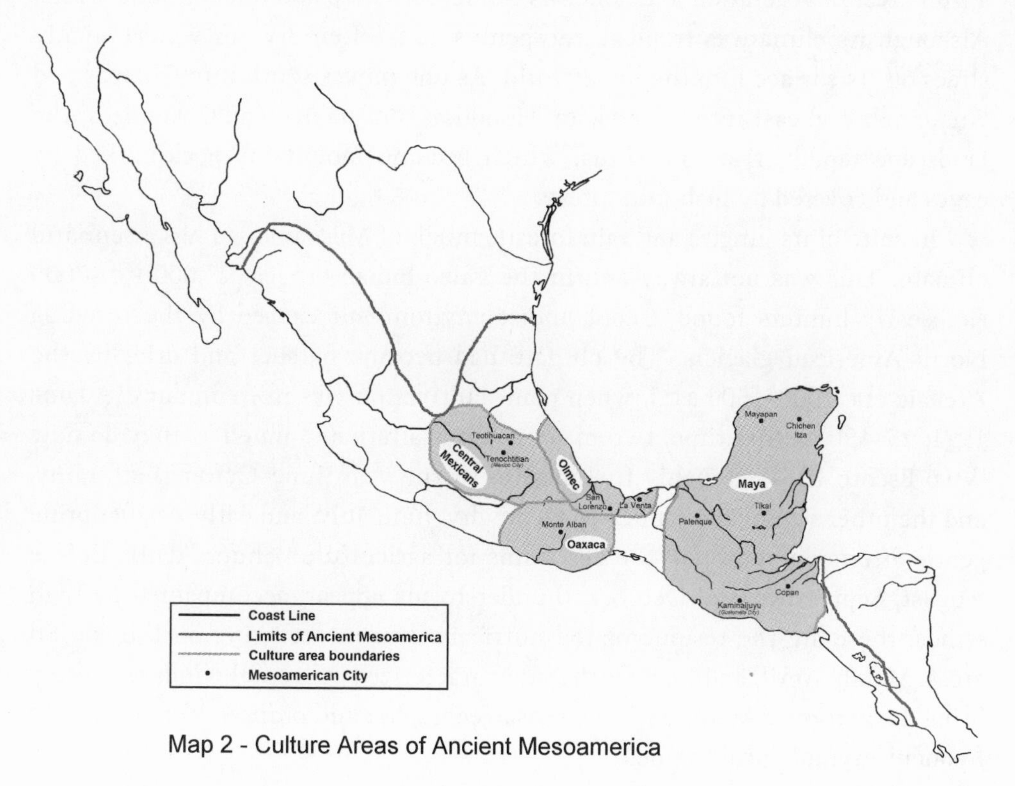

Map 2 - Culture Areas of Ancient Mesoamerica

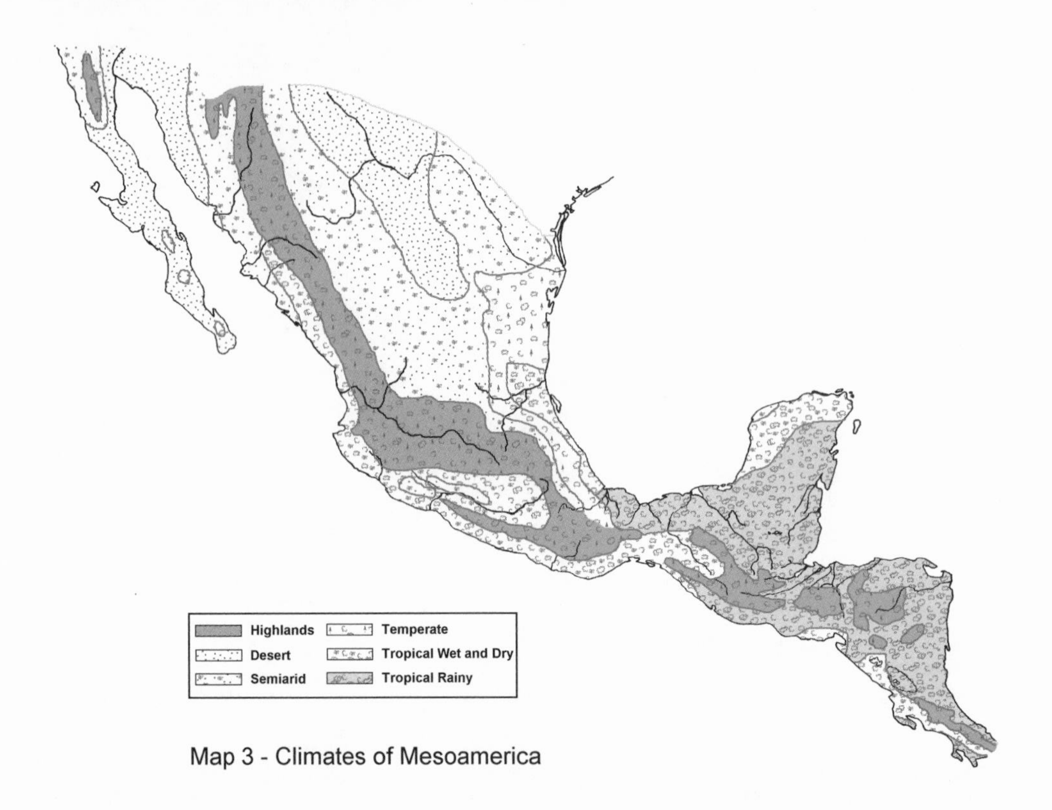

Map 3 - Climates of Mesoamerica

a thin layer of vegetation and conceals numerous caves and underground rivers. Although its climate is tropical, the peninsula is often dry, for water quickly slides off its surface into the underworld. As one moves south into Chiapas and Guatemala and east into El Salvador, Honduras, Nicaragua, and Costa Rica, the landscape rapidly rises into hills, which become mountains pockmarked by caves and covered by lush rain forests.

In spite of its jungles and rain forests, much of Mesoamerica has a semiarid climate. This was not always so. In the Paleo-Indian era (ca. 25,000 B.C.–7000 B.C.), early hunters found a cool, moist environment caused by the receding North American glaciers. The climate had become harsher and drier by the Archaic era (7000–1500 B.C.), when plant cultivation was in its infancy (Adams 1991, 25–45). At that time, two major seasons alternated much as they do now (Vivó Escoto 1964). Roughly five months of the year (June–October) are rainy, and the other seven (November–May) are dry. June, July, and early August bring gentle afternoon showers—the best rains for agriculture—almost daily. In late August, September, and October, thunderstorms appear, accompanied by high winds; these are the residue of the hurricane season occurring on the coastal areas. March, April, and May are driest, characterized by frontal winds that often bring dust storms. As we will see, these geographic and climatic conditions are frequent mythological themes.

Mesoamerican people are as diverse as their many geographic and climatic conditions, and cultural areas are often contiguous with particular geographic regions. Like other Native Americans, Mesoamerica's earliest ancestors probably began migrating from Asia around 30,000 to 40,000 years ago. They first traveled across the Bering Strait, where today just 50 miles separate Asia from Alaska. Back then, however, the earth was locked in an ice age that froze so much water that the oceans dropped up to 300 feet below their present levels, offering these early Asiatic peoples a land bridge of some 1,500 miles. Slowly they worked their way down the American continent to Mesoamerica over many thousands of years. Evidence indicates that nomadic hunters and gatherers inhabited the southern Basin of Mexico about 25,000 years ago. Both of these dates, however, may be overly conservative, and humans may have been roaming Mesoamerica's landscape even earlier. The skeletal remains of the earliest known humans in the area show a body structure much like that of present-day Indians; if dressed in modern clothing, these ancestors would go unnoticed on the streets of Mexico City today (Adams 1991, 29).

Mesoamericans did and do speak an enormous variety of languages. Spanish is now Mesoamerica's official language, but many people speak other tongues as well. For example, there are seven main branches of the Maya family of languages alone, each containing its own variants, many of which are unintelligible to speakers of another variant. A number of varieties of Nahuatl are spoken today in the central region of Mexico, and Oaxaca claims its own particular family of languages. All of these living languages also were spoken in pre-Conquest times, indicating strong forces of continuity at work in spite of the diversity. When appropriate, we will mark this diversity by noting in parentheses the language group or cultural name of the people to whom a mythic tradition belongs.

Beginning with the Conquest, Mesoamerica's mix of people became as varied as one can imagine. Following closely on the heels of the Spanish conquistadores, many others arrived: Dominican, Franciscan, Augustinian, and Jesuit clergy as well as the requisite governmental authorities and sundry opportunists, explorers, and adventurers. By the second half of the sixteenth century, not only had people of Spanish blood been born in New Spain but Indian and Spanish people had intermarried, and Black and Jewish people had joined the mix. Now this interracial and interethnic stew has become even more complex with the addition of many Europeans, Asians, and others from every corner of the world. These people have spread throughout Mesoamerica. As is true elsewhere, the greatest ethnic heterogeneity is found in the cities. And like any other major city in the world, Mexico City experiences all the joys and tensions of such enormous diversity.

How Do We Know about Mesoamericans?

With the introduction of European-style writing in the sixteenth century and the more recent advent of radio, television, video, and the WorldWide Web, numerous resources exist to tell us about Mesoamericans living since the Conquest. But how do we know anything at all about the many ancient peoples living before the Conquest?[3] Unfortunately, the Spanish conquerors destroyed great quantities of indigenous books, buildings, and sculptures. This makes learning about pre-Conquest Mesoamericans very difficult indeed; nevertheless, it is not impossible. One very rich source is archaeological ruins. Another is a few pre-Conquest books written in a pictorial form, which were lucky enough to escape destruction. A wealth of materials collected and recorded by the Spanish conquerors also remains. And numerous post-Conquest materials exist that can be used as analogies for understanding pre-Conquest peoples as well as peoples living after the Conquest. Of course, the closer one gets in time to the present, the easier it becomes. The most recent mythology often appears in newspapers, magazines, movies, and books, and on television. All of these sources report stories told in churches, on buses, around kitchen tables, or in bars. Myths were told like this in pre-Conquest times too, wherever people gathered: at rituals, on the road, around hearth fires, and in plazas.

Some of the best resources on pre-Conquest peoples are archaeological artifacts, such as buildings and urban plans, or other material cultural artifacts, such as pottery and sculpture. Archaeological evidence includes the material remains where Mesoamericans lived, the temples and pyramids where people participated in rituals, the roads where people walked, and the houses where people gathered around the hearths to tell their stories and myths. Unfortunately, the mere viewing, excavating, or reconstructing of this often impressive and beautiful architecture does not necessarily convey the content of ancient myths and stories. Sometimes one is lucky enough to find a written record in stone or clay, such as the stone stelae or columns at Classic Maya sites, which contain royal histories carved in Maya script. Usually, however, one must use other sources—written documents, oral histories, or ethnographic studies of living peoples—to help one interpret the meaning of archaeological remains. If a frieze on a building or a painting on a pot shows figures similar to those appearing in myths from other sources, then one might theorize that the figures are related to these stories, and take an educated guess as to their meaning. Or if a building is found to mark the solstices, then written and oral myths or histories that tell about solstices might help one understand why the builders were marking those particular celestial events.

Sculpture is an important source of archaeological information on mythology. Like people all over the globe, Mesoamericans permanently recorded mythic themes by incorporating them into architectural and self-standing stone sculptures, figurines, and a variety of other sculpted forms. Some of these sculptures were even incorporated into the stories and rituals, thereby structuring how new generations performed, retold, and remembered these myths. Mesoamericans created sculptures of a wide variety of forms and types. For example, a gigantic Sun Stone tells the story of the Mexica five ages. Wall murals found at Teotihuacan depict various stories and myths of individuals and deities; although we know very little about these personages, we can surmise their significance, based on later, written and pictographic texts. In a Preclassic temple at the Maya site of Cerros (Ser´-ros), the shape of the structure and the sculptured masks on its facade are believed to depict the universe itself (Figure 2). Some scholars believe Maya rulers used the temple as a ritual stage to reenact their travels through the Maya mythic world. And at Monte Albán (Mon´tay Al-ban´) in the Oaxaca valley, carefully constructed tombs of Zapotec (Za-po-tek´) rulers display painted murals showing supernatural scenes that might have been of special importance to the people who now rest there. Through the interpretation of artifacts such as sculptural art, we can to some extent rebuild the myths of pre-Conquest peoples.

Figure 2. A Preclassic temple at the Maya site of Cerros; the temple's shape and sculptured masks on its facade depict the Maya universe. (Kimbell Art Museum)

Figure 3. A Classic pottery vessel that depicts a Maya cosmic being; it was probably used in ritual ceremonies and feasting to offer food to deities. (Trustees for Harvard University. Slide 5-089-0055)

Another artistic medium that archaeologists frequently encounter in excavations is that of painted and decorated pottery. Traditionally, different Mesoamerican groups used pottery in ritual ceremonies and feasts during which food was offered to deities, various cosmic beings, and the ritual celebrants (Figure 3). Often they placed food offerings in specially made pottery, plates, bowls, or vases depicting mythic stories and deities. Among the Classic Maya, archaeologists and art historians have identified various scenes on Classic period pottery from the Colonial period K'iche' (Kee-chay')myth known as the Popol Vuh. Other Maya pottery shows scenes from a variety of different stories that we are just beginning to understand. In the Templo Mayor at Tenochtitlan (Te-noch-teet´-lan), archaeologists found incised burial urns portraying Mexica gods. And in one Monte Albán tomb, archaeologists discovered over the tomb's entrance funeral urns modeled into the shapes of Zapotec gods.

Sculpture and pottery are not the only artifacts on which archaeologists find mythic art: Mesoamericans also inscribed their stories on stones, bone, shell, jade, and obsidian. In sum, the only cultural objects that researchers have uncovered among archaeological ruins are those that withstood time and the natural elements and that were not found and taken away or destroyed by the Spanish or by modern-day looters. Soft materials such as cloth fibers or paper generally do not last, and foodstuffs and plant matter are only rarely found. Likewise, stories that were preserved only by their retelling or reenactment in ritual events have not survived the deaths of the people who perpetuated them. The interpretation of cultural artifacts that were removed from their original settings by unknown individuals (Spanish conquerors or looters) is very difficult, for an object's context tells much about its significance. For example, a bowl found in a kitchen area would have had very different uses from a bowl found on an altar or in a grave. Due to factors such as these, the archaeological record is indeed very incomplete. Fortunately, archaeological artifacts are not the only available resource. Much else has been preserved that can be explored in conjunction with material remains.

Pre-Conquest books called codices, for example, also exist (Figure 4). But because so many indigenous cultural artifacts were destroyed by the Spanish, only seventeen codices remain, fifteen of which are known to predate the Colonial era, and two of which originated either before the Conquest or very soon after.[4] Originally, these ancient books consisted of pictographs, sometimes including phonetic elements, that were painted on paper made from either bark or deerskin and folded accordion style, like a screen.[5] Their contents range from the complex Mesoamerican calendrical systems to genealogies, town histories, and descriptions of rituals. Sometimes the contents were acted out ritually, accompanied by oral recitations. Presently, close analytical studies are under way with the goal of decoding these complex texts.

The Spanish conquerors were at once repulsed and fascinated by the cultures they encountered in Mesoamerica, leading them to collect large quantities of information and to record copious impressions of the conquered natives. Military, religious, and governmental officials wrote accounts of "New Spain," gathered texts in the indigenous languages, and commissioned screen-fold codices from native artists. Native and mestizo authors, trained in Spanish schools, wrote books about their fast-disappearing traditions. Of the first group, for example, Cortés left his letters (Cortés 1986), and Bernal Díaz del Castillo (Ber-nal´ Dee´-az del Kas-tee´-yo), an officer serving under Cortés, wrote an account of the Conquest (Díaz 1956). Antonio de Mendoza (An-tone´-ee-oh day Men-do´-za), New Spain's first viceroy, commissioned a codex describing the history of the Mexica, the tribute they extracted from their vassals, and some of their daily

Figure 4. A Pre-Conquest book called a codex (The Codex Fejéváry-Mayor, Art Resource)

practices (Mendoza 1992). Father Diego Durán (Dee-ay´-go Doo-ran´) wrote an entertaining Mexica history based on a number of native histories that have since been lost (Durán 1971, 1994). The Franciscan Fathers André Olmos (Andray´ Ol´-mos) and Bernardino de Sahagún (Bare-nar-dee´-no day Sa-ha-goon´), sometimes collaborating, interviewed numerous natives from various walks of life. Olmos's collection from these interviews (see Maxwell and Hanson, 1992) is unfortunately largely lost, but Sahagún compiled a twelve-volume encyclopedia using his and Olmos's material (Sahagún 1953–1982). Written in Nahuatl and accompanied by loose and highly interpretive Spanish translations, this source is one of the most valuable. Father Diego de Landa (Dee-ay´-go day Lan´-dah) recorded what he understood about the Maya living in the Yucatán (Landa 1941, 1975). Others recorded in the original language the Maya books of the Chilam Balam (Chee-lam´ Ba-lam´), native-style histories based on indigenous calendars.

And in the sixteenth century, an unknown native songster recited the beautiful Maya myth the Popol Vuh (Poe´-pull Voo) to a priest, who wrote it down (Popol Vuh 1985). Of the second group, the indigenous authors Fernando de Alva Ixtlilxochitl (Fare-nan´-doe day Al´-vah Isht-lil-shó-cheet), Hernando Alvarado Tezozomoc (Air-nan´-doe Al-va-rah´-do Te-zo-zó-mok), and the mestizo Diego Muñoz Camargo (Dee-ay´-go Moon´yoz Ca-mar´-go) wrote European-style histories glorifying their respective Central Mexican cities (Ixtlilxochitl 1985; Tezozomoc 1980, 1992) (Muñoz Camargo 1984).

Near the end of the Colonial period, in the late eighteenth century, travelers returning from Mesoamerica to their homes in Europe and the United States stimulated a renewed interest in the region. These cultural tourists also left behind a variety of sources that teach us much about archaeological sites and indigenous peoples. An English nobleman, Lord Kingsborough, used up all of his personal financial resources on collecting and reproducing beautiful hand-colored copies of many of the early codices, and eventually died in a debtors' prison in Britain. In the nineteenth century, New York lawyer John Lloyd Stephens and English architect Frederick Catherwood explored the Maya lowlands together. Catherwood's extraordinary drawings of many hitherto unrecorded ruins and Stephens's lively descriptions of what they encountered were best-sellers in their day and remain superb resources today (Stephens 1841) (Figure 5).

The twentieth century has seen both the growth of ethnographic studies and an integration of various disciplinary approaches to Mesoamerican studies. A wealth of fine studies of indigenous and other peoples exist—far too many to list here. Such studies not only help us understand how some current peoples live but also can provide insight into how pre-Conquest peoples might have lived; for although many changes have occurred in Mesoamerica's long history, much continuity also exists. The husband-and-wife team of Barbara and Dennis Tedlock, for example, have worked with a living K'iche' Maya daykeeper, Andrés Xiloj (*An-drays´* Shee-loh´). This gentleman knows both an ancient calendrical system and the legend of the Popol Vuh, which he tells much as it was recorded in the sixteenth century by his unknown predecessor. Xiloj helped Dennis Tedlock translate this long and fascinating legend from K'iche' into English. Scenes from this same myth also appear on Maya pottery from the ninth century, testifying to this myth's great age. Although ancient Mesoamerica will probably never be completely understood because of its complexity and an often maddening lack of resources, the indication of continuity in a particular myth over the centuries makes the job a little easier. And recent collaboration among Mesoamericans like Xiloj and others from around the world—ethnographers, linguists, archaeologists, and historians who study both art works and written texts—has greatly enhanced our knowledge.

Figure 5. A drawing by Frederick Catherwood of the pyramid called El Castillo from the site of Chichén Itzá in Yucatán, Mexico (see also Figure 19) (Dover Pictorial Archive)

The Mythmakers' Worldviews

If one wanders through almost any of Mexico's crowded and bustling markets today, one can purchase plates, velvet wall hangings, T-shirts, key chains, wallets, and even shoes with an image of the Sun Stone adorning their surfaces (Figure 6). This now famous image was created by the Mexica, probably in the fifteenth century—less than 100 years before the Conquest. Sometimes incorrectly called the Calendar Stone (for it does not depict a calendar), it is really an elaborate example of a solar disk, a common ancient Mesoamerican symbol often associated with rulership.

By exploring the images blanketing the surface of this phenomenally complex and fascinating sculpture, we can gain some insight into the pre-Conquest cosmos, much of which persists today in indigenous and popular religion. The Sun Stone represented a cosmic topography that spoke simultaneously of four religious themes: (1) the world's space; (2) its power-filled inhabitants; (3) the calendrically structured form of transformative time that charted its indigenous history; and (4) the sacrifice that kept the cosmos's beings alive and functioning (Read 1997b, 824).

First, the cosmic topography appears on the stone's surface, where arrow-like solar rays map the cardinal and intercardinal directions, a sky band and two

Figure 6. The Postclassic Mexican Sun Stone (Drawing by Kay A. Read)

fire-snakes encircling the stone's outer edge depict the celestial realms of this cosmos, and jaguar-paw mouths framing the central face mark the terrestrial realms. Second, various power-filled beings inhabit this topography, from the little deities poking their heads out from between the fire-snakes' ferocious jaws, to precious stones of jade, the underworld's jaguars, and the godly face staring out from the center. Third, these beings change and transform according to a particular schedule controlled by a complex calendar. A ring depicting the twenty days founding the Mexica calendrical system joins the stone's celestial and terrestrial realms. And surrounding the central face and jaguar paws lie the emblems of the four ages or "suns" that predated the Fifth Sun, during which the Mexica lived. Each of these four ages was transformed into the next at the appropriate calendrical moment. Fourth, that enigmatic face sits in the dead center of a bull's-eye. Some believe it to be the daytime sun; some, the nighttime sun; and others, both. But all agree that a tongue, which is simultaneously a sacrificial blade, emerges from its toothy mouth as though panting in thirst and hunger for blood and flesh.

These same four themes—cosmic topography, power-filled inhabitants, calendrically determined transformation, and sacrifice—structured much of Mesoamerican life from the Preclassic era (2000 B.C.–A.D. 250), if not before, to the eve of the Spanish Conquest (A.D. 1521). And they have continued in sometimes altered form from the Conquest to the present. Christianity, of course, has played a major role since Fernando Cortés overtook the Mexica capital of Tenochtitlan in the sixteenth century, but traditional ideas of space, powers, transformation, and sacrifice have continued as sometimes subtle and sometimes not-so-subtle parts of what is particularly Mesoamerican in Christianity. And with Christianity came new mythic themes and ideas, which enriched the delicious stew pot of Mesoamerican religiosity.

Cosmic Topography

Traditionally, Mesoamericans live in worlds shaped by mythological visions.[6] These land- and skyscapes are always local in character. Particular mountains, caves, springs, and other terrestrial features define a town's landscape; and the sun, moon, and other celestial bodies create its outermost boundaries by moving along its particular horizon. Such particularity means that each human settlement is formed by its own unique cosmology. Nevertheless, almost all communities have shared certain larger visions, some apparently enduring for thousands of years. Each community enjoys its own version of these visions. One might imagine a grand world extending from the Gulf's eastern horizon to the Pacific's western horizon; northward and southward rise great mountains. Yet this great cosmic landscape contains many smaller ones, each belonging to a specific village, town, or city: each distinctive, yet similar.

Think of these cosmic topographies as containers, metaphoric terrariums in which move gods, other powerful beings, and people living out their lives. Inside these great houses, they eat, defecate, sleep, make love, work, wage war, and play tricks. All life is held within their boundaries. Like the water and gases cycling through a terrarium's space, water, beings, and many various powers flow throughout. And like a terrarium's plants, beings sprout, grow, blossom, die, and rot to nourish beings to come. Life forms continually cycle through this terrarium-house, disappearing only to appear in new forms. In precontact times, as beings moved round and round these containers, living and dying as they moved, each topographic container moved toward its own death, for each also was considered a living being that eventually must die.

Most cosmic houses are squared-off and divided into quadrants; often laid out horizontally like a four-petaled flower whose topside sometimes is called Earth's Surface (Figure 7). The precontact Mixtec depicted this schema in the Codex Fejérváry-Mayer (Figure 4), and the present-day Nahua (Na´-wa) of San Martín use a similar image to describe the underworld, which they call *Tlalocan.* The cardinal and intercardinal directions mark the flower's sides and corners. Each quarter is associated with a particular color, and often with a particular mountain. In many depictions, a great tree sprouts from each quadrant, with a bird perching atop its branches. Particular gods also claim governance over each quarter. Sometimes appropriately colored rain gods send their moist offerings from each; at other times, sets of gods that some call Bacabs (ba-kabs´, Yucatec Maya) and some others call Tlaloques (tla-lo´-kays, Nahua) hold each quarter erect. A powerful center point punctuates this terrestrial flower, and may act as its greenstone heart. Sometimes this center point demands sacrifice to keep the cosmos living. A watery, celestial, upper world arches over Earth's Surface; below extends a dank and rotting underworld. The sun travels through the upper world's waters during the day, and at night, when the moon and stars have taken its place above, through the underworld's caverns.

These cosmic containers were believed to have been created by various deities, who "spread" them out in the same way one pats out tortillas. Surrounding celestial waters "spread" as water spreads in a pan. In the precontact Nahua story of the five suns, each age was "patted out" and "divided" into its proper portions. Today, the Nahua of San Miguel Tzinacapan (San Mee-gel´ Tsee-na-ka´-pan) describe Earth's Surface as a *comal,* the flat pan that Mexicans use for roasting tortillas. The sun traveling above it produces corn with its heat; the sun beneath the comal, in the underworld, is the hearth fire that cooks tortillas made from that corn. And for the Cakchiquel (Kak-chee-kel´) Maya of Panajachel (Pa-na-ha-chel´), the watery sea spreads out to the horizon until it joins with the sky.

The horizontal quartering of precontact topographies seems fairly clear, but there is less agreement about the structure of the vertical plane. Many scholars have described precontact cosmoses as having consisted of either thirteen or nine celestial layers extending upward from the earth's surface and nine terrestrial layers extending downward. Unfortunately, the pre-Hispanic evidence for such hypotheses is slim. Among Nahua sources, for example, this interpretation is drawn from two main postcontact resources: (1) several lists (recorded mostly in Spanish) that enumerate different sets of "sky-waters" (*ilhuicatl*) and "lands-of-the-dead" (*mictlan*), which bear no reference to any topographical locations; and (2) a single pictorial codex (commissioned by the Spanish) that arranges one

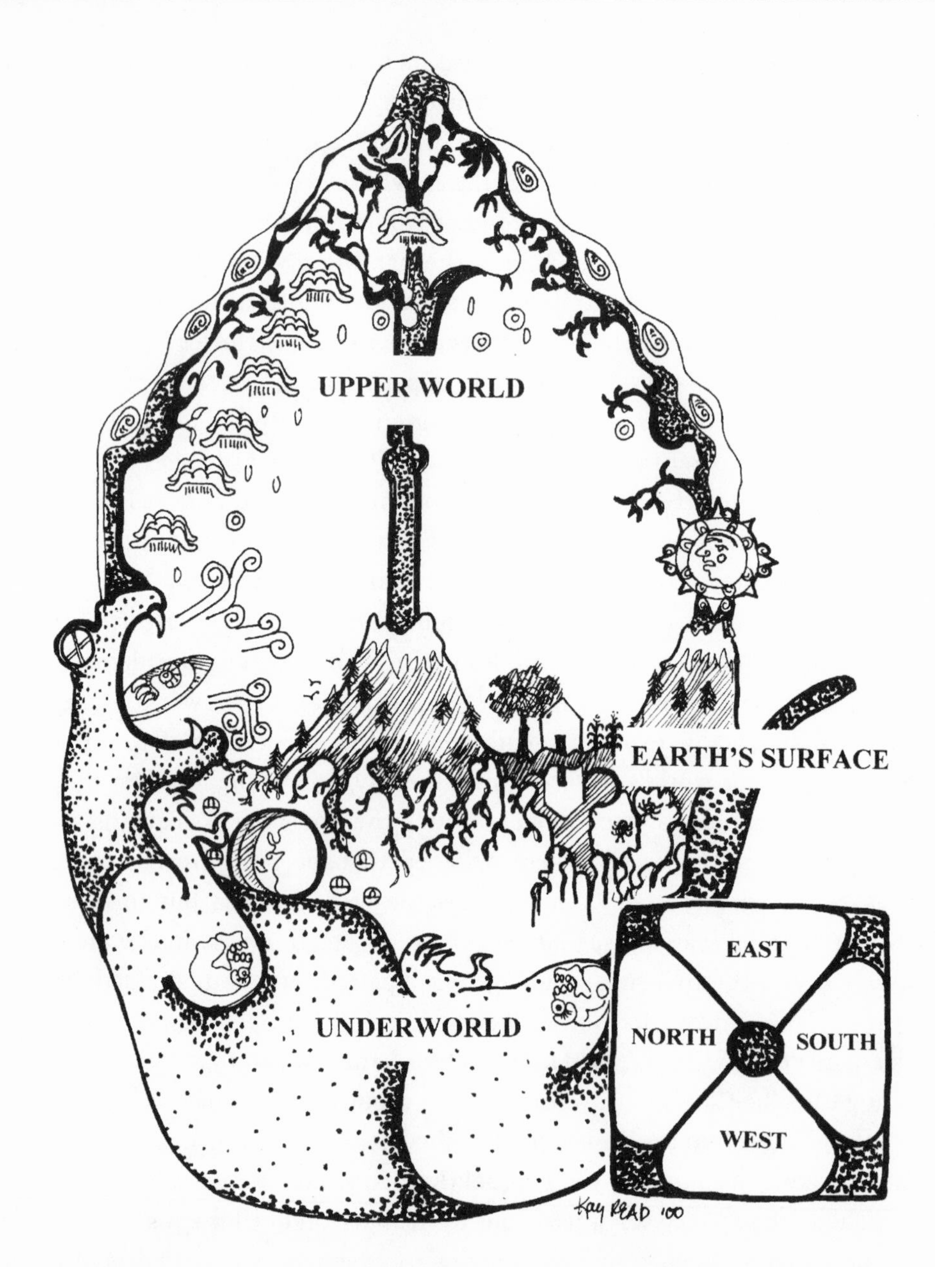

Figure 7. An imaginative rendering of a Mesoamerican mythological cosmos, portraying the upper world, earth's surface, and the underworld as well as the four cardinal directions (Drawing by Kay A. Read)

such set in vertical layers. Its Spanish commentator calls the sky-waters and lands-of-the-dead "heavens" and "hells" and makes explicit comparisons to a medieval cosmology similar to that described by Dante in *The Inferno.* One might ask whether this vertical arrangement of sky-waters and lands-of-death is not the result of Spanish misconceptions attempting to bridge two very different cultures. Today, however, contemporary Maya myths exist that describe the thirteen levels as moving seven up and six down like the sides of a pyramid.

The underworld is the place of death and of rot, a dank reverse of the dry, living surface of earth. The subterranean Land of Death for the sixteenth-century Nahua was walled by water and contained no smoke holes. Yellow dogs carried the dead on their backs across the "the place of nine waters" (also called *Tlalocan,* or the Rain God's Land); there in the Land of Death they "completely disappeared."[7] Today's K'iche' Maya also describe the underworld as a fetid place honeycombed with mountainous chasms and watery channels bearing such names as Pus River and Blood River. It is peopled by unpleasant characters like Seven Death, Blood Gatherer, Pus Master, Skull Scepter, and Trash Master. In the 1930s, the Cakchiquel Maya of Panajachel said that the devil lived inside a hill and lured people to his house, to eat. When he needed laborers, he either bribed weak souls to work for him or he asked God for them; at such times, sickness arose everywhere. Today, among the San Miguel Tzinacapan Nahua, the underworld mirrors the upper, with upside-down villages, and mountains just like those above. The Tzinacapan say that in Mexico City, skyscrapers descend as far into the earth as they ascend above its surface.

Although these trees and mountains are stationary, other living things have the capacity to move through these topographies. Some beings follow predetermined paths; others travel more freely. Like traders carrying bundles of goods, the sixteenth-century Nahua sun and moon bore their burdens of time along paths through the sky and underworld, just as the stars and Venus bore time along ancient, precontact roadways. Running water coursed through this entire Nahua land- and skyscape. Mountains, like pots, held the water that was released by Tlaloc (Tla´-lok, Rain God) or the goddess Chalchiuhtlicue (Chal-chee-oot-li´-kway) in the form of rain or rivers. Water came from the sea via underground rivers to the mountains, changing from salt to fresh as it moved into the land. Thence it burst forth in lakes, springs, streams, and rivers, thereafter to return to the sea, where it formed the celestial walls. Deities and numerous other beings including birds, animals, and people were not confined to certain roadways, and had more freedom.

Temples and churches often mirror these cosmic topographies. Tenochtitlan, the huge Mexica (Nahua) fourteenth-to-sixteenth-century urban center, where the Templo Mayor (Temp´low Mai-yor´, Great Temple) stood, also was apportioned into four quarters, with the main, ritual district in its exact center. As a symbolic mountain, the Great Temple hid the underworld in its many buried caches. These were filled with the sacrificial bodies of all manner of celestial and terrestrial animals; the mountain-dwelling Tlaloc (the Rain God) also was liberally represented.

Many contemporary communities interweave indigenous and Christian elements, creating a new religious tradition. Sacred mountains and water holes mark San Juan Chamula's (San Hwan Cha-moo-lah´) Tzotzil (Tsot-zeel´) landscape. Its church door faces west, and its altar is on the east side. Outside the church, the ritual space is divided in two; on the north is the area of the rainy agricultural season, and on the south, that of dry dormancy. The western, feminine side is where the Christ-Sun descends into the underworld; the eastern, masculine side is where the Christ-Sun rises again.

Whereas some view the underworld as hell and the sky as heaven, others view the under- and upper worlds as equally filled with beneficial or dangerous potentialities. In San Martín (Nahua) the four quarters of the underworld boast mythic roots going back hundreds of years, to the great Classic city of Teotihuacan, and before. Healers and witches travel through its labyrinthine topography to seek help from its powerful inhabitants. But since the Conquest, the upper world has become the home of God, Jesus Christ, Mary, and a host of saints, all of whom can also help or hinder healers and witches in their efforts to meet the challenges of life on Earth's Surface.

In sum, Mesoamerican topographies have both changed and endured through time. With the coming of the Spanish, new themes were introduced; in many places, these themes blended with indigenous perceptions in the most wonderfully complex ways. And along with that blending, a phenomenally multifaceted portrait of Mesoamerican mythology emerged, which has continued to shape and reshape itself up to the present.

Power-filled Inhabitants

Many diverse beings inhabit the traditional topographies.[8] Everything and anything can be animated by a huge variety of powers, whether these beings move on their own accord or not. Mountains, caves, lakes, rivers, and oceans, and the humans, animals, birds, insects, fish, rocks, trees, flowers, and plants that live on, above, and in them, all have the potentiality for life. Because they have the living powers to do so, even the sun, moon, stars, and planets traverse the sky's pathways as though on a journey. Therefore, categories like "animate" and "inanimate" don't really apply to this universe, for all things are in some sense animate. Among the ancient Mexica (Nahua), for example, there were no inanimate things. Instead, the Mexica distinguished between beings that could move on their own, as could people, animals, and various spirits and deities, and those that had to be moved by others, like rocks, corn, and trees, which were rooted to particular spots. Each being had its appropriate path to follow or place to occupy. And each, because it was alive, was born, changed as it went through life eating its appropriate food, and died when its life span had been appropriately completed.

In Mesoamerica, one interacts with various beings on a daily basis; with some, periodically; and with others, only through special rituals (Read 1997b, 825). Forests and deserts might be filled with spirits that can trip one up—or do worse—as one traverses them. In ancient Nahua times, a two-headed deer turned into two beautiful women. One of them seduced a hunter and then ate him. The other chased his brother through the wilderness until she was trapped on a cactus and shot with arrows by some powerful female goddesses of the sky. To keep a tree from falling on him, a Colonial-era Nahua woodcutter might ask it not to "eat him" before he forcibly moved it from its otherwise appropriate spot. A beautiful female spirit lives today in the jungles of El Salvador who is ready to seduce and then kill unsuspecting men with her enormous teeth. In San Martín (Nahua) one might encounter deceased ancestors and neighbors, witches, gods, saints, or even the devil in dreams. Some of these might try to kill one; others are less nasty, and some may even be of help.

In precontact times, good ancestral names had powers to shape a child's personality. And shortly after birth, a baby ritually acquired a calendrical name that gave it both good and bad powers. A girl born during a certain week might carry the powers of the goddess Xochiquetzal (Show-chee-ket´-zal) and so be destined to become a great weaver if she behaved properly. If not, she would fall into bad ways. One young boy of royal Mexica (Nahua) lineage hoped to become a ruler, but only if he could overcome the powers of the day upon which he was first named, for those powers could push him toward indecisiveness or cowardice. For some rulers, part of their right to govern was based on the powers of their mothers, who handed these powers on to their sons when they were installed. Names and royal blood were important because the energies flowing through ancestral lineages bore especially effective powers for governance (lineages and patron deities). And in state ceremonies, Maya rulers drew their own blood in order to offer its life-giving powers to various cosmic beings, including the sun. Among the Nahua in San Miguel Tzinacapan today, marigolds are believed to have powers that link people with the sun. Like their ancient ancestors, the Tzinacapan Nahua believe the flowers bear an internal heat and the force of life because their seeds are mature when the flower is still alive. The bright yellow flowers also represent the hearts of the deceased, and people decorate with marigolds on the Day of the Dead, when the living welcome the dead back to share a feast with them.

Since they believed that everything was alive, ancient Mesoamericans understood the world in particular ways. Before the Conquest, observations of such things as astronomical events and the way a body fell sick and was healed were just as keen among Mesoamericans as in European science during the same era. In fact, Mesoamericans were ahead in some areas. The mathematical concept of zero was understood there before it was in Europe, and Cortés quickly learned that Mesoamerican healers were better at setting the bones of his injured conquistadores than his own medical personnel. But their keen and often accurate observations were and still are performed from a very different vantage point. As Clara Sue Kidwell has noted, Native American science is often based on the idea that all things have wills that must be accounted for if one is to control a situation effectively. So unlike European scientists, indigenous Mesoamerican scientists may not look for the general laws that govern the natural world but for the wills of the beings inhabiting that world (Kidwell 1992, 396). The sun follows a certain path throughout the years not because it is a law but because the sun's will or inborn nature is such that it is appropriately suited to this particular path.

Calendrically Determined Transformation

Because all things have the capacity for life, transformation characterizes all of cosmic reality just as it does all of everyday life (Read 1997b, 825; 1998, 38–39, 84–88). One is not the same as one was when one was born a screaming, red-faced baby. Nor is one the same as one will be when one dies a stooped and wrinkled old woman or man. Nor does one's personality stay the same throughout life; the baby is not the young woman or man, who is not a mature adult with children and grandchildren of her or his own; nor are they the aged for whom others care. Change is a part of ordinary life. And in a cosmos in which all things live, all things are transformed from one life stage to the next, until death causes their powers to change yet again.

A cosmic reality based on transformation also means there is no difference between time and space, for no space can exist that is not timed by its own life span. All things, because they are alive, are born into a particular space; they grow, age, die, and decay through time in a particular space, which also grows, ages, and dies. A baby through time becomes an adult and then an old person in particular places at appropriate times. The tree begins as a young shoot only to grow old and wither away; at its death, its powers pass on to others. Even the living mountains change. They may wear down slowly, or they may suddenly blow out lava and hot ash, irrevocably and quickly changing the landscape and the lives of all who live there. All beings hold within their bodily spaces a living clock that times their living transformations.

Many mythic metaphors express this reality of transformation. Mexica corn grew from seed into a plant, eating the underworld's rotting loam. People then ate corn's mature fruit, digested it, and used their excrement, which came from eating the corn, to fertilize new corn. In the Popol Vuh, when two Maya Hero Twins sacrificed themselves in the underworld, two corn plants that had been growing in their mother and grandmother's house above, on Earth's Surface, died. The boys' bones were ground like cornmeal, from which the twins regenerated themselves in new forms; first, they became fishermen, and later, elderly magicians. At that same moment, their corn above ground grew again. Eventually, the twins rose, transformed into the sun and the moon. Many Mesoamericans believe that because people were created from corn at the beginning of the Fifth Age, they are spiritually the same; and many ancient rulers, like the Maya hero twins, shared the powers of corn and of the sun. In contemporary San Martín (Nahua), healers and witches can shape-shift, turning into the creatures whose powers they share—such as opossums, owls, mice, or even horrible monsters.

"Nothing is forever" in this precontact world of "fleeting moments," where even "jade shatters" and one journeys through life for "just a short time" (Read 1998, 113–114). These words attributed to the fifteenth-century poet Nezahualcoyotl (Neza-wal-koy´-ot), accurately describe the timed impermanence of Mesoamerican existence. In Nezahualcoyotl's time, a living being, whether moving or rooted to a spot, underwent transformative growth and death according to its appropriate life schedule. Even suns' lives were timed. Many saw themselves inhabiting a short-lived fifth sun that had been preceded by four earlier suns. After a set period, each sun found itself changed into the next sun by means of some sort of violent destruction. Numerous variations of sun-age myths appear across Mesoamerica. Some postcontact communities tell stories that include Jesus, Mary, and various saints; others tell about only more ancient deities who do quite different things. Sometimes four sun-ages appear, sometimes five; and the colors associated with the cosmos's quadrants may vary or may not even be mentioned.

"This is the beginning, the Ancient Word, here in this place called K'iche'." And so begins the Popol Vuh intoned by a contemporary Maya daykeeper, or diviner. In the beginning, only gods existed: Plumed Serpent and Heart-of-Sky "who came as three" (Popol Vuh 1985, 73). They made the earth to rise, and then created the first age of animals, causing them to talk each to each, within each kind. But the animals could not say their creators' names, so they were eaten. The gods tried again. In the second age, they molded people from mud, but their efforts were not good. The clay people were lopsided, stupid, and fell apart. They didn't work, so the gods destroyed them. In order to get it right in the third age, the gods first asked Xpiyacoc (Shpee-ya-kok´) and Xmucane (Shmoo-ka-nay´) to count the days and cast lots with corn kernels. Then they created wooden manikins; but these fleshless beings had no hearts and minds, and no memory of their creators. So Heart-of-Sky killed them with a great flood of resin raining down upon them, the animals tore them apart, and even the manikins' own grinding stones and griddles pulverized them. After the Hero Twins balanced life with death and put the fourth age in order, proper humans were finally shaped. Xmucane ground corn for their flesh with water for their blood, and the gods molded the first four couples by means of these "sacrificial" acts.

The Nahua version from the Codex Chimalpopoca (Chee-mal-po-po´-ka) is quite different. This tale was told to a Spanish-employed recorder on 22 May 1558: The first sun-age was called 4-Jaguar, the food was 7-Grass, and the age stretched out for 676 years; jaguars ate this age. The second age was called 4-Wind. Its beings turned themselves into monkeys whose houses were trees and who ate 12-Snake. This age lasted 364 years, until wind blew it away. The third age was called 4-Rainstorm. Its beings turned into turkeys and ate 7-Knife. This age stretched out for 312 years, when Fire Rain burned it up. The fourth age was called 4-Water. The beings of this age ate 4-Flower. This age stretched out for 676 years, until a flood destroyed it. The current, fifth age is called 4-Movement because it moves along a path; the old, wise ones say that earthquake and famine will destroy it and we will all perish.

As in the Popol Vuh, multiple transformative destructions created the world as one knows it. But in the Chimalpopoca's story, each sun's life span is carefully counted out. Each contains its own unique inhabitants who live in unique houses and eat their own food (although no one knows what these foods were). Each sun draws its name from the manner of its destruction. And instead of four ages, there are five. Unlike the Popol Vuh, no moral message appears in this apparently simple recounting of events. This is a calendrical text, not an ethical one, for the arithmetic mirrors the math used to count time. Multiples of 26 count out each sun's time span, and five ages are conflated into four of 676 years by joining the counts of the second and third suns. A Maya daykeeper's divination board is divided just like this, with four parts of 676 counts—one for each of earth's quarters.

Calendrical patterns structured all these various transformations. The tale of the Nahua five suns and the Popol Vuh both are filled with obscure and sometimes hidden calendrical references. They describe not only how the world came to be but also how one calculates its existence according to the motions of particular celestial beings along their appropriate paths. The importance of calendrical calculations cannot be overstated; they are extraordinarily ancient and have permeated all aspects of life for centuries, continuing even today. Not only do things change and metamorphose according to some calendar, but much of daily life was and still can be ruled by calendrical calculations. In ancient times, one did almost nothing important without first figuring out its calendrical meaning. Calendars are even believed to control life's boundaries, for all the diverse beings living in the cosmoses live for particular spans of time that can be calculated calendrically. Even the earthquakes that would end the Mexica (Nahua) cosmos would not come until the Fifth Sun's calendrically calculated life was finished.

Today, calendars are still used to calculate the appropriate times for baptisms, marriages, trips, important business deals, and burials, although much of the complex ancient system has disappeared. The calendrical cycles, especially those governing state rites, were mostly (although not entirely) abolished under Spanish rule because of their political and religious import. Agricultural and divinatory calendars used by healers and daykeepers in remote villages escaped the Spanish because it was easier to hide them from the conquerors' eyes. Complex cycles of church festivals such as saints' days today govern much of religious life in both towns and villages. In El Salvador, this cycle may even replicate the old indigenous state festival calendar that the Spanish thought they were abolishing. And in the Maya area, service to the Catholic church follows the same indigenous calendrical patterns that governed service to the ancient temples. In the sixteenth century, the Spanish did not see such service patterns as religious but as secular; therefore, they did not expend much energy on trying to stamp them out. The indigenous participants at the time, however, probably had a more mythic view of the practice. They continued to serve the cosmos's beings as they had always done; only now some names had changed and new beings had been added.

Sacrifice

In ancient times, sacrifices nourished the living beings of the cosmos, thereby bringing about and controlling transformations (Read 1997b, 826; 1998, 123–155). Many know about the Mexica (Nahua) high state rites in which hearts were cut from the chests of warriors and offered to the sun. Certainly Hollywood and other popular media have made much of these particular rites, but most rites were not nearly as dramatic or gory as Hollywood depicts them. Few know the full variety and complexity of sacrificial practices, the extent of their integration into daily life, or that most offerings were not humans but rather animals, birds, or plants. Ritual blood-letting was one of the most common and widespread practices; small quantities of blood were offered on numerous ritual occasions, from the simple naming ceremonies of Nahua newborns to the high state ceremonies of Maya rulers. Human blood was not always used. The first corn tortilla eaten at dawn was seen as a sacrifice to the sun. Quails, jaguars, crocodiles, ducks, fish, snakes, salamanders, and amaranth cakes also found their way into sacrificial rituals. In fact, just about anything edible might be considered an appropriate sacrifice, although which food would depend on the culinary requirements of the ritual circumstances. The dedication of a new temple often required the blood of warriors captured from enemy cities. But simple amaranth cakes shaped like a god could serve the same purpose in politically less important circumstances.

Sacrificial techniques also varied widely. Extreme forms of human sacrifice included heart extraction, decapitation, drowning, and shooting with arrows. Rituals involved both willing and unwilling participants, from any segment of society—again, depending on the circumstances. Females and males of all ages were sacrificed; sometimes they were foreigners, but often not. The foci of all these rituals were equally diverse; sacrifice was associated with war as well as with the agricultural cycle, and appropriate sacrifices were offered to celestial recipients like the sun, terrestrial ones like the Earth Monster, or those in the underworld who were in need of sustenance. In ancient times, sacrifice permeated all existence from one's daily tortillas to birth and warfare, and it was performed in many ways for many reasons.

Many also are not aware of sacrifice's antiquity in Mesoamerica. Only a short time ago, it was thought that human sacrifice was primarily the invention of the Mexica or Aztecs in the late Postclassic era (ca. 1200–A.D. 1521). But as more and more archaeological data came to light, it became clear that sacrifice had an extremely long history throughout the area. Not only did Mexica priests cut the hearts out of warriors; Maya rulers waged wars after which their human booty was dispatched in similar sacrificial rituals. The sacrificial remains of 32 young men have been found in the foundations of a plaza in a small town in Belize, dating back to the late Preclassic era (ca. 400 B.C.–A.D. 250).

The tremendous diversity of sacrificial rites and their occasionally impressive drama has resulted in a large number of scholarly theories. For perhaps obvious reasons, sixteenth-century Spanish observers tended to overemphasize sacrifice's frequency and violence. Their explanations varied. Some explained indigenous sacrificial rituals as misguided practices originating with the devil; some likened indigenous sacrifice to Christian penance; others saw it as mere superstition. Each explanation depended on the author's own background and on the context and nature of the specific rite in question. Modern explanations have varied even more. Some scholars have viewed Mesoamerican sacrifice as merely one stage in a lengthy evolutionary process. Others, focusing on its environmental, biological, political, social, or psychological functions, have suggested a number of different theories: Sacrifice may have served as a means of population control, as a necessary means of providing protein to supplement people's daily diet, as a way for the elite to maintain power, or as a practice aiding political expansion.

In trying to uncover the religious logic that structures these rituals, others have focused primarily on sacrifice as a coherent system of beliefs. Many of this group of scholars agree that precontact sacrifice involved the ritual sharing of a variety of plant, animal, and human comestibles; sacrifice was a way to feed the many living beings of the universe. Most also believe that sacrifice included some kind of exchange between human and nonhuman entities; such exchanges nourished the cosmos's inhabitants and maintained them in an ordered state of existence. The logic here was simple: If one wanted the cosmic beings to provide food, one had to feed the cosmic beings in return.

A number of scholars have noted the close sacrificial bond between death and destruction and life and creation, a bond that also correlates with concepts of transformation. A close bond exists between eating and transformation in several ways. One must eat to live; eating nourishes life's transformations. If one does not eat, one will die, and the transformation of death will occur. And in order to eat, one must kill something else, transforming that thing into food that is digested and then excreted in a different form. In other words, eating things and thereby destroying them creates new things. Just as the ancient transformative realities saw no difference between time and space, so too those hungry beings saw no difference between life and death or creation and destruction, for one cannot occur without the other.

Some theories of sacrifice do not account for the phenomenon generally but focus almost exclusively on those stupendous high state rituals. None adequately explains this complex, widespread, and ancient phenomenon. For the purposes of understanding the bulk of Mesoamerican mythology, it is probably most helpful to view sacrifice as a transformative exchange that nourishes and maintains the many living beings inhabiting the various Mesoamerican cosmoses. Sacrifice creatively transformed the things of the ancient Mesoamerican world by destructively feeding some beings to other beings. This sustenance allowed gods, spirits, people, animals, plants, and mountains to grow and transform. Rituals following a carefully calculated calendrical system gave order to this transformative process of eating, for they regulated when, where, and why sacrificial transformation should take place. Ancient Mesoamerican beings needed to eat on time if transformation was to be controlled.

With the Spanish, a new kind of sacrifice entered Mesoamerica: the one-time sacrifice of Jesus Christ. For the Europeans steeped in this sacrificial tradition, traditional Mesoamerican practices seemed at once familiar and strange. For some, the killing of humans perverted God's will. One was not supposed to really kill someone and then eat his or her flesh. Sacrifice was to be a symbolic act; God acted through bread and wine, not through actual bodies. Hence, in spite of all the violent bloodshed allowed in their own political wars of conquest, the Spanish considered native rituals of human sacrifice an abomination. But some of the Spanish observers found other forms of sacrifice more understandable because they paralleled their own medieval practices of penance. They seemed to admire them even though the natives directed these apparently penitential practices at the wrong gods, for at least they showed the seriousness of their piety. Like Europeans who willingly chose to suffer in order to demonstrate their intense devotion to God, these natives also were willing to suffer for their gods. Nevertheless, the Spanish promptly outlawed all forms of formal sacrifice addressed to native gods. Only the Christian god could receive offerings, and these must be appropriate to Christian penitential practices.

Still, some traditional sacrificial practices persisted. Sometimes ancient practices were transformed into penitential Christian practices, and sometimes they remained very much the same, only quietly performed out of the sight of the wrong eyes. Today, the ritual sacrifice of chickens and other animals is a common practice. Scattered, infrequent reports and rumors of human sacrifice have continued even up to the present, although the reporters of these tales rarely are able to document and prove them. In the 1930s, in San Martín (Nahua), it is reported that a man was hung from a cross in front of the village church to end a violent feud among the village's healers, witches, and landowners.

MESOAMERICAN CULTURAL HISTORY

Four cultures have played especially important roles in Mesoamerica's history: the Olmec (ca. 2250–300 B.C.); Oaxaca (ca. 1400 B.C.–present); the Mexican highland peoples (ca. 1200 B.C.–present); and the Maya (ca. 400 B.C.–present) (see timeline opposite). Two, the Olmec and the peoples of the Mexican highlands, have exercised influence and sometimes even considerable power over great geographic expanses of Mesoamerica. The Maya and those living in Oaxaca have been somewhat less powerful in the grand scheme of things but nevertheless have made major cultural contributions to Mesoamerican life. Each of these four cultures developed its own distinctive characteristics, yet all have shared a great deal culturally and mythologically over the centuries.

Focusing on these four Mesoamerican cultures, we can distinguish seven historical periods: (1) the Paleo-Indian (ca. 25,000 B.P.–7,000 B.C.); (2) the Archaic (ca. 7,000–2,000 B.C.); (3) the Preclassic (ca. 2000 B.C.–A.D. 250); (4) the Classic (ca. A.D. 250–900/1000); (5) the Postclassic (ca. A.D. 900/1000–1521); (6) the Spanish Conquest and Colonization of Mesoamerica (A.D.1521–1808); and (7)

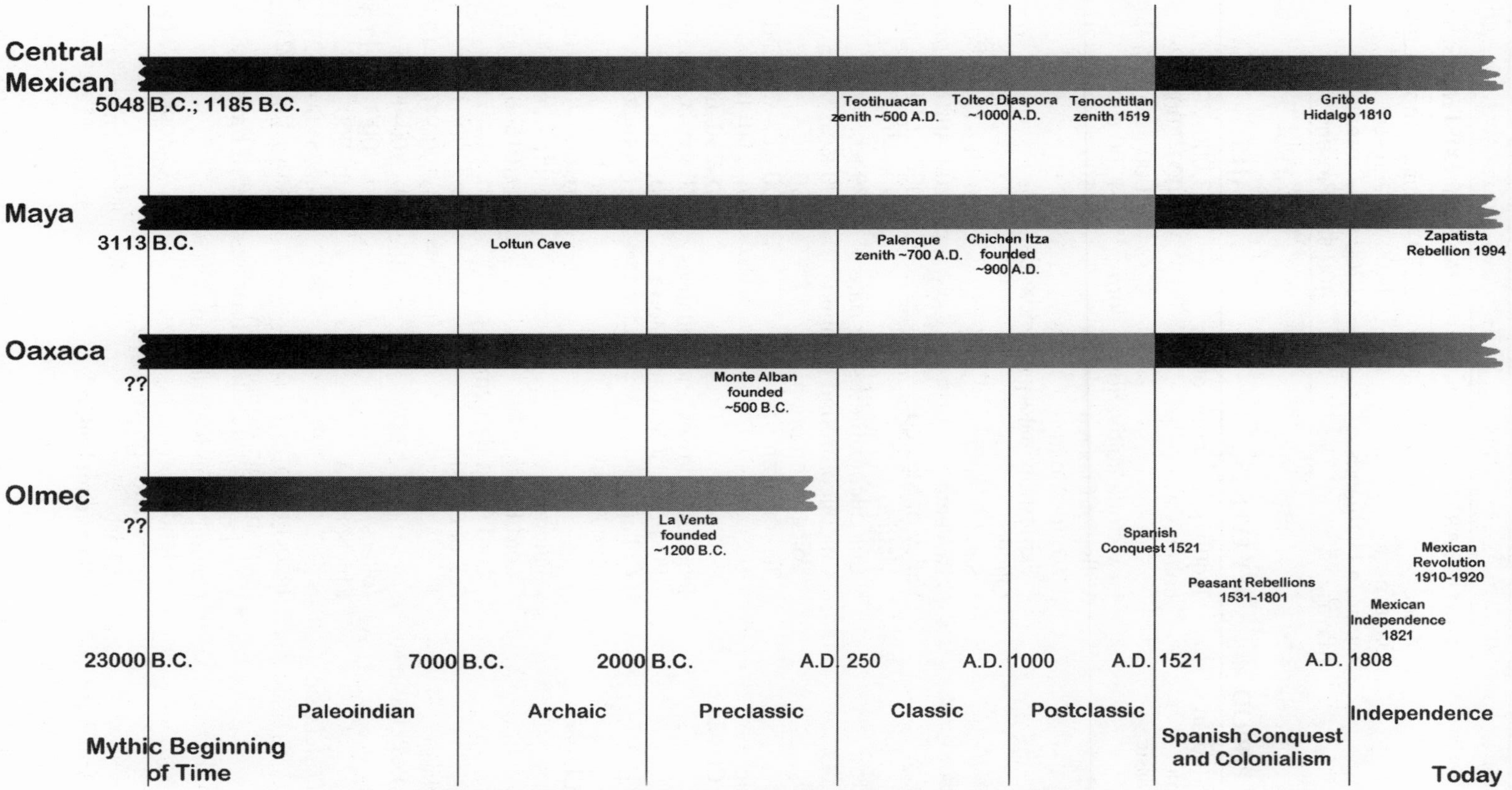

Timeline of Mesoamerican Culture Areas

CHRONOLOGY OF MESOAMERICAN HISTORY

CULTURE AREA	SPANS OF EXISTENCE
Olmec	2250–300 B.C.
Oaxaca	1400 B.C.–Present
Mexican Highlands	1200 B.C.–Present
Maya	400 B.C.–Present

TIME PERIOD	KEY EVENTS	DATES
Paleo-Indian	Tequixquiac, bone of dog	23,000–7000 B.C.
Archaic	Loltún Cave	7000–2000 B.C.
Preclassic		2000 B.C.–A.D. 250
	La Victoria/cultivation of corn	~1500 B.C.
	Valley of Oaxaca	~500 B.C.–A.D. 200
	Monte Albán	
	Earliest divinatory calendar dates	
	Olmec	~2250–300 B.C.
	San Lorenzo	zenith ~1200–900 B.C.
	La Venta	1200–400 B.C.
	Valley of Mexico	6000 B.C.–Present
	Tlatilco	1200–400/300 B.C.
	Cuicuilco/earliest solar date	679 B.C.
	Cuicuilco's round pyramid	400 B.C.
	Volcanic eruption	150 B.C.
	Teotihuacan rises	100 B.C.–A.D. 250
Classic		A.D. 250–1000
Early Classic		A.D. 250–600
	Teotihuacan rises and collapses	100 B.C.–A.D. 650/750
	Pyramids of Sun and Moon	A.D. 150
	Collapse	A.D. 650–750
	Monte Albán	zenith ~A.D. 250–700
Late Classic		A.D. 600–900/1000
	Palenque	zenith ~A.D. 600–700
	Lord Pacal	A.D. 615–83
	Lord Chan Bahlum	A.D. 684–702
	Fall of Classic Maya	A.D. 900/1000
Postclassic		A.D. 900/1000–1521
Early Postclassic		A.D. 900–1200
	Toltecs	A.D. 900/1000–Present
	Chichén Itzá	~A.D. 900–1200
Late Postclassic		~A.D. 1200–1521
	Tenochtitlan	~A.D. 1350–1521
	Spanish begin exploration and conquest	
	Columbus finds Caribbean Islands	12 October 1492
	Cortés lands on Veracruz Coast	8 November 1519
	Fall of Tenochtitlan	August 1521
Spanish Conquest and Colonization		1521–1808
	Encomienda system	1521–1550

TIME PERIOD	KEY EVENTS	DATES
	Approximately 90% indigenous depopulation	by 1600
	Peasant rebellions	1531–1801
	Spanish pressure to take over cofradías	1759
Independence to the Present		1808–2000
	Napoleon occupies Spain	1808
	Grito de Hidalgo	16 September 1810
	Mexican independence	27 September 1821
	Central American Federation	1823–1838
	Cinco de Mayo: Mexicans temporarily resist invading French forces	5 May 1862
	Independence from France	1867
	Protestant missions in Central America	~1900
	Porfirio Díaz	1877–1911
	Mexican Revolution/ Emiliano Zapata	~1910–1920
	U.S. involvement begins in Nicaragua	1909
	Rebels organized under Sandino	1928–1933
	La Matanza/Farabundo Martí	1932
	Augusto César Sandino assassinated	1934
	Guatemalan Revolution	1944
	Overthrow of Arbenz in Guatemala	1954
	Beginning growth of Evangelical Protestantism in Central America	~1960
	Second Vatican Council/Roots of progressive Catholicism	1962–1965
	Nicaraguan Civil War/Sandinistas	1978–1979
	Oscar Romero assassinated	24 March 1980
	Salvadoran Civil War and rise of Farabundo Martí Liberation Front	~1980–1992
	Zapatista rebellion	1 January 1994–Present

Independence to the Present (1808–A.D. 2000). For each period (see timeline and chronology on pp. 33–35), we discuss one or two exemplary sites or myths in order to give the reader an inkling of what it was like to live then. The cultural development of Mesoamerica is the subject of this chapter, which touches only briefly on the development of central mythological themes, symbols, places, events, and figures. Indigenous approaches to time and history are presented in the next chapter.

1. The Paleo-Indian (ca. 25,000 B.C.–7000 B.C.)

Human life in Mesoamerica dates back at least 20,000 to 25,000 years. Some scholars believe it may stretch back even further—from at least 40,000 to 250,000 years; but the extremely early dates come from insecure dating techniques and, therefore, are uncertain. Most scholars agree that until new information is brought to light, 25,000 years is the best estimate.

During the Paleo-Indian era, nomads traveled through a moist, cool landscape, hunting the many game animals roaming the earth's rich surface. They usually bagged small animals, but sometimes people got lucky and caught a stag, a bear, or even a mammoth elephant. Little is known about these early wanderers' mythology because little remains to tell us much at all about any aspect of their lives. But we do know that they were thinking about their world, because at least one small bone carving of a dog-like animal remains from the site of Tequixquiac (Tay-keesh´-kee-yak), in the Basin of Mexico. This little figure may actually date back as far as 40,000 years ago, because it was found at the bottom of a Pleistocene lake. Simple stone scrapers and splinters of mammoth bone at Tequixquiac suggest that people did indeed get lucky at the hunt, and that they stayed here at least long enough to butcher the large beast and maybe to scrape and prepare its substantial hide.

We don't know for sure whether the little bone carving portrayed a mythological figure or simply that of a familiar animal such as a dog, wolf, or coyote. A lack of material remains does not necessarily mean that other kinds of cultural and religious activities were not very well developed. A rich oral tradition may have preserved complex mythological worlds; but of course, this could not have been preserved by the few material remains left us. In other words, there is no way for us to know what religious life was really like. We do know, however, that coyotes and various dogs appear all the way from early times up to the present as both great and minor mythological figures. Perhaps they were important in these earliest of times too. But we can only imagine.

2. The Archaic (ca. 7000–2000 B.C.)

The Archaic period ushered in a warmer climate, a weather pattern very similar to today's (Vivó Escoto 1964). With this new weather pattern came a more settled life. A number of game animals from the Paleo-Indian era disappeared, and others changed their habitats because of the climatic changes. This encouraged people to develop more diverse means of subsistence, including not only hunting and gathering but also agriculture. Except for deer, at first hunters found themselves relying almost exclusively on smaller game—such as opossums, rabbits, gophers, or lizards—and on the plants they gathered. In fact, they probably ate just about anything that walked, crawled, climbed, flew, or swam, as well as any plant that provided sustenance. Some plants, however, were more desired, perhaps because of their abundance, their superior ability to nourish, or their taste. In time, consistent patterns of gathering slowly helped people learn to cultivate certain plants, and encouraged them to remain in the same areas for entire rainy seasons, when the plants were at their best. And as life gradually became more settled, folk began to live in pit houses for at least part of the year. These dwellings were partly dug into the ground, with walls and roofs constructed of wood, reeds, or thatch arching over their cellar-like foundations.

While living this semisedentary life, Archaic folk developed corn from a couple of varieties of wild grasses. Although corn later became one of Mesoamerica's most important mythological symbols, during these very early periods it was not a very important part of the diet. The early corn was very hard and difficult to chew; it took several thousand years of cultivation and development before it tasted good enough to constitute so much as even one quarter of people's diets. It also took several thousand years before people settled down to live in just one place the year around, to concentrate on farming. Yet even with permanently settled lives, a complicated subsistence pattern continued; hunting, fishing, and gathering of wild fruits and vegetables remained as important as agriculture in village life. And as is true of corn and squash (another early plant), hunting and the game one hunted later became important mythological symbols.

At this time, people also began occupying the magnificent caves at Loltún in the Yucatán. Caves held an important place in Mesoamerican mythology. Pocketed by caverns draped with stalactites and stalagmites and crisscrossed by underground rivers, Loltún looked like the moist, dark underworld described centuries later in the Maya tale of the Popol Vuh. People used this cave for hundreds and hundreds of years, and not only for shelter: It seems likely that some of its hidden nooks and watery crannies were the sites of early Mesoamerican rituals. One can still see at Loltún and in other caverns of the area the ancient sinkholes carved out by water rushing through the Yucatán's limestone base, and the bright, crystal clear, blue-green underground pools that are home to exotic species of blind fish. These many shadowy, hidden places have not only sheltered people, fish, bats, and other earthly creatures but also a multitude of gods and powerful beings for millennia.

3. The Preclassic Period (ca. 2000 B.C.–A.D. 250)

The early Preclassic (ca. 2000–900 B.C.) ushered in both a much warmer climate and the development of larger villages and towns. Along with these came a more complex material culture, which occasionally displayed mythological themes that survived through pre-Conquest times, and in some cases, even into the present. Life was rich in communities like La Victoria, which lay in the estuaries of the Pacific Coast. The people of this coastal town feasted on oysters, marsh clams, turtles, and crabs. And at other coastal towns, they enjoyed fish, turtles, iguanas, snakes, various amphibians, a variety of birds, shrimp, and mammals such as deer and racoons, which were hunted seasonally. Villagers also cultivated corn, so that by 1500 B.C. it had begun to take its proper place in Mesoamerican life. Corn now constituted one half of the villagers' diets.

Long-distance contact may have been made by the people of La Victoria with people living as far away as South America, as suggested by certain stylistic commonalities in pottery style. This contact may have been made by boats along the coast, or through overland trade. Or such contact may have come indirectly, as goods were passed from group to group. And as in other villages of the early Preclassic, La Victoria's people did not use pit houses but instead built their dwellings on slightly raised platforms, which kept them above the earth's surface and nicely dry. Moreover, the early Preclassic people at La Victoria and elsewhere raised small temple mounds. For the first time, patterns of architecture developed that were to be repeated for thousands of years to come. Mesoamericans constructed numerous magnificent temple mounds before the Conquest, and many still use house mounds in tropical Mesoamerica.

The Preclassic period gives us the first clear indications of religious life in the material culture. People not only raised small temples to honor gods or other powerful beings (Figure 8), but clearly they were also thinking a great deal about what happens after death. In Preclassic villages throughout Mesoamerica, people sometimes buried their dead in the platforms upon which they erected their houses. Some of the dead were laid out and buried with a few grave goods; others were curled into fetal positions, inside large ceramic jars. Those buried in the platforms under the houses must have had great significance for the people moving through their daily affairs in the homes above. It is possible that these individuals had been particularly important in family and village life; perhaps their heirs wanted to preserve their memory by having them close at hand. Or it may have been more than a matter of mere sentimental memories; during later times, objects (especially bones) were believed to hold various powers that had the ability to affect and alter life on earth's surface. Maybe these buried ancestors held powers that were much needed by the family above.

Figure 8. An early Preclassic temple and mound from Cuello, Belize (N.D.C. Hammond. 1991. Cuello: An Early Maya Community in Belize. *Cambridge: Cambridge University Press, p. 103)*

The Preclassic also saw the rise of the first great urban civilizations. People in the valley of Oaxaca (ca 500 B.C.–A.D. 200), for example, began to level off the Monte Albán ridge in order to shape it into a series of grand plazas around which large buildings could be arranged (Adams 1991, 235–243). The buildings around these plazas included an astronomical observatory and various platforms supporting temples with thatched roofs. Elaborate tombs were erected there to house the remains of prominent people and their slaves and retainers. One of the earliest known examples of calendrics lies in one of these tombs; glyphs from the 260-day divinatory calendar grace the murals of Tomb 72, and urns bear the names of people based on calendrical dates. Monte Albán rose to prominence during the Preclassic period, expanding beyond its original area. This probably explains why war was a well-known activity. A series of famous friezes, now popularly referred to as the *danzantes,* or dancers, appear set into the wall of one of the platforms in the main plaza (Figure 9). These friezes most likely portray war captives who were being tortured.

The Olmec (ca. 2250–300 B.C.), however, are perhaps better known and certainly more influential; many consider them forerunners of all Mesoamerican civilizations (Diehl 1996, 29–33). The so-called Olmec heartland was located on the Gulf of Mexico, in what are now the states of Veracruz and Tabasco; but at their height, Olmec contact and influence spread from the Basin of Mexico, where Mexico City lies today, all the way south to today's El Salvador, Honduras, and western Nicaragua. At one time it was supposed that the heartland was the true center from which all cultural patterns were disseminated. Now, however, scholars recognize that many of its so-called colonies throughout Mesoamerica look more like urban civilizations in their own right and may not

Figure 9. A carved monument called a Danzante, from the Preclassic site of Monte Albán, depicting the lifeless figure of a dead and tortured war captive (Kay A. Read)

have been true colonies at all (Neiderberger 1996, 85–86, 92–93). It's currently thought that the Olmec era was more likely characterized by complex trading patterns among many centers that helped spread cultural patterns along with obsidian, jade, pottery, and other goods.

In its earliest phases, the Olmec heartland was dotted by small villages and towns whose inhabitants occupied the well-drained river levees and mangrove swamps. Like that of other villages in coastal areas, the environment here provided the Olmec with a rich array of foods. They planted corn and beans in small clearings in the high jungle; gathered wild palm nuts and other plant foods; and captured fish, turtles, clams, and other aquatic life. By 1200 B.C., urban centers began to rise that were too large to call villages. The social life in these centers was much more stratified than that in the smaller, more egalitarian villages. A number of centers existed during this time, including San Lorenzo, La Venta, Laguna de los Cerros, Las Limas, and Tres Zapotes (although this last center may have arisen after the demise of true Olmec culture). La Venta, Laguna de los Cerros, and Las Limas may have been the larger and more important centers in Olmec times; however, San Lorenzo is probably the best known to people today.

San Lorenzo was occupied and abandoned repeatedly in its 2,500 years of existence, but its cultural and political zenith was attained around 1200–900 B.C. (Adams 1991, 55–59; Cyphers 1996, 61–71). The city was located in the highest area in the region, where it would be safe from the flooding of the rivers flowing on all sides. This strategic position allowed the inhabitants to control communications, transportation, and trade in the area. By 1200 B.C., San Lorenzo was the main center of the region, with a royal family and various elites, and crafts people, farmers, fishers, and hunters. The immediate center's population was only about 1,000, but there was probably a population in the tens of thousands in the surrounding areas. This scattered urban pattern remained typical in this and the Maya areas until the Conquest. Traditionally, cities in southern Mesoamerica have tended not to have massive populations concentrated at their centers, instead reserving them for a small group of elites and their retainers. The rest of the population usually spread out in the surrounding areas, in house mound clusters, which were probably inhabited by large extended families or small communities of extended families.

Figure 10. An Olmec head monument from the Preclassic site of San Lorenzo, now in el Museo de Antropología de la Universidad Veracruzana in Xalapa, Veracruz, Mexico (Elizabeth L. Fuller)

San Lorenzo is best known for its massive sculptures of giant heads (Figure 10) and other figures carved out of the grey volcanic stone transported from the Tuxtla mountains some distance away. Among a variety of subjects (many of them human), ten giant sculptures portray San Lorenzo's rulers, providing some of the first evidence for the mythological importance of key governmental leaders. Later, the ritual and mythological importance of key governmental figures becomes even clearer, especially among the Maya. The Olmec probably used many of these sculptures ritually, to recreate mythological scenes, moving them around when needed. Perhaps because the stone was so difficult to get, old sculptures were sometimes recycled into new carvings. San Lorenzo's plateau also may have been the site of Mesoamerica's first mythic mountain, a temple mound gone extravagant. Some feel it was shaped like a bird, but others think the mound is now too eroded to tell. Between 900 and 400 B.C., San Lorenzo's importance waned considerably, for reasons as yet not understood. The possibilities range from internal revolt or external invasion to volcanic activity in the Tuxtla mountains, which altered the ecological balance in the area.

Figure 11. Altar 4 from the Preclassic site of La Venta, Veracruz, Mexico, depicting what is probably a ruler emerging from a cave (Kay A. Read)

Olmec occupation of La Venta, another important center, extended from 1200 to 400 B.C., with its apogee occurring around 600 to 400 B.C. (Adams 1991, 59–62; Lauck 1996, 73–81). The original site was large, covering more than 200 hectares (ca. 80 acres). Its central architectural feature is the Great Mound or Pyramid—another mythical mountain. Built atop a platform, the mound is more than 30 meters high, and one can view a panorama of 360 degrees from its summit. Many of the mythic themes of rulership and their relationship to ancestors and caves appear at this site, expressed by a wide variety of stunning sculptures large and small, carved in volcanic stone, jade, and serpentine. As at San Lorenzo, sculptors at La Venta carved great heads; one famous sculpture shows what is probably a ruler emerging from a cave. He appears to be tied to what may be his heirs, by ancestral ropes (Figure 11). This large, square sculpture may have been a throne. If so, the ruler would have sat above his ancestral cave upon a mat woven of reeds, cushioned by jaguar pelts. The giant heads at both sites may even have been carved from thrones such as this one.

Olmec contact and influence extended well beyond the heartland. From 1200 to 700/600 B.C., regional centers in the Basin of Mexico, for example, show strong Olmec presence (Adams 1991, 75–76; Niederberger 1996, 83–93). The Basin of Mexico in the Mexican highlands filled a rich mountain park at an elevation of about 7,200 feet or approximately 2,200 meters. Much of the water in the basin was saline, but the lower ends and some other area lakes were spring fed, offering an abundance of wetland flora and fauna. Ducks, fish, various reptiles, and amphibians such as frogs and salamanders probably were included in the local diet along with corn and other domesticated plants. People living here in the Preclassic era may even have eaten the protein-rich algae, which the Mexica (Nahua) are known to have consumed in this same area some 2,500 years later. As was true elsewhere, civilization had been developing in the region for many millennia, dating back at least to 6000 B.C. By 1200 B.C., the basin supported a culture as complex and sophisticated as that of the Olmec heartland. The Mexican highlands' relationship to the heartland is not completely understood, but it is clear that the peoples of the Basin of Mexico were trading with folk all over Mesoamerica.

Tlatilco (Tla-teel´-ko) served as one of the area's most important centers. Probably a most impressive city, Tlatilco was built on an island in a freshwater lake, as was the Mexica capital Tenochtitlan. Preclassic travelers must have been able to see Tlatilco from miles around. Unfortunately, in the twentieth century, highway construction, the erection of multistoried buildings, and clay excavation for brick manufacturing have destroyed much of Tlatilco's remains, leaving the site in very poor condition. Because so much has been lost, the reconstruction of the city's history is difficult. Nevertheless, a number of significant burial sites have been preserved, which reflect the center's stratified and complex society. Women and children as well as men were buried with considerable grave goods, indicating their importance. Many small ceramic and jade items display the rich mythological landscape of Olmec culture, including images of life and death, human-feline figures, beautiful women, and a variety of birds and other animals. Some of the objects even depict what was perhaps a very early form of pictographic writing.

By 400–300 B.C., Olmec culture had largely ceased to exist. San Lorenzo and La Venta had been abandoned by this time, and the peoples of Tlatilco in their waning years were no longer engaged with Olmec culture (Adams 1991, 107–111; Diehl 1996, 29–33). In the southern end of the Basin of Mexico, a new center had begun its rise to power. Cuicuilco (Kwee-kweel´-ko), a center of about 20,000 people, erected one of Mesoamerica's first round pyramids in about 400 B.C. At this time the town seemed destined for expansion (Figure 12). Previously the center had enjoyed some sort of relationship with the Olmec, and the original calendar round may have begun here on the summer solstice in 739 B.C. The earliest known recorded date, 679 B.C., also comes from this site (Edmonson 1988, x, 20). At the time when Cuicuilco was growing and building its pyramids, six small communities just to the north in the valley of Teotihuacan had just begun to build public architecture (Adams 1991, 109). Interestingly, these building projects were accompanied by a retreat of most communities to defensible

Figure 12. The round pyramid of Preclassic Cuicuilco (David Schavelzon. 1983. La Piramide de Cuicuilco. *Mexico City: Fondo de Cultura Economica, p. 35)*

positions on the hills above the prime farmlands. Competition must have been fairly fierce to force people into places not convenient to their fields; and if the competition was with Cuicuilco, that center seemed to be largely winning. But in 150 B.C. an event happened that altered the course of history in the Basin and perhaps even in all of Mesoamerica: A volcano erupted, completely destroying Cuicuilco and covering the surrounding area with lava. The National University of Mexico now rests atop this enormous lava flow. This disaster effectively cut Cuicuilco out of all competition, and its refugees probably migrated north to the six small towns in the valley of Teotihuacan.

These refugees from Cuicuilco's volcanic disaster may very well have helped give structure to what was to become perhaps the greatest of all Mesoamerican pre-Conquest centers, Teotihuacan (Matos Moctezuma 1990, 19). Such impressive volcanic activity may also explain the frequent appearance of pottery representations of an old fire god at Teotihuacan. By 100 B.C., the six towns had become two towns with a combined population of about 5000. By A.D. 100, the two towns had disappeared, and in their place stood a single great city, Teotihuacan, the population of which had climbed to about 60,000. Teotihuacan's inhabitants began building some of the center's most magnificent architecture; and by A.D. 150, the great Pyramids of the Sun and Moon had been erected, paving the way for the city's rise to fame in the Classic era as the post powerful center in ancient Mesoamerica.

4. The Classic Period (ca. A.D. 250–900/1000)

By A.D. 600, the urban center of Teotihuacan had reached a population of 150,000–200,000; probably larger than any other city in the entire world at the time. At present, many Mexicans call Teotihuacan simply *las Pirámides* or "the Pyramids." But the fifteenth-century Mexica (Nahua) gave it its proper name several centuries after it had collapsed and lay largely in ruins. The name *Teotihuacan* means "the place where the gods were created"; the Mexica visited this powerful site on a regular basis to perform sacrificial rituals on the decaying temple platforms. They thought the city's huge pyramids were the work of giants. No one knows who exactly lived there or what language they spoke, but we do know the city's inhabitants were of average stature. Probably one could have heard on its streets the syllables of numerous tongues, for many different peoples visited its markets and admired its awesome architecture. Some inhabitants even migrated from other parts, far outside the Basin of Mexico, living in tightly packed *barrios,* or neighborhoods within the city's boundaries. People from Oaxaca occupied one such barrio.

In the centuries leading up to A.D. 600, Teotihuacan became a diverse and sophisticated center, with tremendous power and influence throughout all of Mesoamerica. The city probably set patterns for urban structures and relations over a wide area of Mesoamerica. Its peoples traded with folk from as far away as both the Gulf and Pacific coasts and present-day Honduras. They sought obsidian, shells, and sting ray spines for use in various rituals; feathers to be woven into elite and ritual clothing; cacao (Mesoamericans invented chocolate); and cotton, salt, and grinding stones for their everyday needs. Some of these goods probably were gained solely through trade, whereas others arrived by tributary agreements, for Teotihuacan appears to have had a large amount of control over certain other urban centers, such as Kaminaljuyu and Tikal (both in present-day Guatemala). It used to be thought that this control was largely economic, but it's now fairly certain that the Teotihuacanos also waged war, although how much and with whom is not yet clear. The maintenance of their extensive trading

Figure 13. The Pyramid of the Moon at the Classic site of Teotihuacan at the northern end of the Avenue of the Dead, repeating the shape of the mountain behind it (Kay A. Read)

activities would have demanded military activity. Recent iconographic studies of some of the many beautiful murals and friezes decorating the city's buildings also indicate the importance of war.

Teotihuacan's urban pattern replicates its people's unique version of the Mesoamerican cosmos. Oriented 15°25´ east of north in order to align its buildings with the motions of the sun and the Pleiades, its grid pattern spreads out around a roughly north-south street now dubbed the "Avenue of the Dead." The Teotihuacan engineers diverted a river to intersect this avenue at right angles, thereby creating two major sectors, one in the north and another in the south. The Pyramid of the Moon (also a Mexica name) crowns the northern end of the avenue, repeating the shape of the mountain behind it (Figure 13). About halfway down this sector's eastern side, the Pyramid of the Sun rises majestically to the sky (Figure 14). Directly beneath the pyramid's center lies a cave that once held a spring, whose waters may have been channeled to the outside at one time. The cave contains four chambers, like a four-petaled flower. In the early 1900s the great Mexican archaeologist Leopoldo Batres (Lay-o-pol´-do Ba´trays) is said to have located sacrificial burials of children at the four corners of each of the pyramid's levels (Heyden 1975). In the southern sector, on the avenue's eastern side, stands a structure called the Ciudadela. Within it rises a somewhat more modest temple, called the Temple of the Feathered Serpent (Figure 15) because of the many feathered serpent sculptures gracing its four sides. Also decorated with various images of seashells, this monument holds the bodies of around 200 sacrificial offerings of what were most likely war captives. The west side of the southern sector was the site of Teotihuacan's bustling marketplace.

We do not know the languages spoken, much less the mythological stories told, on Teotihuacan's streets; nevertheless, these buildings speak of mythological themes through their images (Heyden 1975; López Austin et al. 1991; Pasztory 1992; Sugiyama 1993). The city's astronomical orientations mark the upper world. The Mesoamerican calendar can be found quite literally in the fundamental building blocks of the city's structures, for the measurements of its major streets and buildings, not to mention the building-stones, were based on classic calendrical calculations. Teotihuacan's builders used the numbers by which they tracked the motions of the sun and stars as the basis for their urban plan.

Figure 14. The Pyramid of the Sun at the Classic site of Teotihuacan (Kay A. Read)

And as it does in many Mesoamerican cosmic conceptions, water flowed through all levels of the city. Teotihuacan's pyramids may have been symbolic mountains enclosing their watery contents. The underworld can be found beneath the Pyramid of the Sun, with its cavern divided into four quarters, like Earth's Surface; and children appear to have been sacrificed to this all-important source of water, just as they were in later Mexica times. In the fifteenth and sixteenth centuries, two Mexica children were sacrificed each spring at the height of the dry season, just before the rainy season was due. As were these Mexica children, perhaps the Teotihuacano children also gave their lives so that the rain gods would have sufficient sustenance to release much-needed water. In some of the many murals at Teotihuacan, a storm deity appears who shares the Mexica rain god's (Tlaloc's) imagery. And at the Temple of the Feathered Serpent, the sea's waters and the warriors' sacrificial blood appear to have been equated in some way. Perhaps the blood of warriors was believed to slake the thirst of the gods, just as the sea provided water to the parched earth. This temple may be a re-creation in imagery of

Figure 15. Temple of the Feathered Serpent at the Classic site of Teotihuacan (Kay A. Read)

the creation of the cosmos and the importance of sacrifice and war to its fertility. The Pyramid of the Sun seems to mirror the underworld and evoke its need for sacrifice, tying it also to the local myth of human origins. For in many Mesoamerican myths, humans first emerged from underground caves; in Olmec sculpture for example, the Olmec ruler emerged from the underworld at La Venta.

Between A.D. 650 and 750, Teotihuacan collapsed, never to rise again. The reasons for its demise, as is true of many other Mesoamerican urban centers, are probably multiple and complex, including a variety of environmental factors such as climatic changes, soil exhaustion, deforestation, and erosion as well as political factors such as rivalry among factions contending for power. By A.D. 600, the city had already begun to pull out of its foreign interests, apparently unable to maintain them. At this time, someone probably sacked and looted the city. Much of the evidence of this destruction has the character of an inside job: The looters clearly knew the exact locations of well-hidden caches of valuables. By A.D. 900, the population of the valley of Teotihuacan was only 30,000. The city's fall initiated a domino effect on other areas of Mesoamerica. On the one hand, its pulling away from foreign interests in A.D. 600 precipitated its loss of power in a number of areas, such as Monte Albán, in Oaxaca. On the other hand, the declining power of Teotihuacan created a space within which certain lesser

Figure 16. The main plaza at the Classic site of Monte Albán, Oaxaca (James A. Schwalbach)

urban centers, such as Palenque, could grow and expand in the latter part of the Classic era.

Monte Albán and Teotihuacan reached their zeniths during the same period, in ca. 250 to 700 (Figure 16), and Teotihuacan's influence is clear in some of Monte Albán's elaborate murals, ceramics, and architectural features (Adams 1991, 243–252). Probably inhabited by the Zapotec, the city of Monte Albán grew tremendously during this period, spreading outward in the Oaxaca valley. More than two thousand terraces occupied the slopes of the main ridge, and many small ravines were dammed for water; the whole area was probably dotted with small ponds and houses. The main center along the ridge top, shaped on a north-south axis, boasted two large platforms on the ends of the main plaza and many pyramid-temples, palaces, patios, tombs (no less than 170!), an old observatory, and a newer ball court and residential building. People moved some of the old sculptures created during the pre-Classic period, including some of the *danzantes* friezes, in order to reuse them in new settings, and new stelae and sculptures appeared. The gods depicted in art at Monte Albán often replicated those of Teotihuacan, including rain and maize gods and the feathered serpent. A bat god appears to have played an important role, and an opossum god also apparently dwelt at Monte Albán. The tombs also display murals hinting at rituals. Above Tomb 103, a fascinating group of figurines offers us a glimpse of one such rite: The mask of a dead man rests on a tiny pyramid, which is surrounded by an orchestra and five priests, while another priest sports the old fire god's garb. We may be witnessing a memorial service for the inhabitant of the tomb below. With the decline of Teotihuacan, the greatness of Monte Albán also began to recede; and by A.D. 700, the rulers had abandoned the center, leaving their dead ancestors alone.

In contrast to Monte Albán, the Maya city of Palenque (seventh and eighth centuries A.D.) began to grow in the latter half of the Classic period, after Teotihuacan's fall. Like Teotihuacan's, this city's layout is instructive of things mythological. Embracing the sides of mountain ridges covered by dense tropical forests, Palenque dominated the southwestern region of the Classic Maya—what is now Chiapas, Mexico (Read 1995, 351–384). The brightly colored, many-staired Temple of the Cross was constructed on the city's northeastern side, its stone structure covered with intricately carved friezes and capped by a tall decoration called a roof comb. Two shorter temples, those of the Sun and of the Foliated Cross, faced each other across the patio on the Temple of the Cross's southeastern and northwestern sides. Downslope a bit and across a small stream, the magnificent Temple of Inscriptions rose, hugging the opposite ridge (Figure 17). Its wide, steep frontal staircase faced slightly east of north. A second, hidden set of stairs led down into the depths of the structure, to the crypt of Lord Pacal, ruler of Palenque (A.D. 615–683). The intricate carving on Pacal's stone sarcophagus depicts the ruler descending the tree that holds up the cosmos's western side. He has just died and now is entering the fleshless, toothy, bony jaws of the underworld monster. Pacal's son and successor Chan Bahlum (Chan Bah-loom´, ruled A.D. 684–702) built the other three temples. These four temples coordinate specific celestial motions with Pacal's death and Chan Bahlum's accession.

At the winter solstice, the sun rose behind the ridge in back of the Temple of the Foliated Cross, illuminating the Temple of the Sun with its beams. Inscriptions and carved images associate the temple with war, captive decapitation, rites of dynastic lineage, and an event that probably designated the six-year-old Chan Bahlum as heir apparent (Carlson 1976, 111). During the solstice, the sun set directly behind the Temple of Inscriptions, marking with its motions the hidden stairs leading to Pacal's tomb. As the sun dipped behind the ridge behind this temple, a beam of light passing to the right of a column in the Temple of the Cross would have highlighted a carved panel depicting God L, a major figure in the underworld. This panel pictures Pacal standing in the west and handing the scepter of rulership to his son, Chan Bahlum (Carlson 1976, 108–111). At their death, Palenque's rulers passed into the underworld as did the setting sun. And at that very moment, a new sun/ruler arose from the underworld. The reasons for Olmec rulers' emergence from the underworld are not entirely clear; but

Figure 17. The Temple of Inscriptions at the Classic site of Palenque (Kay A. Read)

Palenque's rulers appear to have done so because in life they had been equated with the sun, which traveled across the sky in the daytime, and in death, with the sun traveling through the underworld at night. And at the time of year when the days were shortest and the nights longest, as the winter sun paused before beginning its transformation into the summer sun, the dead Sun-Lord Pacal passed his power to the new, living Sun-Lord Chan Bahlum.

The Classic period came to an end between A.D. 900 and 1000. For many years, scholars considered the collapse of the Maya urban centers relatively rapid and mysterious. In fact, neither adjective describes the situation very accurately. Now most believe that Teotihuacan's decline sowed the seeds for the Classic Maya cities' collapse back in A.D. 600. After that point, some centers gained and some lost, but none influenced Mesoamerica to the degree that Teotihuacan had. Toward the end of the Classic era, Maya centers began markedly to decline, at differing rates and for different reasons that included: natural disasters such as earthquakes, hurricanes, and disease; ecological disasters such as the overuse of the land, and soil erosion; the economic isolation of some areas due to changing trade conditions; and sociopolitical reasons such as civil war, raiding among cities, invasion by non-Maya forces, and perhaps the inability of some of the aristocracy to adapt adequately to changing times. Although scholars are only beginning to unravel the complexities of these intertwined factors, it is clear that the ending of the Classic era and the beginning of the Postclassic was a time of great change for everyone, on almost all fronts.

Figure 18. A circular structure called the Caracol at the Postclassic site of Chichén Itzá (Elizabeth L. Fuller)

5. The Postclassic Period (ca. A.D. 900/1000–1521)

The beginning of the Postclassic period saw numerous changes, for people were on the move throughout Mesoamerica. Various Maya groups traveled from the Gulf coast to present-day Honduras, up into the Mexican highlands, and along the coasts of the Yucatán, forging new trading patterns. In fact, coastal trading patterns increased considerably, perhaps even replacing some of the old inland trade networks that had linked the Classic Maya cities. This change in trading patterns may even have contributed to the decline of some Classic cities. Other Maya groups from the Yucatán traveled south into the Maya highlands. And groups from the Mexican highlands traveled into the Yucatán, the Maya highlands, and even as far as present-day El Salvador. Centers such as Cacaxtla (Ka-kasht´-la) and Xochicalco (Sho-chee-kal´-ko) in the Mexican highlands proudly displayed murals and friezes on Mexican themes, in Maya artistic styles. In contrast, Chichén Itzá (Chee-chen´ Eet-za´) in the northern Yucatán displayed friezes and architectural decorations on Maya themes, in the Mexican style. This was a period of regionalization in which no one center or group held power throughout Mesoamerica. Chichén Itzá, however, was one of the more important centers, with close links to the new coastal trade.

Traditionally, scholars have divided the history of human occupation at

Figure 19. The pyramid called El Castillo at the Postclassic site of Chichén Itzá (see Figure 5) (Kay A. Read)

Chichén Itzá (ca. A.D. 900–1200)[9] into two periods, each associated with a different sector of the city. The earlier sector belongs to the Puuc (Pook) Maya who lived in the area, and the later, to the Toltecs (Tol´-teks); the first is seen as more Maya, and the latter, as more Mexican. The earlier, Puuc architecture (Figure 18) shares its style with a number of other centers in the immediate region, but the later, Toltec architecture (Figure 19) is clearly related closely to general Mexican highlands architectural styles, some of it apparently even copied directly from buildings at the Mexican highland city of Tula (Too´-la). Many scholars think that a group whom the Maya called the *Itzá* came to the city from Tula.

One well-known myth suggests that Chichén was invaded by a great Toltec leader named the Feathered Serpent—Quetzalcoatl (Ket-zal-ko´-wat, "Feathered Serpent") in Nahuatl, or Kukulcan (Koo-kool-kan') in Yucatec Maya—who wrested control from its indigenous occupants, the Itzá. Some scholars have pieced together this story from a variety of post-Conquest Mexican and Maya histories (e.g., see Coe 1987, 131–134). They say that political enemies of a ruler named Quetzalcoatl tricked him and then ousted him from Tula, after which he traveled to the Yucatán, capturing Chichén Itzá, where he was named Kukulcan by the Maya. Some say, therefore, that it was the Toltecs who built the impressive Mexican highlands–style buildings. Unfortunately, this version of Chichén's history may be as much the making of a scholarly myth as one of indigenous origin—a rather creative piecing together of scattered textual fragments. The problems with the story's veracity are fourfold. Firstly, the fragmented texts from which this story is drawn are not necessarily connected with each other; secondly, each can be interpreted in a variety of ways differing from this interpretation.[10] Third, if the source was Tula, why are the buildings at Chichén so much better constructed? Usually, copies are inferior to the original. Fourth, although the architectural styles in Chichén's two sectors differ radically, neither is purely one style or another. The Mexican-style buildings display a number of Maya themes, and the Maya-style include some Mexican themes.

New archaeological evidence suggests instead that the city was founded by the Itzá and formed a single, unified entity at the beginning (Henderson 1997, 213, 284 n. 17). Chichén's leaders may have used public architecture to express its increasingly cosmopolitan character, rather than to represent two different peoples. As in cities today in which a number of styles flourish simultaneously, each representing a different group or function, Chichén's distinctive sectors may have existed at the same time, each intended for different purposes. Today's governmental buildings patterned after the ancient Greeks aren't built by Greeks; they merely indicate ideals of government based on current interpretations of Greek governance. In other words, our ideas of classical Greece serve as a mythological model for contemporary governance. Likewise, the buildings at Chichén may represent Maya interpretations of Toltec ideals. Chichén's inhabitants may have had direct links with the Toltecs, perhaps even hiring architects from Tula for a grandiose urban renewal project. We don't really know. But the mere fact that Chichén's buildings look like Tula's is insufficient evidence on which to conclude that Toltecs invaded the city and put up those buildings.

The mythological figure of the Feathered Serpent appears to have been very important at Chichén. His image appears everywhere and in many guises, from feathered snake columns at the Temple of the Warriors (Figure 20) to small heads depicting the Feathered Serpent, mounted on a Puuc-style observatory. Like its many counterparts elsewhere in Mesoamerica, this round observatory tracked the sun's motions and those of Venus (Aveni 1980, 258–269), which as the morning star was often associated mythologically with the Feathered Serpent. Certainly the most impressive display of the great serpent occurs at the spring equinox. Then the setting sun slants its rays across the city to strike the balustrades of the Castillo (Kas-tee´-yo). The shadows coming from this play of light give the appearance of an undulating snake making its way down the pyramid's steps. Although the original inhabitants of Chichén are now gone, new people find this annual mythological display impossible to resist. Today, thousands of people travel to this grand archaeological site each year at the equinox: some just to witness the spectacle, others to perform their own rituals focusing on the great sky-serpent's descent. Kukulkan lives on, although in somewhat different form.

Around A.D. 1350,[11] Tenochtitlan was founded on an island in Lake Texcoco (Tesh-ko´-ko), in the Basin of Mexico (Figure 21). Built near the Preclassic Olmec site of Cuicuilco and the great Classic center of Teotihuacan, Tenochtitlan was to become the capital of the Mexica (Aztec, Nahua) empire and the last great urban center of pre-Hispanic Mesoamerica. At first it was no more than a small town whose inhabitants lived under the heavy thumb of a neighboring center. However, by the time Cortés entered Tenochtitlan in 1519, the population had grown to around 200,000. Not as influential as Teotihuacan had been, the city nevertheless claimed tremendous military and economic power over a huge region extending from the Gulf of Mexico to the Pacific Ocean, and from the modern Mexican states of Queretaro, Hidalgo, Veracruz, and Chiapas to the southeastern borders of Guatemala. Although at this time the Mexica had not yet subdued several major areas within their borders, their ruler Chief Speaker Motecuhzoma II (Mo-te-kuh-zo´-ma) was pursuing the conquest of those regions with an intensity likely to bring him eventual success in some measure (Townsend 1992, 106, 173–191).

Figure 20. The Feathered Serpent columns from the Temple of Warriors at the Postclassic site of Chichén Itzá (Kay A. Read)

Tenochtitlan was a sight to behold for Cortés and his small army (Figure 22). The city was situated in a lush basin surrounded by mountain ranges stretching out for miles and miles. In a fascinating account of the conquest, one of Cortés's officers, Bernal Díaz del Castillo, described what he saw from the top of the Templo Mayor (Great Temple) in the center of the city:

Figure 21. The frontispiece of the Codex Mendoza *depicting the founding of Tenochtitlan (Bodleian Library)*

That huge and cursed temple stood so high that from it one could see over everything very well, and we saw the three causeways which led into Mexico, . . . and we saw the fresh water that comes from Chapultepec [Cha-pool-te´-pek] which supplies the city, and we saw the bridges on the three causeways which were built at certain distances apart through which the water of the lake flowed in and out from one side to the other, and we beheld

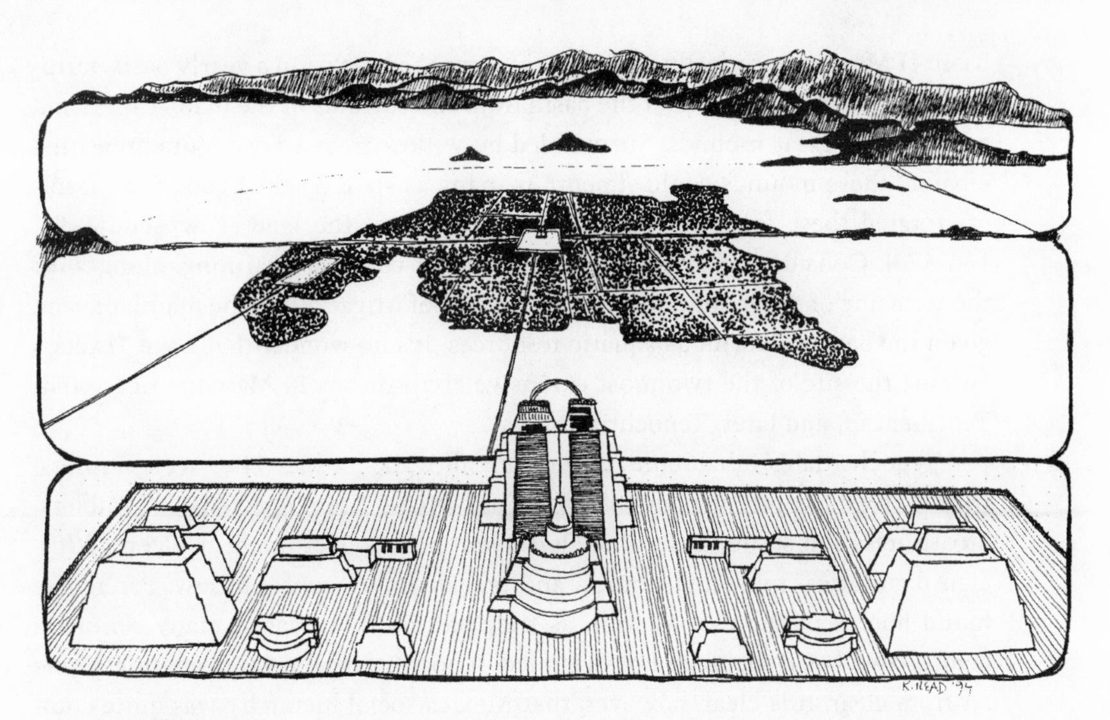

Figure 22. The Postclassic urban center of Tenochtitlan and its ritual center (drawing by Kay A. Read)

> on that great lake a great multitude of canoes, some coming with supplies of food and others returning loaded with cargoes of merchandise; and we saw that from every house of that great city and of all the other cities that were built in the water it was impossible to pass from house to house, except by drawbridges . . . or in canoes; and we saw in those cities Cues [temples] and oratories like towers and fortresses and all gleaming white, and it was a wonderful thing to behold; then the houses with flat roofs, and on the causeways other small towers and oratories that were like fortresses.
>
> . . . We turned to look at the great market place and the crowds of people that were in it, some buying, others selling, so that the murmur and hum of their voices and words that they used could be heard more than a league off. Some of the soldiers among us who had been in many parts of the world, in Constantinople, and all over Italy, and in Rome, said that so large a market place and so full of people, and so well regulated and arranged, they had never beheld before (Díaz del Castillo 1956, 218–219).

The great causeways Díaz describes connected this amazing city to the mainland. Farm fields called *chinampas* (chee-nam´-pas) ringed the urban island. This extremely efficient and intensive form of agriculture was first used in Maya and Olmec areas during the Preclassic period; the wetlands environment of the

Basin of Mexico was ideally suited to chinampa farming. On a yearly basis, farmers dredged up the rich soil of the basin from the bottoms of the many canals and piled it onto great mounds. Surrounded by willow trees whose roots prevented erosion, these mounds could support as many as six crops in a good year; farmers rotated these crops to maintain the fertility of the land (Townsend 1992, 166–173). Considering the high productivity of chinampa farming, along with the terracing of the mountainsides and the use of irrigation on the mainland, and given the basin's enormous aquatic resources, it's no wonder that Lake Texcoco became the site of the two most extensive civilizations in Mesoamerica—first, Teotihuacan, and later, Tenochtitlan.

Tenochtitlan's inhabitants came from all walks of life: They were farmers, traders, craftspeople, vendors, doctors, midwives, ritual specialists, gamblers, prostitutes, and so on. Elite officials served in the government, welcomed foreign dignitaries, mustered armies, and presided over courts of law. Foreigners found homes in the city as well, as they had in Teotihuacan many centuries before. Two basic social groups occupied Tenochtitlan, but their relationship is far from clear. It is clear, however, that Mexica social hierarchy was quite complex and that the elite class, called *pipiltin* (pee-peel´-tin), did not have an overarching control over the commoners, who were called *macehualtin* (ma-say-wal´-tin).[12] Not all elites had power, for some worked for other, more influential elite employers; at the same time, some nonelite merchants could wield a great deal of influence, and under certain circumstances, even elites shared the status of commoners. Moreover, two different schools educated the city's young men, who enjoyed upward social mobility if they showed talent either in school or at war. Social group membership appears to have been closely linked to a mythological ancestry. Tenochtitlan was divided into four quarters. In the middle of each quadrant stood a small temple housing the patron god, the ancestral progenitor of the quarter's inhabitants. Whether linked by blood ties or not, all of the inhabitants of each sector were seen as genealogically related and could trace their mythic heritage back to the city's patron god, the deity that gave life, power, and direction to their existence: Huitzilopochtli (Weet-zee-lo-pocht´-lee), the Mexica war god.

A huge ritual district sat at the crossroads in the center of Tenochtitlan. The Templo Mayor, from which Díaz surveyed the city's bustling scene, dominated both the city and this ritual district. Two sets of stairs mounted its western facade, each leading to a small house at the top, belonging to a god. The northern building housed Tlaloc, the rain god. Sacrificial hearts were placed in the bowl held ready by the hands of a stone figure called a *chacmool* (chak-mool´), which was positioned in front of Tlaloc's house (Figure 23). If rain was to come, the rain gods who released it from the mountains that held it had to be fed, for everything

Figure 23. A Chacmool that sat in front of the Postclassic site of the Templo Mayor, Tenochtitlan (Kay A. Read, Museo del Templo Mayor, Mexico City)

was alive in this cosmos. As had the people at Chichén Itzá, the Mexica copied their chacmool from the Toltec one that stood at Tula. The southern building housed Huitzilopochtli. When warrior sacrifices were made in front of this temple, the bodies were decapitated, dismembered, and flung down the steps toward the large, round panel at its base. This panel depicted the conquest and sacrifice of Coyolxauhqui (Ko-yol-shauw´-kee), the sister of Huitzilopochtli. Mexica rulers were genealogically related both to the Toltecs and to Huitzilopochtli.

This great cosmic temple-mountain marked the two seasons that the sun carried on its back as it journeyed along its annual path. The northern house marked summer's rainy season, when the sun rose from behind the northern half of the eastern mountain range. The space between the two houses marked the year's two middle points, the equinoxes. And the southern house marked the sun's rising from behind the southern half of the eastern mountain range, in winter's dry season. When the sun was in Tlaloc's house, the time had come to plant crops and tend the fields. But when the sun moved to Huitzilopochtli's house, the season of war had arrived. The fields of war were considered a plentiful source for harvesting the human sacrificial offerings needed to sustain various nonhuman beings in the cosmos. Summer was a time to concentrate on feeding humans; winter, a time to feed other important beings. Of course war had more purposes than feeding various gods and other beings. It also served to expand or consolidate the Mexica domain. But the growing of crops was so important that Mexica rulers deemed it wise to direct their energies toward the agricultural fields in the summer and not toward the fields of war; to do otherwise was considered foolish. As one ruler told his three sons and possible heirs to the throne:

> And especially take care of the ridge, of the ditch. Plant and sow in the field. . . . If you dedicate yourself only to nobility, if you do not plant in the ridges, in the ditches, what will you give anyone to eat? What will you eat? What will you drink? Where have I seen nobility [help] anyone rise from bed or go to sleep?[13] Sustenance [to eat and drink] is life; most truly it is said: [by it] one rules, one governs, one conquers. Where have I seen an empty-gutted one [one with no intestines], a non-eater, who rules, who governs?[14]

But within just a few years, Mexica (indeed, all Mesoamerican) nobility would be almost eradicated by the very visitors who had found Tenochtitlan so amazing—the people who called the Templo Mayor "cursed." They razed the city's magnificent buildings to the ground, using the stones as foundations for new buildings and the rubble to fill in Tenochtitlan's canals. In just a short time, a completely different city stood in its place—one built on a grid pattern, not on the four cardinal directions of the cosmos. Spanish governmental buildings rose where Motecuhzoma's palace once stood. And the central ritual district housed a large cathedral marking the heavens and celebrating the single sacrifice of Christ rather than a temple marking the sun's journey along the horizon and the sacrificial sustenance of a multitude of human, nonhuman, and cosmic beings (Figure 24). For no longer did those in power view the sun and all other things as alive and in need of food. A radical change was taking place.

6. The Spanish Conquest and Colonization of Mesoamerica (1521–1808)

On 3 August 1492 Christopher Columbus set sail from Palos, Spain, in search of a quick western route to the vast trading riches of the Indies, which at the time included much of India and Asia (Figure 25). Believing that China lay a mere 5,000 nautical miles to the west, he expected to sail first to the Canary Islands off the coast of Africa, and from there only 2,400 nautical miles more to the easternmost islands of Japan. There he meant to establish a trading town. Of course, this never happened. Many more miles later than expected, on 12 October 1492, Columbus

Figure 24. The main Catholic Cathedral in Mexico City with the ruins of the Templo Mayor in the foreground (Kay A. Read)

found himself not on the shores of Japan but on those of a Caribbean island probably populated by the Taino people. Two decades later the Europeans realized their mistake; but by then the word *Indians,* which they had used to describe the local inhabitants of what they had thought were the Indies, had become habitual, and it would remain so for centuries. Because the first Indians the Spanish saw were village farmers who wore little clothing in their hot climate, all Indians henceforth were viewed as simple primitives, even after Cortés encountered the impressive expanses of the Mexica empire. European cartographers named this territory *America,* after Italian navigator Amerigo Vespucci, whose accounts of his travels to this "New World" were widely read throughout Europe.

A new myth had been born that was to endure for at least the next five centuries. Of course, this was a European myth, not a Mesoamerican one. The land was not new to the people who had been its discoverers 24,000 years or more before, none of whom called themselves Indian or their various lands America, and none of whom viewed themselves as uncivilized. Nor should they have. A culture with the sophistication and antiquity of Mesoamerica certainly was not primitive. Tenochtitlan rivaled any European city of the time in both size and complexity; and Mesoamericans were skilled mathematicians, astronomers, doctors, and artists, sometimes surpassing European abilities in those areas. This

Figure 25. A sixteenth-century painting of Columbus and his ships in first contact with the New World (Library of Congress)

was not a case of a civilized nation overcoming a few primitive people but of one complex civilization confronting another in what was eventually to become an enduring battle over whose way of life had the right to exist. Because of the power of myth to create reality, the European names stuck, along with the assumptions behind them. After all, the new myths were certainly convenient and effective foundations for conquest. They have continued to serve as useful legitimating tools for those in power up to the present, often at the expense of the indigenous populations at whom these myths were and sometimes still are directed.

On Holy Thursday in 1519, Cortés and about 600 men landed on the coast of Veracruz. From there they began a march inland to Tenochtitlan, the center of the Mexica ruler Motecuhzoma II.[15] On 8 November 1519, Cortés and his forces entered Tenochtitlan as guests of Lord Motecuhzoma. Almost two years later, in August 1521, Motecuhzoma II was dead and the current ruler Cuauhtemoc (Kwaw-te´-mok) had surrendered to the Spanish invaders. The battle had not really been as easy as many historical myths suggest. The Conquest came at great cost and absorbed many resources: help from thousands of Indian warriors opposed to the Mexica, brought in by alliances that often were arranged by an Indian woman named Malinche (Ma-lin´-chay) or Doña Marina (Don´-ya Maree´-na); severe losses to the Spanish when they retreated from heavy fighting in Tenochtitlan in June 1520, during a night they called *La Noche Triste* ("The Sad Night"), following an intensive, three-month siege of the city; and finally, the hugely debilitating effects on the Mexica of smallpox, a new disease from Europe against which the indigenous people had no natural resistance. Cortés also had had to destroy his ships in order to prevent some of his own men from leaving for home before the march on Tenochtitlan (he later salvaged the iron fittings to make new boats with which to attack the island stronghold). It had taken nearly two years, thousands of Indian allies, enormous struggles, and a major epidemic to defeat the Mexica (Figure 26).

Once in power, the Spanish put into effect vast changes in the land they now called New Spain.[16] The conquistadores received rewards for their work from Cortés in the form of tribute and land grants. The *encomienda* (en-kom-ee-en´-da) system also allowed the Spanish conquerors to acquire grants of people in return for their education in the Christian faith and supposed protection. The conquerors often abused these privileges and doled out extremely harsh treatment to their Indian laborers in spite of orders from the Spanish government not to do so. Around midcentury, the Spanish government took more control over colonial affairs and freed the Indians, making them citizens of Spain, and instituting policies of protection that helped somewhat to alleviate abuses. Still, by the end of the sixteenth century, some estimate that the depopulation rate among Indians was close to 90 percent, due to repeated smallpox epidemics, harsh labor practices, maltreatment, and the enforced separation of male from female laborers, which contributed to a lower birthrate.

The vast economic inequities begun with the encomienda system in the early part of the sixteenth century were furthered by the growth of haciendas (ah-see-en´-das), a system particularly suited to the world's economic conditions in the seventeenth and eighteenth centuries (Cosío Villegas, Bernal, et al. 1995, 57–58). Huge ranches and farms swallowed up large expanses of Indian lands. The loss of their land forced Indians into labor on the ranches, in mines, or in the cities, creating a dependence among them on goods produced by others. Laborers on the ranches and mines found themselves paid so little that they had to go into debt to the owners, who sold the laborers basic goods for more than they earned. This assured that they could not leave their employers. Those in the cities could find themselves working alongside black slaves and prisoners in

*Figure 26. An indigenous illustration of the Conquest of Mexico (*Lienzo de Tlaxcala, *pl. 42, Museo Nacional de Antropología, Mexico City)*

factories, where supported by harsh labor laws the exploitation was even worse than in the countryside. By 1800, Mexico had become one of the richest countries in the world; but although it had tremendous wealth, vast numbers of extremely poor people lived there in misery. Sixty percent of the population was still Indian; 20 percent was mestizo (mes-tee´-zo, of mixed European and Indian heritage); blacks and mulattoes (of mixed European and black heritage) remained a very small percentage; and Creoles (poor immigrants from Spain) constituted 16 percent. The Creoles slowly developed into a small middle class. More than 80 percent of the population lived in severe poverty, and the top 4 percent held the major part of the wealth.

It is no wonder, then, that the poor frequently rebelled against their harsh conditions, especially since the majority of poor people lived in isolated areas that had not yet been fully conquered. Between 1531 and 1801, various indigenous peoples rose against Spanish rule more than 38 times (Castro 1996, 124–125). The specific reasons for rebellion varied. Some wanted to destroy the Spanish, expel everything Spanish (even their chickens, cats, and dogs), and effect a complete return to what in most respects had become a mythic pre-Conquest past. Others viewed such a return as impossible and appropriated particular European cultural innovations as marks of a better form of liberty: Such things as cattle husbandry and mining techniques might be seen as new and useful tools, in the hands of Indians. Other movements sought greater equality and did not necessarily seek to expel the Spanish. Much could be and was accepted by indigenous populations, even in rebellion. In the insurrection of Canek (Kan-ek', Maya), in 1761, it was thought that warriors who died in combat would be resurrected, like Christ; and in other uprisings, rebels celebrated masses with tortillas and pulque (a fermented drink made from the agave cactus). In 1712, the Tzeltales (Tsel-ta´-lays, Maya) created a theocracy for a short time, modeled on the Spanish hierarchy, with native bishops, vicars, and a royal superior court. The Indians called themselves "Spanish," and the vanquished Spanish, "Indians"; "Indian" women were required to marry the "Spanish" victors and work in their households. Other indigenous rebels hoped for a major, cleansing catastrophe and the arrival of a new era. Some of these millenarian movements sought the return of the creator of the sky and earth, Lord Motecuhzoma. Saints, including the Virgin of Guadalupe, led still other insurrections. Toward the end of the Colonial period, many Indians thought they had the help of the King of Spain. After all, was not he the great protector of the people, the symbol of good, whose picture was so proudly hung in schools, government buildings, and churches? It could not be he who was the root of their problems but only corrupt leaders closer to home.

If the political conquest of the indigenous populations of New Spain was not complete, neither was their spiritual conquest (Figure 27). Conversions to Christianity occurred so rapidly that their superficiality was unavoidable. The first Catholic fathers sometimes performed mass conversions of thousands of Indians at a time. Moreover, these conversions took place under conditions of defeat; and when defeat had occurred in pre-Conquest times, the people believed that their own patron god was defeated by the victor's god but nonetheless continued to exist. In Tenochtitlan's ritual district stood a kind of jail, in which dwelt the many patron gods whom Huitzilopochtli had defeated. Hence, Mesoamericans may very well have seen Jesus as the victor over their now defeated but still living gods. Later their gods rose again in rebellion; or as more time passed, Jesus,

Figure 27. The Catholic Cathedral in the town of Mitla, Oaxaca, with the earlier pre-Conquest temple seen directly beneath the foundation (Jason J. González)

Mary, and the saints joined with ancient gods in an enlarged and even more complex cosmos. The result was not a simple overlay of Christianity on indigenous traditions or even a mixture of the two but the creation of many new, theologically complicated religions forming continuities with both Catholicism and the ancient traditions (Ángeles Romero 1996, 226). A variety of religious forms arose in the different regions: Earthly landmarks now might house local deities as well as saints; the devil set up housekeeping inside particular mountains; and the old deities inhabited the underworld, whereas the saints inhabited the sky. In some places, saints took over for the patron gods as the heads of ancestral lines. The old traditions were not completely lost, nor was Christianity totally rejected; instead, each enriched the other. Today, many villagers still bless the four quarters when they grill the first tortilla, watch out for scary beings inhabiting woods and rivers, nourish various "souls" (a Christian concept)[17] with sacrifices of chickens, and attend church on Sundays. Some people view these activities as mutually contradictory; others consider them a unified tradition. When these folk-Christian religious traditions of *el pueblo* clearly claim allegiance with Catholicism, current scholarship generally views them as part of the "Popular" or "People's Church" (*Iglesia Popular),* and recognizes that they may be severely at odds politically and theologically with the Church hierarchy and its approved doctrines.

As with everything in Mesoamerica, continuity and invention were intertwined—in social and group activities as well as in personal actions. People served the church now in the same socially patterned ways in which they had served the temple. This service translated into indigenous understandings of communal property as well (Ángeles Romero 1996, 225–231; Castro 1996, 109–110). Traditionally, property had always been held communally and work done cooperatively. So in post-Conquest times, groups called *cofradías* (ko-fra-dee´-as) developed. Those who served the church also guarded a chest or *cofra* in which were kept cash; records of which lands, produce, and cattle herds were communal; and records of who produced and maintained them. These groups fulfilled the role of governing bodies in villages, towns, and city neighborhoods. But in 1759, the Spanish king Charles III began to pressure the groups to move their assets to federal banks so that the government might gain greater control over money and power in local communities. This pressure, coupled with a famine in 1756 and with other forces, helped move New Spain toward revolution and a bid for independence. And in 1808, events in Europe helped make independence a reality.

7. Independence to the Present (1808–2000)

The occupation of Spain by Napoleon in 1808 weakened the Spanish hold on the Americas.[18] By this time, many Creoles had gained a modern education, having been trained by Jesuit priests in humanist philosophy, and some had begun to move into the wealthiest social strata. Inspired by the successful revolutions in the United States (1776) and France (1789), they argued strongly for independence and played a major role in mobilizing local forces against Spain. Conservatives remained loyal to Spain, but their voices were overcome by the more vociferous liberals who deeply resented Spanish intrusion into community affairs, taxes, and trade restrictions, and who wanted to be masters in their own houses. On Sunday morning, 16 September 1810, the Jesuit-trained Father Miguel Hidalgo y Costilla freed the prisoners in his village of Dolores, Mexico, and locked up the Spanish authorities. Calling his parishioners to mass, the elderly priest urged them to join with him in overthrowing the bad government (Figure 28). Within days, his 600 followers had swelled to 100,000 workers from the mines and haciendas; and when the Bishop excommunicated him, his followers forced the cathedral council to lift the ban. This outcry, or *grito de*

Figure 28. A mural painting by Juan O'Gorman depicting Hidalgo crying from the church steps, surrounded by his followers (Corbis-Bettmann)

Hidalgo, launched the revolution. Mexico officially gained its independence on 27 September 1821, just twelve days after the other Central American countries had declared their independence. From 1822 to 1823, what are now the countries of Costa Rica, El Salvador, Guatemala, Honduras, and Nicaragua were legally parts of Mexico.[19] But in 1823, they broke ranks with Mexico and formed the Central American Federation, which lasted until 1838, when it broke into the five countries we know today.

Inequities between the haves and the have-nots continued into the nineteenth and twentieth centuries, exacerbated by almost continual political conflicts. Throughout the nineteenth century, liberals and conservatives fought each other politically and militarily in both Central America and Mexico; frequent coups, military dictatorships, unstable political alliances, and continuing indigenous uprisings defined the entire region. These constant political tensions undermined the economy, causing suffering especially among the poor. Moreover, the United States and European powers repeatedly inserted themselves into

Mesoamerican political and economic affairs. War with the United States resulted in Mexico's loss of its northernmost lands.[20] France, under Napoleon III, seized power for a brief period, placing the young, romantic Hapsburg prince Maximilian and his beautiful Belgian wife Carlotta in power. But pressure from the United States and fear of war in Europe weakened France's hold. On 5 May 1862, Mexican defenders drove the invading French back (a victory that is still celebrated today in Cinco de Mayo festivities); and in 1867, Benito Juarez executed Maximilian and rode victorious into Mexico City. Carlotta, who had returned to France to plead unsuccessfully for Napoleon's support, went insane from worry and grief. The Mexican chaos was temporarily stanched in 1877, when Porfirio Díaz took control of the country by force, asserting an extremely efficient rule that lasted 30 years. As Mexico began to attract foreign capital, its economy gradually improved.

By the late nineteenth century, coffee had been introduced into Central America and southern Mexico, and it soon became a major product of those regions. Euro-U.S. powers increasingly sought to control coffee and fruit growing interests as well as mining and oil concerns in all Mesoamerican countries. External powers also funded and promoted the shipping enterprises needed to export those products, by building railroads and lobbying for canals. By the early twentieth century, the United States had become the dominant player in these politico-economic battles, and Porfirian Mexico (which benefited economically from U.S. interests) was a model of peaceful development for the region.

As in earlier periods, however, only a minority enjoyed Mexico's great wealth under the Porfirian regime, and Indians lost more and more of their lands to big investors. To make matters worse, Díaz suggested the possibility of free, democratic elections toward the end of his reign, but then did not follow through with that suggestion. The poor economic conditions for most Mexicans, and the younger generation's resentment of Porfirian autocracy, resulted in revolution and the ousting of the 80-year-old Díaz in 1911. Led by the mythic Virgin of Guadalupe, and in part by the Indian guerrilla rebel leader Emiliano Zapata (d. 1919; see Figure 29), the revolution ended in 1920, after a decade of intense fighting. A lasting stability was finally established nine years later with the institutionalization of political rule under the leadership of what is now called the Institutional Revolutionary Party (PRI).[21] But almost two decades of considerable chaos had left the economy a shambles. Working against strong opposition from landowners and foreign investors, Álvaro Obregón, the first Mexican president (1920–1924, before the PRI), and President Lázaro Cárdenas (1934–1940, after the creation of the PRI) instituted limited social and land reforms that addressed some of the inequities, but these efforts did not radically alter the situation.

Throughout most of the twentieth century, Central American countries remained under the control of military dictators supported by small classes of

Figure 29. Emiliano Zapata—detail of a mural by Diego Rivera in Cuernavaca, Mexico (Archivo Iconografico, S.A./Corbis)

very wealthy landowners who cooperated with the heavy presence of the United States. This foreign presence was largely economic, but it was sometimes supported by direct political and military intervention. For most of the century, from the 1920s to the years of Ronald Reagan's presidency (1981–1989), much of U.S. involvement centered on sometimes real but just as often imagined fears of Communist influence in Central America. Harsh economic sanctions were placed on governments that were not sympathetic to U.S. interests, whereas sympathetic governments received tremendous amounts of foreign aid, including military support. None of this did anything to help the huge numbers of poor living in these countries; instead, the foreign presence often exacerbated already poor living conditions. Because social inequities were not adequately addressed, civil wars broke out in Nicaragua, Guatemala, and El Salvador in the late 1970s and early 1980s.

U.S. involvement in Nicaragua was particularly marked in the early part of the century. In 1909, the United States sided with rebels to drive a ruler from power who was not cooperating with U.S. interests in building a canal from the Atlantic to the Pacific. Marines were sent to Nicaragua in 1911 to protect U.S. interests and supervise elections, and a Marine force remained there almost continuously until 1933. These early incursions into the government's operations were resisted by rebels led by Augusto César Sandino, who was later assassinated by U.S.-trained Nicaraguan troops. In the 1970s, widespread protests against the forty-year-old rule of Anastasio Somoza began to build. Somoza had been sympathetic to U.S. economic interests and had done little to relieve the social and economic inequities. By 1978, the tensions had grown into civil war, and by 1979, the rebel guerrillas, including a group called the Sandinistas (named after Sandino), had won the war. The new government headed by the Sandinistas undertook many reforms designed to help the poor and improve the economy, but recovery was slow. In the 1980s, rebels called the contras sided with old Somoza forces in stepping up antigovernment attack, and in 1983, they launched an all-out war. President Reagan claimed that the Sandinista government was communist, and awarded U.S. support to the contras, ordering mines to be placed in Nicaraguan harbors and slapping an embargo on the country. Short-lived negotiations between the two sides fizzled and fighting resumed in 1989, only to cease after an anti-Sandinista president was elected. Since then the Sandinistas continue to influence politics in the country, although they have not been able to recapture the presidency.

In El Salvador, the United States backed the government during a twelve-year civil war in the 1980s. Here too, the roots of war lay in longstanding economic inequities that governmental policies had exacerbated. As elsewhere in the early 1900s, coffee had been introduced into El Salvador. This precipitated reforms in 1908 that removed many lands from peasant farmers and placed them in the hands of a small but wealthy minority. A system was set up very similar to the hacienda system of the previous two centuries, and by the 1920s, governmental and Church pressures successfully had eradicated the cofradías. In the early 1930s, the world plunged into economic depression. The poor suffered most because they had the least to begin with and governmental policies failed to support them. Economic suffering, the overthrow of a reformist leader, and the events of the preceding two decades had caused enormous resentment toward the government. As a result, in 1932 the communist trade unionist Farabundo Martí led peasants against the government of President Maximiliano Martínez, demanding reforms. The response was a massacre now called *La Matanza* (La Ma-tan´-za, "the Slaughter"), which killed an estimated 10,000 to 30,000 people, most of them peasants. In its aftermath, all overtly indigenous cultural patterns were outlawed; one could be killed for merely speaking Pipíl (Pee-peel´, a dialect of Nahua), for wearing native dress, or for producing indigenous crafts.

La Matanza and Martí's name became rallying cries for civil war in the 1980s. The war ended with a United Nations brokered peace accord in 1992. As in other Central American countries, enormous economic and social inequities underlay the Salvadoran civil war. Before the war, 1 percent of the population held 70 percent of the land, and 8 percent of the population received 50 percent of the national income, whereas 20 percent owned no land and received only 2 percent of the national income. Moreover, 70 percent lived in absolute poverty, mostly working on hacienda-like plantations; their wages could not provide enough food to meet even minimum health requirements. In the 1970s, when the world entered a major economic recession, many faced starvation on a daily basis. Peaceful demonstrations were countered by massacres, and by 1980, the

Figure 30. FMLN (Farabundo Martí National Liberation Front) painted on the side of what was left of a bombed bridge in El Salvador (Kay A. Read)

peasants were engaging in guerrilla warfare (Figure 30). Although great numbers of peasants who joined the rebel forces of the Farabundo Martí National Liberation Front (FMLN) did not even know what communism was, much less adhere to it, the Reagan government supported the Salvadoran government, accusing the rebels of being communist-inspired and -controlled.[22] Hundreds of millions of dollars flowed into the country from the United States, and they trained Salvadoran military personnel in Honduras and the United States. While wealthy Salvadoran landowners set up extra houses and large bank accounts in places like Miami, massive numbers of refugees fled the country to Nicaragua and Honduras. Others came legally and illegally to the United States. Most were fleeing death squads that systematically tortured and murdered anyone speaking out against the government, as well as other abuses of human rights (such as massacres of whole villages).

After the demise of the Soviet Union and its communist satellite nations, U.S. interest in El Salvador waned, causing the withdrawal of U.S. support from the Salvadoran government. The FMLN fought government forces to a stalemate, leaving the country in disarray. The war had claimed some 70,000 lives, in a country about the size of Massachusetts. From 1992 to 1995, the United Nations oversaw a moderately successful reconstruction that sought to accomplish necessary, substantive reforms. More recently, new industries and economic policies based on free trade appear to be changing conditions in El Salvador. But the country still faces high unemployment, and the gap between the rich and poor is growing again. El Salvador is far from healed, and many remain suspicious that the new policies are only a repeat of policies of earlier centuries, benefiting foreigners and small groups of the wealthy elite while leaving the vast majority of the population in a state of exploitation and poverty.

Guatemala, the home of many Maya groups, has experienced the same social and economic problems as Nicaragua and El Salvador, and is no stranger to civil war. As elsewhere, private owners gained control of peasant lands, turning them to coffee and fruit production, thereby forcing landless peasants to work in hacienda-like conditions. In 1951, the reform government of Jacobo Arbenz Gúzman began taking over much land that was owned privately by a small minority, in order to redistribute it to landless peasants. These lands included large areas owned by the United Fruit Company, which maintained close ties to business interests in the United States. The U.S. government, fearing communism, supported a rebel attack against Gúzman, forcing him to retire. After a decade of chaos and military rule, civilian rule was restored under Julio César Méndez Montenegro in 1966. But violence grew during his regime, with terrorist raids killing many. By the late 1970s, the violence had become widespread. Antigovernment groups included many poor Indians and peasants who like the Salvadoran and Nicaraguan rebels sought a better quality of life. As tensions mounted, many Indians fled deep into the Guatemalan mountains, to Mexico, and to the United States. In 1996, the Guatemalans finally signed a peace agreement, ending some thirty years of violence.

As elsewhere, conditions in Mexico had always adversely affected the poor, but they increasingly were affecting the nascent middle class, as the poor became poorer. In the early 1960s, 10 percent of the population received almost 50 percent of the national income, and 40 percent of the population, barely 14 percent. By 1977, 10 percent of the middle class had become poor, and the poor were receiving less (Cosío Villegas, Bernal, et al. 1995, 154); economically based class distinctions were becoming more marked. The Mexican economy, by the early 1980s, was on the verge of collapse due to a decline in the oil market. Severe austerity measures were imposed, including a devaluation of the peso that left many middle-class and poor people destitute and many others living on the edge. Moreover, corruption at the highest levels of the Mexican government had increased dramatically since World War II.

It was in this environment that a new mythic political figure was born. Shortly after the institution of the North American Free Trade Agreement (NAFTA), it became painfully clear that President Carlos Salinas de Gotari (who had assumed office in 1988, after elections that were rumored to have been fixed) was implicated in major economic scandals. His brother Raul had been jailed for amassing huge sums of money from drug racketeering. Accused of stealing the equivalent of billions of dollars from Mexico and placing them out of reach in foreign banks, Carlos Salinas eventually was forced into exile. He quickly became the mythic cause of all of Mexico's economic woes. Dolls, masks, and T-shirts mocking him appeared overnight in the markets, and street dances and plays satirized him as the latest symbol of the decadent and exploitative rich.

Given the enduring poor economic conditions throughout Mesoamerica, it is not surprising that indigenous and peasant rebellions continued throughout the nineteenth and twentieth centuries. From 1847 to 1855, Maya Indians in the Yucatán rebelled in response to racism, the destruction of communal life by governmental attempts to disband cofradías and take over communally owned lands, and other forms of exploitation, such as hacienda-type working conditions (Bracamonte y Sosa 1994, 109–159). One also can count the 1932 rebellion in El Salvador as a peasant rebellion. And most recently, on 1 January 1994, just a few hours after NAFTA went into effect, largely indigenous populations revolted in Chiapas, Mexico. They called themselves Zapatistas in honor of Emiliano Zapata, the fabled revolutionary reformer. Mexico's economic austerities in the 1980s had caused much suffering to many of Chiapas's poor; and like many post–civil war Central Americans, the rebels felt that NAFTA was a return to the old, unfair policies of the past, dressed in new clothing. The revolt used NAFTA as a symbol of centuries-old racism and economic and social injustices. Far less violent than many other revolts, it lasted only a short time before the sides began negotiations, which predictably brought little result. The rebels' restraint might in part have resulted from a skillful use of computerized technologies to quickly communicate with supporters all over the world, and from the fact that Mexico could ill afford adverse publicity that would discourage the foreign investment that people hoped NAFTA would bring. The rebellion's mysterious poet-leader, subcommander Marcos, and his partner Ramona, have become folk heroes in Mexico (Figure 31), representing a mythological opposition to Carlos Salinas. As of summer 2000, the political environment had altered in Mexico. For the first time since the creation of PRI in 1929, a non-PRI candidate was elected for presidency; free elections in Chiapas offered the possibility for change through less violent means. Substantive reforms, however, had not yet occurred and deep-set tensions were building in other parts of the country.

The recent popularity of mythic figures like Carlos Salinas and the Zapatista leaders mirrors a rise in respect for those who have suffered at the hands of the influential, for the concerns of *el pueblo.* Included in these many and diverse peoples are the indigenous groups. Events like the 1992 Quincentennial celebrations of Columbus's discovery of America, which were followed by the Year of the Indigenous sponsored by the United Nations, fostered new mythic attitudes toward indigenous peoples in Mesoamerica. Only a short time ago, for example,

Figure 31. Subcomandante Marcos (left) and Comandante Moises of the Zapatista army at a press conference in La Realidad, Chiapas, August 1996 (AP Foto/Jorge Nunez)

many claimed that Catholicism had entirely replaced traditional religions. Now, new voices, not the least of which are those belonging to indigenous peoples themselves, offer very different visions. Catholicism may have been the most influential religious tradition in Mesoamerica since the Conquest, but neither the indigenous nor their mythic traditions simply rolled over and died when the conquistadors marched into Tenochtitlan.

Moreover, the increased emphasis on the concerns of the poor expressed by the Second Vatican Council (1962–1965) helped Catholics focus on the problems of ordinary people (Peterson and Williams 1996; Peterson 1997). Prior to this time, the Catholic Church in Mesoamerica tended to side with the influential and well-to-do, especially in Central American countries such as Nicaragua, El Salvador, Guatemala, and the adjacent states of Mexico. Thus, these areas felt the influence of reform movements inspired by post-Vatican II, progressive Catholicism more than some others. Progressive Catholicism took the Council's preferential option for the poor very seriously. Largely independent Catholic religious orders—often viewed as subversive by local church factions that sided with the upper classes and opposing governmental forces[23]—sponsored programs that combined spiritual formation and community building with training in literacy and in political affairs. Drawing their strength and resolve from biblical myths such as Exodus and stories of Christ's life, many common folk soon made their desire for liberation from suffering heard by their active participation in peaceful or in violent protests. No longer did they think that their rewards must wait until heaven; now their religion allowed them to believe that Christ himself had fought for an end to earthly injustice and suffering. And in their view, like Christ and the early Christians, they did not openly seek martyrdom, but they were willing to accept it if that is what it took to improve their lot (Peterson 1997, 79–80, 83, 85–88, 174).The most famous martyr of all was not a peasant but Oscar Romero, archbishop of El Salvador. Assassinated by a pro-government death squad while saying mass on 24 March 1980, Romero was a strong and effective spokesman for the poor. Since his death, grateful Catholics have attributed numerous miracles to him, and the Church is considering him for sainthood.

Now, however, one can no longer say that all countries are exclusively Catholic. The rapid growth of evangelical Protestantism since the 1960s indicates important changes in Mesoamerica's religious character. Mainline and evangelical Protestants primarily from the United States began missions in the region at the end of the nineteenth and beginning of the twentieth centuries; at the time, they exerted only a very small influence. But in the 1970s, evangelical movements gained enormous momentum, drawing many new converts, especially in Central American countries such as Guatemala. Some postulate that evangelical Protestantism has had less success in Mexico because of the popular view there that Protestantism supports the economic policies of the United States, and because of the Virgin of Guadalupe's past mythic support for revolutionary reform and her close mythic association with Mexican national identity (In conversation, Peterson 1998). In Mexico, even nominal Catholics may not be eager to convert to another tradition, because they cannot abandon their Virgencita.

And so life in Mesoamerica continues to change and be transformed in ways that sometimes repeat the past and sometimes produce entirely new creations. Myths also are changing along with everything else. But, the historical view presented in this chapter is not necessarily the one many Mesoamericans would describe. Mythical time does not always march forward in such a neat, straight line; it can curve back or twist inward on itself, destroying any sense of linear momentum. Dates may be important, but for different reasons, just as reality may be based on somewhat different premises. We turn now to an exploration of history from a more mythic viewpoint.

NOTES

1. According to the sixteenth-century historian Fray Diego Durán, the Mexica were first called the Aztecs because they came from a place called Aztlan. Later they were called Mecitin, or Mexicans, after their leader, whose name was Meci—a name that seemed to stick so well that even Tenochtitlan was renamed Mexico City by the Spanish, and the

country, Mexico (Durán 1994, 21). Since the word *Aztecs* is a nineteenth-century revival that refers imprecisely to a variety of peoples who weren't even Mexicans, *Mexica* has been the preferred term in more recent times.

2. My thanks to Nora Carrol, who told me this story and gave me permission to use it (even though I changed it a little because I could not remember it exactly).

3. See Adams (1991, 3–9) for an excellent survey of many of the main resources on ancient Mesoamerica. See Keen (1971) for resources on central Mexicans.

4. Four pre-Conquest Maya pictorial codices have survived, as have five Mixtec from western Oaxaca and six others from a disputed area (probably southern Puebla, western Oaxaca, or the Gulf coast). The *tonalpohuallies,* or divinatory calendars, of the *Codex Borbonicus* and the *Codex Aubin* are both probably very early post-Conquest texts done in fairly authentic pre-Conquest style (see Robertson 1959; Wauchope 1964–1976, vol. 14, pt. 3).

5. The Mesoamerican pictographic writing often used rebuses, in which a picture is used to represent the sound of a spoken word. Many readers will have seen (perhaps in their childhood) a rebus—for example, a picture of an eye being used to indicate the sound for "i" or the word *I*.

6. See Read (1998, 137–144) for a description of Mexica topography.

7. Translation by Kay Read and Jane Rosenthal from the Nahuatl in Sahagún (1953–1982, bk. 3, pt. 4, 41–46).

8. See Read (1998, 144–151, 157–161) for a description of Mexica cosmic beings.

9. John Henderson (1997, 213) suggests a different set of dates for Chichén Itzá: the Terminal Classic era, or ca. A.D. 800–1000.

10. Others suggest that some of these myths represent the motions of the star Venus (e.g., Aveni 1980, 261–262).

11. 1350 is an estimated date. The dates suggested in various sources for Tenochtitlan's founding range from 1140 to 1372. The earliest dates (all of which come from a single source) are probably off, and the rest cluster around 1350.

12. This suggestion comes from Frederick Hicks (in conversation, November 1997).

13. The father is asking the sons how they expect the fact of their nobility to sustain them.

14. Translation by Kay Read from the Nahuatl found in Sahagún (1953–1982, bk. 6, pt. 7, 90–91).

15. See Díaz del Castillo (1956) for an account of the Conquest.

16. The following has been drawn from Cosío Villegas, Bernal, et al. (1974); and Liss (1975).

17. For Nahua speakers, the idea that beings should have souls was such a foreign concept that a Spanish word *(anima)* was borrowed to describe the soul. In pre-Conquest times, beings appear to have had multiple centers in their bodies that contained a variety of animating forces able to do different things. These forces could continue after death by migrating into other bodies or to various places. But nowhere does any one force exactly match Christian beliefs in a single soul that outlasts the body. See López Austin (1988a, 203–236), and Read (1998a, 111–112, 114–115, 159, 202, 206, 208).

18. See Cosío Villegas, Bernal, et al. (1974) for a good summary of Mexican history.

19. New Spain was divided into two major sectors. Ruled from Guatemala City, the first included what are now Guatemala, Honduras, Nicaragua, El Salvador, Costa Rica, and Panama. Controlled from Mexico City, the second included what are now Mexico, California, the southwestern states of the United States, and Texas. Belize had been brought under implicit British control over a period 150 years after shipwrecked British sailors established a colony there in 1638. By 1821, it was more British than Spanish. In 1862, Britain formally declared the area the Colony of British Honduras, and it gained independence in 1981.

20. California, the southwestern states, and Texas were acquired by the United States, and the current boundaries were established in 1848, as a result of the Mexican War.

21. In 1929, at its establishment, the party was named the National Revolutionary Party. In 1938, it was restructured and given the name Party of the Mexican Revolution. Another restructuring in 1946 resulted in the present name.

22. Although some (though not all) FMLN leaders were socialists, the majority of rank-and-file members were peasants seeking concrete economic gains and greater access to political processes.

23. The accusation of subversive activities made against various progressive clerics and religious lay workers at times had consequences as serious as torture and death.

2

MYTHIC TIMELINES

Mythic timelines are based in both tangible and intangible worlds. On the one hand, the idea of time is founded on actual human experiences of tangible change. After all, we all experience a great deal of unavoidable transformation from birth to death. As babies we are not the same as when we are children; and as children, we are not exactly like what we will be as young adults. We change when we marry and have children of our own, and again when we reach the age at which our children care for us. People experience change on a daily basis: This year's summer is different from last year's, yesterday was different from today, and morning is different from night. Flowers grow from seeds; eventually they wither and die, and new ones take their place. Change is a simple fact of life. And it often seems to occur in a moving line of moment-like events, one leading to the next, with past events slipping away as present ones replace them. Many say that these kinds of common experiences characterize time; they are what time is made of.

On the other hand, from a somewhat less tangible position, time can be much more than a mere march from one moment to the next. For although life's changes seem to occur sequentially, moving from beginning to end, mythically people do not always view change that simply. While one's life progresses from one's beginning in birth to one's end in death, one encounters mythic moments along the way—moments in which one can pick up part of the past and make it present. Many families tell mythic stories about what particular individuals did in the past, helping shape their own familial image as well as that of the individuals in question. Stories about a grandparent who fought heroically in a war lend a treasured aura both to grandpa and his family; or stories about a child who early on proved particularly talented in music help mold the child's personality and future career as well as express familial pride and the value the family places on music.

Even history contains many mythic elements, although more than any other kind of time it seems to speak about moving from some objectively true past to the present. But histories are never simple, unobjective recordings of past events; they tend to be particular to the people who tell them. The mythic elements in historical narrations reflect ideals and help people recapture past moments, making them present once again. People pick and choose events they wish to remember, often elaborating on or sometimes even altering them to fit the story they want to tell. In its official history, a nation may count its independence as its birth, and then mark all those past events up to the present that its influential people deem important. But the less influential may tell an unofficial counterversion of the same nation's history, focusing on events the influential would be happy to forget. Each individual also can tell his or her own personal history from a particular standpoint, or a family may trace its historical lineage back to a particularly important founding figure, leaving past mistakes or family skeletons quietly locked in the closet. This careful scripting of history helps people to create ideal models for the present, for what they wish life would or would not be like. And by so doing, they may even successfully shape the future according to those ideals.

Mesoamericans often use the past in these ways, and like others, they frequently participate in rituals drawing on mythic models gleaned from the past. They even sometimes hope with luck to use the past together with the present to mold the future by means of both their ordinary and ritualized actions. As for many around the world, modern astrology is one way for Mesoamericans to account for the present and future. One's daily horoscope is based on one's birth and the convergences of the stars, but its outcome may depend on how one acts on the astrologer's advice. Similarly, prophetic and other types of rituals based on specifically Mesoamerican calendrical systems draw on influences such as one's ritual naming day at birth, one's ancestry, one's dreams, the convergences of heavenly objects and particular calendrical counts, and one's own actions. As with modern astrology, people often hope to use this information to act effectively, sometimes altering future events such as travel or career plans, marriage, or business deals. Mesoamericans also have used past events not only to effect the future but sometimes to predict their own demise as individuals or as a people. Throughout one's lifetime, change may proceed from beginning to end, but before one reaches the finish line, one will momentarily bring the past into the present many times—whether in the form of memories, dreams, the circumstances of one's birth, or one's familial or national histories. In this way, the past both prefigures and shapes one's future life and events. Later, we will explore in more detail how Mesoamerican rituals and mythic histories could bring forth the past into the present and predict the future. But first, two indigenous mythic histories need to be told, for it is through such stories that Mesoamericans organize and express their ideas about time. Because of this, these historical tales can offer us good insight into Mesoamerican temporal concepts.

TWO MYTHIC HISTORIES: K'ICHE' AND NAHUA

Many indigenous Mesoamerican histories follow a particular pattern: (1) The present world is created after three or four other ages have lived and died. The gods, who already exist, both shape each age and participate in its destruction. (2) Events performed by nonhuman beings and gods create the important things of the present age, such as the sun, moon, and food. (3) Then the gods create human beings. (4) The story moves on to tell of the migratory travels and settling down of a particular group, usually those to whom the story belongs. Finally, (5) the history is given of the group's royal lineage—who its rulers were and what they did. The K'iche' Maya Popol Vuh provides us with a wonderful resource because it presents these five elements in great detail. The situation is somewhat more difficult for the Nahua because no one source offers all these elements with the same richness and depth as the Popol Vuh, although the "Legend of the Suns" (Codex Chimalpopoca 1992b, 141–162) offers quite a bit. In the following narrative, we have summarized the stories of both the Popol Vuh and the "Legend of the Suns"; in the case of the latter, we have supplemented the story with tales from other sources.

K'iche' Maya History

The epic legend of the Popol Vuh begins with these words:[1]

This is the beginning of the ancient word, here in this place called Quiché.[2] Here we shall inscribe, we shall implant the Ancient Word, the potential and source for everything done in the citadel of Quiché, in the nation of Quiché people.

And here we shall take up the demonstration, revelation, and account of how things were put in shadow and brought to light

by the Maker, Modeler, named Bearer, Begetter,
Hunahpu [Hoon-ah-poo'] Possum, Hunahpu Coyote,[3]
Great White Peccary, Tapir,
Sovereign Plumed Serpent,
Heart of the Lake, Heart of the Sea,
Maker of the Blue-Green Plate,
Maker of the Blue-Green Bowl,[4]

as they are called, also named, also described as

the midwife, matchmaker
named Xpiyacoc [Shpee-ya-kok'], Xmucane [Shmoo-ka-nay'],

defender, protector,
twice a midwife, twice a matchmaker,

as is said in the words of Quiché. They accounted for everything—and did it, too—as enlightened beings, in enlightened words. We shall write about this now amid the preaching of God, in Christendom now.[5] We shall bring it out because there is no longer a place to see it, a Council Book,

a place to see "The Light that Came from Across the Sea,"'
the account of "Our Place in the Shadows,"
a place to see "The Dawn of Life,"

as it is called. There is the original book and ancient writing, but he who reads and ponders it hides his face. It takes a long performance and account to complete the emergence of all the sky-earth:

The fourfold siding, fourfold cornering,
measuring, fourfold staking,
halving the cord, stretching the cord
in the sky, on the earth,
the four sides, the four corners,[6]

as it is said,

By Maker, Modeler,
mother-father of life, of humankind,
giver of breath, giver of heart,
bearer, upbringer in the light that lasts
of those born in the light, begotten in the light;
worrier, knower of everything, whatever there is:
sky-earth, lake-sea.

After this preamble, the storyteller goes on to retell this long, ancient tale, beginning at the beginning, with the creation of the four ages, and ending at the end, with the coming of the K'iche' lords.

1. The First Three Ages.

At first only the sky and sea existed. The great knowers all enclosed in a sea of bright blue-green quetzal feathers and called Plumed Serpent—the Maker and Modeler, the Bearers and Begetters—met with the three Thunderbolts, also called Heart of Sky.

Figure 32. A Classic Maya vase portraying a mythic story or event with animals from the Popol Vuh (Justin Kerr Archives, File no. 3413)

"How should it be sown, how should it dawn? Who is to be the provider, nurturer?" the gods all asked (Popol Vuh 1985, 73).

They decided that earth must first be emptied of water so that humans would have a place to work. For without humans, no one would exist to sing out bright praises for the gods' work and designs. And so by simply calling its name, the gods caused earth to rise up through the water, instantly covered with mountains, trees, and rivers.

Age One: Once this was done, the gods created animals to inhabit the earth. The animals could multiply, but unfortunately they all spoke to each other only according to their own kind. They hummed, buzzed, chirped, cackled, snorted, barked, and whined (Figure 32).

"'Talk, speak out. Don't moan, don't cry out. . . . Name now our names, praise us. We are your mother, we are your father. Speak now,'" the gods all said to the animals (Popol Vuh 1985, 78).

But the animals only kept squawking, chattering, and howling.

"'This hasn't turned out well,'" the gods said (79).

So they told the animals that they would simply have to be transformed, that it would be their place to be of service to others by becoming their food. And so the animals were killed and eaten.

Age Two: The gods tried again. They had to work fast because the time of planting was drawing near. This time they tried with mud, but the body they made did not look so good. It kept going soft, crumbling, and falling apart. Its head wouldn't turn, and its face was lopsided and twisted. It could talk only nonsense. It could not walk or procreate. So they just let it dwindle away, finally taking it apart completely; they let it become just a "thought" (80).

Figure 33. A Postclassic probable Maya daykeeper throwing lots with corn (Museo de América/Art Resource)

Age Three: Then the gods summoned Xpiyacoc and Xmucane, Hunahpu Possum and Hunahpu Coyote, and other daykeepers. They asked them to count the days, to count the lots, to throw the corn kernels in order to see how it was to be done (Figure 33).[7] The daykeepers told them to make wooden manikins. This the gods did. The man they carved of coral tree wood, and the woman, of reeds. The manikins could walk, talk, and multiply. But there was nothing in their hearts or minds; they had no memory of their creators, the gods. They became the first of many peoples here on earth's face, but they accomplished nothing. So Heart of Sky created a great flood of resin to destroy them. Then various beasts and beings gouged out their eyes, snapped off their heads, crunched their flesh, and tore them open. Even their dogs went after them because the manikins never fed them enough. They were smashed and pulverized because of their incompetence. It is said now that monkeys are made of wood and look like humans, but they are really a warning that we people must have a heart.

2. The Hero Twins and 7-Macaw

Once the three ages were completed, preparations for the fourth and present age became possible. This story, however, does not begin at the beginning; instead, it appears to begin with a story plucked out of the middle of a longer tale about the birth and feats of the twin boy heroes Hunahpu (Hunter) and Xbalanque (Sh-ba-lan-kay', meaning Jaguar Deer). This particular story begins after the Hero Twins are already beyond childhood. Holding special powers, they defeat 7-Macaw, an overly prideful ruler who claims to be the sun. First they break his jaw by shooting it with a blowgun; then, enlisting the help of an old grandfather and healer, they "cure" this bird-lord by plucking out his bejeweled eyes and teeth, after which he loses his luster and, along with his wife, dies. Again using trickery, the Twins also defeat Seven Macaw's sons: Zipacna (Zee-pak-na'), who claimed to have created the mountains, and Earthquake, who said he could scatter them. Both are buried now, one under a mountain and the other in the earth. The Twins defeated these three because of their self-glorification and false claims.

3. Exploits in the Underworld

Now the tale turns back to the past, to the time of the Twins' father 1-Hunter and their uncle 7-Hunter. Also twins, 1-Hunter and 7-Hunter were born of the old couple who threw lots before the Third Age, Xpiyacoc and Xmucane. The lords of the underworld—1-Death, 7-Death, Pus Master, Bone Scepter, Jaundice Master, Bloody Claws, and so on—summoned the Twins to play ball. They endured several tests, only to be defeated and sacrificed by the lords, who buried them in the ball court and hung One Hunter's head in a calabash tree (Figure 34). A daughter of one of the lords, an innocent young maiden named Blood Woman, went to the magical tree to pick its fruit, not wanting its sweetness to go to waste. But the skull of One Hunter spoke to her:

"'You don't want it,'" he said.

"'I do want it.'"

"'Very well. Stretch out your right hand here, so I can see it,'" said the skull (114).

She did, and the skull spit a bit of saliva into her palm, which promptly disappeared. The skull told her:

"It is just a sign I have given you, my saliva, my spittle. This, my head, has nothing on it—just bone, nothing of meat. It's just the same with the head of a great lord: it's just flesh that makes his face look good. And when he dies, people get frightened by his bones. After that, his son is like his saliva, his spittle, in his being, whether it be the son of a lord or the son of a craftsman, an orator. The father does not disappear, but goes being fulfilled. Neither dimmed nor destroyed . . . he will leave his daughters and sons. So it is that I have done likewise through you" (114–115).

Upon learning that Blood Woman is pregnant, her enraged father tries to sacrifice her. But with the help of some owls, Blood Woman escapes to the upper world. She goes to the house of her mother-in-law Xmucane and her twin brothers-in-law. Xmucane does not believe her story any more than her father did. But when Blood Woman prays to the goddesses of the field, she proves her unborn sons' heritage by bringing the old woman a huge bag full of corn gathered from just one measly stalk. The babes are born, and even though their uncles try to

Figure 34. A Mesoamerican ballcourt at the Classic site of Monte Albán, Oaxaca (Elizabeth L. Fuller)

kill them by placing them first on an anthill and then on some brambles, the infants not only survive the ordeals but sleep peacefully through them. When the boys grow older, they get their revenge by enticing their uncles to the top of a tree, where they turn them into monkeys.

As young adults, the Twins decide to become farmers, but this turns out to be a bad career choice. Every day they plant corn (Figure 35), which magically matures by evening, but animals eat it in the night. Finally they catch a rat, who—after they singe his tail, try to choke him, and promise him food—tells them that they are meant to be ball players like their fathers (Figure 36). He helps them get their ball playing equipment down from the rafters where their grandmother had hidden it. As his reward, the rat receives many seeds and kernels, as well as the household garbage.

But as had their fathers, the boys disturb the underworld lords by playing ball over their heads; so the lords summon the Twins below. This worries both their mother and grandmother, for this is how their father and uncle had died. In an effort to stall their leave-taking, Grandmother sends the summons with a tiny, slow-moving louse. But Louse is eaten by Toad, who is eaten by Snake, who is eaten by Falcon, who flies swiftly to the ball field with the message in his belly. There Falcon vomits up Snake, who vomits Toad, who just sits there and drools. So the boys squash Toad's rear end and pry open his mouth, where they find Louse stuck in his teeth. Louse tells the boys that they must go to Xibalba (Shee-

Figure 35. A farm field, or "milpa," with corn, beans, and squash (Carmen C. Arendt)

Figure 36. A Classic depiction of the Hero Twins as Ballplayers (Israel Museum, Jerusalem)

bal-ba'), the underworld, to test themselves against the lords there. To assuage their mother's and grandmother's worry, they each plant a corn seed in the middle of their house. If they die, the plants will die; if they live, so will the plants.

In Xibalba, the lords cannot trick the Twins into defeat as easily as they had their father and uncle (Figure 37). After passing a few minor tests, the Twins are sent to six different houses to spend six successive nights in various trials. In the Dark House, they trick the lords into thinking they are smoking a single cigar all night without burning it, by "lighting" it with a firefly. In the Razor House, the boys give the great chopping knives who dwell there the flesh of all the animals

Figure 37. A Classic depiction of the Hero Twins in Xibalba (Justin Kerr Archives, File 1742)

to eat so that the knives will not chop them up. In the Cold House, they shut out the drafts and hail, making it warm. In the Jaguar House, they give the ferocious cats bones to eat, thereby saving their own skins; in the Fire House, the Twins merely simmer, they don't boil to death. But Hunahpu meets his match in the Bat House. There a bat chops off his head, which is taken to the ball court to become the ball. All the animals come to help Hunahpu, who is lying helpless in the Bat House. Each brings his own kind of food; Coati brings a pumpkin. While Possum holds back the dawn by painting it with red and blue streaks,[8] they fashion a fake head from the pumpkin for Hunahpu. Then the boys go to play ball with the lords. At a good moment, Rabbit diverts the lords' attention; he rolls off like a ball, making them chase him. Quickly the Twins make a switch. Placing Hunahpu's proper head back on his shoulders, they turn the pumpkin into a ball. The game begins again, but this time Xbalanque rapidly ends it by kicking the "ball" and smashing it to pieces, releasing its seeds. With this, Hunahpu and Xbalanque defeat the lords of death and disease.

But they have not yet really won. The lords hope to trick the Twins into falling into a big fire, but the Twins thwart the lords by willingly leaping to their death in the conflagration. An aged seer who is secretly working for the Twins advises the lords to grind the boys' bones and sprinkle them on the river. As a result, on the fifth day, the Twins reappear as catfish; and on the sixth day, they appear as two old vagabonds. Of course these are no ordinary vagabonds but magnificent entertainers who can dance many dances, burn houses down and make them reappear, and bring sacrificed dogs and people back to life. After the boys sacrifice themselves and return to life, Lords 1-Death and 7-Death become caught up in the magical dance and shout:

"Do it to us! Sacrifice us! Sacrifice both of us!" (Popol Vuh 1985, 153).

The Twins sacrifice the two lords but do not bring them back to life. Upon seeing this, all of the other lords immediately surrender, and the boys reveal their true identity. Instead of killing the remaining lords, the boys tell them that as inciters of evil, the lords of the underworld henceforth can feed on only the creatures of meadows and clearings, and not on humans;[9] and that only the guilty and violent will come to them. Next the Twins go to the Place of Ballgame Sacrifice, where their father still lies. There they try to put him back together again; but they only partially succeed, because he cannot remember all the names of his body parts. So they leave him there as he is, promising him that he will be the first to be consulted and worshiped, thereby somewhat comforting him. Then, ascending into the sky, one twin becomes the sun, and the other, the moon.

4. The Creation of People, and Their Migrations

After the Hero Twins rise as the sun and moon, the cosmos is now ready for the fourth and present age. And with the promise of the first dawning, the gods' thoughts on how to make proper humans now appear clearly. Fox, coyote, parrot, and crow bring them white and yellow corn, along with the news that the mountain at Broken Place, Bitter Water Place holds all manner of sustenance: corn, cacao, zapotes, anonas, jocotes, and nances, all sweet and delicious. All of the edible fruits, great and small, are there.

Xmucane then grinds the white and yellow corn. The gods model human flesh, arms and legs from the cornmeal. Water becomes human blood, and the water in which Xmucane rinsed her hands becomes human fat. The first humans are not born of any woman but by the sacrifice and genius alone of Builder, Sculptor, Bearer, and Begetter. These new human creatures, made of the food that will sustain them, are the final and most successful creation. They talk in words, look and listen, walk and work; and most importantly, they praise and thank the gods for having been created by them. Yet all is not quite right. These first humans can see with such intensity that their knowledge is perfect, they understand everything, they understand too much, as much as the gods themselves. So the gods dim their eyes as a mirror's face is dimmed when one breathes upon it, taking back some of their knowledge. Now humans can only see things nearby, not those far away.

First the gods mold four men, and then they shape their four wives. Thus the first human pairs are created: Jaguar Quitze (Keet-zay') and Celebrated Seahouse, Jaguar Night and Prawn House, Mahucutah (Mah-hoo-koo-tah') and

Hummingbird House, and True Jaguar and Macaw House. Lots of people come about then, many lineages are created, black and white, of many faces and languages. Each can trace itself to one of the first four men; the K'iche' trace their lineage to Mahucutah. All these people stand around at the edge of the sky, watching for the first sunrise. While waiting at this place called Tollan (Tol'-lan),[10] a place of seven caves, each lineage receives its own language and gods. Among others, the K'iche' receive Tohil (Toh-heel'), a great god of fire who is worshiped by others as well. Then, dressed in nothing but animal skins, they all leave and begin migrating to their various homelands; along the way, they create shrines for their gods, whom they pack on their backs. And all this time they await the sun's rising. Finally, like a person, the sun shows its face, which is so hot that it dries out the soggy earth. Then the first sacrifices to Tohil begin. After several other adventures, the first four men come to the time of their deaths. Knowing this, they leave instructions for their wives and sons, telling them to press on to their true homelands.

5. More Migrations, and the Coming of the K'iche' Lords

Remembering the words of their fathers, they move eastward, toward their fathers' birthplace. The only son of Mahucutah, Coacutec (Kwa-koo'-tek), leads the K'iche'. They visit many places on their travels. At one, the lord of Nacxit, keeper of the royal mat, bestows upon them the signs of lordship, such as a canopy and throne, bone flute, jaguar's paw, nosepiece, and parrot and heron feathers. As the groups travel, they carry these things along with the writings about Tollan. The first four women die, but the four groups continue traveling. Eventually they become so numerous that each group splits into various lines. The K'iche' split into four lines that multiply, becoming great, with numerous lords. Lord Plumed Serpent, of the fourth generation, is particularly great, able to go up into the sky and down into Xibalba. At other times he transforms himself into a great jaguar, a serpent, an eagle, or a pool of blood. Bit by bit, the K'iche' lords take lands from others whom they have conquered, erect houses for their gods, and create lovely things from jade, metal, and feathers. Now there have been fourteen generations of K'iche' lords living in K'iche'; the Spanish appeared during the twelfth. At that time Tonatiuh, or Pedro de Alvarado (Pay'-dro day Al-va-ra'-do) arrived.[11] Now K'iche' is called Santa Cruz (San'-ta Kroos).

Nahua History

The Mexica Nahua also tell a tale beginning with the creation of the cosmos in a series of ages and ending with the coming of their lords. Most of this story is preserved in the "Legend of the Suns."[12] Although the latter lacks the richness of the Popol Vuh, several other texts offer more detailed variations of the individual stories.[13] The legend, which the teller relates on 22 May 1558, begins with what may seem to many readers an odd little tale. This now unknown songster first explains: "They divided the earth into one portion each. . . . Thus it is known how all things originated. Everything existed as the Sun's time and place for 2,513 years."[14] The Narrator then goes on to tell about four different ages that were created before the present one.

1. The First Four Ages

Age One, whose name was 4-Jaguar, lasted 676 years before Jaguars ate it up in the year 1-Reed, on the day 4-Jaguar. Its inhabitants ate 7-Grass for their food. We are not told much more about this age, nor are we told what kind of food 7-Grass was. 7-Grass is a date in the Mexica calendar; since the ancient Mesoamericans often used calendrical dates for names, this phrase could have referred to any number of things. It could have been, of course, something they actually ate (which is now called something else), or it could have been the name of a god. That particular day might have carried special powers rather as astrological signs carry powers, so that its "food" is mythically real but not actually so. Or 7-Grass could have been referring to a specific period of time that was passing—hence, being "eaten" metaphorically. We really don't know. But we are told that when the man-eating jaguars ate this age, people turned themselves into monkeys to escape into the second age. The next three ages all follow the same pattern: Each disappears in a particular year, has a name based on the day and manner of its own destruction, and has inhabitants who eat something with a calendrical date for a name. Probably each age had a house too, because in the second age, the monkeys' houses are mentioned. Our problem is that the ancient songster may have offered his or her Spanish interrogator a highly abridged version, and this is all we're left with now.[15]

The second age, named 4-Wind, existed only 364 years before it was blown away by the wind in the year 1-Knife, on the day 4-Wind. The wind was so strong that it blew away the monkeys' tree houses too. During this age, the monkeys ate something called 12-Snake, and turned themselves into turkeys to escape the wind. The third age, 4-Rainstorm, existed only 312 years before a great volcanic rainstorm of fire burned everything up. Like the second, this age also disappeared in the year 1-Knife, but on the day 4-Rainstorm. During this age, the turkeys ate 7-Knife, and turned themselves into nobles when their age was destroyed. The fourth age, 4-Water, existed for 676 years before being destroyed by a huge flood in the year 1-House, on the day 4-Water. During this age, the nobles ate 4-Flower, and turned themselves into fish to escape certain death when the flood poured in. Then water spread out for another 52 years, while the gods rearranged the cosmos into four parts.

Unlike the Popol Vuh, this curious little story's main concern lies less with the nature of various beings, than with counting out time's passing as things disappear or transform themselves. The Popol Vuh made it clear that proper human beings were to have a heart and mind capable of praising their creators but not so great as to compete with them. No such moral message exists in the Nahua version, which contains only objective observations voiced mythologically. Because the Mexica lived in the fifth of five ages, how and when each age would end was of great concern, for it indicated when their own age's end would come due. Each age is only very briefly described, but at the same time, quite carefully counted out. The significance of this story lies in its calculation of how long each age lasted and how its destruction transformed it into something else; it describes the mathematics that structure the cosmos. Like the people at Teotihuacan, who built their city's buildings according to math based on celestial patterns, the Mexica also lived in a world built on celestial calculations.

2. First Couple[16]

Once the cosmos had been laid out in four parts, it came time to create the fifth age and the beings who would inhabit it. As in the Popol Vuh, the creation of humans does not occur after just one try. The first attempt goes like this:

The great god, Titlacahuan,[17] called to the first couple, Tata [Tah'-ta] and Nene [Nen'-nay], and asked,

"Children, do you want anything more?"

"Make a very big hole in a cypress tree[18] and put us in it when the vigil begins and the sky falls." This he did. And when he was finished he told them,

"You will have one cob of corn each to eat. When you have finished all the kernels, then you will see that the water is all gone and that your cypress trunk has stopped rocking."

When the corn was gone and the cypress trunk had stopped rocking, Tata and Nene emerged and found that they were saved. Using a drill to start a fire in some small sticks, they roasted a few fish. But this was not appreciated by the gods because it smoked up the sky, making it black. Titlacahuan-Tezcatlipoca [Teet-la-ka'-wan/Tez-kat-lee-po'-ka] bawled them out for their error. He then cut their heads off at their necks and sewed them back onto their buttocks. This turned them into dogs, the first ancestors of all those living in the Fifth Sun.

The sky was smoked by these dogs in the year 1-Rabbit. Afterward, it was dark for 25 years. Then [in the 26th year], which was called 2-Reed, Tezcatlipoca lit the fire drill and smoked the sky once more.

As with the early attempts of the Maya gods to make people, this trial was not entirely successful. But the gods' next attempt worked out a bit better.

3. Creation of People[19]

And then the gods consulted among themselves. "Who will be the ones to settle there?" they asked. "The sky has been spread out, the earth lord has been spread out. Oh gods, who will settle there?" [All the gods including] Quetzalcoatl and Titlacahuan were not happy.[20]

Then Quetzalcoatl went to Mictlan [Mict'-lan] (Land of the Dead). Upon arriving, [he met] Mictlanteuctli [Mict-lan-tay-ooct'-lee] and Mictlancihuatl [Mict-lan-see'-wat] (the Lord and Lady of Death). He said, indeed he [spoke] like so:

"I have come for the precious greenstone bones that you are guarding. I have come to take them away."

"What will you do with them, Quetzalcoatl?" [Mictlanteuctli] asked.

He answered once again, indeed he [spoke] like so: "The gods are unhappy; who will settle there on earth?"

Mictlanteuctli again responded, "Oh, very well! Blow my conch-shell horn and encircle my precious enclosure four times. And may the shell horn not have holes."

Immediately [Quetzalcoatl] summoned worms who drilled holes in it. Then bumblebees and honeybees entered it. When he blew it, Mictlanteuctli heard it.

"Oh, very well! Take them!" Mictlanteuctli once again replied. Right away Mictlanteuctli said to his messengers, the Micteca (the People of the Land of the Dead), "Gods, tell him that he has to leave them here!"

Quetzalcoatl responded, "No, I'm taking them once and for all!"

Just then Quetzalcoatl's *nahualli* [na-wal'-lee][21] spoke to him. "You tell him that you have left them." So [Quetzalcoatl] said to [Mictlanteuctli], he called out to him, "I've left them!"

Quickly rising, Quetzalcoatl took the precious greenstone bones. A man's lay in one place and a woman's in another. Immediately, Quetzalcoatl gathered them up, wrapped them up, and carried them off.

Once again Mictlanteuctli said to his messengers, "Gods! Quetzalcoatl is actually taking the greenstone bones! Gods! Quickly, make a pit!" They wanted to make him fall down.

He fell right into that pit, he whacked himself and the quails startled him. He passed out from that fall, spilling all the greenstone bones. The quails chewed them; they ground them to bits.

Then, Quetzalcoatl was revived. He howled out, he said to his *nahualli*, "My *nahualli*, how will they be?"

He told him how it would be: "Really, he messed things up. However it actually goes, is how it goes."[22]

Then [Quetzalcoatl] gathered them up, he picked them up and wrapped them. Like so, he carried them to Tamoanchan. When he delivered them, the [goddess] named Quilachtli [Kee-lacht'-lee] who is called Cihuacoatl here,[23] ground them and bathed them in a greenstone bowl. Quetzalcoatl bled his member on them. Then all the gods in that place gave them merit. . . .[24]

And then they said it: "The gods and commoners were born because they gave us merit."

4. Creation of Corn[25]

After the commoners were created, the gods wondered what they would eat. The ant went and got a kernel of corn from inside the Mountain of Produce.[26]

Meeting this ant, Quetzalcoatl asked him, "Tell me where you mean to take that corn you are carrying." But the ant didn't really want to tell him. So Quetzalcoatl questioned him very firmly, and eventually the ant gave in. "Over there," he said.

Instantly Quetzalcoatl turned himself into a black ant and followed the red ant, helping him to carry the corn.

He carried the corn to Tamoanchan. It is there that the gods chew it up and place it on our lips. In this manner, we [who live now] grew strong.

The gods asked, "What will we do with this Mountain of Produce?" Quetzalcoatl wanted to carry it on his back. He tied it up and tried, but he couldn't do it.

So Oxomoco [Oh-sho-mo'-ko] and Cipactonal [See-pak-to'-nal] cast fortunes with corn (Figure 38). They also cast fortunes of the day.[27] They said, "Nanahuatl [Nah-Na'-wat] will be the one who strikes open the Mountain of Produce."[28] They knew this because they had "opened up" the fortune.[29]

Immediately, the Tlaloques [the fierce rain and lightning gods of the mountains] piled up: the green Tlaloques, the white Tlaloques, the yellow Tlaloques, and the red Tlaloques.[30] Instantly Nanahuatl struck the mountain and the Tlaloques snatched out all the food—the white, black, yellow, and red corn, beans, chia, and amaranth, all of it they snatched away.

5. Creation of the Fifth Sun[31]

Now the earth's surface has been prepared, and both people and their food exist. All that is missing is the dawning of the fifth age. The story goes like this:

Figure 38. Oxomoco and Cipactonal casting lots with corn (Codex Borbonicus, *fol. 21, Museo de América/Art Resource)*

I.
Here it is, the story in which it is told how the
little rabbit is stretched out on
the Moon's face.
The Moon, it is said, was played with like so:
Like so they whipped his face,
Like so they beat his face,
Like so they wrecked his face,
Like so they killed his face,
The gods did all this.
When later he came out, he was spread out flat.

II.
It is said that:

When it was still the dark-place time,
When there was not yet warmth,
When there was not yet day,
They met together,
They all consulted together,
The gods did all this at Teotihuacan.

They said it, they took counsel:
"Please come here, oh Gods!
Who will carry it?[32]
Who will bear it:
The warming,
The dawning?"[33]
And then, like so:
He says it,
He steps forth,
He makes it clear,
Tecuiçiztecatl [Te-kwi-seez-tay'-kat] did all this.
He said it: "Oh Gods! Indeed I, I will be the one!"

Yet a second time, the gods said it:
"Who will be another one?"
Like so, then,
They, altogether, look at each other,
They look closely at each other.
They take counsel with each other.
"How will this thing be there?
How will we do it then?"

No one was daring.
No other would step forth there.
All men were frightened.
They were turning tail.
And still, not even one man would present himself there.
There, in the company of all,
Nanahuatzin was listening to what was being said.
Like so, the gods called to him there.
They took counsel.
"You! You will be it, Nanahuatzin [Na-na-wat'-zin]!"

Quickly he responded to their rallying cry.
He accepted it with pleasure.
He said to them:

"Indeed, this is good, oh Gods!
You have done me a great favor!"

III.
Like so, then,
They set forth,
Preparing themselves to celebrate the rituals.
They fasted for four days,
The two of them together,
Tecuiçiztecatl [and Nanahuatzin].

Also then,
The fire was set in order,
Burning there in the fire pit,
They call that fire pit[34] the "God Oven."

And he, Tecuiçiztecatl,
He was preparing himself with very precious things:
His ritual branches were of quetzal feathers,
His grass heart was woven of gold,
His spine was of greenstone,
Likewise,
The bloodletting,
Blood-covering instrument was of coral,
And, his incense was copal, a very fine copal.
As for Nanahuatzin,
His ritual branches were made only of
green grass and green reeds,
Tied in three bundles,
Bound bundles of nine each, three in all.
And his grass ball was woven only of pine needles,[35]
And his bloodletting spine was only a maguey thorn.
He was bloodying them well with his own blood.
And his incense consisted of only scabs that he was twisting off.

For those two,
For each one,
Their mountain was made.
There, where for four nights,
They had been ritually celebrating,
It is said that now there are pyramid-mountains:
His pyramid, the Sun's;
His pyramid, the Moon's.

When they had completed
four nights of ritual celebration,
They hurled them down,
They dashed them down,
Their ritual branches,
Everything with which they had celebrated.

This was done:
When it was their lifting up.
When it was just getting dark.
They would serve as slaves,
They would create gods.

And when midnight arrives,
They arrange them,
They adorn them,
They prepare them.

To Tecuiçiztecatl, they gave
His tall, round egret headdress and his vest.
But to Nanahuatzin, they gave only paper.
Like so:
They braided his hair,
They bound his head with its name,[36]
His paper hair,
His paper robes and
His paper loincloth.

And, when midnight arrived,
All the gods made a procession around the fire pit,
They spread out around it.
They praised it as the "God Oven."[37]
The fire burned there for four days.

The gods lined up on both sides.
And Nanahuatzin and Tecuiçiztecatl
were placed in the middle.
They stood up very straight.
These two together were called,
Nanahuatzin and Tecuiçiztecatl.
They faced each other.
They stood facing each other,
At the fire pit.

IV.
Then the gods spoke.
They shouted at Tecuiçiztecatl:
"Oh do it, Tecuiçiztecatl!
Fall down!
Hurl yourself into the fire!"

Like so, then,
He is now going!
He will throw himself into the fire!

The fire became a heated thing,
A thing not to be faced.
A thing not to be tolerated.
A thing not to be suffered.
The fireplace was burning well.
The fire was going well.
The fire was in good order.
Because of this, he was growing frightened.
He stops!
He retreats!
He turns back!
Once again he goes, but:
He struggles!
He tries his hardest to throw
himself into the fire!

But he dares not to approach that heat!
He retreats!
He turns tail!
He cannot do it!
Four times, four times.
He tries to do it.
But it was not possible to throw
himself into the fire.
Nevertheless, he persisted four times.
And he drew back four times.

Like so, then, they called to Nanahuatzin there.
The gods called to him:
"You!
Quickly, you!
Oh Nanahuatzin, on with it!"

Nanahuatzin was the only one who dared.
He completed it.
His heart strengthened him.[38]
He closed his eyes, but not because he was afraid.
He did not stop.
He did not turn back.
He did not retreat.
He simply threw himself down.
He hurled himself into the fire.
Like so it goes well!

Like so, then, he burns.
He blossoms.
His flesh sizzles.
And when Tecuiçiztecatl saw him burning,
He hurled himself after him.
And they say,
It is said that,
Then an eagle also rose out of the fire after them.
He threw himself into the fire.
He hurled himself into the fire.
The eagle is arranged well everywhere because of this.
His feathers are darkened.
They are smoky.
But the jaguar was last.
Then the fire was no longer very well arranged.
He fell.
Like so,
He was barely burned,
He was burned just a little,
He burned here and there.
The jaguar was not arranged completely.
Because of this:
He was painted.
He was sprinkled with black soot.
He was spattered with black soot.

It is said that because of those things:
The traditional words spread out there,
They were considered there.
In this way,
He who was brave was named.
"Eagle-Jaguar" was his name.

That one, the eagle, came first.
It is said,
They say that:
This is because he went first into the fire.
But the jaguar is only last.
Therefore they say it [as one word]:
"Eagle-Jaguar."
Because of these things, the jaguar fell into the fireplace afterwards.

V.
When, in this way,
The two had both thrown themselves in the fire,
When they had burned,
Then the gods sat waiting to learn
from where Nanahuatzin would emerge.
He was the first to fall into the fire,
So he would be the first to shine,
Like so, he would light up first.
For a long time they stretched out there,
They sat waiting.
The gods stretched out there.

Then, like so, it begins.
Everywhere it becomes red,
Everywhere was surrounded,
The lighting of dawn,
The reddening of dawn.[39]
Hence, it is said that the gods knelt down.
Like so, they will wait
For the place from which the sun will emerge.
It was done.
They would look for it everywhere.
They keep on turning around.
Nowhere were they well united.
Their traditional words,
Their oration:
Nothing which they said was good.

Some thought he would emerge
from the Place of the Dead.
They spread themselves out to look there.
Some thought the Place of Women,
Some thought the Place of Thorns,[40]

They expected this because
Dawn's reddening encircled everything.
And some did well,
They spread out to look for him at the Place of Light.[41]
They said it:
"Already he is way over there,
Already he is there,
The sun will be emerging!"

Their words were very true,
Those words belonging to
Those who waited there,
Those who pointed there. . . .

And when the sun was emerging, he was spreading like red dye[42]
He was spreading in an undulating way.[43]
He could not be faced.
He dazzled a great deal.
He shines a lot,
He shimmers.
His shimmering rays were coming from everywhere.
He arose.
His warm rays entered everywhere.

And afterwards,
Tecuiçiztecatl came to emerge
from the Place of Light.
He could only follow him,
He came to be spread out like the sun.
As they fell into the fireplace,
So too did they come out.
In this way, they followed each other.

VI.
They say that the gods talk over many things.
They discuss and discuss it.
[The suns'] appearances were just alike.
Thus they were shining when seen by the gods.
Just alike were [the suns'] appearances.

Then once again it was discussed over and over.
[The gods] said: "How will these two [suns] be, oh Gods?
Will both of them follow the same road?

Will both of them shine in the same way?"
And the gods all gave their opinion.
They said it:
"Like so it will be, this thing.
Like so it will be done."

Then like so, a person fled from the gods.
Like so, he beat Tecuiçiztecatl in the face with a rabbit.[44]
Thus, they wrecked his face.
Thus, they killed his face.
In this way now,
Like so, he appears.

Right then, like this:
When they were both spread out,
It was still not possible for them to move.
They still did not follow their paths.
They were only spread out.
They were only spread out on the edge.[45]

Like so, once again, the gods say it:
"How will we live?
The sun does not move.
Will we live a life mixed up with the commoners?[46]

This one, the sun:
May he go on.
May he be revived [or born].
May we all die!"
Then, like so, that one, Ehecatl, did his work.
Right away he kills the gods.

But they say that Xolotl [Sho'-lot] did not want to die [Figure 39].
He tells the gods: "Let me not die, oh Gods!"
For this reason,
He was crying a great deal.
His eyes were very swollen.

His eyelids were very swollen.
Right then Death quickly comes forward,
Xolotl fled to the field of young corn, diving into it.
There he transformed himself into something else.

*Figure 39. Xolotl (*Codex Borbonicus, *fol. 19, Museo de América/Art Resource)*

He turned himself into the young maize with two stalks.
This is called "Xolotl of the Field."

But he was seen there in the field of young corn.
Once again, Death quickly comes forward,
Again he entered the maguey field.
Like so he turned himself into the double maguey.

Its name is "Maguey Xolotl."
Right away once again, he was seen.
Again he entered the water place.
He turned himself into the "Water-Xolotl."[47]
Right away, there they went to seize him.
In this way, they killed him.

VII.
And they say that, even though all the gods died,
In truth, still he did not move.
[It was] not possible for the Sun, Tonatiuh,
To follow his path.

In this way,
Ehecatl did his work.
Ehecatl stood up straight.
He grew extremely strong.
He ran and blew lightly.
Instantly, he moved [the sun].
Like so, he follows his path.

And when [the sun] was following his path,
The moon was left behind.
When the sun was going to go into his entrance again,[48]
Like so, the moon came forth.

In this way, they exchanged with each other.
They separated from each other.
In this way, the sun emerges once,
He takes one whole day.
And the moon shoulders his work for one whole night.
He shoulders his work for one night.

Like so, he appears there.
It is said that, certainly,
He, the moon, Tecuiçiztecatl,
Would have been the sun
If he had fallen into the fire first.
Because, indeed, he offered himself first.
With all precious things,
He celebrated the rituals.

Here it ends, this thing:
The tale,
The ancient fable,
In this way, they used to tell it,
The old ones whose charge it was.

6. Birth of Huitzilopochtli[49]

Now that the fifth age has begun, the patron god of this age's inhabitants, the Mexica, can be born.

On the top of Snake Mountain, Coatlicue [Ko-wat-lee'-kway] (Snake Skirt) was performing her rituals by carefully sweeping up, keeping the mountain tidy [Figure 40]. As she swept, some feathers dropped from above. She picked them up and placed them in her clothing near her waist. But when she had finished sweeping and reached for them, the feathers had disappeared. It was in this manner that she became pregnant.

When her daughter Coyolxauhqui and her four hundred sons from the south found out about this mysterious pregnancy, they became very angry and wrathful, accusing their mother of having gravely dishonored them. Calling her wicked, they determined to kill her.

This really frightened the poor woman, who had done nothing more than ritually sweep the mountain. But her unborn child, Huitzilopochtli, spoke to her from her womb, comforting her, "Do not fear, I already know what I am going to do about this!"

Coyolxauhqui led her brothers in the attack. But a traitor warned Huitzilopochtli about their plans. He told him about every movement Coyolxauhqui and

Figure 40. Statue of Coatlicue (Museo Nacional de Antropología de Mexico, Mexico City)

her army made, about each place they passed on their way to Snake Mountain.

Just as this fearsome army with Coyolxauhqui in the lead scaled the heights of Snake Mountain, Huitzilopochtli was born. He was magnificently arrayed! He carried his magical shield, his darts and dart thrower. His faced was painted with diagonal stripes and his upper arms and thighs were striped blue. Feathers were pasted on his forehead and ears. The sole of his one thin left foot also was coated with feathers.[50]

Suddenly, the turquoise snake burst into fire. Commanding it, Huitzilopochtli pierced Coyolxauhqui and then quickly chopped off her head. Her body fell over the edge of Snake Mountain and crashed to the ground, breaking apart as it fell; her legs and her arms each came off.

Then Huitzilopochtli charged his 400 brothers. He plunged after them, scattering them from the top of the mountain. He chased them down and around the mountain four times. He made them turn tail. He destroyed them well, he completely enveloped them in clouds and thoroughly finished them off with smoke.[51]

Even after all that he continued to chase them. They cried out piteously to him, "Please, let this be enough!" But he continued after them, and only a few escaped back to the south, whence they had come.

7. Migration

The time had come for Huitzilopochtli to lead his people on their travels in search of their homeland. Fray Diego Durán tells the following story. The seven peoples of the Valley of Mexico all originated in the Place of Seven Caves, or

Chicomoztoc (Chee-ko-moz'-tok). One by one, each group exited their subterranean home to migrate to the valley. The Mexica were the seventh and last to leave, led by their patron god Huitzilopochtli, whom they carried hidden in a bundle on their backs. They were called Mexicans in honor of Meci (Me'-see), a priestly lord who led them forth. They also called the Place of Seven Caves Aztlan (Azt'-lan). In this delightful land, people lacked nothing; they lived in leisure there and never grew old. Aztlan was a place of beautiful lagoons filled with reeds and all manner of waterfowl and fish. But once the Mexica left there, life became very hard. The stones became sharp, wounding them; the bushes became prickly and the trees thorny. Everything turned against them, and they no longer could remember how to return to this beautiful place. Along the way, the Mexica stayed in many places. At one time, the Mexica were related to the people of Malinalco (Ma-lee-nal'-ko), just west of the Valley of Mexico. But Huitzilopochtli had a falling-out with his sister Malinalxochitl (Ma-lee-nal-sho'-cheet):[52]

This woman was very beautiful, had a charming disposition and was so intelligent that she became skilled in the magical arts. She was very cunning, however, and did harm to the people, causing them great fear. They suffered her presence and gave her respect only because she was the sister of Huitzilopochtli. [Eventually, however, things became so bad that] they decided to ask their god to rid them of her for everyone's sake.

In the usual manner, the priests consulted Huitzilopochtli through dreaming[53] and passed on these revelations to the people:

"Your god sees your affliction. He says that his sister, with her cunning ways and bad talk, endangers you. He is disturbed and very angry to see the powers she has acquired by illicit means. She has power over fierce and dangerous beasts. She kills all who anger her by magically sending snakes, scorpions, centipedes, or deadly spiders to bite them."

"Since she is so dangerous, and since your god loves you so much and has no wish to bewitch or harm you, he says you should leave her. After she has fallen asleep, you should depart, leaving no one behind to tell her the way."

So all of those who were not Malinalxochitl's followers went away. They abandoned her and her attendants while they slept.

Malinalxochitl, not being able to follow the departed Mexicans because she did not know where they had gone, went on to found the town of Malinalco. There she bore a son she named Copil [Ko'-peel]. When Copil was old enough, she told him the story of how she was so cruelly abandoned by the followers of her brother, Huitzilopochtli. Her son was moved by his mother's tears, and his heart was so filled with wrath that he promised to seek revenge.

Seeing Copil's determination, she helped him to prepare by inciting all the nations against the Mexicans and teaching Copil her own wicked tricks and sorcery.

While the Mexicans camped at Chapultepec,[54] Copil set out, passing from town to town, turning many hearts against the Mexicans and inciting the nations to destroy them with their most fiendish skills and cunning.

But events came out exactly opposite to what Copil had hoped. His uncle, Huitzilopochtli, learned of Copil's bad intentions and warned the Mexicans. He told them that before Copil had a chance to surround their hill, they must take him by surprise, kill him, and give his heart to him, their god.

Shouldering their idol [Huitzilopochtli], the Mexicans successfully stalked and slayed Copil. But when the Mexican priest presented the captured heart to Huitzilopochtli, he was told to cast it as far as he could into Lake Texcoco. It is said that the heart landed in a place . . . where a prickly pear cactus sprouted out of it. It is in that same spot that Mexico City [Tenochtitlan] was later built. It also is said that hot water began to gush forth from the place in which Copil was killed. These springs are now called . . . "Water of Copil."

After visiting many more places and fighting a few battles, the Mexica settle down on land owned by the people of Colhuacan (Ko-wah'-kan).[55] The land is very poor and filled with venomous snakes. But the Mexica solve the problem by eating the snakes, and live there in peace and contentment. The lord of Colhuacan had been so sure that the snakes would kill them, he is disturbed by this turn of events, and just a little bit frightened of the Mexica. So when they request permission to trade in the city, he feels obliged to grant their wish. They even intermarry with the city's people. But Huitzilopochtli views Colhuacan as his enemy and determines that they should depart from this place in a manner that would be anything but peaceful. He instructs the Mexica to ask for one of the lord's daughters to serve Huitzilopochtli as a living goddess, to which the ruler agrees. But as soon as the maiden comes to the Mexica, they sacrifice her, and then invite her father to a festival in her honor. After the lord and his entourage had received their fine hospitality, the Mexica invite him into an inner chamber to view their god Huitzilopochtli and his goddess Toci (To'-see), his daughter. When to his horror he sees a Mexica youth dressed in his daughter's flayed skin sitting next to Huitzilopochtli, he flies into a rage and calls for vengeance. The people of Colhuacan chase the Mexica out of the city and into the marshes of Lake Texcoco.

This is actually good fortune in disguise, for after a bit of soggy wandering, the Mexica finally find their true homeland on an island in the middle of the lake. Huitzilopochtli tells them to search for the signs that will tell them where to build Tenochtitlan. First, they find a spring out of which runs one stream of water as red as blood, and another bright blue and extraordinarily thick. Soon after, they discover a prickly pear cactus, on which stands a magnificent eagle basking in the bright sun; in his talons he grasps a very fine bird (Figure 41).[56] This was the sign. It was here that they built their city of Tenochtitlan and elected their first ruler, Acamapichtli (A-ka-ma-peecht'-lee). The city and its people enjoyed a very long and successful history, with many rulers who performed many astounding feats.

*Figure 41. The Eagle and Cactus (*Codex Mendoza, *frontispiece, Bodleian Library)*

8. Return to Aztlan

But all good things must come to an end. And the Mexica know this. One of their greatest rulers, Motecuhzoma I, in the midst of his successes, received a warning to this effect:[57]

After the king, Motecuhzoma I, had established himself in his office and was very rich and well off, he wanted to find the home of his ancestors. He had heard that Huitzilopochtli's mother, Coatlicue, was still alive and living there. Since he wanted to find her and give her a fine present, he called his associate, Tlacaellel [Tla-ka-e'-lel]. Tlacaellel told him that he would need many priest-shamans, because according to history, this Place of Seven Caves was very well hidden by huge rock roses, thorny and tangled plants, and lagoons with thick reed beds. Moreover, it was a place inhabited by their fathers and grandfathers who were described not only as agreeable and delightful but also as very vicious.

So Motecuhzuma gathered a quantity of mantles, women's clothing, rich rocks, precious jewels, much cocoa, the aromatic *teonacaztli* [Tay-o-na-kazt'-lee] plant,[58] cotton, flowers of the vanilla plant, and the biggest, most beautiful, and finest feathers he could find. He sent his priest-shamans off with these gifts, to look for Aztlan. When they arrived at the hill called Coatepec in the province of Tula, they drew circles around themselves and anointed their bodies with salves so they might call down the gods and be changed into birds and fierce beasts, into lions and tigers and terrible cats. In these forms, they arrived on the banks of the place of their ancestors. There they changed themselves back into human beings.

A number of people of the earth were there, fishing from their canoes and farming. Upon encountering them, these strange people of the earth asked in the Mexica-Tenochca's own language what the newcomers were doing there.

"Sirs, we are from Mexico and we have been sent by our lords to look for the place of our ancestors."

"Whom do you worship?"

"We worship the great Huitzilopochtli. The great Motecuhzuma and his associate, Tlacaellel, have sent us to search for the mother of Huitzilopochtli, whose name is Coatlicue, and for the place of our ancestors which is called Chicomoztoc (Place of Seven Caves). We have presents for her, if she still lives, and if not, for the fathers and tutors who served her." The people told the Mexicans to wait and then went to the tutor of Huitzilopochtli's mother.

"O venerable sir, some people have arrived at the shore who say they are Mexicans sent by a great lord called Motecuhzuma and another called Tlacaellel. They say they have gifts for the mother of their god, Huitzilopochtli, and that they have been sent to present them to her personally."

The ancient one replied, "It is good they have come. Go back and bring them here."

So in canoes they were brought to the island. There they went to the foot of the hill of Colhuacan, where the house of the ancient one stood. It is said that in the middle of the top of this hill there was a tiny, sandy spot that could not be mounted because it was so soft and so deep.

"O venerable aged one and sir, here we have arrived, your servants, at the place where your word is obeyed and the desires of your mouth are revered."

"It is good you have come, my children. Who has sent you?"

"We have been sent by Motecuhzuma and his associate, Tlacaellel, whose other name is Cihuacoatl."

"Who is this Motecuhzuma and who is Tlacaellel? No one by those names left here. . . . [S]even went out as leaders of each . . . neighborhood. Four marvelous tutors of Huitzilopochtli also left here . . . and two others."

"Sir, we must confess that we do not know these gentlemen. We have never seen them. We have only a memory of them, for they have died. I have heard them mentioned."

The ancient one was amazed. "O lord of the born! What killed them? Why are all of us whom they left behind still living? Why has none died? Who are those that live now?"

"We are their grandsons."

"Who then is now the father and tutor of Huitzilopochtli?"

"A great priest whose name is Cuauhcoatl [Kwaw-ko'-wat]."

"Have you spoken with Huitzilopochtli?" the ancient one asked.

"No, we were sent by our king and his associate."

"When will Huitzilopochtli return? He told his mother that he would, and the poor woman spends each day waiting and crying with no one to console her."

"We only have been sent by our lords. But we have a present for the great lady, and we would like to give it to her and bring her our greetings. We want to bring her the loot and riches that her son enjoys."

"All right then, get it and follow me." And he moved off with such great agility that they had difficulty in keeping up with him.

When they reached the sandy place at the top of the hill, the Mexicans sank into it, first to their knees and then to their waists, as they struggled forward. Finally, they could not move.

The old one returned to where they were stuck and asked, "What have you been doing, Mexicans? How have you made yourselves so heavy? What do you eat there in your country?"

"We eat the food that is grown there and we drink cocoa."

"These foods have made you heavy. They do not allow you to visit the place of your fathers and they have resulted in death. And these riches that you carry, we don't use them here. We are poor and simple folk. Now, give them to me and wait while I go and see if the lady of this house, the mother of Huitzilopochtli, will see you." He took their ample gifts, carrying them on his shoulders as though they were no more than a tiny straw, and climbed the hill with ease.

When he returned, they were able to continue to the top because they were no longer weighed down by all their goods. There Coatlicue appeared. She was a lady of great age, her face was blackened, and she was as ugly and dirty as one could imagine. Crying bitterly, she said, "It is good that you have come, my children."

Full of fear and trembling, they replied, "Great and powerful lady, we have been sent by our lords and your servants, the king, Motecuhzuma, and his associate, Tlacaellel Cihuacoatl, to search for the place where our ancestors lived. We bring you kisses for your hands. Motecuhzuma is not the first king. . . . [He] is the fifth, and remains in your service.

"The four previous kings have suffered much hardship, hunger, and work. They paid tribute to other provinces, but now they have their own city and are prosperous and free. They have opened roads to the seacoast and all of the earth. And now Mexico is the lord and prince, the head and queen of all the cities. They have discovered mines of gold and silver and of precious rocks, and they have found the house of rich feathers. And as you can see, we have been sent with these things, which are the goods and riches of your marvelous son, Huitzilopochtli, who is brave and strong with a good head and heart, the lord of the born and of the day and the night. And with these gifts, we have completed our mission."

Her weeping somewhat assuaged, she replied, "I congratulate you, my children. I greet you, my children. Tell me, are those who left with my son still living?"

"Madam, they are not of this world any longer. They are dead, and we did not know them. We only have them in our memory."

Her weeping returned. "What killed them? Here all their companions are still living! And tell me, children, this that you carry, is it food?"

"Madam, it is eaten and it is drunk. The cocoa is drunk, and the rest of it is mixed with it and, at times, eaten."

"You have become attached to it, my children, and this is the reason you could not climb up here. But tell me, my children, is the clothing of my son the same as these rich, feathered mantles?"

"Yes, Madam. They are crafted elegantly and are richly arrayed, for he is the lord of us all."

"This is very good, my children. My heart is at peace. But I tell you, I am in much sorrow because it is difficult to be without him. Look at me now, a penitent who fasts for your cause. He told me when he left:

"'Dear Mother, I will be gone only as long as it takes me to establish the seven *barrios* [neighborhoods] in the places that have been promised them so that they can live on and populate this earth. And then I will return. The assigned years of my migration will expire after I have waged war against all the provinces, cities, villages, and hamlets and have placed them in my service. But then I will lose them to strangers in the same order that I won them, and I will be expelled from this earth.

"I will return after that, because those whom I have subjected with my sword and shield will turn against me, and I will be turned on my head, and my weapons will be thrown on the ground. Whereupon, Mother dear, I will return to your lap. But until then, do not feel sorrow. Give me two pairs of sandals, one to go with and one to come back with; four sandals, two with which to leave and two with which to return."

"I congratulated him and told him that he should not linger so that the time would be completed and he could return. But I think he must be happy there, for he does not remember the sadness of his mother. So tell him that his period is now completed and it is time for him to come home. To help him remember his mother, please give him this mantle and loincloth made of maguey fiber."

They took the mantle and loincloth and descended the hill. When they had arrived at its skirt, she called to them:

"Wait a minute and see how, in this land, no one grows old! Watch my old tutor!"

The ancient one descended the hill; the lower he got, the younger he became. Then he turned to ascend. And as he climbed, he grew older.

"This is how we live here, my children," he said. "And this is how your ancestors lived. No one dies here. We can rejuvenate ourselves whenever we want. Now look, your problems have been caused by the cocoa you drink and the food you eat. They corrupt you and rot you. And these rich clothes and feathers, they ruin you. But because you cannot take this manner of attire back with you, come and take from what we have to offer."

And he offered them all the wonderful game and fruits of the earth that grew in that place. Then he gave them two mantles and loincloths of maguey, one each for their king, Motecuhzuma, and his associate, Tlacaellel. Telling them please to forgive them, for they had nothing better to offer, he left.

They took their presents, drew their circles around themselves, and turned into the same animals as those they had come as. When they arrived at Coatepec, they turned themselves back into human beings. Twenty members, one-third of their party, had been decimated. Some said that the fierce beasts and birds that they had encountered had eaten them.

They returned to Mexico and told their story to Motecuhzuma, giving him the gifts. They told him how Coatlicue awaited the return of her son, how his time would be completed when all the towns that he had conquered were lost again in the same order.

Motecuhzuma then called Tlacaellel and related the whole story to him; about the abundance of Aztlan and how their own food and things weighed them down, corrupted them, causing death. Crying because they were remembering the ancestors and wanted very much to see this place, they told those who had gone on the mission to rest and then gave them the gifts that they had brought back. Finally, they gave the mantle and loincloth of maguey to Huitzilopochtli because his mother had sent it to him.

9. Destruction of the Fifth Age

Just as the four previous ages had come to an end and the reign of the Mexica was foredoomed, so too will the fifth age end. When its time is up, it will end, in this way:[59]

Like so is the Fifth Sun.
Four Movement is its day sign.
It is called Moving-Sun because
It moved,
It follows a path.
The old ones say that,
On Four Movement, it will be done like so.
The earth will quake.
They will be hungry.
Like so, we will perish.

MYTHOLOGICAL TIME

These two indigenous histories are very different from the history of Mesoamerica presented in Chapter One. Even if we had begun that history with the creation of the cosmos, as these began, they still would have been different. Not only are their main actors gods, animals, and humans with some pretty unusual powers (all in true mythic style), but in addition, time in these stories does not simply march onward. True, time moves in a kind of line; but it also sometimes both doubles back on itself and springs forward. Under the names Hunahpu Possum and Hunahpu Coyote, the Maya twin heroes appear at the beginning of time as two of the daykeepers who cast lots to see how people should be made; yet they are not even born yet, for that doesn't happen until the next age. Also before they are born, they destroy Zipacna and his two sons. In the Nahua myth, each age (including the present) will self-destruct according to a cosmic mathematical plan; and the Mexica magicians will return to the place of their origin in Aztlan, only to find out about their own future demise. Moreover, in that strange place of Aztlan, the normal aging processes do not operate; one can become young or old simply by running down and up a hill. How can what hasn't yet happened act in the present, transforming it? How can one know what is to come before it gets there? And how can one manipulate time, making it move backward and forward at will? A Euro-American historical timeline would never operate like this.

But time for indigenous Mesoamericans is not always like Euro-American time.[60] Euro-Americans base their calendar on only one celestial object, the sun; therefore they count the moments linearly, like beads on a rope. The sun was born a long time ago and will die many years from now; in the meantime, our lives tick onward like the hands of a clock, never turning back. But Mesoamerican calendrics are not based on just one but on many calendar rounds and on numerous celestial cycles, all moving according to their own paths. These all operate simultaneously, creating a very complex system. Moments do not line up like beads on a rope; instead, time is more like the rope itself, in which many fibers of differing lengths spin together. Now some fibers overlap and others do not; now others overlap that before had not.

As though one is weaving all the same points together into a coil of rope, rituals collapse many past and future moments (or fibers) into one moment (or rope section). By so doing, they bring all those moments' powers to bear on the present. This binding creates a unique meshing of many moments, just as a single binding of many points on a rope's coil ties together a number of unique sets of fibers. The present moment, which contains many past and future ones, is identical to no other moment that ever existed or will exist, just as a particular group of bound fibers on a coiled rope contains different fibers from other groups that could be bound. In this way, present moments reach backward and forward simultaneously, picking up all the powers of specific years, deities, days of times past and future. By manipulating different calendrical bindings, one can control the present, shape the future, and even reshape the past.

Thus, because these different moments could in fact converge, the Hero Twins could exist both at the beginning of time, helping to create some of the first beings, and still be newborns long after that creation was completed. As their father One Hunter told their mother Blood Woman, "The father does not disappear, but goes being fulfilled. Neither dimmed nor destroyed." One lives on in one's heirs, but this was more than simply a father's heritage carried on in his sons. Just before rising as the sun and the moon, the Twins also partially put their father back together again—not quite the same as he was before, but almost. Most importantly, he could still talk to them, just as he had to his daughter-in-law years before. The Twins' dead father was different from how he had been before, but he was not really dead; and even though he had been transformed, he also transformed the present, and was promised a future of continuing to do so. Transformation or change creates new things out of old things, and some of the old continues to live actively in the new. The father simultaneously lives in his sons, alongside his sons, and for them, long after he has died. The past still lives in, along with, and for the present.

Time's Purpose

Calendars help control the transformative change that is a natural part of life, because each moment holds particular powers able to shape and mold tangible events. By combining and recombining various moments, people can create new

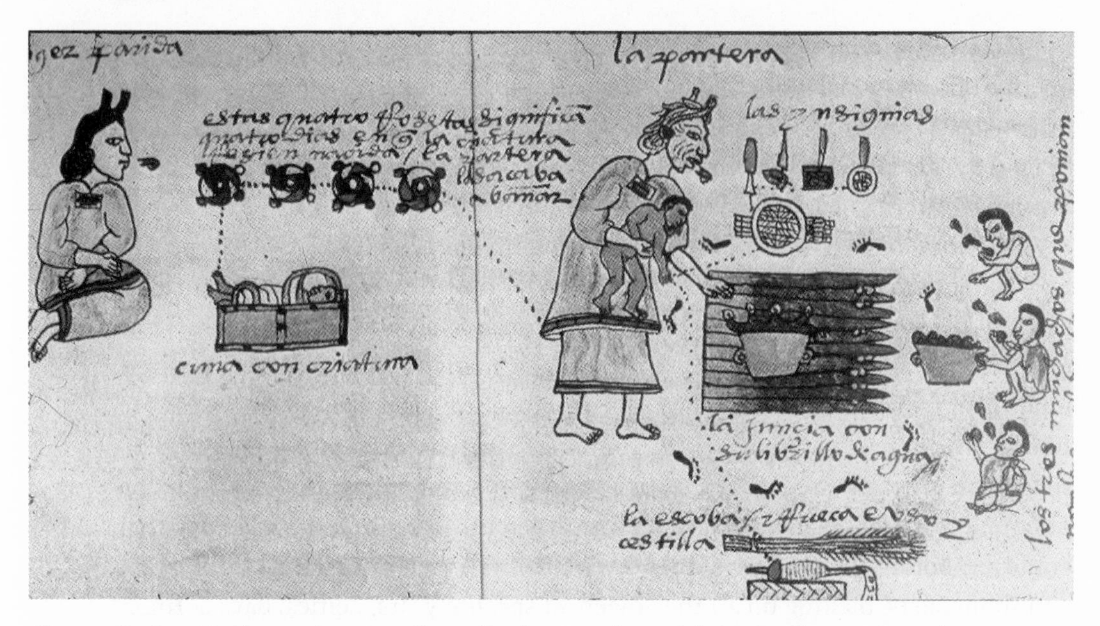

*Figure 42. A midwife naming a newborn (*Codex Mendoza*, fol. 57, Bodleian Library)*

moments that will prove propitious for certain activities. Conversely, some combinations are unlucky for certain things, and are avoided. The points in life when change occurs are linked to the calendrical system through rituals, which are timed to coincide with the most effective moments for their success. Thus, calendars help shape everything from the changes a new birth brings upon a family to the transformation of a dead leader's power into that of a new leader. Calendrical rituals exist for successful planting and harvest, marriage, travel, business transactions, waging of battles, and conduct of diplomatic missions. In ancient times, people's personal identities were partially formed by temporal calculations, for a calendrical name given at birth gave a child positive and negative traits (Figure 42). These traits became part of a person's personality and destiny, along with the effects of other life-changing calendrical rituals, other names (a person could have many), actions of the gods on a person, that person's own deeds, and his/her physical constitution—all of these, if properly controlled, came into existence at positively charged moments. Their sum total was called one's *merits.*[61] And because time changes, so too did one's merits.

Histories usually were tied directly to the elite classes and could be manipulated calendrically to create more favorable stories. However, when a particular city was conquered by another, these historical stories and the calendars on which they were based often ceased to function. Such was the case with the Classic Maya. Their elites used a particular calendar called the Long Count to tell their histories; this calendar was not used for any other purpose, and only those in control had the right to use it (Figure 43). Extremely accurate, the Long

Count could pinpoint events to the day within a several-thousand-year span. Maya elites used the count to shape their future and remain in control. But when the Classic Maya cities disappeared, so too did the Long Count, for no powerful rulers existed any longer to use it. Although the Maya were the only people who used the Long Count, other groups used a variety of calendrical systems for similar purposes. The Mexica rewrote their history in order to manipulate the calendar's powers to their benefit. Given the transformative powers possessed by particular dates, this was more than a mere reworking of self-image (although that was important too); by changing how they coordinated historical and celestial events, the Mexica believed they could literally change their past, present, and future, because the past always prefigures current and future events. It both foretells and shapes what is to come; and what is happening now happens because of what happened earlier.

Figure 43. A Maya Long Count date from the Temple of the Sun, Palenque, Chiapas, Mexico (drawing by Jason González, from frontispiece by Frederick Catherwood in Stephens, 1841)

Time's Workings

At one time, mathematics structured almost everything in Mesoamerica; and even today, calendrical concerns govern much of daily life, especially in villages and the countryside. Since indigenous calendars are neither simple nor all the same, we won't go into much detail here, but a small glimpse into how three or four cycles mesh might prove helpful to understanding how moments in the past, present, and future can converge. All Mesoamerican calendars are based on a running count of twenty days. Each day is named for and bears the powers of a particular deity (calendar dieties). The basic calendar was and still is the divinatory calendar, called the Tzolkin (Tsol-kin') in Yucatec Maya and the Tonalpohualli (To-nal-po-wal'-lee) in Nahuatl. Its age is very long and its origin quite obscure; possibilities range from a lunar cycle to a baby's gestation period, or the length of the rainy

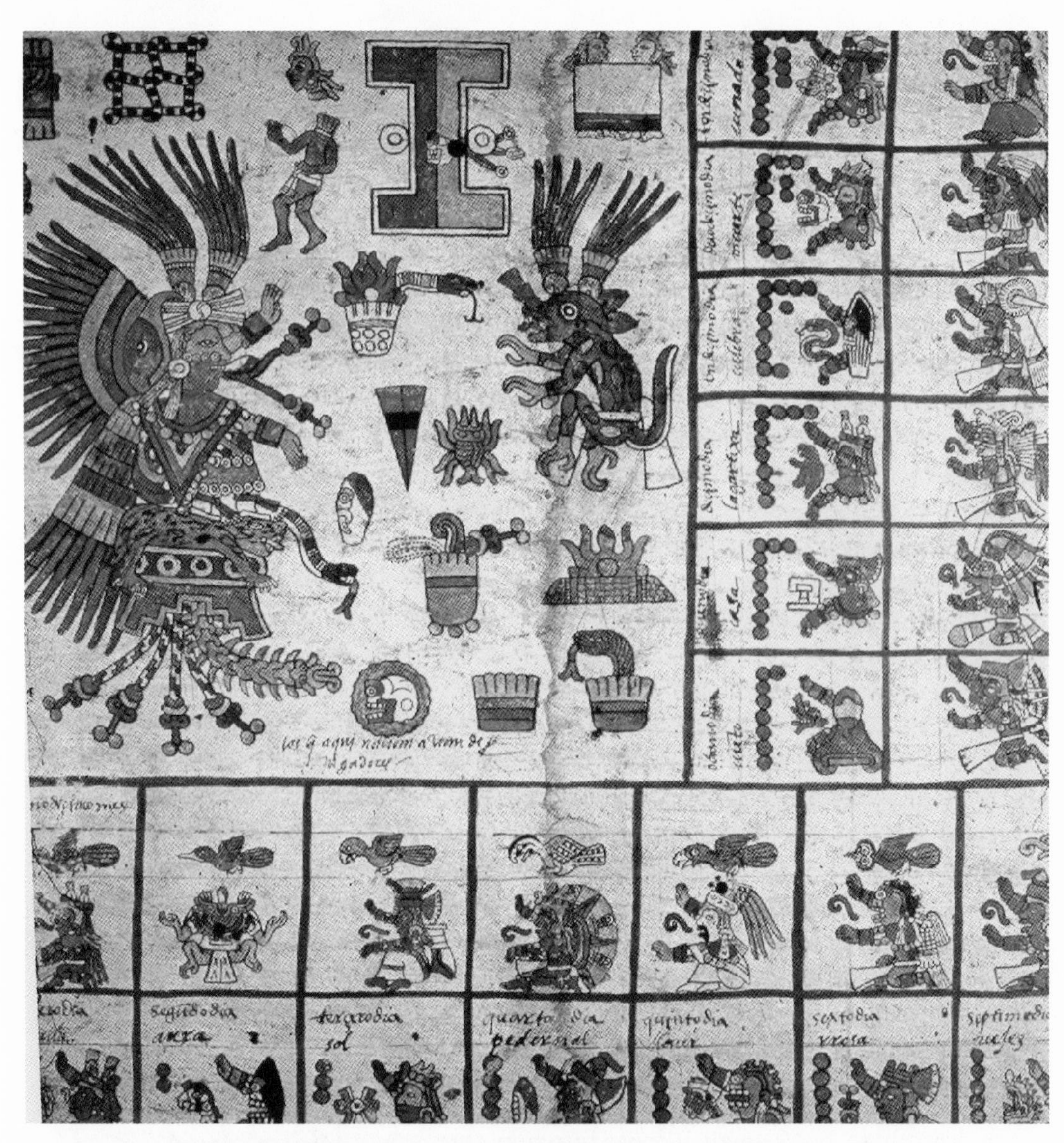

*Figure 44. Week 18 from a Mexica Tonalpohualli (divinatory calendar) (*Codex Borbonicus, *fol. 19, Museo de América/Art Resource)*

season to the period between zenith passages of the sun. People use the divinatory calendar for prophesying individual and communal events. This is the calendar one consults if one wants to know when to name one's baby, marry, or make a business deal: 260 days long, the round consists of 20 "weeks" of 13 days each (20 X 13 = 260). The basic 20-day count (each day indicated by a deity) lines up with each week's count of 1 to 13 (marked by dots). The Mexica version of this looked something like this (see Table 2.1 and Figure 44 and Table 2.1).

Another basic round is the solar calendar, called the Haab (Hahb) in Yucatec and the Xiuhmolpilli (Shee-ooh-mol-pee'-lee) in Nahuatl. In ancient times, this

TABLE 2.1. THE ROTATION OF TWENTY DAY SIGNS AND THIRTEEN *TRECENA* DAYS IN THE *TONALPOHUALLI*

Day-Signs	Dots, Thirteen Days of each *Trecena*
1. Crocodile	1 dot, *Trecena 1*
2. Wind	2 dots
3. House	3 dots
4. Lizard	4 dots
5. Snake	5 dots
6. Death	6 dots
7. Deer	7 dots
8. Rabbit	8 dots
9. Water	9 dots
10. Dog	10 dots
11. Monkey	11 dots
12. Grass	12 dots
13. Reed	13 dots
14. Jaguar	1 dot, *Trecena 2*
15. Eagle	2 dots
16. Vulture	3 dots
17. Movement	4 dots
18. Knife	5 dots
19. Rain	6 dots
20. Flower	7 dots
1. Crocodile, etc.	8 dots, etc.

calendar controlled the yearly agricultural cycle and was often used for high state rites; today local communities still use it to govern their civic events. It consists of 18 "months" of one 20-day round each, plus a period of 5 days generally considered dangerous; in pre-Conquest times, those five days were not even officially marked ([18 X 20] = 360 + 5 = 365). Every fifth name of the 20-day round was also a solar year name. For the Mexica, these were House, Rabbit, Reed, and Knife (underlined in Table 2.1 above). The mathematics of the system assured that every 365 days, the year would end on one of these days, and each of these four days would appear in succession every four years. Like the weeks in the divinatory calendar, this count went up to 13, and then started again with 1. In the Mexican Highlands, a 52-year round was counted out using this system, with each count of 13 being aligned with one of the 4 cardinal directions (4 X 13 = 52). For the Mexica this worked like so (see Table 2.2 and Figure 45).

The Mexica divinatory and solar rounds ended on the same day every 52 years. At that very same moment, the Pleiades reappeared in the sky after having disappeared for six weeks, and the sun rested at its nadir. Moreover, this happened in November, when the rainy season of agriculture ended and war's dry season began. At this power-laden conjunction of several celestial and seasonal moments, a ceremony took place in which a new sun was given birth, for it was said that the

TABLE 2.2. THE 52-YEAR CYCLE OF THE *XIUHMOLPILLI*

Southern Quarter Dots-Year Sign	Eastern Quarter Dots-Year Sign	Northern Quarter Dots-Year Sign	Western Quarter Dots-Year Sign
1-Rabbit	1-Reed	1-Knife	1-House
2-Reed	2-Knife	2-House	2-Rabbit
3-Knife	3-House	3-Rabbit	3-Reed
4-House	4-Rabbit	4-Reed	4-Knife
5-Rabbit	5-Reed	5-Knife	5-House
6-Reed	6-Knife	6-House	6-Rabbit
7-Knife	7-House	7-Rabbit	7-Reed
8-House	8-Rabbit	8-Reed	8-Knife
9-Rabbit	9-Reed	9-Knife	9-House
10-Reed	10-Knife	10-House	10-Rabbit
11-Knife	11-House	11-Rabbit	11-Reed
12-House	12-Rabbit	12-Reed	12-Knife
13-Rabbit	13-Reed	13-Knife	13-House

Note: Read each column down, beginning with the southern quarter (on the left), move right to the eastern quarter, then the northern quarter, and end with the Western quarter. This cycle repeats every fifty-two years.

life of a sun lasted only fifty-two years. This ceremony, called the Binding of the Years, or the New Fire Ceremony, took place on a hill overlooking Tenochtitlan (Figure 46). All fires in the entire domain were snuffed out, houses swept clean, and old clothing and household goods thrown away. At midnight, a specially trained priest cut out the heart of a distinguished war captive (a man, probably 52 years old), and then sparked a fire in his chest cavity. His heart was fed to the fire, which also consumed his entire body. If the fire was not successfully lighted, creatures of the night would descend and eat up the age; but if it was, a new sun would rise. Because the years had been properly bound, like the Hero Twins containing something of their father One Hunter, this new sun would contain something of the old sun but would still be a different entity. And like the Hero Twins, Nanahuatzin, and Tecuiçiztecatl, this new sun had risen out of the ashes.

In the Nahua five mythic ages, time spans also were calculated on the 52-year cycle: 13 X 52 = 676 years, the length of the first and fourth ages; 312 + 364 = 676, the length of ages two and three combined. Remember that in the Nahua myth ages two and three both ended on the same year, 1-Knife. Like the two suns in the myth about the birth of the fifth age, they were named the same and so were considered the same. While this was inappropriate to the creation of the fifth age, which needed only one sun at a time, here it was appropriate because the two ages needed to be made the same. Mathematically joining them left 676 years for the fifth age to live—years that otherwise would have been used by a previous age. By juggling numbers in this way, those skilled in calendrics could manipulate the calendars to create their own realities. If four ages have already

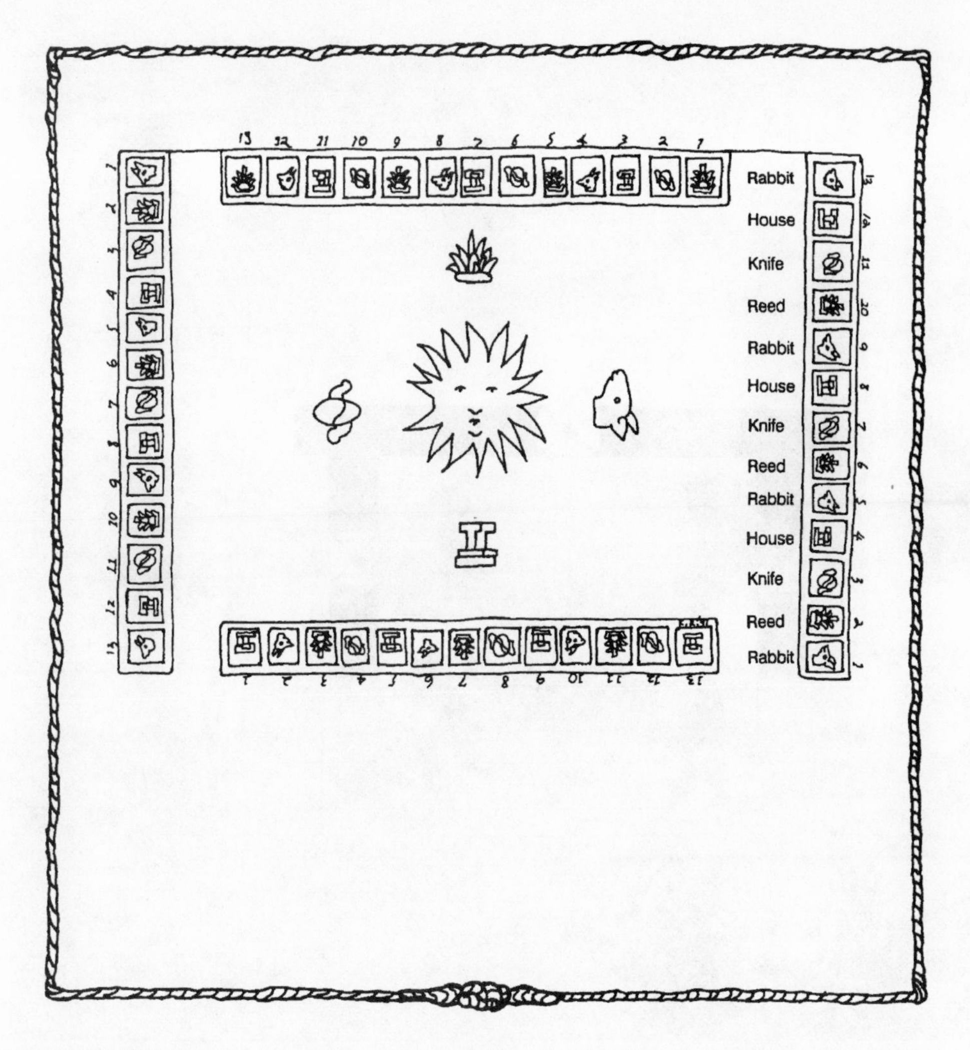

Figure 45. The Mexica fifty-two-year round (drawing by Kay A. Read from the Codex Aubin*)*

occurred, then simply take two past ages and bind them together; join the two in order to create room for a future, fifth age that now needs to be made present.

This is what Mesoamerican calendrics were and are all about: the chance to manipulate life's events by coordinating them with the motions of celestial events governing time. Calendars provide the tools by which the many cosmic powers could and can be controlled in order to improve the quality of one's existence. Calendars are not and never were rigid mathematical systems, unyielding to any outside shaping. Not only are they guides for one's journey through life, but one can even use them to mold the very landscape over which one travels.

So while some Mesoamericans tell a story of time that begins at the beginning and builds moment by moment to the present, others tell a story of time

*Figure 46. Binding-of-the-Years or the New Fire Ceremony (*Codex Borbonicus, *fol. 34, Museo de América/Art Resource)*

that presents a more complex picture. In the indigenous timeline, the present can pick up moments from the past and make them real again; time also can join past and present moments with the future, binding all three together. Thus is life controlled and transformed at the very same time as it moves forward, carrying one from birth to death. The past predicts and even molds what is to come; and present events happen because of what happened in the past.

NOTES

1. I base my retelling of this story on the Popol Vuh translated and annotated by Dennis Tedlock (1985, 71–72).

2. *Quiché* is an alternate spelling of *K'iche'*. Depending on the circumstances, this word might refer to the people, their language, their homeland, or all three.

3. Hunahpu Possum and Hunahpu Coyote are names for the Hero Twins who, in the form of vagabond dancers and magicians, later defeat the lords of the underworld (*Popol Vuh* 1985, 342).

4. The Maya creator gods are many.

5. The original text, which was translated by Dennis Tedlock with the help of K'iche' day-keeper Andrés Xiloj, was first recorded in the mid-sixteenth century *(Popol Vuh* 1985, 28). Xiloj knew this same tale very well and told it almost the same as it had been told 400 years before.

6. The storyteller is describing the measuring-out of the horizontal and vertical dimensions of the cosmos's four quarters as one might measure out a house under construction.

7. Modern daykeepers like Andrés Xiloj cast lots using corn kernels and pieces of coral, rather like some people use dice or cards to judge fate. This is done by coordinating the count of kernels as they fall with the count of days in a calendar called the divinatory cycle. Ideally, the best divinations are believed to be those performed by a male and female pair working together (*Popol Vuh* 1985, 370).

8. Because of Possum, the dawn now is streaked with red and blue.

9. According to Tedlock, this means that the lords of the underworld will be denied human sacrifices (*Popol Vuh* 1985, 293).

10. Tollan—or in an alternate spelling, Tula—is the home of the ancient ancestors in many Mesoamerican mythic traditions. Mexica myths indicate that the Toltecs, or people of Tollan, may have lived at an actual city called Tula. More likely, however, the Toltecs were mythical, and more intangible than tangible.

11. *Tonatiuh* is a Nahuatl word meaning "sun." This was the name the Nahua of the Mexican Highlands gave Pedro de Alvarado, one of Hernan Cortés's main men (*Popol Vuh* 1985, 366).

12. For a full English translation (by John Bierhorst) of the "Legend of the Suns," see *Codex Chimalpopoca* (1992b).

13. Most of the Nahua stories included here appear in Read (1998, 48–84), in either the same form or an expanded form. We have taken the liberty of eliminating some of the more technical information and have included phonetic spellings for foreign words. Some stories are translated in full, and others are retellings. All translations from the original Nahuatl were done by Kay A. Read and Jane Rosenthal.

14. Summary based on Read (1998, 67). Original translation by Kay A. Read and Jane Rosenthal (*Codex Chimalpopoca* 1992a, 87).

15. Many other versions of this tale of five ages exist, some of which are a bit more detailed than this one. See Moreno de los Arcos (1967) for a discussion of these versions.

16. From Read (1998, 70), retold from the Nahuatl in the *Codex Chimalpopoca* (1992a, 88).

17. This is one of the many names of the god Tezcatlipoca, a major deity who was sometimes paired with Quetzalcoatl and sometimes identified as the Mexica god Huitzilopochtli.

18. The cypress tree, or *ahuehuetl,* can grow to an enormous height and live hundreds of years. In Mesoamerican myth, the tree is a symbol of rulership.

19. Read (1998, 71–72), retold from the Nahuatl in *Codex Chimalpopoca* (1992a, 88–89).

20. Like those of the Maya, the Nahua creator gods are many.

21. *Nahualli* can mean a lot of things. Often it means "magician" (or shaman or medicine person), or the transfiguration of that magician into some other form. In this passage, *nahualli* also means an extra spirit that can act independently of the magician himself.

22. He's saying "que será, será," or "whatever will be, will be."

23. This bit of added information indicates that the narrator was from out of town.

24. Merit is the sum total of one's powers received through birth, various rituals, circumstances determined by the gods, and as the result of one's own actions (Read 1998, 114–116, 254 n97).

25. Read (1998, 73), retold from the Nahuatl in the *Codex Chimalpopoca* (1992a, 89–90).

26. Like the K'iche' Maya, the Nahua told stories about a mythic mountain filled with good things to eat.

27. Oxomoco and Cipactonal, like Xpiyacoc and Xmucane in the *Popol Vuh,* are daykeepers who use corn kernels to throw lots.

28. In modern versions of this Nahua myth told by the Nahua of Yaonahuac and Huitzilan, Nanahuatl is lightning, and he strikes the mountain with his head, cracking it open (Taggert 1983, 88–92).

29. "To cast fortunes" also means "to open something," which implies that the future can be opened.

30. There were four sets of Tlaloques, one for each cardinal direction.

31. Read (1998, 49–58). Translation by Kay A. Read and Jane Rosenthal from the *Florentine Codex* 1953–1982, bk. 7, pt. 8, chap. 2:3–9, app. 42–58.

32. They are asking who will govern this age ("to carry" also means "to govern"). Many metaphors describe the ruler as governing the city by carrying it on his back as one might carry a child.

33. The burden to be borne will be time itself, and the sun and the moon will be the bearers because they are the ones governing these periods.

34. This fire pit is a cooking fire in which three stones were used, as they still are today in many parts of Mesoamerica, to support cooking vessels.

35. Balls, usually woven of grass, were used to catch blood flowing out during bloodletting ceremonies.

36. A headdress bore on it the image, or name, of a particular god. As with all names, this image was imbued with that god's power. Hence the name belonged to the god and not to Nanahuatzin.

37. "Praising" also means the ritual summoning of gods and various powers.

38. This passage probably means that because Nanahuatzin has a good heart, he has the power to do the deed he needs to do; his merit is of a good variety.

39. In Nahuatl, this first phrase describes the lighting of a house (the cosmos was thought of as house in which people lived). The second describes dawn's first rosy rays as doves the color of burning embers, perhaps the embers of the fire from which the new sun has just emerged.

40. These are the cardinal directions, described in a counterclockwise order, beginning with the north (the Place of the Dead) and moving to the west (the Place of Women) and then to the south (the Place of Thorns).

41. This, as one might expect, is the east.

42. The dawn is metaphorically a red sacrifice, and *dye* also refers to blood.

43. "Spreading in an undulating way" is a rich metaphor for the growing light of dawn. The sun's rosy hues are twisting and bending like red dye or sacrificial blood spreading out in a body of water. Since the walls of the cosmos were made of water, this seems particularly fitting.

44. If one looks carefully, one can see a rabbit on the moon rather than a face. Viewed from the United States the rabbit is crawling up the left side, but seen from Mesoamerica he runs along the bottom just as he should.

45. In other words, they spread on the earth's eastern horizon or edge.

46. Gods and people are not supposed to be living together on the same level, as that would literally mess things up.

47. The *axolotl,* or salamander, is not really a fully developed salamander but is still in the larval stage. This particular variety is known as the mole salamander *(ambystoma talpoideum)* in the United States. But in Mexico, it never loses its gills, and remains fully aquatic. The creature looks like a full-grown salamander, apart from the huge, feathery gills on each side of its head.

48. The sun's daily path (ending in the west) is established and he will now continue to set there. From now on, he will enter the earth each night and travel through the underground before emerging again in the east.

49. Read (1998, 75), retold from the Nahuatl in the Florentine Codex (bk. 3, pt. 4, chap. 1:1–5).

50. Huitzilopochtli, like his close counterpart Tezcatlipoca, often is depicted with one small or oddly shaped foot.

51. This imagery depicts a powerful mountain storm, with Huitzilopochtli wielding a comet or lightning-like weapon and throwing up huge storm clouds to defeat his enemies.

52. Read (1998, 76–77), retold from Durán (1994, 24–25, 31–33).

53. Dreaming is probably analogous to the longstanding tradition of vision questing among North American native peoples, in which youths who are coming of age seek visions by "dreaming." These visions might be thought of as extrasensory visual experiences by Westerners. They are acquired through a wide variety of ritual practices. In ancient Mesoamerica, sometimes visions were induced by fasting, bloodletting, dancing, or the use of hallucinogenic drugs.

54. Chapultepec was situated on a rocky outcropping on the shore of Lake Texcoco, just to the west of Tenochtitlan—the site of today's Chapultepec park and zoo, in Mexico

City. In pre-Conquest times, the site included a magnificent garden. Then springs flowed from the rocks, and Mexica rulers visited there.

55. This summary is based on Durán (1994, 34–57).

56. The text says that the eagle grasped a bird, but the picture in Durán shows a snake in the great bird's grip (ibid., plate 6). One must remember that Durán was a Spaniard retelling Nahua stories and didn't always get things right (although he didn't always get them wrong, either). The current Mexican flag depicts the image in Durán's picture. This picture from the *Codex Mendoza* shows nothing in the eagle's grasp.

57. Read (1998, 78–82), retold from Durán (1994, 212–222).

58. This is a beautiful plant with yellow flowers and a lovely aroma that was used to perfume cocoa when it was made into a drink.

59. Read (1998, 83–84). Translation by Kay A. Read and Jane Rosenthal from the Nahuatl in the "Anales de Cuauhtitlan," one of two other texts contained along with "The Legend of the Suns" in the *Codex Chimalpopoca* (1992a, 5).

60. See Read (1997a, 821–824; 1998, 211–235) for more information on Mesoamerican time and calendrics.

61. The Nahua word for this is *mahceua*. Read (1998, 114–116, 151, 185, 203, 246 n19, 264 n1).

3

DEITIES, THEMES, AND CONCEPTS

ACAMAPICHTLI, LORD

Time period: Postclassic

Cultural group: Nahua-Mexica

Lord Acamapichtli (A-ka-ma-peecht´-lee) was the first Chief Speaker of the Mexica or Aztecs (Nahua; ruled ca. 1369–1403), and mythically represents the origins of Mexica greatness. He and his reign symbolize the official beginning of the Mexica as an independent political entity, for without its own royal lineage, a city could not aspire to any real power. Acamapichtli's father was a Colhua nobleman, his mother the daughter of a Mexica ruler, and he married a Colhua noblewoman. Through this Colhua heritage, he linked the Mexica royal line with that of the fabled Toltecs and their patron deity Quetzalcoatl, whose ancestry gave them a civilizing legitimacy. And he acted as the "likeness" of the Mexica patron deity Huitzilopochtli, who was closely associated with the great god Tezcatlipoca. This first ruler therefore embodied two of the most powerful deities in the Nahua cosmos, Quetzalcoatl and Tezcatlipoca, and thus served as a harbinger of the Mexica's later power.

For years the Mexica remained too weak to throw off the control of neighboring city Azcapotzalco, whose territory they occupied. It is told how, during Acamapichtli's reign, the Azcapotzalco ruler Tezozomoc demanded the Mexica pay a seemingly impossible tribute for this privilege: a floating raft sown with maize, chiles, beans, squash, and amaranth. They succeeded in this task with the magical help of Huitzilopochtli. Then Tezozomoc raised his demands, this time requiring that duck and heron chicks hatch from their eggs the moment another garden-raft floated into Azcapotzalco. Again Huitzilopochtli helped, this time predicting the future demise of Azcapotzalco. Impressed with their ability to accomplish the impossible, Tezozomoc declared that the Mexica were the chosen people of their god and some day would rule over all other nations, a prophecy that came largely true.

See also Huitzilopochtli; Quetzalcoatl; Tezcatlipoca

Suggested reading:
Codex Mendoza. 1997. As reproduced in the *Essential Codex Mendoza.* Commentary and edited by Frances Berdan and Patricia Rieff Anawalt. Berkeley: University of California Press.
Durán, Fray Diego. 1994. *The History of the Indies of New Spain.* Trans. Doris Heyden. Norman: University of Oklahoma Press.
Townsend, Richard Frazer. 1992. *The Aztecs.* London: Thames and Hudson.

AHUITZOTL, LORD

Time period: Postclassic
Cultural group: Nahua-Mexica

As the eighth Chief Speaker of the Mexica or Aztecs (Nahua, ruled ca. 1486–1502), Lord Ahuitzotl (A-weet´-zot) expanded the Mexica or Aztec domain tremendously and consolidated their power at a time of potential weakness. He was the third son of Lord Motecuhzoma I (Ilhuicamina), the fifth Chief Speaker (ruled ca. 1441–1469), and he sired the last true Chief Speaker, Cuauhtemoc (ruled ca.1520–1524), whom the Spanish captured and executed. Ahuitzotl, with his energy of youth and great capabilities, symbolizes the return of Mexica power. At the same time, he represents the limitations of all people, including rulers.

When Chief Speaker Tizoc died from poisoning after a short and rather ineffectual rule (ca. 1481–1486), political wolves in the form of Tenochtitlan's neighbors were barking at Mexica doorways. The Mexica desperately needed a strong ruler; Ahuitzotl, a high-ranking military leader, proved to be their man.

Stories surrounding Ahuitzotl often stress his youth, skills, energy, strength, and audacity. Fray Diego Durán tells a magical tale of his election, in which he is not an experienced military leader, but a mere youth, one who requires training from the Tlacaellel, a leader often ruling in partnership with the Chief Speaker. Ahuitzotl is so young that, upon election, the electors fetch him from school. Yet, he comports himself with the maturity of an elder, and although inexperienced, returns victorious from his first war. The Mexica became so strong they could secretly invite their enemies to the celebration of the rebuilding of their main temple, and shower them with extravagant gifts. Durán also claims that Ahuitzotl sacrificed 80,400 war captives at this celebration, in spite of the impossibility of both doing this in the manner Durán describes, and that disposing of that many bodies would have caused serious environmental damage. These myths' exaggerations stress Ahuitzotl's strength, ability, and wealth, as well as Mexica power and ruthlessness, and the invincibility of their patron god Huitzilopochtli.

Yet Ahuitzotl's own invincibility went only so far. In another story, against the advice of his counselors, he murders the magician-ruler of Coyoacan because

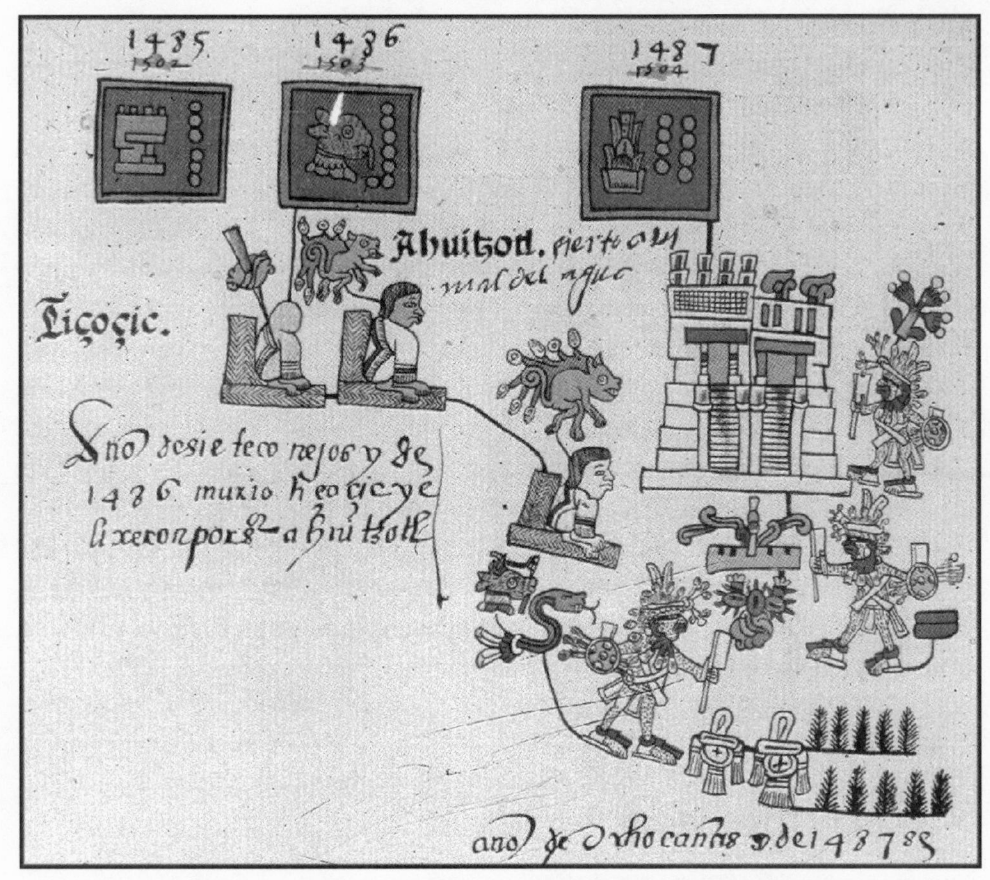

*Figure 47. Ahuitzotl's sacrifice at the Templo Mayor (*Codex Telleriano Remonsis, *fol. 39, Bibliotheque Nationale/Art Resource)*

he wants the control of his spring. Ahuitzotl builds an aqueduct and brings the water to Tenochtitlan, only to flood the city forty days later. His counselors bade him to stop the flow and make offerings to the water goddess Chalchiuhtlicue, who was clearly offended by the ruler's death. Ahuitzotl also died unnaturally young from a strange disease perhaps brought on by poison, an event reminiscent of his predecessor's death. The moral is that both the incompetent and arrogant will fall, and even the strong can die.

See also Chalchiuhtlicue; Cuauhtemoc, Lord; Motecuhzoma I, Lord; Tizoc, Lord; Tlacaellel

Suggested reading:

Codex Mendoza. 1997. As reproduced in the *Essential Codex Mendoza.* Commentary and edited by Frances Berdan and Patricia Rieff Anawalt. Berkeley: University of California Press.

Durán, Fray Diego. 1994. *The History of the Indies of New Spain.* Trans. Doris Heyden. Norman: University of Oklahoma Press.

Townsend, Richard Frazer. 1992. *The Aztecs.* London: Thames and Hudson.

AJITZ C'OXOL

Time period: Contemporary

Cultural group: Tzutuhil Maya

Ajitz C'oxol (A-heets´ K-h-o-shol´) also goes by the names K'ek Co'xol and Huitzil. A myth from the town of Tzutuhil San Jose la Laguna describes him as a red witch of the K'iche' King Tecun Uman. He had a red face like a devil and lived in a nearby hill called Paquixquil. San Jose used to be a wealthy place where one had only to lift up a stone to find gold, and everyone was contented. However, when Ajitz arrived he berated the Tzutuhiles, calling them dead fish and crab eaters and poor excuses for men. After many years of this abuse, the Tzutuhiles got tired of it. One day, all the witches and *nahuales* gathered and changed into animals that flew or had four legs. The flying animals caught Ajitz and dropped him over a large stone, where the four-legged ones tore into him; but Ajitz was very strong, and they could not kill him. After the animals had repeated this punishment a number of times, Ajitz repented; he finally left them, cursing the people of San Jose to eternal poverty and taking their wealth with him to the town of Santa Clara.

See also Nahual

Suggested reading:

Sexton, James D. 1992. *Mayan Folktales: Folklore from Lake Atitlan, Guatemala.* New York: Anchor Books, Doubleday.

BACABS

Time period: Postclassic–Contemporary

Cultural group: Yucatec Maya

These four Maya deities hold up the heavens; in fact, a creator god placed these skybearers at the four corners of the universe for this very purpose. Because each stands at one of the four cardinal directions, each claims a specific color and particular years of influence in the Maya calendar that are symbolically linked to that direction. The eastern Bacab (Ba-kab´) claims the color red, Kan years, and the name Hobnil; the northern Bacab, the color white, Muluc years, and the name Can Tzicnal; the western Bacab, the color black, Ix years, and the name Zac Cimi; the southern Bacab, the color yellow, Cauac years, and the name Hozanek. In Yucatec Maya cosmology the Bacabs also control the rain and wind and often serve as patrons of beekeeping and divination.

According to the sixteenth-century historian Diego de Landa and the Chilam Balam de Chumayel (a mythic history from the town of Chumayel), the Yucatec creator deity Hunab Ku created the Bacabs when the gods made the universe in the third and previous age. A great deluge destroyed that age. These four brothers escaped, received new names, and once again took up their places at the four quarters of the cosmos when the gods created the fourth and present age. Landa tells us that each Bacab received "one of the four dominical letters [the four days on which a new year could start]. They also indicated the miseries or happy events which they said must occur the year of each one of them" (Landa 1941, 144–145). According to the Chilam Balam de Tizimin (a mythic history from the town of Tizimin): "The Bacabs planted five trees. They stretched out the earth, planted a red Imix in the east, a white Imix in the north, a black Imix in the west, a yellow Imix in the south, and a green Imix in the center of the country" (Makemson 1951, 23).

Figure 48. Two Bacabs with their hands in the air holding up the universe (Thompson, J. E. S., Peabody Museum of American Archaeology and Ethnology)

These four brothers appear relatively late in Maya history. Scholars have identified Postclassic sculpture at the site of Chichén Itzá as the Bacabs. There they appear with their hands outstretched above them. Bacabs also appear in two Postclassic documents, the Madrid and Dresden Codices, which contain divination almanacs. We also know stories of the Bacabs from historical documents such as Landa's *Relaciónes,* the Chilam Balam de Chumayel, and Tizimin. In the modern era, people living at Chan Kom in the state of Yucatán, near the ancient Maya ruins of Chichén Itzá, continue to make ritual offerings to the Bacabs, hoping for more rain and better crops.

Much of our understanding of the Bacabs comes from stories found in Landa's descriptions and the various Chilam Balams. Throughout the colonial period and into the modern era, the stories and myths of the Bacabs have metamorphosed. At some point in history they became joined with the figure of Chac, a Maya rain god with an extraordinarily long mythic history. The Yucatec

Maya of Chan Kom believe in four Chacs, each associated with one of the four corners of the universe, and each having a cardinal direction and color. Besides their task of bearing up the sky, these Chacs/Bacabs of Chan Kom bring rain. However, their duties as patrons of beekeeping have changed. For at Chan Kom, different deities, the Balams, maintain bees; they also stand at the four quarters, along with the Chacs/Bacabs. Like many other deities, the Bacabs are important in divination ceremonies for both ancient Maya and modern Maya. One might approach the Bacabs with questions about future rain or wind, or maybe the health of one's beehive. In response the skybearers might foretell what is to come or might help with one's needs.

See also Chac and the Chacs; Earth, Agricultural, and Hunting Deities; Hunab Ku; Rain and Water Deities; Tlaloc and the Tlaloques

Suggested reading:

Landa, Diego de. 1978. *Yucatan before and after the Conquest.* Trans. William Gates. New York: Dover.

Roys, Ralph L. 1965. *Ritual of the Bacabs: A Book of Maya Encantations.* Norman: University of Oklahoma Press.

Thompson, John Eric Sydney. 1970b. *Maya History and Religion.* Norman: University of Oklahoma Press.

BATS

Time period: Classic–Contemporary

Cultural group: Mesoamerica

Bats mark the Underworld, death, rottenness, and destruction in Mesoamerican mythology, perhaps because these creatures travel the sky by night and hide in caves by day. In many although not all myths, bats also are associated with male sexuality; and as blood-sucking beasts, they sometimes serve as mythic agents of sacrifice. Not all bats suck blood, of course: 118 of the 120 species inhabiting Mesoamerica suck only the nectar of flowers or eat fruit and insects, and only two tropical species of vampire bats (Desmodontinae) suck blood.

Classic Maya ceramists often pictured bats as pop-eyed males, associated with human skulls and bones. In the Postclassic era, Central Mexicans sometimes depicted bats sporting snouts that resembled sacrificial knives and carrying severed human heads. In some representations, the starry eyes of the night sky decorated their wings; and occasionally they appeared alongside other dangerous nocturnal beasts, such as scorpions and owls. Among the Postclassic Zapotec, depictions of bats appeared frequently with funerary goods and bore some characteristics of the Jaguar, another figure of night and the Underworld. An impressive, life-size ceramic bat-man has been unearthed from the Templo Mayor in the center of the Mexica capital of Tenochtitlan. This god of death has a human body, but his clawed feet and hands are those of a bat. His bulging, humanoid eyes peer menacingly from a bat-like head, reminding one of the Zapotec images. Huge fangs protrude from his gaping mouth, and his mouse-ears are incongruously large. This is not a beast one would want to meet in the dead of night. In contrast, contemporary representations of bats bear a much less threatening character, although some still associate bats with death and the Underworld.

The Hero Twins of the K'iche' Maya Popol Vuh came up against the cunning and destructiveness of bats in their contest with the gods of the Underworld. In their last house of trials, the House of Bats, the boys hid in their blow-guns to prevent themselves from being decapitated by the monstrous snatch-bats with snouts like knives. All night the creatures flew around them, screeching as they rushed through the night air. Then the wily beasts stood very still for awhile, tricking the boys into thinking that dawn finally had come. Hunahpu peeked out from his blow-gun to see if light was coming. Instantly a bat swooped down and plucked off his head almost as though it were a piece of fruit hanging from a tree. Hunahpu's head rolled off to the ball court, to serve as the ball for the gods' next game. Xbalanque, with the help of Opossum and the other animals, fashioned a makeshift head for Hunahpu from a pumpkin. Only then could the boys continue their task of unseating the Lords of Death.

An ancient Nahua story says that the first bat was born when Quetzalcoatl's semen dripped onto a rock while he was washing. The gods sent the bat to bite out the vulva of the young goddess Xochiquetzal, from which they grew nasty-smelling flowers to present to Mictlantecuhtli, lord of the Underworld Land of Death. In some stories, Xochiquetzal appeared as the Sun's wife, so this odd little tale may refer to celestial and terrestrial journeys. Quetzalcoatl, as the morning star that heralds the rising sun, inadvertently had spawned an Underworld servant, who through a sacrificial act forced upon the Sun's wife, created the fruits of the rotting, foul-smelling Land of Death. Like the Hero Twins, the Sun would travel through that same nasty underworld every evening, abandoning the pleasant upper world to the creatures of the night.

Death continues as a theme in contemporary myths about bats. In the 1930s, the Cakchiquel Maya said that the bat was the Devil's cook. Every night she went out from the Hill, or the Devil's Underworld home, to collect blood from animals, which she then brought back to make into delicious dishes for her boss. Dead sinners spent time laboring for the Devil to pay off their debts before going to heaven, so perhaps the bat too was a sinner.

A contemporary story from Oaxaca is more benign. Oaxacans say that one day the bat complained to God that he was cold, although in truth he was jealous of all the birds' fine plumage. God reluctantly asked each bird to donate one feather to keep the bat warm. Because of all these feathers from so many different birds, the bat became the most beautiful flying creature around; he spread color through the sky both day and night, and he could even create a rainbow. As a result, he became insufferably proud. Fed up with the bat's arrogance, the birds flew up to heaven to have a little talk with God, who then summoned the bat so that he might see all of the wonderful things he was doing on earth. As the bat performed his marvelous feats, his feathers fell out one by one, leaving him exactly as he was before. And to this day, the bat remains so ashamed of his ugly body that he comes out only at night, when he flies rapidly back and forth, looking for his lost feathers.

See also Hero Twins; Opossums; Quetzalcoatl; Sun; Underworld and Caves, Deities of the

Suggested reading:

Henestrosa, Andres. 1994. "The Bat." Pp. 33–37 in *Myth and Magic: Oaxaca Past and Present.* Palo Alto: Palo Alto Cultural Center.

Tedlock, Dennis, trans. 1985. *Popul Vuh: The Definitive Edition of the Mayan Book of the Dawn of Life and the Glories of Gods and Kings.* New York: Simon and Schuster.

BLOOD WOMAN

Time period: Postclassic–Contemporary

Cultural group: K'iche' Maya

Blood Woman (Xquic, or Little Blood) appears in the Popol Vuh legends as an underworld maiden, the daughter of Blood Gatherer, one of the death lords. Having been impregnated with the Hero Twins Hunahpu and Xbalanque, Blood Woman secretly migrated to Earth's surface so that her sons could carry out their destiny: the destruction of her own male relatives, the lords of death, and the creation of the world as we know it.

Blood Woman's pregnancy was miraculous, as she remained a virgin even after conception: According to myth, she was impregnated by the calabash head of Hun Hunahpu. After the Twin's father and uncle were sacrificed, the Xibalba lords placed Hun Hunahpu's head in a barren tree as a victory trophy. Immediately, this tree burst into new leaf, blossomed, and became laden with calabash gourds, one of which was Hun Hunahpu's head. One day Blood Woman heard of this magical tree, and even though her father warned her away from it, she had to see it for herself. Just as she was about to pick the tree's fruit, Hun Hunahpu's calabash head talked to her, telling her that she did not really want to take it. He then spit into her hand as a sign of what was to come. His spittle caused Blood Woman to become pregnant.

Her pregnancy angered her father and the Xibalba lords, who did not believe that she could have conceived without knowing a man. They demanded that Blood Gatherer discover who the father was; if Blood Woman refused to divulge his identity, then her father was to sacrifice her. Although she was visibly pregnant, Blood Woman insisted that she had not lain with any man. Her father then ordered the Death Lord's messenger owls to kill her and to bring her heart back to him in a bowl. But Blood Woman convinced the owls instead to bring back the sap of the croton tree, which was shaped like a heart and bled red liquid as a real heart would. Seeing the fake heart, the Xibalba lords believed her dead, and she was able to escape to the world above.

See also Hero Twins; 1-Death and 7-Death; Sky Deities and Beings; Underworld and Caves, Deities of the

Suggested reading:

Tedlock, Dennis, trans. 1985. *Popol Vuh: The Definitive Edition of the Mayan Book of the Dawn of Life and the Glories of Gods and Kings.* New York: Simon and Schuster.

CALENDAR DEITIES

Time period: Prehistoric–Contemporary

Cultural group: Mesoamerica

Each day, week, month, and year—each calendrical count—holds particular powers and so is considered a deity with special capacities and characteristics, both negative and positive. Dates can serve as patrons for people born on their day, month, and year, as well as hold prophetic powers over human and cosmic events. What may be the earliest recorded date, 679 B.C., came from Cuicuilco in the Valley of Mexico. Of course we do not know for sure if this date was also a deity at that time, but we know that calendrical dates operated as such by the time of the Conquest. Then documents such as Landa's *Relaciones de las Cosas* and Sahagún's *Florentine Codex* describe the nature of many of the calendar deities. Today, similar ideas about the calendar deities continue among indigenous groups in many parts of Mesoamerica, although each may have its own distinctive calendar and names for their deities.

Calendar deities have a great deal to do with dreaming and prophecy. Because of them past, present, and future moments can relate to each other, and sometimes even collapse into each other. Hence once an event is placed into the calendar, earlier events are seen to have prefigured it, while the event itself becomes a prophecy of future happenings. Ancient Nahuatl speakers began and ended migrations, and founded cities on the year 1-Knife, for that year marked foundational moments for Mexica history. In 1695, the Itzá Maya sent word to the Spanish that they were ready for conversion to Christianity because, according to the count of their calendar deities, this was the same year the Spanish had conquered them; first the physical conquest, then the spiritual conquest, each governed by the same calendrical powers. On a more personal level, traders consulted the calendar deities with the help of diviners to know when to travel, and warriors to know when to go to battle. Families even named babies on days propitious to the future development of their character.

The ancient Mexica, for example, said the day 1-Death held largely good powers. The great war god Tezcatlipoca received honor then, and people sacrificed quail and made other offerings to him on their home altars and the altars of the city's district temples. But, if people failed to show Tezcatlipoca honor, then he could turn on them, withdrawing his favors. A child born on this day would prosper, and those wishing him dead would die instead. If that child failed to perform the requisite rituals for Tezcatlipoca, however, the child would harm the god's day sign, receiving harm in return. Slaves also claimed 1-Death as their sign, and received very fine treatment on this day. If one did not properly honor the slaves on this day, then one would be covered with pustules and sores, struck and beaten like a slave, and chased from place to place, never to settle down.

The contemporary K'iche' Maya use certain phrases like "at dawn," "opening," "to blame," "conceal," "lie," or "trick" to help them remember the qualities of the day-lord Foredawn. On Foredawn, one performs rituals such as the opening rites for new priest-shaman students. Young men and their families also mark the beginning of planning for his marriage with rituals, and begin negotiations with the young girl's family on Foredawn. A child born on Foredawn will be wealthy and verbally skillful but also possibly a liar, cheat, or complainer. The babe will be blessed with an extra body-soul called lightening, which will enable him/her to talk directly with animals, plants, and other powerful beings. Because of such attributes of his/her nahual, or character, the child may grow up to be a priest-shaman, community elder, or perhaps a marriage spokesman.

Dennis Tedlock, a contemporary anthropologist from the United States, reports that once he had trained as a K'iche' daykeeper skilled in interpreting the calendar, he could not help but use it to seek the meaning of his daily events, even when living in the United States. He now spontaneously feels the "sheet lightning" a daykeeper feels, slight twinges like small electric shocks that produce invisible spasms and stir his blood. Combined with his dreams and the portents of particular calendar deities, these twinges relay important information to him about future events. Thus by studying with Maya teachers, he learned to live by both a Western calendar and the invisible powers behind it that the many Maya calendrical deities govern.

See also Fifth Sun; Nahual; Tezcatlipoca

Suggested reading:

Edmonson, Munro S. 1988. *The Book of the Year: Middle American Calendrical Systems.* Salt Lake City: University of Utah Press.

Sahagún, Fray Bernardino de. 1953–1982. *The Florentine Codex: A General*

History of the Things of New Spain. Books IV, V. Trans. Arthur J. O. Anderson, and Charles E. Dibble. 12 books, 13 parts. Monographs of the School of American Research no. 14. Santa Fe: School of American Research; Salt Lake City: University of Utah Press.

Tedlock, Barbara. 1982. *Time and the Highland Maya.* Albuquerque: University of New Mexico Press.

Tedlock, Dennis. 1990. *Days from a Dream Almanac.* Urbana: University of Illinois Press.

CANEK

Time period: Classic–Modern

Cultural group: Maya

Canek (Kan-ek´) served as the name for both an ancient form of pre-Conquest Itzá Maya rulership and a post-Conquest culture hero who was to save the Itzá from their conquerors. In ancient times, the name stood more for an ancestral lineage and office of rulership than any one particular person; in Colonial times, however, a mythic royal figure called Canek repeatedly and miraculously reappeared to lead the Itzá in revolt against their oppressors. These salvific reappearances were based on predictions made in the Chilam Balams (native mythic histories), which described an ancient, deceased Maya ruler called Canek as returning to life in order to drive foreigners out of Maya Lands. Thus, through time, this culture hero transformed from a form of governance, to a messianic rallying cry of numerous Maya colonial uprisings; moreover, the mythic Canek remains a symbol of hope for many today.

Shortly after the conquest of the Mexican Highlands, Hernán Cortés traveled with his conquistadors through the Itzá lands on his way to what now is Honduras. Although the Itzá, at an earlier time, had lived in northern Yucatán in the area of Chichén Itzá, by the time of Cortés's travels, they had migrated to the central Petén in the southern lowlands of Guatemala. Spanish reports from that trip and the reports of others who followed indicate that the Itzá called their rulers Canek (or Can Ek). Apparently, conquest of the Itzá did not come easy, for every twenty years or so, a person called Canek would meet with Spanish officials or priests either to express Itzá defiance of the Spanish or discuss an alliance with them. In fact, the Spanish did not fully conquer them until 1695, making the Itzá the last of all Maya groups to give up their independence. Only after their conquest did the figure of Canek take on messianic import, when he became a reborn ancient Maya ruler.

The pre-Conquest name Canek served both as a title and lineage marker. Given common indigenous perspectives on death and ancestry, a living pre-Hispanic Canek may have inherited portions of the previous, deceased Canek's powers, which he carried in his own physical body. If this were so, he would have received his ancestors' powers, just as he inherited his nose or mouth from them. In some sense, then, the old Caneks might have been reborn at least partially in the body of the current Canek. They both looked similar and could accomplish similar things, so they were similar (even almost the same) beings. This idea may have helped form the messianic image that Canek acquired after the conquest of the Itzá, for such an idea probably meshed nicely with Christian concepts of rebirth.

With conquest came oppression and a longing for lost freedoms. The Itzá's long political resistance to the Spanish now transformed into a new mythic resistance that continued to fuel further political resistance up to the twentieth century. Moreover, Canek-inspired rebellions were not confined to the Itzá alone. More than one Maya prophet or would-be rebel leader adopted the name Canek to evoke popular support. In these prophetic leaders, a deceased ancient ruler called Canek was said to have been reborn in a manner reminiscent of both the pre-Conquest ideas of ancestry and Christ's own rebirth.

In 1761, rebels subscribing to the prophecy set down in the Chilam Balams anticipated the imminent return of the Itzá king of the royal lineage of Canek to rescue them from their Spanish oppressors. Their Maya leader assumed the name of the prophet Jacinto Canek, and in an attempt to make the prophecy come true, he and his followers tried to drive the whites into the sea. However, the Spanish squelched Canek's uprising and he was publicly drawn, quartered, and burned in the plaza of Mérida. From that time forward, "Jacinto Canek" became the rallying cry of Yucatec Maya rebellions and separatist movements. The latter flowered most notably in the Caste Wars, which began in 1848 and lasted until the twentieth century.

The Caste Wars were a series of semisuccessful rebellions by the Yucatec Maya against the Mexican government. Although rebels forced the government to allow them autonomy in their villages and personal lives, they were unsuccessful in gaining true independence, and the rebellion eventually was crushed by the Mexican military. By the beginning of the twentieth century, the government had forced the various Maya villages in the state of Quintana Roo, where the Caste Wars were centered, back into the national political system.

In more recent years, modern Mexican authors have created new myths about this hero figure. For example, Ermilo Abreu Gómez, in a small collection of short stories titled *Canek: History and Legend of a Maya Hero,* tells about the friendship of a Creole boy and a Maya boy named Jacinto Canek, growing up together on a henequen plantation just before the Caste Wars. Because of this book and other stories, *Canek* continues to be a powerful name among the Maya, symbolizing unity, resistance, and cultural independence.

See also Ahuitzotl, Lord; Christ; Motecuhzoma I, Lord; Motecuhzoma II, Lord; Pacal

Suggested reading:

Abreu Gómez, Ermilo. 1979. *Canek: History and Legend of a Maya Hero.* Trans. Mario L. Davila and Carter Wilson. Berkeley: University of California Press (English ed. of *Canek* [Mexico City: Ediciones Canek, 1940]).

Carmack, Robert M., Janine Gasco, and Gary H. Gossen. 1996. *The Legacy of Mesoamerica: History and Culture of a Native American Civilization.* Upper Saddle River, NJ: Prentice-Hall.

Jones, Grant Drummond. 1989. *Maya Resistance to Spanish Rule: Time and History on a Colonial Frontier.* Albuquerque: University of New Mexico Press.

CHAC AND THE CHACS

Time period: Preclassic–Contemporary

Cultural group: Lowland Maya

This Maya deity of rain and lightning served as a patron or protector of warriors, sacrificers, and fisherman; and because of his close association with water, he was also the patron deity of agriculture. He possessed a long, pendulous nose ending in a curl; a scroll design under each eye; and a mouth sometimes depicted as lacking teeth. Chac (Chak) appears both singly and as a set of four gods, one for each cardinal direction. Each of the four aspects bore a different name and color: Chac Xib Chac was the red Chac of the East; Sac Xib Chac, the white Chac of the North; Ek Xib Chac, the black Chac of the West; and Kan Xib Chac, the yellow Chac of the South. Because both the Bacabs and the Chacs were associated with the four colors and the four cardinal directions, one might assume that their present close connection always existed. However, in ancient times, it did not; Bacabs served as skybearers, whereas Chacs served as gods of lightning. Only in more recent times have the Bacabs and Chacs merged into more general rain deities under the name *Chacs* or *Chaacs.*

In Postclassic codices or ritual almanacs, Chac is found wielding serpents, axes, and conch shells to create rain, lightning, and thunder. These books often identified him as the patron of fishing, where he used lightning to kill and catch fish. Chac taught agriculture and breadmaking to humans, and ruled over the farm fields and crops. Perhaps Chac figured so prominently in these divinatory almanacs because farmers needed to predict the appropriate times for their ritual and agricultural activities.

The Chacs' importance centers primarily around concepts of rain and water. They make the water fall from the sky, beginning in the east as they move through the heavens, and tip their conch shells filled with rainwater. According to early myths, one could see Chac also on earth: in streams, waterfalls, or cenotes. Many stories describe Chac as central to Maya farming activities. The colonial Maya credited him with breaking open a rock and retrieving the first maize plant. Another story, from the Chol Maya, tells how Chac once stood above the water after it had rained. He asked his servant to fetch a cloth from his wife. However, when the servant looked around, he saw only toads—Chac's wife's children—and not Chac's wife. After much searching, he finally found Chac's wife, and she gave him some cotton. However, the cotton was really a cloud, which rose above the earth, taking the rain back up to heaven, where it might again fall to water the earth.

Maya perceptions of Chac have changed over time. Even though we do not know the prehistoric Maya myths and stories of Chac, prehistoric pictures suggest what those stories might have been. Early images of Chac depict him in close association with water symbols, as do images dating from the Colonial and modern periods. They show no fourfold configurations, with a different Chac for each cardinal direction. At this time, a fourfold manifestation was more typical of Tlaloc, a similar rain deity belonging to the Nahua of Central Mexico, whose culture was influential during the Postclassic era. The Maya Chac may have borrowed Tlaloc's cardinal directionality.

Chac is one of a few Maya deities with a particularly long history. His image appears on Preclassic sculpture at the Maya site of Izapa, and reappears in Maya art and sculpture throughout the Classic period among the lowland Maya. Later, in the Postclassic period, we know Chac existed as a mythical figure because of the glyphic texts and pictures in the Maya codices describing him. It was during this time that he may have gained his fourfold character. Today, myths and stories of Chac and the four Chacs continue to circulate among the Maya.

See also Bacabs; Chalchiuhtlicue; Earth, Agricultural, and Hunting Deities; Rain and Water Deities; Tlaloc and the Tlaloques

Suggested readings:

Freidel, David, Linda Schele, and Joy Parker. 1993. *Maya Cosmos: Three Thousand Years on the Shaman's Path.* New York: William Morrow.

Taube, Karl. 1992. *The Major Gods of Ancient Yucatan.* Washington, DC: Dumbarton Oaks Research Library and Collection.

Thompson, John Eric Sydney. 1970b. *Maya History and Religion.* Norman: University of Oklahoma Press.

CHALCHIUHTLICUE

Time period: Postclassic–Contemporary

Cultural group: Nahua, Central Mexico

Chalchiuhtlicue (Chal-chee-oot-lee´-kway) governed the waters of the ocean, rivers, springs, and lakes; and she cleansed and protected newborn children and cured the ill. Like her husband, brothers, or children Tlaloc and the Tlaloques,

*Figure 49. Chalchiuhtlicue (*Codex Borbonicus*, fol. 5, Museo de América/Art Resource)*

she lived in mountains, releasing her waters when appropriate; and as with all rain and water deities, Chalchiuhtlicue served an extraordinarily important role for the Postclassic Nahua of Central Mexico; Fray Diego Durán, the sixteenth century historian, says that she was "universally revered" (1971, 261). Today's water sirens and goddesses living in local rivers, lakes, and mountains such as Malinche share a number of traits with Chalchiuhtlicue.

Her relationship with Tlaloc and the Tlaloques varies with the mythic source. Some myths call Chalchiuhtlicue Tlaloc's wife, others the elder sister of Tlaloc and the Tlaloques, and still others their mother. Like them, she resided inside the mountains. From these cavernous pots she released various ground waters, both positive and negative. She could send calm water, which heaved to and fro, gently splashing and spattering the shore or, if there was no wind, spread very quietly. But her waters could also become restless, tossing and crashing, overturning boats and drowning people.

Like her various waters, Chalchiuhtlicue appeared in both positive and negative forms. She could provide the waters necessary for growing crops, in which case, she associated with a young virgin the corn goddess Xilonen; or if she chose to withhold her moist bounty, drying the earth and killing the crops, then she associated with the slavering snake goddess Chicomecoatl. Like many water deities, Chalchiuhtlicue often appeared with Quetzalcoatl who, as the wind, moved the waters. Certainly the wind helped churn the waters into a dangerous place for boaters, but Chalchiuhtlicue also could act alone, stirring herself up into whirlpools and great waves that dangerously swallowed or rocked hapless vessels. On Lake Texcoco in the Valley of Mexico, these phenomena probably were due to unstable geological conditions underlying the basin, which sometimes produced fissures and earthquakes.

Two children were sacrificed to the rain deities, including Chalchiuhtlicue, at the height of the dry season just before the rains were due. It was felt that the gods—as living entities—needed nourishment if they were to produce rain at the appropriate time. Moreover, this was a debt payment, for people owed their lives to the rain gods, without whom all would die of thirst. Drought loomed as an ever-present danger for the entire cosmos. Therefore, on the same day that a six or seven year-old boy was sacrificed to Tlaloc on his mountain just east of Tenochtitlan, the Mexica sacrificed a young girl to Chalchiuhtlicue in Lake Texcoco at Pantitlan, where a whirlpool sometimes suddenly engulfed boaters. They say that Motecuhzoma II's lost treasure, which disappeared during the Conquest, still lies buried at Pantitlan.

As the patroness of birth, Chalchiuhtlicue cleansed newborns of harmful things like disease. At a baby's birth, the midwife quietly said: "Our Lady Chalchiuhtlicue, Chalchiuhtlatonac, the tail feather, the wind feather has arrived. Receive him/her" (Sahagún 1953–82, bk. VI, 176–77). She then gently immersed the child into Chalchiuhtlicue's blue and yellow waters, telling it to descend and be cleansed. When she had swaddled the babe, and placed a jade strand around its neck, the midwife told the child that it had come to a difficult life of many sorrows. In a few days when the child was named, the midwife placed a bit of water in its mouth to cleanse its insides. If it was a boy, he received the implements of war; if a girl, the tools for weaving. The midwife then told the babe that Chalchiuhtlicue continually watches over it, washing harm away with her waters.

Indeed Chalchiuhtlicue's waters washed much harm away. Not only new mothers and their babes bathed in her preciousness, the ill also washed in Chalchiuhtlicue's gifts; and all left offerings of small jade figurines of frogs, fish, ducks, crabs, and turtles in springs and rivers. Today's many water sirens share a great deal with Chalchiuhtlicue. They too reside in rivers, springs, lakes, and mountains. They too can protect the young, wash disease away, and make crops grow and can either release or withhold their bounty from earth's inhabitants, depending on how one treats them.

See also Bacabs; Chac and the Chacs; Earth, Agricultural and Hunting Deities; Malinche; Motecuhzoma II (Xocoyotzin, Lord); Quetzalcoatl; Rain and Water Deities; Tlaloc and the Tlaloques; Underworld and Caves, Deities of the

Suggested reading:

Durán, Fray Diego. 1994. *The History of the Indies of New Spain.* Trans. Doris Heyden. Norman: University of Oklahoma Press.

Sahagún, Fray Bernardino de. 1953–1982. *The Florentine Codex: A General History of the Things of New Spain.* Trans. Arthur J. O. Anderson, and Charles E. Dibble. 12 books, 13 parts. Monographs of the School of American Research, No. 14. Santa Fe: School of American Research; Salt Lake City: University of Utah Press.

CHRIST

Time period: Colonial–Contemporary

Cultural group: Mesoamerica

The traditional Christ, with a bit of a local twist, is easily recognized in Mesoamerican Christian stories, but in other "unofficial" tales, Christ bears little resemblance to the more "official" or orthodox representations. In early Colonial times, Christ and his Cross became the first two and most widespread indigenous saints. Like other Mesoamerican Catholic saints in the unofficial, Popular Church, Christ and the Cross appear to the faithful in concrete forms, such as statues; serve as the patrons of particular localities; establish landholdings; and give communities their identities. Representations of the sacrifice and the resurrection of Christ often contain distinctly indigenous symbolism. Christ's most common Mesoamerican persona is the Sun, who fights darkness and provides light. Because Christ and the Sun also helped create the world and many of the things in it, in some myths the Christ-Sun appears to have taken over the tasks of the ancient Hero Twins in the Popol Vuh. Christ and his Cross heal the sick, protect those in danger, affirm the worth of traditional life, and support peasants fighting against vast inequities.

Indigenous peoples of the Colonial era understood the Cross, Christ, and his story in their own particular ways. They embraced both the Cross and Christ as repositories of sacred power, capable of performing miracles of all kinds. Then, as now, the Cross itself was personified: It could answer the faithful's pleas by taking action or by speaking to them; and it sometimes appeared draped in a traditional skirt and petticoat. Crosses marked Colonial plots of land, claiming them for particular families or communities. Stories even told of how people could die if they objected to a cross being located on a parcel of land; if the Cross wanted to be there, then so it must. Generally speaking, Colonial human souls went to God and Jesus in Heaven, but people's lands remained on earth in the care of the Cross and other patron saints. Among the Maya, Christ's Cross became the living World Tree standing in the center of the world. Early Christian travelers made the reverse analogy: For them, because of its visual similarity, the Maya World Tree was a manifestation of the Christian Cross, evidence of the universal presence of Christ.

Creative interpretations of the Christ story take many forms in Mesoamerica. Christ's relationship with Mother Mary and God the Father could follow distinctly indigenous family patterns. As a Nahua mother, the Colonial-era Mary did not want her son to leave her; but his father God said he must, and the ancestral prophecy declared that he would. Caught between opposing familial duties, Jesus decided to follow his prophetic destiny in spite of his mother's distress (Burkhart 1996, 89–95). The Colonial-era Christ was a distinctive saintly figure, completely separate from the other members of the Holy Trinity. Even today, the Trinity is understood by some Mesoamericans as three separate brothers whose names are Father, Jesus, and Spirit.

The Spanish brought with them scenes of Christ's harrowing in Hell, in which Hell was pictured as a great monster with a large, open, toothy mouth. This very European bestial figure naturally became the mouth of the indigenous Underworld; and Christ, upon his death and entombment, passed through that world just as the Sun, rulers, and the Hero Twins had in ancient times. Louise Burkhart tells us that in Spanish-Christian terms, Christ traveled to the Underworld to redeem Adam and Eve and others lost in limbo; but for the colonial Nahua, the lost became the ancestors who prophesied his sacrifice and transformation into the Sun. In one sixteenth-century tale, it was Quetzalcoatl rather than Christ who lay in a stone sepulcher while he traveled through the Underworld, before rising as the Morning Star—a reasonable act for a deity who had often followed the ancient Sun on its path. The Nahua were not alone in identifying Christ's death with ancient prophecy or in linking him to the Feathered Serpent: The Maya Chilam Balam of Chumayel predicted Christ's appearance in association with the return of Kukulkan at Chichén Itzá on the date Katun 4 Ahau.

The Sun-Christ, a common figure throughout Mesoamerica, fights the forces of darkness and evil that take on the forms of night, devils, and people who lived in a bygone age. The colonial Nahua called the nails pinning Christ to the Cross his blood-letting thorns, and said that his sacrificial death brought the world into a new and peaceful age, much as sacrifice caused the transformation of previous ancient sun-ages.

A twist on the Sun-Christ story comes from Chiapas, where the members of the Trinity are three brothers. The elder is named God and the middle one Jesus; but the youngest, named K'osh, proves the most clever of the three. K'osh turns his elder brother God into a pig by placing a tortilla on his nose. The middle brother Jesus runs off into the forest after becoming a wild boar. In the end, K'osh becomes the sun and his elder pig-brother becomes the moon because he cannot walk as well.

More commonly in such tales, Jesus is transformed into the Sun. The Kanhobal Maya say that when Christ died on the Cross, he climbed into Heaven on a golden ladder so that he could shine down upon earth. The Jacalteca Maya say that when Christ arose, the sun became real, and the Spaniards fled into caves and under the water, where they all eventually died. According to the Tzeltal Maya, during the Third Creation (or third age), Christ offered to become the sun because Lucifer the Devil could not give enough light or warmth (after all, he lived in the dark, damp Underworld); Christ ascended into the sky to become the sun, while his mother Mary became the moon. Yet they also say that Grandmother Moon fights the Sun during an eclipse because she wants things to stay the same; she does not want Lord Sun to become angry and kill all of the people who have done wrong. For this reason, the people say that she bears their sins. According to the Nahua, various birds betrayed Christ to a group of nasty policemen before his death and resurrection. Not surprisingly, the miscreants were roosters, doves, and other birds that typically herald the dawn with their singing.

Christ also acts as a creator of the current world and many of the things in it. The Mam Maya say that in the Third Creation, St. Joseph made a perfectly flat earth; and then, because it was very dark, he created the sun and moon. Jesus was born to the Blessed Virgin Mary and grew to full size in just four days. He told his father: "Do not be troubled, for I am going to make another world, and you will be able to help me." Then Jesus made mountains, valleys, canyons, and rivers; he even made the moon less bright than the sun so that people could sleep at night. But in a Tzeltal version of the story, Christ unfortunately also created three Ladino couples to lord it over the Indian workers.

In the Maya area, Christ often appears as a pair of brothers who act like the ancient creator pair, the Hero Twins; and two infant boys appear in many Maya Christmas creches. In San Miguel Acatán, Jesus convinced his elder brothers to climb a tree that just kept getting taller and taller as they climbed; they became monkeys, just like the Hero Twins. But unlike in the Popol Vuh, here Jesus also stripped bark from the tree and used it to form a lake at its base. According to Linda Schele, every February, in Chamula's New Year's celebrations, the Sun-Christ confronts the forces of darkness in the form of monkeys who belong to the previous age or world. Following the Path of God or the Sun's path across the sky, the Jesus-Gods overcome the monkey-gods of the age before them. Evoking the Hero Twins' self-sacrifice by fire, which enabled them eventually to become the sun and the moon, the individuals playing the Sun-Christ's part in these celebrations race across a road strewn with burning thatch (Friedel, Schele, and Parker 1993, 120, 290–292, 331–334). K'osh, the clever younger brother of the Trinity in Chiapas, repeatedly burned his field to clear it, only to find every time that it had grown back the very next day; the same occurred to the Hero Twins before they realized they were meant to be ballplayers and not farmers. One day, K'osh picked up his flame, and instead of going to his field, he went to where the day meets the heaven; similarly, the Hero Twins eventually went to the east, where they rose as the sun and moon.

Christ is not always so inept a farmer; indeed, he often produces material things, agricultural and otherwise. In Santo Tomás Chichicastenango, they say that when Jesus was crucified, he turned around, and white, yellow, and black corn sprouted from his bare back. In another story from Chiapas, Jesus and Mary couldn't get corn to grow because the Devil's children watched over it. So they tricked the Devil by throwing a party, enticing him in with good music and dance. Mary got the Devil drunk, distracting him while Jesus sneaked off to their field. There, making the sign of the Cross, he killed all the Devil's children and seized control of the land. And, so it is true that we are Christ's children, and that people say liquor is one half God and one half the Devil. In yet another story, the Tzeltal say that liquor came from Santa Lucia's bath water, which Christ gave to the community; but in another version, liquor comes from Christ's own bath water. Even dirty saintly water can hold impressive powers. Among some Nahua, Christ also is responsible for the various winds, which, like liquor, are both good and bad. These winds are people who, because they put their hands on Christ, are now condemned to live in some unpleasant place such as a cave or ravine. For some, the entombed Christ—perhaps because he travels through the Underworld—carries the powers of the fertile rain god Tlaloc.

Christ's suffering at the hands of the Romans parallels the suffering of peasants at the hands of Ladino or White oppressors in some regions, making Christ a symbol and source of power for resistance. During El Salvador's civil war in the 1980s, Jesus was seen as an ordinary person with a weather-beaten face; one who, like the peasants, sweated as he toiled. The martyrs who died in the war repeated Christ's sacrifice, and Christ was resurrected in every martyr's death.

Some Mesoamerican Christs are Black, which may be a result of Latin America's African heritage; there also were and still are dark-faced Indian Christs. At Tila in Chiapas, a white Christ appeared three times when the villagers were building their church. Each time he told them that the spot upon which they were erecting the building was bad for some reason, either because it was too wet or had too many ants. In the end they followed his advice, erecting the town and its church on top of a mountain. But during the rebellion of 1712, Christ fled from people who were looting his churchly home, taking refuge in a cave across the valley. Eventually he reappeared on his own accord back in the church, but he had returned black! Meanwhile, a stalagmite resembling Christ was left behind in the cave. Later, this same Christ miraculously lightened himself to mulatto tones, preempting a priest's threat to paint him even lighter. Like the Cross and other Mesoamerican saints, Christ often represents his particular people and locality very well. Moreover, he can transform to meet local needs—sometimes by means of violent sacrifice, and sometimes in gentler ways.

See also Feathered Serpents; Hero Twins; Kukulkan; Quetzalcoatl; Saints; Sun; Underworld and Caves, Deities of the

Suggested reading:

Bricker, Victoria Reifler. 1981. *The Indian Christ, The Indian King.* Austin: University of Texas Press.

Burkhart, Louise M. 1996. *Holy Wednesday: A Nahua Drama from Early Colonial Mexico.* Philadelphia: University of Pennsylvania Press.

Friedel, David, Linda Schele, and Joy Parker. 1993. *Maya Cosmos: Three Thousand Years on the Shaman's Path.* New York: William Morrow.

Nash, June. 1985. *In the Eyes of the Ancestors: Belief and Behavior in a Mayan Community.* 2nd ed. Prospect Heights, IL: Waveland Press.

Thompson, John Eric Sydney. 1970. *Maya History and Religion.* Norman: University of Oklahoma Press.

CIHUACOATL

Time period: Postclassic

Cultural group: Nahua, Central Mexico

The goddess Cihuacoatl (See-wa-ko´-wat), or Snake Woman, appeared in many places and took on many guises. She was a powerful woman warrior whose battlefield resided in the sky; a patroness of agriculture who dwelt on the earth's surface, and an inhabitant of the underworld. Some cities, including the Mexica city Tenochtitlan, claimed her as their primary matron, watching after the city's household. As a warrior, she often played the role of a supreme strategist both on military battlefields and those of childbirth. And, she appeared as a harbinger of death, wailing out bad omens in the night.

Sometimes known as Quilaztli, Cihuacoatl both watched over the agricultural fields and helped create human beings. She did this in the same way one would make corn tortillas. The god Quetzalcoatl retrieved some jumbled up bones from the land of the dead, and brought them to Cihuacoatl in the women's house by the western tree or the cosmos's western quadrant. Taking them, she ground them like corn kernels, wetting them with blood from Quetzalcoatl's

Figure 50. Cihuacoatl (drawing by Kay A. Read from the Florentine Codex, *bk. 1, no. 6)*

member. Thus ancient Nahua people were made of godly corn and sacrificial blood.

Cihuacoatl served as the patroness of midwives, so women invoked her powers to help them through the battle of birth. Midwives called on her especially for difficult births, exhorting their charges to have the courage of Cihuacoatl, and using her powers to carefully plan the strategy required for a successful campaign. If the woman unfortunately died, she turned into one of the Eagle Women or honorable women warriors who, each noonday, captured the sun from dead male warriors. These women took the sun to their house in the west, where the People of the Dead captured it at dusk, they kept it until dawn when the male warriors recaptured it. If the woman lived, she could receive much fortune from Cihuacoatl, perhaps even the capture of twins who were said to have come from her.

Because of Cihuacoatl's powers at war, young male warriors tried to capture the middle fingers and hair from the bodies of women who had died in childbirth; they attached these potent trophies to their shields to make them valiant and paralyze the feet of their opponents. Cihuacoatl wore the eagle plumes of the great warrior god, Mixcoatl. She carried a shield of eagle plumes and wielded a weaving batten like a weapon. The Tlacaellel, a governor of Tenochtitlan who could hold as much power as the ruler, dressed in her clothes for ceremonies, and thus acquired her skills at war to use for his city's gain.

She also could bring bad news about death and destruction. Usually she wore her hair up in the manner of a matron, but sometimes she wore her hair loose, dirty and tangled in the manner of a woman in mourning. At these times, she also wore the jawbone of the death deities and the underworld, and lived in a dark house in which all the gods were kept. Dressed thus, she could appear at night crying out warnings for all to hear. Cihuacoatl delivered such a warning twice to the Mexica before the Conquest. Then she wailed: "Dear children, soon I am going to abandon you! We are going to leave you" In this guise she is a forerunner of La Llorona, the woman who at present still cries out in the night.

See also La Llorona; Quetzalcoatl; Tlacaellel

Suggested reading:

Durán, Fray Diego. 1994. *The History of the Indies of New Spain.* Trans. Doris Heyden. Norman: University of Oklahoma Press.

Read, Kay A. 2000. "More than Earth: Cihuacoatl as Female Warrior, Male Matron, and Inside Ruler." Pp. 51–67 in *Goddesses and Sovereignty.* Ed. Elisabeth Benard and Beverly Moon. New York: Oxford University Press.

Sahagún, Fray Bernardino de. 1953–1982. *The Florentine Codex: A General History of the Things of New Spain.* Trans. Arthur J. O. Anderson, and Charles E. Dibble. 12 books, 13 parts. Monographs of the School of American Research, No. 14. Santa Fe: School of American Research; Salt Lake City: University of Utah Press.

CIZIN

Time period: Classic–Contemporary

Cultural group: Maya

Cizin (See-zeen´), also known as Yum Cimil, is the principal lord of the Yucatec Maya underworld and presides over the deceased. He has been depicted throughout Maya history, to the present day, as a skeletal figure with a prominent skull and disembodied eyeballs hanging in his hair or around his neck. By means of this imagery, the Classic and Postclassic Maya art suggests Cizin's close association with putrescence and filth. According to a Lacandon Maya myth, after a person dies, Cizin burns the soul on its mouth and its anus. When the soul complains, Cizin drenches the soul in ice water, causing further protests, which causes Cizin to burn the soul again, and so on, until the soul disintegrates from this cycle of hot and cold. Cizin has counterparts throughout Mesoamerica. Among the Highland K'iche' a similar figure, called Hun Came (1-Death), is found in the Popol Vuh; and among the Mexica, Mictlanteuctli mirrors Cizin.

See also Devil; Mictlanteuctli; 1-Death and 7-Death; Underworld and Caves, Deities of the

Suggested reading:

Taube, Karl. 1992. *The Major Gods of Ancient Yucatan.* Washington, DC: Dumbarton Oaks Research Library and Collection.

Thompson, John Eric Sydney. 1970. *Maya History and Religion.* Norman: University of Oklahoma Press.

COATLICUE

Time period: Postclassic–Contemporary
Cultural group: Mexica, Central Mexico

Coatlicue (Ko-wat-lee´-kway) or Snake Skirt was the mother of the sixteenth-century Mexica patron and warrior god Huitzilopochtli, and his sister and rival Coyolxauhqui. Coatlicue's symbolic associations included agricultural fertility, war, and governance; and she probably was a warrior woman who, like Cihuacoatl, warned the Mexica of their eventual demise. Today, as some reinterpret the early sixteenth century indigenous myths, she has become a representative of fierce feminine strength and the dark power of the unconscious.

Coatlicue was celebrated (along with other deities) in two pre-Hispanic Mexica rituals. The first, a spring ritual called Tozozontli, occurred when the rains began to fall heavily. It ended an earlier ritual in which sacrificial offerings were flayed, and it celebrated the first fruits of the season. Among other things during this ritual, the flayed skins were placed in a cave, bones of dead war captives received special attention, and it was believed that the ritual cured the sick. During the second, an autumn ritual focused on hunting called Quecholli, a woman impersonating Coatlicue was sacrificed. These two rituals suggest that agricultural and hunting fertility along with sacrifice and war may play roles in Coatlicue's symbolism.

Her mythic imagery highlights primarily themes of sacrifice, war, and governance. Here, Coatlicue represents the maternal source of Mexica heritage and power gained through war. It is said that one day a ball of feathers floated down from the skies above while Coatlicue swept the top of Snake Mountain. Picking up this ball, she tucked it into the belt of her skirt; this act impregnated her with Huitzilopochtli. Accusing her mother of incorrect behavior (for proper babies do not drop from the sky), the enraged Coyolxauhqui led her 400 brothers, the Centzonuitznaua, against her. But just as they approached the top of Snake Mountain, Huitzilopochtli spoke from the womb, telling his mother that she shouldn't worry because he would vanquish her attackers. Indeed, at the last moment and dressed in full battle array, he sprang from her womb, slaying his sister and routing his brothers.

In a counter myth, Coatlicue warned the Mexica of their eventual demise. In this tale, which happened when the Mexica were rising to power, she was waiting in her home Aztlan or Chicomoztoc (The Place of Seven Caves) for her son Huitzilopochtli to return. The great Mexica ruler Motecuhzoma I (ruled ca. 1440–1469) sent sixty magicians to visit her, for Aztlan was the Mexica place of origin. There the magicians met Coatlicue's aged tutor who agreed to take them to her, but they were unable to climb a tall, sandy hill to meet her because they were too heavily laden with gifts. So, the ancient tutor picked up their burdens and ran up the hill as though carrying no more than a few straws. On top, they found Coatlicue weeping because she missed Huitzilopochtli. Asking after those Mexica ancestors who originally had left Aztlan many years before, she was shocked to learn of their deaths, for people in Aztlan do not die. Moreover, she told them that the reason they could not carry their own burdens was because they had grown too heavy from all their rich foods and beautiful clothing. She then said that Huitzilopochtli would lose all the cities he had conquered for the Mexica in the same order that he had won them. Only then would he return to his mother's side, abandoning the Mexica to their fate. She gave the magicians two simple grass capes and two pairs of sandals to encourage her son to return. The returning magicians gave them to Motecuhzoma and Tlacaellel, who placed them on Huitzilopochtli's shrine; both leaders were greatly saddened by Coatlicue's strong admonitions, and her grim prediction.

A Mexica sculpture of Coatlicue depicts her as an aging warrior woman (Figure 40). Perhaps a column supporting the roof of a temple, this massive structure portrays a woman dressed in a warrior's skirt of netted rattlesnakes. She has been decapitated; sprouting from her neck, two coral snakes face each other, together forming a new fearsome face. Snakes also form her arms and hands, and another snake coils between her feathered legs. She wears a necklace of hands and hearts with a skull medallion. Her limbs sport signs of the underworld and, on the bottom of her taloned feet, where nobody can see it, the toadlike underworld monster spreads its legs and open maw. Here one envisions the horrors of war, sacrifice, and death. One might read this as representing the entire cosmos, as have some; or one might see it as the power of the Mexica to overtake their enemies, for they often portrayed the conquered as warrior women. Or one might even see the reverse, the threat of its temporarily conquered enemies waiting for revenge. After all, some day Huitzilopochtli will abandon the Mexica to their fate, and go home to his mother Coatlicue.

Primarily a Mexica deity, Coatlicue nevertheless was known by others. In Tlaxcala, she sometimes took the place of another mythic female warrior and chief named Chimalman, whom the great male warrior Mixcoatl was unable to kill because this clever woman moved too quickly. Eventually grabbing her, he forcibly impregnated her; from this union, came the god Quetzalcoatl.

In more recent times, the Coatlicue sculpture has served as a philosophical and poetic starting point for women struggling to comes to terms with the modern world. Here she represents the force women can have, and the dark, hidden underside of one's subconscious. Gloria Anzaldúa has said that by delving deep into her own Coatlicue consciousness and being cradled in the earth mother's arms, she can confront her own fears and make the leap into the dark unknown. There like a seed in the underground, she is regenerated, and slowly becomes able to straddle the various borders of her own ancient-modern, patriarchal-feminist, and southern-northern Hispanic heritage. By confronting herself in Coatlicue's eyes, she becomes whole.

See also Blood Woman; Coyolxauhqui; Earth, Agricultural, and Hunting Deities; Huitzilopochtli; Motecuhzoma I, Lord; Quetzalcoatl; Tlacaellel; Underworld and Caves, Deities of the

Suggested reading:

Anzaldúa, Gloria. 1987. *Borderlands/La Frontera: The New Mestiza.* San Francisco: Aunt Lute Books.

Durán, Fray Diego. 1994. *The History of the Indies of New Spain.* Trans. Doris Heyden. Norman: University of Oklahoma Press.

Sahagún, Fray Bernardino de. 1953–1982. *The Florentine Codex: A General History of the Things of New Spain.* Trans. Arthur J. O. Anderson, and Charles E. Dibble. Monographs of the School of American Research no. 14. Santa Fe: School of American Research; Salt Lake City: University of Utah Press.

CORTÉS, FERNANDO (HERNÁN)

Time period: Conquest–Contemporary

Cultural group: Mesoamerica

Fernando (Hernán) Cortés (Kor-tez´, Fer-nan´-doe [Her-nan´]) became the first European to establish colonial power in Mesoamerica, conquering the Mexica in 1521, in the name of Spain. He was reputedly a highly skilled and creative leader, with an extraordinary ability to adapt to changing conditions in an alien land. A bit greedy and unwilling to brook any competition, he nevertheless operated by clear (although sometimes brutal) ethical standards common to sixteenth-century European warfare. Against the wishes of his monarch, Cortés perpetuated the terribly ruthless encomienda system, thereby richly rewarding both himself and his men for risking their lives. Cortés also supported his own offspring, whether Spanish or mestizo, in high style.

The Cortés of popular myth is an amorphous character, representing different things to different people at different times. This one man has come to symbolize both the civilizing and the brutalizing effects of the Conquest in folk and literary traditions. Conquest mythology describes his uncanny military and leadership powers. With shipwrecked sailor Jerónimo de Águilar and a native woman known as Malinche acting as his translators and advisers, Cortés manipulated the desires and fears of various indigenous groups to further his goals. He also managed to turn opposing Spanish forces to his side. In the end, after much effort and many reversals verging on defeat, Cortés, his men and supporters, and his many Indian allies subdued the Mexica, opening the way for tremendous, jarring shifts in Mesoamerican world realities. Myths expressed the fears these shifts produced in the indigenous people. Various stories suggest that the Mexica leader Motecuhzoma II found Cortés both puzzling and unsettling. Some sources describe Motecuhzoma repeatedly testing Cortés: Was he the returning Quetzalcoatl, or not? Given that he would not partake of human sacrificial blood, could he be trusted? Was the demise of the Mexica close at hand, and if so, could Cortés help Motecuhzoma escape to the underworld? Whether these stories have a basis in fact is unclear. Other stories describe many Mesoamericans as less intimidated, some even taking advantage of the Spaniards' presence, allying with them in order to advance their own causes.

Stories about Cortés often suggest that the Conquest was inevitable. Early on, some indigenous people might have viewed Cortés as a model conqueror. Susan Gillespie (1989, 226–230) suggests that the Indians saw him as the next ruler, a kind of boundary figure whose time had come to replace the old line of Motecuhzoma–a perspective reflected today in a number of folk dances. Indeed, at least one indigenous informant said Cortés had acquired a Tlacochcalcatl, or native judge, in Cempoala, and noted that a native woman had brought him to Mexico. Others believed that Cortés was a reincarnation of Quetzalcoatl—a sort of sixteenth-century Moses ushering in a New Israel. Literary sources often have painted Cortés as the bringer of Christianity and/or European technological superiority, as though the Conquest were ordained by God or scientific progress. A number of histories have suggested that the superstitious Indians fell down in awe before the Spaniards' strange horses and powerful weaponry—their authors having forgotten how long the Conquest actually took, the thousands of native allies assisting the Spaniards, the numbers of Mexica claimed by smallpox, and how close the Spaniards came to defeat. These histories, many of them quite recent, frequently have stressed Cortés's early mythological link to Quetzalcoatl, without noting how Cortés's own grasping behavior quickly dispelled that honorable connection.

Positive images of Cortés also developed among his native allies, for whom his name quickly came to symbolize New World nobility. Cortés sponsored numerous native leaders, who as a gesture of gratitude gave his name to their sons at baptism; this quickly made *Cortés* the most common Indian noble surname in colonial New Spain. And within 150 to 200 years after the Conquest, traditional lordly rhetoric in Nahuatl had fused with Spanish titles to create a picture of a noble past. For example, a group of local Chalcan officials argued for land entitlement by prefacing their request with the phrase: "Cortés don Luis de Velasco Marqués brought us the true faith." They then argued that this gentleman of lengthy title had ordered them to build a church, for which purpose they needed land (Lockhart 1992, 123, 412).

In 1539, a sumptuous play was performed in Mexico City called the *Conquest of Rhodes,* in which Cortés probably played himself successfully leading a troop of Christians against an infidel army of Moors. But not all accounts describe Cortés so positively. Later that same year, a play in Tlaxcala entitled the *Conquest of Jerusalem* reversed this image, placing a fictitious Cortés and his second-in-command Pedro de Alvarado at the head of the Moorish army instead! A troop of Indians soundly defeated the Moors, expressing in theatrical disguise the conquered peoples' resentment. Less complimentary images also appear hidden in contemporary folk dances. In *La Danza de la Pluma,* performed today in Oaxaca during annual Catholic festivals, the figure of Cortés plods around with an army of very small boys, all dressed in rather boring costumes, while Motecuhzoma and his adult warriors dance magnificently, in splendid dress. At the dance's end, Cortés finds himself abandoned by his consort Marina and defeated by a resurrected Motecuhzoma. Moreover, the 1992 quincentennial celebration of Columbus's entrance into the New World raised many people's consciousness of the plight of Mesoamerican natives. Since then, Cortés's name has enjoyed far less worshipful treatment than in past eras, symbolizing the continuing Euro-American brutalization of embattled yet resistant noble indigenous traditions.

See also Malinche; Motecuhzoma II, Lord; Quetzalcoatl

Suggested reading:

Cortés, Hernán. 1986. *Letters from Mexico.* Trans. and ed. A. R. Pagden. New Haven, CT: Yale University Press.

Díaz del Castillo, Bernal. 1956. *The Discovery and Conquest of Mexico: 1517–1521.* New York: Farrar, Straus and Giroux.

Gillespie, Susan. 1989. *The Aztec Kings: The Construction of Rulership in Mexica History.* Tucson: University of Arizona Press.

Harris, Max. 1997. "The Return of Moctezuma: Oaxaca's *Danza de la Pluma* and New Mexico's *Danza de los Matachines.*" *Drama Review* 41, 1 (T153): 106–134.

Lockhart, James. 1992. *The Nahuas after the Conquest: A Social and Cultural History of the Indians of Central Mexico, Sixteenth through Eighteenth Centuries.* Stanford, CA: Stanford University Press.

Sahagún, Fray Bernardino de. 1953–1982. *The Florentine Codex: A General History of the Things of New Spain.* Trans. Arthur J. O. Anderson and Charles E. Dibble. Monographs of the School of American Research, no. 14. Santa Fe: School of American Research; Salt Lake City: University of Utah Press.

COYOLXAUHQUI

Time period: Postclassic

Cultural group: Mexica, Central Mexico

Coyolxauhqui (Koy-ol-shauw´-kee) was either the mythic sister or mother of the sixteenth-century Mexica patron and war god Huitzilopochtli. In either case, she symbolically represents the Mexica's first victorious conquest, for in both, Coyolxauhqui challenged Hiutzilopochtli, only to be defeated. In the first case, it is told how she led her 400 brothers, the Centzonuitznaua, in an attack on her mother, Coatlicue, because Coatlicue had become pregnant by mysterious means. But just as Coyolxauhqui and her forces were about to strike, Huitzilopochtli was born in full war regalia. He immediately killed his sister, decapitating her and chopping off her limbs and throwing them down the sides of Mount Coatepec, and then he routed his brothers.

Figure 51. The Coyolxauhqui Stone from the Postclassic site of Tenochtitlan (drawing by Kay A. Read)

In the second case, Huitzilopochtli took Coyolxauhqui as his mother. At this time, the Mexica were living at Coatepec or Snake Mountain, for they had not yet found their island home of Tenochtitlan. Coatepec was very beautiful, for the Mexica had dammed a river, creating a wonderful, rich marshland full of frogs, fish, and water birds. It was so pleasant that, when Huitzilopochtli ordered the Mexica to leave and continue searching for their real home, Coyolxauhqui and her brothers, the Centzonuitznaua, objected, wishing instead to remain at Coatepec. This did not sit well with Huitzilopochtli, for he did not like being told what to do. Late that night a huge commotion arose from the ball court; and in the morning, the Mexica found that Huitzilopochtli had decapitated Coyolxauhqui and eaten her heart. In one version, Huitzilopochtli then became a demon of darkness and burrowed into the ground, draining all the water from the lagoon; in another, he ordered the Mexica to break the dam. In any case, without water, Coatepec dried up and the Mexica were forced to continue searching for their final settlement.

A huge, impressive shield-shaped stone frieze has been unearthed from the base of the stairs on the Huitzilopochtli side of the Templo Mayor. Coyolxauhqui spreads out on her side, wearing nothing more than a warrior's belt knotted from a double-headed snake. Her head, arms, and legs have been chopped off, the bones poking out from the flesh. Her hair sports balls of eagle down; from her ear hangs the Mexica year sign; a bell graces her cheek; she bears the marks of the underworld on her joints; and as with her mother Coatlicue, her belt ties a skull to her back. An earlier frieze also has been found, and although she does not appear nude on this one, Huitzilopochtli's weapon, a xiuhcoatl or fire-serpent, pierces her chest.

Some have thought she is the moon, who has been vanquished by the sun; but others feel she is the goddess of the Milky Way. Even if her celestial associations are less obvious, her vanquished eagle warrior status seems clear. The Nahua called defeated cities fallen warrior women, and said they lay on the ground like shields dropped in battle, just as Coyolxauhqui now lies. In fact, warrior ritual sacrifices imitated her myths. As Huitzilopochtli had decapitated Coyolxauhqui and chopped off her limbs, flinging them down the side of Mount Coatepec, so too were war captives ritually treated. First, the captives' hearts were cut out, then they were decapitated, their limbs chopped off, and finally their bodies rolled down the steps of the temple to land on the great Coyolxauhqui stone.

Of course, as with any good myth, multiple meanings are simultaneously possible; Coyolxauhqui may have represented simultaneously the cities Tenochtitlan defeated in battle, and either the moon or stars defeated by the great sun warrior Huitzilopochtli.

See also Coatlicue; Huitzilopochtli; Ix Chel; Moon; Sky Deities and Beings; Underworld and Caves, Deities of the

Suggested reading:

Codex Chimalpahin. 1997. As reproduced in *Codex Chimalpahin: Society and Politics in Mexico Tenochtitlan, Tlatelolco, Texcoco, Culhuacan, and other Nahua Altepetl in Central Mexico: The Nahuatl and Spanish Annals and Accounts Collected and Recorded by Don Domingo de San Antón Muñón Chimalpahin Quauhtlehuanitzin.* Edited and translated by Arthur J. O. Anderson and Susan Schroeder. Norman: University of Oklahoma Press.

Durán, Fray Diego. 1994. *The History of the Indies of New Spain.* Trans. Doris Heyden. Norman: University of Oklahoma Press.

Sahagún, Fray Bernardino de. 1953–1982. *The Florentine Codex: A General History of the Things of New Spain.* Trans. Arthur J. O. Anderson, and Charles E. Dibble. Monographs of the School of American Research, No. 14. Santa Fe: School of American Research; Salt Lake City: University of Utah Press.

CUAUHTEMOC, LORD

Time period: Postclassic

Cultural group: Nahua-Mexica

Lord Cuauhtemoc (Kwaw-teh´-mok) was the eleventh and last pre-Conquest Chief Speaker of the Mexica (ruled 1520–1524), and the son of the great Lord Ahuitzotl (ruled ca. 1486–1502). He surrendered to Fernando (Hernán) Cortés on 13 August 1521, after a year of strong resistance. Cortés hanged him in 1524.

Cuauhtemoc symbolizes the ending of Mexica hegemony and the fall of a valiant pre-Conquest indigenous life. The Spanish viewed his conquest as justified and proper; the indigenous saw it as simply tragic.

The Mexica elected Cuauhtemoc to rulership in the midst of war, after Cortés's principle captain Pedro de Alvarado massacred hundreds of Mexicans. Responding to this tragedy, the angry Mexica elected Cuitlahuac to replace Lord Motecuhzoma II (Xocoyotzin) whom they considered a traitor, and rebelled against the Spanish, expelling them from Tenochtitlan in a bloody battle. But soon after, Cuitlahuac succumbed to smallpox, and Cuauhtemoc replaced him. A strong opponent, Cuauhtemoc held the Spanish and their thousands of allies at bay, causing them considerable damage.

Most stories describe Lord Cuauhtemoc as noble, valiant, intelligent, and sometimes cunning. It is said that he fought to the death, carrying on the warring tradition of his deceased father Lord Ahuitzotl. When the Spanish attacked the city with a catapult, Cuauhtemoc dressed one of his finest warriors in his father's power-laden attire to instill bravery into his discouraged troops. Apparently Ahuitzotl's powers still held, for they won the battle.

But different authors sometimes describe him in different ways. The Spanish claim he deceived them by attacking after saying he wanted to surrender; more indigenous sources, however, say he met with his council who dissuaded him from giving in. Spanish sources say that, when Tenochtitlan fell, he tried to escape in fifty canoes laden with wives and goods, was hoodwinked into capture, and then dramatically pleaded with Cortés to kill him because he had failed. Indigenous sources say that, after discussing with his council what tribute they would offer, he went willingly to surrender to Cortés in a single canoe with only two companions. Spanish sources say he was hanged because he plotted rebellion; indigenous sources say he was falsely accused by Malinche, Cortés's influential indigenous translator. Thus Spanish historical mythology creates an image of a mostly worthy, but appropriately vanquished opponent; and indigenous sources a valorous, but tragic figure.

See also Ahuitzotl, Lord; Cortés, Fernando; Malinche; Motecuhzoma II, Lord

Suggested reading:

Díaz del Castillo, Bernal. 1956. *The Discovery and Conquest of Mexico: 1517–1521.* New York: Farrar, Straus and Giroux.

Durán, Fray Diego. 1994. *The History of the Indies of New Spain.* Trans. Doris Heyden. Norman: University of Oklahoma Press.

Sahagún, Fray Bernardino de. 1953–1982. *The Florentine Codex: A General History of the Things of New Spain.* Book XII. Trans. Arthur J. O. Anderson, and Charles E. Dibble. 12 books, 13 parts. Monographs of the School of American Research, No. 14. Santa Fe: School of American Research; Salt Lake City: University of Utah Press.

DEAD, DAY OF THE

Time period: Colonial–Contemporary

Cultural group: Mesoamerica

The dead return to visit the living on the Day of the Dead, also called *Todos Santos,* or All Saints' Day. The "day" is actually a festival beginning on 31 October and usually lasting until 2 November. Many communities extend the ritual until 8 November or longer by linking it with other rites performed throughout the year for the recently deceased. Traditionally, people welcome back the souls of the departed to family hearths with lavish meals, new clothes, and delightfully elaborate and idiosyncratic altars, or *ofrendas,* commemorating them. Families share food and drink with their relatives and neighbors. These spectacular repasts include everything from figurines and skulls made of sugar and chocolate to special breads, stews, and tamales; fresh fruits; beer and soda pop; and even junk food, depending on the tastes of both the dead and the living. An ofrenda may include pictures and portraits of the dead, important saints, or Mary and Jesus; flowers, especially marigolds; lacy paper cutouts depicting skulls and skeletons; and papier-mâché dolls of skeletons doing everything from dancing and singing to typing, cycling, or riding in cars and buses, cooking, or using the facilities. In fact, in recent years the rite has spawned a head-spinning array of public and private displays both humorous and serious, which can be made out of everything from traditional palm-frond weaving to white plastic and neon lights. Rural displays tend toward the traditional, reflecting the serious purpose of the original rites; but in cities, there are no limits to the imagination, and displays there often diverge far from the festival's personal commemorative purposes. In recent years, the festival even has begun to merge with Halloween.

Contemporary ritual use of skulls and skeletons suggests a relationship to pre-Conquest sacrificial traditions; however, the similarities are only superficial. The ancient Nahua, for example, honored the dead on a number of occasions throughout the year, not just in the fall, and skulls were not necessarily part of their celebrations. Sometimes food was offered, as it is today. Such practices are also common to many ancient folk traditions in Europe. Soul concepts, furthermore, have changed radically from pre-Conquest times to today. Ancient Mesoamericans, like many Native Americans, tended to understand a human as containing not just one sole soul but multiple "souls" or living forces that scattered upon a person's death: one went with the body's ashes (if cremated) or the bones; some remained with the deceased's names, which could be passed on; some might go with particular gods or birds and butterflies; and one went into the woods, to threaten the living. Although some of these and other pre-Conquest conceptions of death have survived to the present, often melding with Christian worldviews, the idea of a single spirit that remains intact after the body's disappearance is more Christian than indigenous. Today, souls generally are regarded as singular rather than multiple entities, as reflected in the celebration of Todos Santos.

Many of the specifics of All Saints' Day can be traced directly to Europe. The sugar figurines have predecessors in celebrations of All Saints' Day in twelfth-century Naples, and they still appear in Palermo, Sicily today. The earliest Mesoamerican sugar skulls did not appear until the nineteenth century and may have been related to an indigenous practice in the Yucatán. There the intrepid traveler John L. Stephens reported in 1843 that skulls of the dead were housed in a local church at Kabah; each bore the deceased's name on its forehead, along with a short prayer. Today one can buy sugar skulls with a space on their foreheads for the name of a deceased loved one or a living friend. Humorous skeletons appearing today may have gotten their start with the skeletons used for political satire in the early twentieth century. Before that, skeletons on carts represented the Grim Reaper in celebrations of death cults, which originally grew up in plague-infested medieval Europe; but these festivals are distinct from All Saints' Day celebrations.

Of course this does not mean that no pre-Conquest elements whatsoever survive in today's rites. The sugar figurines and skulls may have replaced earlier amaranth and honey figures frequently used in pre-Conquest rituals. The art of paper-cutting claims a centuries-long tradition; and the ancients used marigolds ritually for centuries, believing that they bore the sun's warmth and power. Today, one still finds the bright yellow-orange flowers arranged on altars and church floors as an offering, not just for the dead, but for others as well. At San Miguel Tzinacapan, marigolds sown between Saint Antoni Tixochit's Day (13 June), when the sun is said to be in the underworld, and Saint John's Day (24 June), when the sun appears in the sky, are used specifically for the Day of the Dead.

The variation among Day of the Dead rites is enormous. The rites now span all of Mesoamerica and its diaspora in the United States. Many say that if you do not honor the dead, they will return to bother you; or you might actually see the dead, and then die yourself. Typically, the souls of small children are believed to return first, sometimes as early as 30 October, followed by older children on 31 October and by adults on 1 November. Often a path of marigolds shows the dead the way to the front door, which is left open to welcome them; but those who died a violent death by murder or were drowned may be kept outside the house because they are considered dangerous. Because the returning spirits normally can only be sensed and not seen, they only absorb the food's essence, after which the family distributes the meal among grandparents, relatives, and neighbors. Some food may be brought to the cemetery, where the graves may be decorated elaborately on 2 November or some other day during the festival. In some areas, a night-long vigil takes place in the cemetery.

In the 1930s, at the cemetery in Chan Kom, which had reached its capacity, bones were dug up on the Day of Dead after two or three years in the grave. They were sprinkled with holy water and placed in cloth-lined boxes, and prayers were said over them. People then carried the boxes to their homes, and placed them on decorated tables. More prayers were said and food offered, and the celebrants drank chocolate that evening. Again holy water was sprinkled over the bones, and then they were deposited in a house in the cemetery. It is said that the bones were stored there for some time, until one day when strange sounds began coming from the building, after which people moved the bones outside.

A story from Oaxaca tells about a man whose wife had disappeared. A vulture took him to a strange church, where he recognized his wife. He followed her home and asked her where she had gone. She replied that she couldn't tell him but he should take their money and cook a turkey on All Saints' Day, and she would return to eat it with him. This he did and waited patiently, watching the door. Tiring after a while, he looked around the room, and lo and behold, he saw a great snake with a pot on its head. Afraid, he took up his machete to kill it; but as soon as he approached the creature it disappeared. Still not seeing his wife, he called the vulture and asked to visit her again. Upon arriving at the church, he asked why she hadn't come to visit him. She responded that she had been there but he had chased her away with his machete!

Today, among the Totonac, the dead who died tragically are believed to suffer punishment at the hands of the god of death. They must wander for four years, sometimes appearing at streams as voices that try to trap the living. Every morning, the dead help the sun to escape the god of death residing in the underworld; by turning into birds, butterflies, clouds, stars, and planets, they help the sun move across the sky to its death and reentry into the underworld at sundown. On the Day of the Dead, insects who eat the festival food are believed to be the dead returning for their annual visit. At Huaquechula, the altars vary with the neighborhood. Some ofrendas rise as high as 10 to 12 feet and are covered in white satin or plastic. At Iguala, one might hire actors to perform a living tableau representing scenes from the life of Christ. And in Mexico City, stores paint their windows with humorous skeletons; bakeries sell countless sugar figurines, breads, and chocolate skulls; the markets are filled with skeletons and paper-cuttings, many amusing and satirical; and businesses and local groups sponsor competitions for the best ofrendas.

Many from the United States return to Mexico for Todos Santos; others remain to celebrate in their own fashion. In Los Angeles, traditional foods are sold; ofrendas appear everywhere, decorated with both local and imported offerings; and a big parade and fiesta are held. Throughout the United States, Hispanic churches celebrate with marigolds, pictures of the deceased, and spoken remembrances of the year's dead. Museums hold exhibits, artists create elaborate displays, and many schools offer special programs. North of the border, the Day of the Dead embodies a Mexican sense of national identity and cultural pride as well as providing a chance for mourners to remember their lost loved ones. Certainly the creativity with which the dead are welcomed home is astounding both north and south of the border. The Mesoamerican festival's roots may lie largely in Europe; but after five centuries of practice, the American celebrations have developed their own wonderful character, unlike that of All Saints' celebrations anywhere else in the world.

See also Sky Deities and Beings; Underworld and Caves, Deities of the

Suggested reading:

Carmichael, Elizabeth, and Cloë Sayers. 1991. *The Skeleton at the Feast: The Day of the Dead in Mexico.* London: British Museum Press.

Furst, Jill Leslie McKeever. 1995. *The Natural History of the Soul in Ancient Mexico.* New Haven, CT: Yale University Press.

Parson, Elsie Clews. 1936. *Mitla, Town of the Souls: And Other Zapteco-Speaking Pueblos of Oaxaca, Mexico.* Chicago: University of Chicago Press.

DEER

Time period: Prehistoric–Contemporary

Cultural group: Mesoamerica

Deer are encountered throughout the Americas, both physically and in mythology. They range from northern Mexico and the southwestern United States to Central America. White-tailed deer are the most common; mule deer are found mostly in the northern regions of Mesoamerica; and the small brocket deer are found only in the tropical lowlands. Although people have hunted them for centuries, deer are not easily domesticated. The sixteenth-century historian Fray Diego de Landa reported that the Itzá Maya had domesticated deer; but these particular deer probably looked less like cows grazing in a pasture and more like Sami reindeer, roaming free until people rounded them up to count and cull them. The animal's wide-ranging habitat and general resistance to domestication, as well as the age-old traditions of hunting this game for food and clothing, may help explain the plethora and variety of mythological deer. People have had centuries to spin tales around these familiar animals, as they have around dogs. But unlike the highly sociable canine, a deer interacts with humans only from a distance, and so always remains somewhat unknown; and not knowing much can stimulate the creative imagination wonderfully. One of the twenty days in many calendars is named for the deer; and in some calendars, one of the four years bears its name. Beyond that, there seems to be little mythological homogeneity among the many deer stories, although diverse themes may randomly intersect; the subjects range from deer tails and myths of cosmic fatherhood and female sexuality to fables depicting the animals as downright silly.

The Popol Vuh says that deer have short tails because of something that happened back when the Hero Twins still thought they might like farming. Deer and other animals ate up the corn the twins had just planted, but when they tried to catch the deer by grabbing them by their tails, the tails broke off and the beasts leapt free. The present-day Tzeltal and Chol tell a tale in which the first family kept deer, peccaries, and rabbits as pets, all bound together by their tails. One day they left them alone with Grandmother, warning her that if she laughed, they would break loose. She did, and they did, leaving their tails behind them. The Chamula say that during the time of the first father and mother, the father cut off the deer's ears and tail because he was caught eating from the family's cornfield.

Deer are depicted as having been present at the beginning of time. A deer was the father of the sun and the moon; another carried the sun into the sky; and others were used or abused by the solar deity. In one contemporary story from Oaxaca, the sun and moon are described as two very bad children who, feeling ashamed that their deer stepfather is a mere animal, kill him and stuff his hide with wasps. When the twins' stepmother comes along and strikes her stuffed husband with a stick because she mistakenly thinks he is making fun of her, the wasps swarm out and sting her. She comes home very angry with the twins. To avoid punishment, the two terrible children lock her in a small sweathouse used for bathing, and there she dies. In another tale, from the Kekchi, the Lord Sun tries to win the hand of a maiden by impressing her with his hunting prowess. He shoots a deer and carries it past the girl's house. Then he skins and stuffs it, each day thereafter lugging the same dead beast past her. This impresses the girl, who thinks he is a great hunter, but her father is a little more suspicious. He tells the girl to throw some water on Sun's path the next time he parades by. Using the slippery lime water from her corn preparation, she does; Sun slips in it and falls, breaking open the fake deer. Fully exposed and embarrassed, he runs away to escape her laughter.

Sometimes deer are linked with sexual or warring powers. The contemporary Mopan and Kekchi say that the deer trampled on the Moon Goddess when he escaped from a log in which the sun and moon had imprisoned him. In the process, he split the goddess, thereby forming her vagina; hence, today the deer has cleft hooves. In an ancient Nahua story, two hunters, Mimich and Xiuhnel, chased two deer, each with a double head; but by the end of the day, the deer had worn the hunters out, so they stopped for the evening. Then two beautiful women appeared, calling the hunters to come eat and drink. Xiuhnel succumbed to one of the deer-women's enticements; but after making love, she killed him. Frightened, Mimich started a fire and ran through it. The other deer-woman followed, chasing him all night and all morning. At noon, a barrel cactus descended from the sky, and the woman fell into it and was pinned down by its spines. Mimich shot her full of arrows. Then Mimich led the Fire Lords to a goddess named Itzpapalotl. They burned her, and four great flints burst forth: blue, white, yellow, and red. Mimich took the white one because it held Itzpapalotl's spirit, which made him a great warrior (thereafter, he was called Mixcoatl). The pre-Conquest Nahua also sometimes said that the single-headed goddess and warrior-woman Cihuacoatl was named Deer of Colhuacan.

Other narrators also spun two-headed deer stories. A present-day Tzotzil tale explains that weird creatures called Charcoal Crunchers no longer exist because, way back when, a man got rid of his charcoal crunching wife. Every night, his wife's head would leave her body and bounce over to the fireplace to eat hot charcoals; sometimes, she would bounce out of the house and thud around the neighborhood. One night he rubbed salt on her empty neck, so that when she returned, she could not stick her head to her body again. Annoyed, she bounced up on his shoulder and stuck there, which caused him no end of physical and psychological discomfort. A week or so later, he convinced his wife to bounce off temporarily so that he could climb a tree to gather pine nuts for her. But then he refused to come down, and she could not bounce high enough to reach him. "Go die somewhere else!" he told her. Banging around the tree, she accidentally crashed onto the shoulder of a passing deer and stuck there. The startled deer ran off, carrying the last Charcoal Cruncher with it.

Just as the hare once lost a race with the tortoise, the supposedly swift deer sometimes loses races with other proverbial underdogs. In a contemporary Zinacatecan story, Deer is distracted by Mosquito, who keeps buzzing around, telling him what to do, and in the end Deer is worn out by Toad, who just keeps going. In a modern Nahua story, Hummingbird asks Deer to keep an eye on him. Deer follows him wherever he goes, but suddenly Hummingbird disappears. Where has he gone? Deer hears him call. Oops! There's Hummingbird, sitting on his antlers. And so the many stories spin on, explaining why the animal has such a short tail, and weaving together various tales of hunting, sex, war, two-headed beasts, stuffed deer, or just plain silliness.

See also Cihuacoatl; Dogs; Hero Twins; Moon; Sun

Suggested reading:

Codex Chimalpopoca. 1992. As reproduced in *History and Mythology of the Aztecs: The Codex Chimalpopoca.* Trans. John Bierhorst. Tucson: University of Arizona Press.

Sexton, James D. 1992. *Mayan Folktales: Folklore from Lake Atitlán, Guatemala.* New York: Doubleday.
Thompson, John Eric Sydney. 1970b. *Maya History and Religion.* Norman: University of Oklahoma Press.

DEVIL

Time period: Colonial–Contemporary
Cultural group: Mesoamerica

The Devil evolved a multifaceted, distinctively Mesoamerican personality after he migrated to the New World in the sixteenth century. At his early appearances in the friars' stories and plays, he still looked quite European, but the locals quickly claimed him as their own, and today, one often can catch only glimpses of his European ancestry. In the 500 years since the Conquest, the Devil has adopted many personae.

A contemporary Nahua tale tells of his incessant changeability. Late one night while walking home, a good Christian Nahua man found himself being harassed by the Devil. First the Devil appeared to him as an elegant gentleman dressed in a black cape and a great, flat hat; then the gentleman yanked on his hat, and it became a mariachi musician's sombrero, and his teeth grew as big as those of a horse. The musician rolled his hat up, and it became two big horns on his head; then he mounted a great black horse that struck sparks from the ground with its hooves. Finally, after the poor villager passed the church, the Devil reappeared as Pontius Pilate. Unable to take anymore, the man went home, got his machete, and attacked the nasty apparition, slicing him through a good twenty times.

While this shape-shifting, shifty character (see Nahual) rarely appears twice in the same form in all the years of his existence, his home and area of influence have remained pretty much the same. Like his European counterpart, the Mesoamerican Devil usually claims a portion of the Underworld as his domain, deals with the dead, and punishes those who step outside the boundaries of propriety; but unlike the European Devil, his Underworld home remains uniquely Mesoamerican, and he sometimes also offers sinners a route to redemption.

The Devil meant different things to the sixteenth-century Christians and their indigenous converts. For the Spanish, the Devil became a convenient way to explain the presence of evil in a world created by a completely good deity. In this worldview, the New World's pagans had perverted God's plan, having allowed themselves like ignorant children to be led astray by the Devil. Christ now offered them redemption, but only if they would let the friars lead them from their sinful ways. In his earliest appearance in a play in Tlaxcala, the Devil and three demon companions vied for people's souls (the Devil went after

Christ's). Not being too smart, the Devil, who had dressed up as a hermit, failed to hide his horns and his clawed feet and hands.

This early manifestation would have seemed somewhat familiar to the indigenous audience, as it evoked native depictions of both the ancient earth monster with its clawed feet and hands, and the nasty, skull-headed, underworld god of death. Thanks to similar, more explicit comparisons by the Spanish clerics, the Nahuatl word *tlacatecolotl,* which once meant a shaman who drew on the powers of the horned owl, today means "devil." In ancient times, the nocturnal bird of prey was believed to be an agent for the Lords of Death and to bring misfortune. Drawing on this powerful mythic association, the early friars called the great Mexica god Tezcatlipoca *tlacatecolotl,* but they never translated the word properly as Owl-man, instead telling the Mexicans that it meant "devil." And so it came to be.

Creatures of the Mesoamerican night were also creatures of the underworld and caves, and visual representations soon appeared that combined European devils with these indigenous dark, subterranean features. A popular Spanish image of Hell as a great monster from whose open, toothy mouth Christ first pulled Adam and Eve and then others in need of redemption, was painted on the walls of outdoor chapels where the newly converted came to hear priests' lectures. Although the depiction itself was a direct copy of a Spanish prototype, the native understanding of its meaning seems to have been a somewhat less exact replica. A play translated into Nahuatl by a native scholar for a celebration on Corpus Christi showed the Devil in Hell, having been imprisoned there by Christ, who thereby liberated Adam and Eve and others from Satan's servitude. However, the ancient figures whom Christ liberated became, in the indigenous mind, more than simply Adam, David, or Moses of Old Testament times; they were ancient ancestors who offered prophecies from a past era, predicting that their indigenous heirs would receive the same redemption (Burkhart 1996, 125, 244).

Medieval European theological dualism translated into a complex cosmological dualism for indigenous Christians. They quickly came to understand that the Devil stood in opposition to Christ, and that Church authorities did not like the Devil in any size, shape, or form; so the Devil took up residence on the edge of native homes. One found him and the entrances to his subterranean home in the forests far from human habitation, the pre-Conquest location for nocturnal, Underworld beings. But that did not mean that people paid him no attention. In the native world, life-giving creation cannot happen without death-producing destruction. The Devil, as the representative of death, the Underworld, and night, must continue to exist in order to give power to life, the upper world, and daylight. As Fernando Cervantes points out, in the indigenous mind it wasn't an issue of evil versus good; without the Devil, the world would swing out of whack because destruction could no longer balance out creation. Indeed, the world already had become unbalanced, for disease and death were everywhere. If devils were like the old gods, who brought disease when they were neglected or in need, then people should make sacrificial offerings to them in order to right things. Priests caught some people in the Mexican highlands imitating the crucifixion, with a chicken as sacrificial victim (Cervantes 1994, 50). Significantly, this rite occurred at midnight, when the night shifted to day, and when pre-Conquest prayers traditionally were said to Tezcatlipoca and other deities. Cervantes also reported that one indigenous man had tattooed a picture of Christ on one arm and the Devil on the other, to remind him not to worship one when he was worshiping the other (Ibid., 49–50). With the introduction of Christian deities, the Devil had been transformed into the nocturnal, Underworld counterpart of the solar-based, diurnal Christ.

The Devil thus came to be explicitly equated with various Underworld gods. In seventeenth-century Oaxaca, no less than five deities took on the Devil's characteristics: a god of death, and two apparently distinctive male and female deity pairs of disease and misfortune. In the midnight sacrifices mentioned above, part of the offerings were given to the Devil in the form of either the old Fire God or the God of Thunder (who could bring corn), and another part to the Church. In other cases, St. James was invoked as both the Devil and the God of Thunder. A whole host of native rain and water deities dwelt inside the mountains. If the Devil was the master of this subterranean realm, then he must be the one who controlled water in its many forms. Even today, some say that when lightning strikes a house it is because the Devil wants to kill the people inside.

Many of these themes find echoes in contemporary mythology. The Devil today is very human, although his powers certainly exceed those of normal people. He still lives in the underworld and plays the counterpart of Christ; causes disease and death by disrupting the status quo; and enslaves the dead, especially those who have sinned in some way (which includes just about everybody). As with the European Devil, people sometimes turn the tables by tricking him, and some even get away with it. In numerous and significant ways, however, this rich, rather wonderful trickster has grown closer to the ancient gods than to his European ancestor; for even when one might recognize a European mythic genre, the details quickly mark these stories as distinctively Mesoamerican.

The Nahua of Amatlán say that Tlacatecolotl (or an owl-man devil) is the elder brother of Toteotsij, who is God, the Sun, and Jesus all rolled into one; therefore, darkness has the upper hand. But among the Sierra Nahua, the story is a little different. The Devil got annoyed with God at this world's creation because he made crickets that chattered all night. In the process of arguing with God, he made and lost a bet that limited his rule; henceforth, when the rooster crowed at dawn, the Devil had to return to his underworld home. During labor in Tecospan, God and the Devil duke it out in the birthing room's hearth fire. If God wins the battle, the baby's *tonalli,* or shadow-soul, will be strong and win a place in Heaven; if not, it will weigh heavily, fail in earthly endeavors, and go to Hell. Disease often is attributed to the Devil or devils. When bidden, the Maya Ah Yacax will send worms and flies into people's noses. In Amatlán, a number of disease-causing devils exist. Besides Owl-man and his wife, there is also his partner who commands the spirits in the Land of the Dead; another, the brother of Death, flies like a butterfly and can attack and kill whomever he meets. Before a healer can accomplish a cure, he must use these beings to balance out the disequilibrium. Often disease-bearing devils arrive as ill winds. The Nahua of Amatlán, the Chortí and Yucatec Maya, and people of Mitla in Oaxaca all say that the Devil hides himself in whirlwinds, which make people sick.

The Cakchiquel Maya of Panajachel in the 1930s said that everything was reversed inside the Underworld home of the Devil, which they called the Hill; for example, if one drinks a lot here, one will drink nothing there. One went to the Hill either to be cleansed in its fires or, more commonly, to work hard at paying off one's debt before being admitted to Heaven. Only saints like Francis, who didn't mind poverty, could avoid involvement with the Devil; so pretty much everyone landed in the Hill at least for a time. Merchants had to work an especially long time because their debts were huge; and Ladinos never got out because they worshiped the Devil. These people did not sin in the usual small ways, for both groups clearly did not work in life but came by their wealth through their allegiance to the Dark Chief's tempting powers. When the Devil found himself short on labor, he asked God for more workers, and then there was lots of sickness. Like the pre-Conquest rain god's land of Tlalocan, the Hill had its own inner landscape, with beautiful rivers, streams, trees, plants, and birds. One entered this place through certain caves, rocks, and trees; one could even hear its dogs barking, cocks crowing, and church bells ringing if one of these windows opened up. The forest was a dangerous place, so if one heard such sounds, one had to get out fast. The Devil, that paradigmatic rich landowner, was always looking for more workers to enslave.

Various animals are associated with the Devil. The Cakchiquel said that the bat sucked blood in order to cook the Devil delicious dishes, and the mosquito gathered the Devil's wine. Throughout Mesoamerica, the Devil might appear as a jaguar, caiman, or snake that kills and eats livestock; or he might send his coyote to reward a brave hunter who managed to survive a wild bull ride across the Oaxacan landscape. But if one accepts such rewards, one is in trouble, for one will surely find oneself paying for them later with one's own backbreaking labor.

Stories abound of the Devil's attempts to trick people into his employ. He may entice a stubborn and arrogant Maya girl into marriage by sporting the two gold teeth she wanted to find in her future husband's mouth. Or the poor might be tempted by his other riches. He sometimes helps people by having them cure a king's illness that he himself has induced. The healer's fortune is made when he succeeds where doctors have failed. But if he breaks the contract, or when he dies, he will have to serve the Devil. Teofila from Oaxaca once called to the Devil, out of desperation, to help her out of her poverty. To her surprise, that night he turned up, suave, handsome, and riding a beautiful honey-colored horse. He apologized for being late and offered her a bag of money, which she wisely refused. But he said, "Are not your brother and friend coming to visit? Here is a chicken to feed them when they come." Teofila had not been expecting any guests, but they did indeed arrived; and the Devil—visible only to Teofila—slipped into the house with them to join in on the fun. This happened night after night, for the Devil had fallen in love with her. Still, she would not accept his money. He even built himself a ramshackle house in her front yard and camped out there. Slowly she weakened and became sick; finally, she confessed to the priest. He blessed her house with holy water and raised a cross in her door. The Devil then left, his shack disappeared, and Teofila lived to a ripe old age, with her children supporting her.

The Devil often appears as a rich, handsome landowner who rides a beautiful horse, and the outcome can be quite pleasant. In another Oaxacan story, one evening he came riding up on a great white horse to a tired ranch foreman snoozing peacefully on his front porch.

"Aren't you going to the fiesta in town?" he asked.

The startled foreman explained that he was not because he had worked his mule all day and she was too tired to travel the 35 leagues to town. Moreover, he would never be able to make that distance and return in time to work again the next morning.

"But it will be great fun! Come with me, my horse is very fast and we can get there in plenty of time to drink a few rounds with your friends and still return for work tomorrow morning. Anyway, it's no problem, because I too have work tomorrow. Look, I'm your friend, and here are ten pesos to prove it."

The man, after vacillating a bit, took the money and finally said yes. He thought of the fun drinking with his buddies, and he was just a little curious about this strange, obviously well-off gentleman. So off they went. In a twinkling they had covered the 35 leagues, even with a short stop to pick up some mescal. They boozed all night with the foreman's friends, and with the first streaks of dawn's light, the strange man said it was time to return. So they mounted his horse and absolutely flew back. The gentleman graciously took his leave and disappeared on his marvelous steed. Just then the foreman woke up on his own front porch, exactly where he had been the night before. Had this really happened, or was it just a dream? He reached into his shirt pocket, and there were the ten pesos! The foreman and his boss were great friends, so he told him what had happened. Both of them agreed it would be great fun if that strange man on the white horse returned, but he never did.

Sometimes a person tricks the Devil and wins. The Maya woman who wanted to marry a man with gold teeth quickly found out that she had made a big mistake. Her new husband refused to work, and kept popping into little containers like glasses of water or kettles and disappearing instead. Upon the advice of a shaman, she convinced him to pop into a gourd jar, and then slapped a lid on it, trapping him. She tossed the jar in the rubbish heap, where he sat for several days, stuck. Finally, a drunk came along and let him out, having been promised a reward. The Devil helped him become a healer by curing (you guessed it) a sick king. The story ends with the comment that some think shamans can cure better than doctors, but they're mostly drunks who are in cahoots with the Devil.

Occasionally, the stories are simply silly. In Amatlán, the crazy, sometime-saint Pedro was always getting into trouble. In his saint aspect, Pedro could revive the dead; but when his stupid shepherd assistant (acting against orders) tried to do it on his own, the Devil locked him up in a suitcase. In one story, as a mere mortal, Pedro secretly tied the tails of a bunch of devils together and then shouted "Holy Mother Mary!" They all leaped up at once, falling over each other in a great jumble. Wishing to meet his saintly namesake, Pedro went to heaven; but they didn't want him there. They slammed the door shut; having just stuck his head in, he was decapitated. His head stayed in heaven, while his body went back to the devils. Once upon a time, the Devil peed in the pulque at a dance, getting people really drunk and raucous. A young, awesome violinist whipped the dancers into a frenzy; then losing all restraint, he kidnapped a young girl. The next morning, his new wife asked him to play the violin again, but he said he couldn't because he had no instrument. So she got out her father's violin, but he still couldn't play. The devil's pee had bewitched him!

The Mesoamerican Devil often seems to express aspects of human life that are out of control, for he brings hard labor, disease, and death. He also preys on people's natural limitations by tempting and tricking them. But at the same time, the Devil occasionally offers a second chance, perhaps even a route to redemption. Admit your faults, pay your debts to him, and you too can go to Heaven. After all, if only saints could attain perfection, then only saints would be redeemed; and that was never how *el Pueblo* understood the Christian message, even back in the sixteenth century. It might be said that in this case, the Popular Church took the old theology offering them rewards after death and subtly turned it to their own advantage. The Devil belonged to them, not the priests;

and if rewards could not be enjoyed in this life (or even immediately in the next), at least imperfection could be savored now, with a chance at redemption later!

See also Bats; Christ; Rain and Water Deities; Saints; Tezcatlipoca; Underworld and Caves, Deities of the

Suggested reading:

Burkhart, Louise M. 1996. *Holy Wednesday: A Nahua Drama from Early Colonial Mexico.* Philadelphia: University of Pennsylvania Press.

Cervantes, Fernando. 1994. *The Devil in the New World: The Impact of Diabolism in New Spain.* New Haven, CT: Yale University Press.

Sandstrom, Alan. 1991. *Corn Is Our Blood: Culture and Ethnicity in a Contemporary Aztec Indian Village.* Norman: University of Oklahoma Press.

Wisdom, Charles. 1940. *The Chorti Indians of Guatemala.* Chicago: University of Chicago Press.

DOGS

Time period: Paleo-Indian–Contemporary

Cultural group: Mesoamerica

Long ago, a Paleo-Indian living at Tequixquiac in Mexico shaped a cameloid bone into a doglike creature. We don't know for sure whether the object depicts a mythological beast or a familiar animal; unfortunately, its material remains cannot tell the stories that may have been spun around it. Nevertheless, we know that dogs were one of Mesoamerica's first domesticated animals and that they have provided fodder for mythological tale-spinning for many centuries.

Like cows and sheep in Europe, dogs in Mesoamerica were considered useful farm beasts, not family pets. Many of these dogs were of hairless species, and they were often used in the hunt. The colonial Yucatec Maya even bred a barkless hunting dog. Dogs themselves also served as food: Before the Spanish Conquest, male dogs frequently were castrated and force-fed in preparation for one feast or another. Dogs also could become sacrificial offerings, especially in funerals. These various uses may explain why people often still differentiate between cosmologically important dogs and those considered common yard beasts, sometimes even giving them different names. In ancient Nahuatl, for example, the calendrical and ritual dog was always referred to as *Itzcuintli,* whereas other dogs were *Chichimeh.* The calendar also indicates dogs' great mythological age, for the tenth day of many ancient and current twenty-day counts is called "dog." Mesoamerican dogs participate in three broad mythological streams: the first, concerning the creation of people; the second, food—particularly, the discovery of maize (in which dogs sometimes overlap with coyotes, foxes, or opossums); and the third, the underworld, death, the evening star and Quetzalcoatl. Occasionally, dogs also are the butt of jokes.

Dogs date to the first periods of mythic creation. The Popol Vuh describes how dogs and turkeys killed the people of the second age because the people always beat them; those folk who escaped turned into monkeys. The Tzotzil and Tzeltal say that in the Third Creation, a white dog mated with Eve to produce Ladinos, whereas a yellow dog sired Indians. Dogs also often appear as trickster figures. When the pre-Conquest Nahua Fourth Sun disappeared in a great deluge, a man and woman called Tata and Nene survived inside a great cypress log. When the log stopped rocking in the water, they climbed out on a beach, caught some fish and built a fire to roast them. The fire smoked the sky, upsetting the stars Citlallatonac and Citlalicue; this, in turn angered Tezcatlipoca. He bawled the two out for making such a mess, then chopped off their heads and sewed the heads onto their rumps, thereby turning them into dogs. This is how the first cooking fire came to be. During the Fifth Sun's creation, Death hunted the Nahua dog-god Xolotl. Xolotl first eluded Death by turning into a small green maize sprout, hiding in a field; when Death found him there, he ran away and turned into the parrot-like leaves of a young maguey plant; when found again, he hid as a salamander in a pool. But there Death cornered and killed him. Thus, three important native foods were born from a dog's shape-shifting body (see Nahual).

Figure 52. A dog figurine (Kay A. Read/Museo de Antropología e Historia, Puebla, Mexico)

A number of stories exist today in which a coyote or fox discovers corn; after all, dogs and their relatives are great scavengers. The Cakchiquels believe maize first grew from the entrails of a dead coyote. The K'iche' say the coyote was one of four animals to discover corn; the Mopan, Kekchi, and Pokomchi say that a fox made the discovery, although some think this fox was really an opossum. Like Xolotl's twin Quetzalcoatl, this fox met some ants carrying corn seeds back to their nests. After eating some of these seeds, Fox returned to the other animals. When he broke wind, the other animals smelled a difference, and they accused him of having found a new food, which he denied. So they followed him back into the forest, where they discovered Mesoamerica's most important form of sustenance.

Dogs roam the underworld in a number of guises. Perhaps the best known is Xolotl, who as a manifestation of Venus, teams up with the sun by following its path closely. Among the pre-Conquest Nahua, Quetzalcoatl played the role of Venus in its Morning Star phase, moving with the rising sun; his twin Xolotl played the role of Venus as the Evening Star, moving with the setting sun. A graphic depiction in the *Codex Telleriano Remensis* shows Xolotl opposite a figure called Tlachitonatiuh. In this cosmic image, the earth monster (see Earth, Agricultural, and Hunting Deities), fanged mouth gaping wide, swallows the sun. Sun, after being eaten, will travel through Earth's body at night before emerging at dawn, and Xolotl will travel with him until Quetzalcoatl takes over. A contemporary Totonac story tells how Moon, who thought he was the lover of all women and master of all, was led on a wild goose chase through the underworld by a little dog. This gave Sun enough time to escape and emerge first from the underground. Now, Moon must follow Sun. The Popol Vuh tells how the Hero Twins sacrificed a dog and then brought it back to life in order to impress 1-Death and 7-Death, the lords of the underworld. The dog was so grateful to live again that he wagged his tail.

When they die, people often go to the underworld accompanied by a dog. As early as the Preclassic, the Chupicaro buried dogs with the dead. Dogs also went with the Classic Maya to the underworld, for they appear both in tombs and in underworld scenes painted on pottery. The Maya believed the dead needed a dog to cross a body of water. Likewise, the Postclassic Nahua believed that a yellow dog waited by a body of water to carry a dead person across, after which the deceased completely disappeared. Only yellow dogs could do this; white dogs said they couldn't because they had just washed themselves, and black ones said no because they had just finished carrying themselves over. In the funeral ritual, a yellow dog was killed and cremated before the cremation of the deceased. Today, the Huitzilan say a dog takes a dead man across the water to reach the Devil's underground home; the Tarascan dog-god Uitzimengari saves the drowned by taking them to the Land of the Dead; and the Mixquic offer pictures and effigies of dogs to their deceased.

Dogs also can become the butt of jokes; after all, like Tata and Nene, one might say they were created to think with their behinds. One contemporary Nahua farce tells the tale of a grandmother and her dog-like grandson. Grandmother happens to come by a gourd full of fermented agave juice. Because she wants it all for herself, she tells the dog it is poisonous. She then goes out for a while. While she is gone, her grandson drinks the juice; becoming drunk, he thinks he's dying. Upon Grandmother's return, he tells her that thousands of dogs came and drank it, so he had to try it too. Angry, she beats him with a stick as she would a dog. Nevertheless, not all dogs or dog-like people are depicted as fools: Without dogs, people and maize might not exist, hunting might be less successful and meals more boring, the sun might not rise properly, the dead might lose their way, and some good jokes might never be told.

See also Devil; Earth, Agricultural, and Hunting Deities; Fifth Sun; Hero Twins; Nahual; 1-Death and 7-Death; Quetzalcoatl; Sky Deities and Beings; Sun; Tezcatlipoca; Underworld and Caves, Deities of the

Suggested reading:

Bricker, Victoria Reifler. 1973. *Ritual Humor in Highland Chiapas.* Austin: University of Texas Press.

Quiñones Keber, Eloise. 1995. *Codex Telleriano Remensis: Ritual, Divination, and History in a Pictorial Aztec Manuscript.* Austin: University of Texas Press.

Sahagún, Fray Bernardino de. 1953–1982. *The Florentine Codex: A General History of the Things of New Spain.* Trans. Arthur J. O. Anderson and Charles E. Dibble. Monographs of the School of American Research, no. 14. Santa Fe: School of American Research; Salt Lake City: University of Utah Press.

EARTH, AGRICULTURAL, AND HUNTING DEITIES

Time period: Preclassic–Contemporary

Cultural group: Mesoamerica

Earth's Surface, sandwiched between the skies above and the underworld below, is the space in which people live and eat, in which they grow crops and hunt animals. Like the Underworld, the Earth's Surface in much Mesoamerican mythology is divided horizontally into four parts aligned with the cardinal directions, but the precise point at which the Earth's Surface ends and the underworld begins is difficult to ascertain. This may be because the Earth's Surface generally forms either the roof of the Underworld or the skin of the Earth Monster that contains the subterranean realm. Moreover, many of the same deities who govern sustenance—rain, the crops, domestic animals, and game—move freely between Earth's Surface and the Underworld, blurring the distinctions even further. Sometimes Earth appears as a being in its own right, a forceful creature who requires care and demands respect. At other times, Earth's Surface is a landscape in which people, various animals, and other beings dwell along with powerful agricultural and hunting deities.

The mythology of Earth extends at least as far back as the Preclassic Olmec, and probably farther, although direct evidence from the earlier period is lacking. Among the Olmec, Earth was pictured as a great dragon floating on the sea, whose body sustained and nourished a vast array of plants. The Olmec also claimed a maize god with a cleft head from which corn sprouted—possibly an artful depiction of a mythological mountain in which the Olmec believed maize originated. The Classic Maya divided Earth into four quarters, one each for the four cardinal directions. Each quarter housed a great tree atop which perched a bird, and a fifth tree stood in the center. They also depicted the maize god Yum Kaax as dead and surrounded by ears of corn. This symbolic link between corn and death echoes the common bond between creation and destruction in Mesoamerican mythology. By

Figure 53. An ancient Hill of Seeds perhaps portrayed as the goddess Xochiquetzal from a mural at Teotihuacan (Kay A. Read/Museo Nacional de Antropología)

the Postclassic era, Yum Kaax had been joined by many other agricultural tales linking life with death, and creation with destruction.

The Postclassic Mixtecs continued to divide the earth into four portions: the east was that of light and the rising sun; the north, the place of the dead; the west, the dwelling of women and the setting sun; and the south, the place of thorns. In each, a pair of deities flanked the quarter's tree and bird (see Figure 4). The Nahua of this period told a story reminiscent of the Olmec dragon and the themes of life and death imaged by Yum Kaax: Seeing the great female creature called "Water-Earth Deity" (Atlalteutli) floating on the sea, Tezcatlipoca and Quetzalcoatl transformed themselves into snakes. One grabbed her right foot and left arm, and the other grabbed her left foot and right arm; and together they pulled on her until she was torn in two. One half produced the sky, and the other, the Earth. From her hair and hide came the trees, flowers, and plants. From her eyes and nostrils came springs and caves, and from her mouth came the valleys and mountains. But she cried out from this simultaneously destructive and creative act, and would not be quieted until fed human hearts; and she could not produce fruit unless watered with human blood. So, for people to continue eating the fruits of Earth, they must in turn feed her body with something from their own bodies. This respect was marked by ritual sacrifices that fed the earth with human hearts, rulers who ceremonially let their own blood to water it, and people who offered a sign of respect by taking a pinch of earth to eat before speaking to a great ruler or lord. When praying for a newborn child, the midwife called upon this great beast with the phrase "Our Mother, Our Father; Tonatiuh [Sun], Tlaltecutli [Earth-Lord]"—an apparent example of the sexual dualism so common to Mesoamerican mythology.

The Nahua also told a tale of the Mountain of Seeds, which was reminiscent of the Olmec maize-mountain god. Quetzalcoatl was the first to discover this mountain, by following a red ant into its depths, but he was not strong enough to crack it open. It took a god named Nanahuatl, who was probably lightning, to break it apart. As soon as he did this, the Tlalocs (fierce lightning and rain deities) snatched out all the food: the corn of the four directions, white, black, yellow, and red; beans; chia; and amaranth. And so, while food-filled mountains existed on earth's surface, it was the rain gods dwelling inside the mountains who governed all sustenance. Cinteotl was the Nahua maize god, comparable to Yum Kaax. A number of female deities governed corn in all its developmental phases: Cihuacoatl governed the raised fields and wetlands in the Valley of Mexico in particular; the goddess Toci was called the heart of the Earth; and the god Camaxtli served as patron of the hunt. By the seventeenth century, Oaxacans were honoring a god of lightning and rain, as well as a solar deity whose benefits were avidly sought by hunters; they also offered sacrifices of birds to a maize god and a wealthy Guardian of Grain.

Figure 54. Agricultural deity (Kay A. Read/Museo del Templo Mayor, Mexico City)

Many of these earthly themes of sustenance have survived until recent times, albeit sometimes in altered form. The Cakchiquel Maya of Panajachel in the 1930s said that when God first made the world, everything was flat, and it was too easy to travel from place to place. Afraid that people might forget him, he thought it would be better if they had it a bit harder. So God made mountains, hills, ravines, and volcanoes to make sure people would remember to pray to him. Now when people are facing a steep climb or a gorge that must be crossed, they say: "May God will that we arrive safely!"

As a deity, Earth's need for respect is clear. In Panajachel, they said that Mother Earth was like God himself, for she used her eyes and ears to judge the world. Before one did anything (bad or good), one needed to ask permission of both God and Earth by praying to them from either the patio or the crossroads. To do so, however, was a very serious act, because Earth was severe and unforgiving, and never had to be asked twice. Bad people did not last long because Earth would open up and simply swallow them. It was said that one day, a bad person from Santa Apolonia was riding his horse when, all of a sudden, a great hole opened up before him. He fell into it, and it closed over him, leaving only his hat and his horse's ears showing above ground. The tale's teller went on to say that these could be seen today because they had turned to stone. For this reason, people used to show Earth great respect. They prayed first to God to dispel any evil before they began to work the land, and then kissed a pinch of dirt before striking the Earth with any tool. She was very touchy then, and would cry out in pain when anyone hit her if not given respect first; they also risked her retaliation if they mistreated her. The Cakchiquel said that because people are made of earth, Earth knows the needs of the body; so a pinch of dirt can heal a wound caused by any earth-working tool. The Nahua of today's Amatlán, when talking about the Hill of Postejtli, whence comes all sustenance, say that Earth must be respected and that people tire her out by walking on her, but many people don't care, and make no offerings on the Hill, and even pee on it; but if one paid more respect, rain would come and the crops would do well.

These ideas of respect and judgment extend to stories about grain as well as other plants and animals of sustenance, and some even include the implements people use to prepare food. The Popol Vuh tells of the Third Age's wooden people, who had no heart or memory. They did not offer proper respect to the gods' creations. Because of this incompetence, a great resin from the sky rained upon them, and nasty beings snapped off their heads and ate their flesh. Everything complained to them: their cooking pots, griddles, grinding stones, and water jars. "Everyday you rub and rip our faces. Pain, that is all we get!" they shouted. Their dogs and turkeys asked: "Why can't you give us food? All you do is beat us for our troubles!" So they too attacked the people and smashed their faces in, scattering them. Today, this is why monkeys exist as a sign for humans; they look like people, but are made of nothing but wood and have no hearts.

Similarly, contemporary Tzutuhil Maya say that once upon a time complaints issued from many of the produce gods. Numerous people didn't pay proper respect to God for his creations, so a judgment was passed, and God threatened to end the world. But first God interviewed all the produce to learn exactly how people treated them. Corn and Beans griped bitterly, saying that their lives were full of torment. "Day and night people burn us in the fires and grind us to make corn tortillas and bean burritos, and then they chew us up and turn us into poop! Please make justice on them!" The grinding stones and griddles agreed that they too suffered from having their faces burned all the time. But then Tomatoes and Chilies told God that not all people were bad; and Squashes and Pumpkins said that, indeed, good people existed, Corn and Beans were just jealous because they received less respect. Sweet Potato agreed. The bad, disrespectful people became frightened and ran into caves to hide—whereupon God turned them into burrowing rodents and coyotes. These animals now are enemies of all who obediently till the earth.

Contemporary Nahua still tell tales about a Hill of Seeds, which sometimes contains domestic animals as well. In Amatlán, a variety of stories are told about a hill called Postejtli. In one story, the Virgin Tonantsi, or Our Honorable Mother, called the Gods of Thunder to destroy the Hill because ants kept cutting its flowers. The Hill's destruction resulted in seeds, but nobody could get them to grow. So St. John raised clouds from the sea, which watered them, causing the birth of black and yellow maize. In a second story, they say that God became annoyed because lawless men went up to the Hill to see what bad things they could do, so God decided that the Hill needed to be knocked down. He

Figure 55. A Mazahua child making tortillas (Kay A. Read)

called Woodpecker to do it, but the Hill proved too tough for Woodpecker's pecking. Then he called in old San Juan, who in spite of his age split the Hill into seven pieces with a single rumble of thunder and a bolt of lightning. The pieces burned by lightning became black maize, and those that had been white became yellow maize. This is what God had prayed for. Yet another story tells of two children who had killed their grandmother because she wouldn't let them marry each other, and who had hidden inside the Hill. Those who went looking for them knocked the Hill down, but they found that the lightning gods had burned them and they were no longer children. Now they were Seven and Five Flower, from which all of the crops sprang: black and yellow maize, beans, squash, and melons—every food that grew in the region.

Among the Chortí, the Earth God Ihp'en personifies earth, soil, plant growth, riches, and property in general. Ihp'en, both male and female, joins San Manuel with the Virgin. Ritually buried in the fields, s/he guards a family's possessions, and the union of these two brings about the birth or sprouting of their children, all cultivated plants. Maize is male, and the consort of beans. Because the male and female gods produce these comestible male and female offspring, people eat the male maize and the female beans together. Among the Mopan, Huitz-Hok, the mountain-valley god, along with Morning Star and Moon, receives prayers and offerings for good crops. In parts of highland Mexico, Malinche protects both animals and produce. But in Chan Kom in the 1930s, the Yucatec Maya said that the Balams guarded both the fields and the villages. Sometimes they had no definite form; other times they appeared as little old men wearing sombreros, sandals, and local dress. Balams behaved themselves when people offered them proper gifts and prayers; they could turn nasty if people didn't, bringing sickness to both the field and its owner. If jilted, they might even live off children's souls. If the Balams cried out during the night, then someone was going to die.

In addition to crops, Earth's Surface supports trees and shelters the animals that people hunt. Before felling a tree, a Colonial Mexica logger would respectfully ask a tree not to "eat" him. Similarly, the Yucatec Maya of Chan Kom requested permission to cut trees, and made offerings to the Kuiob Kaaxob, forest deities. Hunters of seventeenth-century Oaxaca petitioned two deities: one, the solar deity Licuicha, and another named Lexee, who protected them and sent them dreams. Today, the Itzá Maya tell a story about a hunter who went out shooting deer every day. One day he shot a very large deer, but only wounded him; the deer turned and ran off into the forest. The hunter followed his trail of blood into a great, door-like cave at the base of a hill. Inside he found a big ranch, and the wounded deer standing with a number of other deer. Among them stood an old man who was giving the animals food. The man looked at him and said:

"You are the one who shoots my animals. Now you see how you have hurt and wounded them. I have had to cure them all. Next time you shoot a deer, shoot it well, don't shoot it badly! Otherwise, you will have to come back here, and I will be waiting. All right, I will take you home now, but don't tell anyone anything about this!"

The old man told him to shut his eyes, and in an instant, the hunter found himself back outside at the base of the hill; the cave-door had disappeared. When the hunter arrived back home, his wife and children broke into joyful tears. Although he was positive he had been gone only a few hours, they told him he had been gone for three months, and they were sure he was dead!

And thus life is sustained on earth's surface, often with the help of those living below, who nourish the corn with water and the things of death, or who guard the living grain, plants, and animals so necessary to life above. If one is not careful to show the proper respect for the forces that help life continue, then one may find oneself in deep trouble, perhaps even face Death itself. After all, the living eat things that feed off the goods of the underworld; it is only fair that they should feed those subterranean forces in return, and carefully honor that relatively small terrestrial portion visible to human eyes—Earth's surface.

See also Chalchiuhtlicue; Cihuacoatl; Deer; La Llorona; Moon; Quetzalcoatl; Rain and Water Deities; Saints; Sky Deities and Beings; Sun; Tezcatlipoca; Underworld and Caves, Deities of the; Yum Kaax

Suggested reading:

Codex Chimalpopoca. 1992. As reproduced in *History and Mythology of the Aztecs: The Codex Chimalpopoca.* Trans. John Bierhorst. Tucson: University of Arizona Press.

Joralemon, Peter David. 1996. "In Search of the Olmec Cosmos: Reconstructing the World View of Mexico's First Civilization." Pp. 51–59 in Elizabeth P. Benson and Beatriz de la Fuente, eds., *Olmec Art of Ancient Mexico.* Washington, DC: National Gallery of Art.

Sexton, James D. 1992. *Mayan Folktales: Folklore from Lake Atitlán, Guatemala.* New York: Doubleday.

Tedlock, Dennis, trans. 1985. *Popol Vuh: The Definitive Edition of the Mayan Book of the Dawn of Life and the Glories of Gods and Kings.* New York: Simon and Schuster.

Read, Kay A. 1998. *Time and Sacrifice in the Aztec Cosmos.* Bloomington: Indiana University Press.

Wisdom, Charles. 1940. *The Chorti Indians of Guatemala.* Chicago: University of Chicago Press.

FEATHERED SERPENTS

Time period: Preclassic–Contemporary

Cultural group: Mesoamerica

Feathered serpents—powerful beings, combining features of the quetzal bird with those of the rattlesnake—claim a lengthy history stretching back into the Preclassic era. These zoomorphic characters often both help create the cosmos and associate closely with humans, thereby joining cosmic elements with human events. Feathered serpents appear only rarely until the Classic era, when a few begin to grace some of Teotihuacan's walls. They become a stronger theme in the Postclassic era, when they appear in an area stretching from the Mexican highlands to the Yucatán and Guatemala. Their most famous representative, the Nahua Quetzalcoatl, claims the greatest ascendancy, having been linked mythologically during the Conquest with the Spanish and with Christianity. Eventually, however, that mythology was reversed, and Quetzalcoatl now represents Mexican nationalism and its noble indigenous heritage.

Among the Preclassic Olmec, the feathered serpent appears in his most basic form, as a rattlesnake wearing feathers or a winged element on the back of his head. Overshadowed by many jaguar images, the Olmec feathered serpent's infrequent appearances suggest that he was not the most central deity. The occasional snake appearing paired with a jaguar may foreshadow the Postclassic partnership of Quetzalcoatl and Tezcatlipoca's jaguar aspect; and as did Postclassic feathered serpents, Olmec versions usually appear with humans, but this does not mean the Preclassic feathered serpent is identical to his Postclassic relative. On Monument no. 19 from La Venta, a rattlesnake wearing a feather headdress gracefully encircles a priest holding a ceremonial bag and wearing the snake's mask, its jaws framing his head. In small sculptures from Guerrero and Guatemala, coiled bird-snakes also appear framing human faces with their jaws. In still other depictions, feathered serpents and jaguars devour humans. Scholars can only make educated guesses as to what these various images mean. Priests likely dealt with ceremonies involving feathered snakes; and given the feathered serpent's later Postclassic association with ritual practices and its reputed shape-shifting capacities, perhaps the feathered serpent served some Olmec priests as their nahual. But the word for "serpent" in Maya languages also means "sky," so this figure also may have been a celestial deity.

The feathered serpent does not really become a featured figure until the Classic era, when he appears on a few of Teotihuacan's buildings. His most famous portrayal is on the walls of the Feathered Serpent Temple in the Ciudadela (see Figure 15). There his body flows through the water with shells and marine animals; his own head alternates with another imposing portrayal of an unidentified figure. This second head could represent a number of things: the rain god Tlaloc, although he bears few of Tlaloc's distinctive features; a war headdress, although it bears only a few resemblances to other headdresses; a firesnake representing war; or a crocodile, perhaps like the Nahua Cipactli, from whom Quetzalcoatl and Tezcatlipoca formed the earth. Thus some feel that the two figures together may represent the wet and dry seasons; for in later times, Quetzalcoatl, in his wind form, was closely associated with rain and water gods, and the dry season was considered the season of war. Others suggest that the whole temple refers back to the beginning of time, when the earth was formed. What is more clear is that the temple probably was situated in a residential complex for Teotihuacan's rulers and other elite. Their deceased may have been buried in the temple, although no clear evidence of nobles' tombs has yet surfaced. A massive burial of war captives and other burials of women and children have been found inside the temple, but the only indication of a possible royal burial is an interment that was long ago thoroughly stripped by looters.

At other sites that originated at the end of the Classic and beginning of the Postclassic eras, the feathered serpent usually is displayed with important people. At the Mexican highland site of Xochicalco, a Teotihuacan-like feathered serpent snakes beneath seated rulers who appear to be Maya; likewise, he usually is depicted with elite individuals at Cacaxtla and at Chichén Itzá. Nahua tales of Quetzalcoatl suggest that his name had become a title for rulership; perhaps these sites testify to his association with elites. Quetzalcoatl also has a creator aspect, which may link rulers with cosmic responsibilities such as making sure rains arrive on schedule. A Preclassic Olmec frieze from Chalcatzingo, Morelos, shows an elite person, probably a ruler, seated inside the cave-like mouth of the earth monster. Mist and clouds come from this mouth, and rain falls on crops below. Postclassic Mexica rulers also held responsibilities for maintaining crops, assuring a good climate, and playing priestly roles in rain ceremonies; moreover, drought indicated a ruler's personal failure. Just as he did in the Preclassic, the feathered serpent in the Postclassic era joined cosmic and human events; thus, it seems likely that as a deity of both sky and waters, he was believed to endow human rulers with his special powers.

The feathered serpent comes into his own in the Postclassic era, when depictions bearing both Toltec and Maya traits appear at various sites, from the Mexican highlands to the Yucatán and Guatemala. He also emerges in stories collected just after the Conquest from those areas. By then, it's obvious he has become a complex figure with both a creative-cosmic side and a rulership association. As Gukumatz in the Popol Vuh, he cooperates with the deity Jurakan to create the first K'iché world; later, he enjoys a priestly keeper, who watches out for his ceremonial needs. Quetzalcoatl creates the Nahua world with Tezcatlipoca, helps shape the first humans, discovers corn, forms the prosperous Toltec civilization, and lends his name to its line of rulers. Fray Diego de Landa wrote that Quetzalcoatl, as Kukulcan, came from the West and founded Mayapan, a new city near Chichén Itzá in the Yucatán. He wrote that after Kukulcan returned to Mexico, he built himself a memorial on the sea at Champotón. At one time, scholars created their own tale by linking Landa's with one about Quetzalcoatl's departure from Tula in the Mexican highlands; in that story, he left because of sexual transgressions. Scholars suggested that a real person named Quetzalcoatl journeyed from Tula to the Yucatán. More recently, new archaeological evidence has cast doubt on this assumption.

With the Conquest, Quetzalcoatl enjoyed an extraordinary popularity. At first, Cortés became the returning Quetzalcoatl ready to vanquish Tezcatlipoca's Mexica, although this myth did not live for long. In the centuries that followed, however, many mythic permutations occurred in literary traditions. Quetzalcoatl became Saint Thomas evangelizing the New World; the Mexican national representative of a noble indigenous heritage; and finally, the triumph of that heritage over an imposed European culture. But by the twentieth century, the feathered serpent largely vanishes from folk traditions. Now Gukumatz appears only rarely among the K'iche', and the Lacandon say he is the large, malevolent pet snake of their principle sun deity. In a number of places, San Sebastian appears to have taken over his wind shrines; among the Nahua, various wind gods still move storm clouds as did Quetzalcoatl; and some Maya tales now attribute Quetzalcoatl's past sexual transgressions to Saint Thomas. Even where the folk feathered serpent does not survive in name, his actions are remembered.

See also Cortés, Fernando; Gukumatz; Jurakan; Kukulcan; Nahual; Quetzalcoatl; Rain and Water Deities; Saints; Sky Deities and Beings; Tezcatlipoca; Tlaloc and the Tlaloques

Suggested reading:

Codex Chimalpopoca. 1992. As reproduced in *History and Mythology of the Aztecs: The Codex Chimalpopoca.* Trans. John Bierhorst. Tucson: University of Arizona Press.

Joralemon, Peter David. 1996. "In Search of the Olmec Cosmos: Reconstructing the World View of Mexico's First Civilization." Pp. 51–59 in *Olmec Art of*

Figure 56. Jaguar from a wall mural at Teotihuacan (Kay A. Read)

Ancient Mexico, eds. Elizabeth P. Benson and Beatriz de la Fuente. Washington, DC: National Gallery of Art.

Pasztory, Esther. 1997. *Teotihuacan: An Experiment in Living.* Norman: University of Oklahoma Press.

Tedlock, Dennis, trans. 1985. *Popol Vuh: The Definitive Edition of the Mayan Book of the Dawn of Life and the Glories of Gods and Kings.* New York: Simon and Schuster.

FIFTH SUN

Time period: Postclassic

Cultural group: Nahua-Mexica

The Mexica lived in the Fifth Sun, the Nahua age of life and power. When the sun died, their life would also end. Following the demise of the fourth age, the gods created the fifth yearly calendar deity through their sacrificial activities at the great city of Teotihuacan. Two gods were chosen to sacrifice themselves, a very rich but somewhat overly proud god named Tecuiçztecatl, and a poor but very humble god named Nanahuatzin. Both performed preparatory rituals, the first with implements and attire made of gold, precious stones, and fine feathers, the second with objects made only of paper and grass. When finished preparing, they threw their goods down on the ground into great piles, thereby creating the Pyramids of the Moon and the Sun. One can still visit these pyramids just outside of Mexico City today.

Once preparations had been made, the gods called to Tecuiçiztecatl to jump into a great bonfire burning brightly there, but he could not make himself do it. Then the Gods called to Nanahuatzin, who willingly performed his duty by leaping bravely into the conflagration. This inspired Tecuiçiztecatl so much, that he gained the courage to also make the leap. Nanahuatzin rose from the fire as a well blackened eagle, but Tecuiçiztecatl arose only as a partly spotted jaguar; he had not burned as well because the fire had died down before he leapt into it. Then two suns appeared, each exactly the same, sitting on the eastern horizon. The gods solved this duplication problem by smashing one with a rabbit thereby dimming its light, but still neither orb moved. After food had been created, and all the other gods had been sacrificed, Quetzalcoatl gently blew the sun into motion. The moon with its rabbit face followed suit. Thus the Fifth Age was born. It is said that Tecuiçiztecatl would have been the sun if he had jumped into the fire first. The tale also is told that this sun will die from famine and earthquakes when it is 676 years old. Hence people call the Fifth Sun 4-Movement, for it will die by motion.

See also Calendar Deities; Moon; Quetzalcoatl; Sun

Suggested reading:

Codex Chimalpopoca. 1992b. As reproduced in *History and Mythology of the Aztecs: The Codex Chimalpopoca.* Trans. John Bierhorst. Tucson: University of Arizona Press.

Sahagún, Fray Bernardino de. 1953–1982. *The Florentine Codex: A General History of the Things of New Spain.* Trans. Arthur J. O. Anderson, and Charles E. Dibble. 12 books, 13 parts. Monographs of the School of American Research no. 14. Santa Fe: School of American Research; Salt Lake City: University of Utah Press.

GOD L

Time period: Classic–Postclassic

Cultural group: Maya

God L is a deity represented as an old man dressed in a muan bird (an owl or another raptor) headdress; often black in color, he is closely linked with the underworld. His animal counterparts are the jaguar and the muan bird, both creatures of the night and caves, which are gates to the underworld. Unfortunately, we do not know his given Maya name, so scholars have simply designated him by the letter *L.* However, because of the consistent presence of the muan bird and sky symbols in his headdress, some scholars have suggested his name may have been Muan Chan, or "Misty Sky."

The Maya often viewed God L as a deity of death and destruction and associated him with war and conflict. However, like many other Mesoamerican deities who bore multiple traits, he was not just a god of death but also one of merchants and trade, frequently appearing with riches, a merchant bundle, and a staff or spear. In addition, in many artistic renditions, God L has water, rain, and agricultural fertility associations. A common figure in Classic art and iconography, God L clearly served as an important figure in Maya myths and lore during this period. Many Classic scenes show the moon goddess taking the regalia of God L, illustrating a mythic scene from an oral story that no longer exists. By the Postclassic period, God L is a far less important deity, appearing only infrequently in art and Maya codices.

Figure 57. God L from the Dresden Codex (Museo de América/Art Resource)

See also Earth, Agricultural, and Hunting Deities; Moon; Rain and Water Deities; Sky Deities and Beings; Underworld and Caves, Deities of the

Suggested reading:

Sharer, Robert J. 1994. *The Ancient Maya.* 5th ed. Stanford, CA: Stanford University Press.

Taube, Karl. 1992. *The Major Gods of Ancient Yucatan.* Washington, DC: Dumbarton Oaks Research Library.

GUADALUPE, VIRGIN OF

Time period: Colonial–Contemporary

Cultural group: Mesoamerica

Like all Mesoamerican saints, the Virgin of Guadalupe possesses a personality and powers that are unique to the particular locale; but unlike other saints, this particular representative of Mary the mother of Christ also has a national cult: Her powers are believed to be directed toward helping the nation of Mexico as much as individual communities and individuals. As a result, there are two contrasting ways of understanding Guadalupe and two different, traditional ways of interacting with her. Guadalupe invokes strong emotions, and her interpreters typically have taken either a markedly sympathetic, believing view of her or a strongly unsympathetic stance based on an entirely different worldview. People

Figure 58. The Virgin of Guadalupe (ng.netgate.net/~norberto/materdei.html)

have interacted with her in two different but related ways: either as a follower of her national leadership, or as a simple worshiper with loving gratitude, hopeful supplication, and humble awe of her powers.

The historicity of the events surrounding the mythological Guadalupe remains unproven by scientific or scholarly means, but the effect of Guadalupe's myth on national and personal events is profound and undeniable. As with all powerful myths (any of the myths described in this volume), the truth and the reality of Guadalupe lie outside of the methods contemporary historians have at their disposal. Even if it could be proven that Guadalupe never existed in reality, what people actually have done with her powers in real life would remain irrefutable; both the national history and personal biographies provide ample evidence of it.

According to Guadalupe's Mexican myth, early one morning in December 1531, the Virgin miraculously appeared before a shepherd and Christian convert named Juan Diego. This apparition occurred on Tepeyac, a hill just a few miles north of the center of Mexico City, or Tenochtitlan, the traditional center of the entire Mexica domain. As did the Juan Diego at Ocotlan, Tepeyac's Juan Diego heard strains of beautiful music and a lovely lady calling to him: "Juanito, Juanito! The least of my sons, where are you going?" He told her he was going to church. She then told him that she was the "Virgin Mary, Mother of the true God," and that she wanted a church built for her right there on Tepeyac. She also promised to reward his faithfulness.

Juan Diego hurried to Mexico City to make the Virgin's request known to Bishop Zumarraga, but the good father dismissed the shepherd's story as nonsense and sent him away. Juan Diego went back to the lady at Tepeyac to explain the problem; she sent him back to the bishop, who again rebuffed him. Then he was sidetracked by his uncle who had fallen mortally ill with smallpox. On his way to find a priest to administer last rites, Juan encountered the Virgin again. She told him she had already cured his uncle. Then she directed him toward the normally dry, cactus-ridden hilltop, where he was to pick some unusually lush roses. After he had done so, she arranged the flowers carefully in his cloak, telling him to take them back to the bishop, for they were a sign. When Juan Diego opened his cloak at the cleric's house, the roses tumbled to the floor, revealing a lovely painting of the Virgin that had not been there before. The bishop carried this amazing cloak to the chapel and hung it on the wall. The next morning, he rode with Juan Diego to the latter's house, where they found his uncle in perfect health. His uncle reported that the Virgin had appeared to him the previous evening, had cured him, and had informed him that she wanted to be called "Guadalupe." The bishop was finally convinced, and had a chapel built to honor the Virgin of Guadalupe. As the story goes, the Indians had already been acquainted with this Lady for many years and called her Tonantzin, which means "Our Honorable Mother" in Nahuatl.

Such is the mythic history of Guadalupe. Scholarly historians suggest a somewhat different story. The Virgin of Guadalupe is said to have appeared first in Extremadura, Spain. A small wooden statue of her was supposed to have been hidden during the Moorish invasion, but a shepherd recovered it in the thirteenth century, and the shrine of Guadalupe eventually became a popular pilgrimage site. The name "Guadalupe" is Arabic in origin, but its meaning remains uncertain. Columbus and the conquistadores (many of whom came from Extremadura) brought the Virgin's cult with them to the New World. Indeed, she rode into Tenochtitlan emblazoned on a flag carried by Cortés's men.

The chapel at Tepeyac, dating to 1555 or 1556, originally was dedicated to the Virgin Mary. Early on it received the popular name of Guadalupe because of the similarity between the chapel's image of Mary and the one in Extremadura. Some interpreters claim that the site was the location of a pre-Conquest goddess called Tonantzin, but as many scholars have noted, the evidence for that is almost nonexistent. The sixteenth-century scholar Fray Bernardino de Sahagún did express his disapproval of the veneration of the Virgin at Tepeyac, saying that it constituted idolatry and played on the ambiguity of the name Tonantzin. He may not have been far wrong, for the Nahuatl word *tonantzin* was and still is a form of reverent address used for numerous female deities, not just one; today, people often address Mary this way. The Tepeyac site itself may or may not have been an ancient place of pre-Christian worship (we can't be sure); but in any case, the site clearly encouraged an indigenous form of piety that worried Sahagún. At about the same time, the Franciscan provincial Francisco de Bustamante also issued an intense condemnation of popular devotion to Guadalupe, claiming that her image had been painted by an Indian named Marcos. There is no clear documentary record of any physical manifestation of the Virgin of Guadalupe during the next hundred years (Poole 1997, 1536). However, others embraced her cult, if not her apparition; Jacques Lafaye has suggested that the Virgin of Guadalupe signaled the creation of a "Western Paradise" legitimizing the European hold on the New World (Lafaye 1976, 228). These arguments for or against her veneration, which often reflected tensions between the clerical orders operating in New Spain at the time, have continued in various forms to the present.

In spite of all the arguments over her, Guadalupe did not really come into her own until 1648, when Miguel Sanchez published a book apparently retelling oral tales about her because he could find no written references. He related her to the founding of Tenochtitlan, which was depicted as an eagle standing on a cactus (this image now appears on the Mexican flag; see Fig. 41). Transforming Guadalupe's Spanish image, Sanchez turned an angel at her feet into a Mexica-like cactus, and the angel's wings into eagle feathers. This transformation, combined with stories of the Virgin of Guadalupe, made the Virgin instantly appealing to the criollo population (European immigrants' children born in New Spain), who had been living betwixt and between two worlds, longing for their own legitimacy. Sanchez gave them a Virgin who combined both the Old and the New Worlds, a saintly validation of both their heritages. The next year his book was published in Nahuatl, but this edition, *Nican mopohua,* never caught on with the Indians. Guadalupe remained a largely criollo saint throughout the seventeenth century.

In the eighteenth century, and even more so in the nineteenth, devotion to Guadalupe took off as the criollos' descendants appropriated her as a mascot for their nationalist aspirations. In 1810, Hidalgo chose her as the symbol of rebellion and liberation. Of course, many Mesoamerican saints have led rebellions, but few have led one that succeeded as well as this one; Guadalupe led the Mexican people through a full-scale revolution to independence. After Independence, the ruling and intellectual classes made the Virgin an icon of Mexican identity and a unifying focus in a fragmented society; even the anticlerical Benito Juarez respected the symbolism of Guadalupe's chapel. For indigenous peoples, she also became a source of intensely personal devotion. This "Queen of Peace" and "Queen of Mexicans" requested that her devotees give themselves over to "Mary and to Jesus through Her," and do everything "by Mary, with Mary, in Mary, and for Mary" (Lafaye 1976, 287).

Anticlericism flourished among certain sectors of Mexican society in the nineteenth century. Some said Guadalupe was nothing more than a way for the power-mongering clerics to maintain control over the simple folk. The history of the tale had been questioned since the seventeenth century, but the controversy surrounding it had since become so inflamed with passions that any scholarly investigation was impossible. In this debate, two worldviews and two camps were pitted against each other—Christian mythology against humanist myths of objectivity and rationality, and those who supported the Church as a valid institution against those who saw it as an evil force that oppressed humanity. The debate became so intense that one premier historian, Joaquin Garcia Icazbalceta, abandoned his research altogether near the end of his life, too tired and discouraged to deal with the controversy swirling around his biography of Zumarraga (which omitted any mention of Guadalupe's apparition) and a subsequent letter he wrote that strongly questioned her myth's historical validity.

Although passions abated in the twentieth century, the issue of Guadalupe's historical veracity continued to be questioned. In 1922, historian Mariano Cuevas popularized the idea that *Nican mopohua* was an eyewitness account dating from the time of the apparition. However, his claim that the original document had been looted by the Americans during the Mexican-American war was discredited, and other historians continued to question the myth's historicity. In this century as in the past, Guadalupe has had her defenders and detractors, but now there is a trend toward more balanced historical treatments.

Today's devotion to the Virgin of Guadalupe remains central to Mexican national and religious life in spite of scholarly debates. A metro stop at the Basilica of Guadalupe is clearly marked on the subway heading to this northern suburb of Mexico City. The Basilica itself is a huge, ultramodern affair in which the traveler to Tepeyac can view both the cloak and a fine old painting of the Virgin. There she stands in a blue cape upon a crescent moon, with solar rays emanating from behind her. The explanation for this painting, other images of her, and Sanchez's earlier criollo adaptation can be found as easily in a biblical reference as in indigenous tradition. Revelation 12 describes an apparition of a woman clothed with the sun, the moon at her feet, and a crown of twelve stars; she was threatened by a serpent and received two wings of an eagle. Guadalupe's association with the moon also links her to some indigenous, pre-Christian lunar goddesses, and her solar rays often are painted in the ancient style. Moreover, until quite recently, pilgrims could be seen crawling on their hands and knees up to the basilica in an expression of extreme piety; some had come from miles away. Such contemporary pilgrimages echo the ancient journeys people took to various shrines throughout ancient Mesoamerica. Indigenous piety may have shaped these practices of veneration of Guadalupe.

Guadalupe seems to have special meaning for a number of contemporary Mexican-American women. Jeanette Rodriguez has reported that Guadalupe provides women with positive models of an ideal self, nurturing, strongly connected with the family and community, and self-controlled. Yolanda, one of the women Rodriguez interviewed, said that Guadalupe represented strength, hope, and optimism, and that she belonged particularly to *los latinas.* Another interviewee, Edyth, said that Guadalupe belonged to everyone, that she was a "Mexican Mother, waiting, caring, unselfish." At the same time, Rodriguez noted that negative ideas, such as the conforming child and critical parent, also resulted from her veneration (1994, 106, 109). This echoes what other feminists have said about her. For some, she represents strength and liberation; for others, subjugation—arguments that mirror those surrounding Guadalupe throughout previous centuries. The fact that Guadalupe's historicity continues to be questioned suggests the power of history itself to form mythic realities.

See also Christ; La Llorona; Malinche; Moon; Saints; Sun

Suggested reading:

Florescano, Enrique. 1994. *Memory, Myth, and Time in Mexico: From the Aztecs to Independence.* Austin: University of Texas Press.

Lafaye, Jacques. 1976. *Quetzalcoatl and Guadalupe: The Formation of Mexican National Consciousness, 1531–1813.* Chicago: University of Chicago Press.

Poole, Stafford. 1997. "Virgin of Guadalupe and Guadalupanismo." Pp. 1535–1537 in *Encyclopedia of Mexico: History, Society, and Culture,* vol. 2, ed. Michael S. Werner. Chicago: Fitzroy Dearborn.

Rodriguez, Jeanette. 1994. *Our Lady of Guadalupe: Faith and Empowerment among Mexican-American Women.* Austin: University of Texas Press.

GUKUMATZ

Time period: Postclassic–Contemporary

Cultural group: K'iche' Maya

Gukumatz (Goo-koo-mats´) is the K'iche' Maya version of the highland Mexican feathered serpent deity Quetzalcoatl, found throughout Postclassic Mesoamerica. In the K'iche' creation myths, called the Popol Vuh, Gukumatz is one of the gods who helps create the universe and the first human beings.

Gukumatz has six major symbolic representations in K'iche' myths and stories. First, he appears as a plumed serpent, for his name translates to "feathered serpent." Second, the K'iche' Maya viewed Gukumatz as an eagle. Third, some K'iche' myths recount his transformation into a jaguar. Fourth, one story records his transformation into a pool of blood. Fifth, sometimes the K'iche' represent Gukumatz as a conch shell or snail. And sixth, the K'iche' associated Gukumatz with a flute made of bones.

The Popol Vuh describes him as one of the creator deities, who threw lots to decide the fate of the people they had created, and what kind of relations these new creations would have with the gods. Gukumatz probably was borrowed either from the Toltecs of highland Mexico (Quetzalcoatl) or the Yucatec Maya (Kukulkan). The K'iche' gave him a secondary role as a creator god and blended him with other deities. In addition, some of the myths in the Popol Vuh and elsewhere indicate an association between the creator deity and a historically known ruler or individual named Lord Gukumatz. This person may have been so named because he drew some of his powers from Gukumatz.

See also Feathered Serpents; Kukulkan; Quetzalcoatl

Suggested reading:

Preuss, Mary H. 1988. *Gods of the Popol Vuh: Xmucane, Kucumatz, Tojil, and Jurakan.* Culver City, CA: Labyrinthos.

Tedlock, Dennis, trans. 1985. *Popol Vuh: The Definitive Edition of the Mayan Book of the Dawn of Life and the Glories of Gods and Kings.* New York: Simon and Schuster.

HERO TWINS (HUNAHPU AND XBALANQUE)

Time period: Classic–Contemporary

Cultural group: K'iche' Maya

Hunahpu (Hoon-ah-poo´) and Xbalanque (Sh-ba-lan-kay´), known as the Hero Twins, are the main figures in two of the five myths from the Popol Vuh, the K'iche' legend of creation. The Hero Twins are not creator deities or gods that control the fates of ordinary humans but rather trickster figures that outsmart and defeat morally questionable supernatural figures. First, they defeat those who tried to magnify themselves over the creator god Jurakan; and second, they trounce the unsavory underworld lords of Xibalba. These contests were disputes within a single family, for Hunahpu and Xbalanque share the same genealogy as the gods. These two twins are the sons of Vucub Hunahpu (Yum Kaax, or the diving god), often interpreted as a maize god, and Blood Woman, a daughter of one of the underworld deities. Moreover, they are the grandsons of Xmucane and Xpiyacoc, the Grandmother and Grandfather deities responsible for helping Jurakan create the universe and for grinding the maize from which the first humans came.

Hunahpu and Xbalanque appear primarily in the Popol Vuh's second and third sections. In the second, the Hero twins defeat three self-glorifying gods, 7-Macaw, Zipacna, and Earthquake. 7-Macaw claimed to be the sun, Zipacna claimed to have made the Earth, and Earthquake claimed to have the ability to bring down the sky and destroy the Earth. Because of their evil self-aggrandizing over the true creator deities, each was defeated by Hunahpu and Xbalanque through deceit. The third myth describes the birth of the Hero Twins; the death

Figure 59. Hero Twins, Hunahpu and Xbalanque, talking to 1-Death, Hun Came, in Xibalba (Justin Kerr Archives, File no. 1183)

of their uncle and father at the hands of the lords of Xibalba, and the Hero Twins' entrance into the underworld, where they outwitted and defeated the Xibalba lords by tricking them into wanting to be sacrificed. After they tricked the underworld gods, they partially resurrected their father, Vucub Hunahpu, and rose into the sky to become the sun and the moon. Among other things, one can see this myth as a metaphor for the cycles of the sun and moon, which also enter the underworld at the end and the beginning of every day and reappear victorious after their travels and trials in Xibalba. In like fashion, a ruler such as Pacal, who bears the sun's powers, enters the underworld at death, to rise as a new sun with the next ruler.

The origins of the Popol Vuh stories and the first myths of Hunahpu and Xbalanque remain unclear. However, among the Classic-era ruins of the lowland Maya, archaeologists and art historians have found painted images of the Hero Twins on pottery depicting not only scenes from the Popol Vuh but also scenes from stories that cannot be identified because they no longer exist. Hunahpu and Xbalanque were important to the prehistoric Classic Maya just as they are critical figures among today's K'iche' Maya, who continue to tell stories about them.

See also Blood Woman; Earth, Agricultural, and Hunting Deities; Jurakan; Moon; Pacal; Quetzalcoatl; Sky Deities and Beings; Sun; Underworld and Caves, Deities of the; Yum Kaax

Suggested reading:

Preuss, Mary H. 1988. *Gods of the Popol Vuh: Xmucane, Kucumatz, Tojil, and Jurakan.* Culver City, CA: Labyrinthos.

Sharer, Robert J. 1994. *The Ancient Maya.* 5th ed. Stanford, CA: Stanford University Press.

Tedlock, Dennis, trans. 1985. *Popol Vuh: The Definitive Edition of the Mayan Book of the Dawn of Life and the Glories of Gods and Kings.* New York: Simon and Schuster.

HUITZILOPOCHTLI

Time period: Postclassic

Cultural group: Nahua-Mexica

Huitzilopochtli (Weet-zee-lo-pocht´-lee) was the Mexica patron and war god. His name means "Hummingbird on the Left." Mythically, he was said to be instrumental in the creation of the cosmos; he led the Mexica to their island home of Tenochtitlan and brought both victory and defeat to the Mexica on the battlefield. In fact, his defeat meant the demise of the Mexica. He stood for cosmic creation, success in war, strong governance, and good trade. Historically, he was probably a relatively young deity, and perhaps not even a terribly central one; but in post-Conquest times he found himself elevated to a position of extreme importance by Spanish commentators who misunderstood his role in Mexica mythology.

One story of cosmic creation describes how Huitzilopochtli was one of four sons of the ancient creator couple Tonacateuctli and Tonacacihuatl; the other three brothers were the red and black Tezcatlipocas and Quetzalcoatl. It's said Huitzilopochtli was born with only bones and no flesh; and that, of the four, he was the smallest and his place lay on the cosmos' left side. After 600 years, Tonacateuctli and Tonacacihuatl told Huitzilopochtli and Quetzalcoatl to put the world in order. Together they made fire; a sun that did not shine much; the first man and woman, Oxomoco and Cipactonal; they put Mictlantecutli and his woman Mictlancihuatl (the Lord and Lady of the Land of the Dead) in the underworld; created the earth from the crocodilian creature Cipactli; and created Tlaltecutli and Chalchiuhtlicue from whom the deities of water were born.

Another story describes how he was born magically in full war regalia to the fierce goddess Coatlicue; his first act was to destroy his sister Coyolxauhqui who led her brothers, the Centzonuitznaua, against their mother on Coatepec Mountain. Still other stories tell how he led his people, the Mexica, from their island place of origin Aztlan or Chicomoztoc (Place of Seven Caves). Traveling often, they settled temporarily in many places; and after several incidences establishing his primacy, Huitzilopochtli finally led them to their proper settlement on their new island home of Tenochtitlan.

But Huitzilopochtli would not always remain victorious; his defeat meant the defeat of the Mexica. It's said that in Motecuhzoma I's time, magicians went to Aztlan only to be told that Huitzilopochtli would lose all the cities he had conquered for the Mexica in the same order he had won them. Then he would return to Aztlan, abandoning them. Before the Spanish arrived, one of Huitzilopochtli's temples burned down in an uncontrollable fire; throwing water on the flames only made them worse. This presented the Mexica with an omen of their impending demise, for the burning of a patron deity's temple was the sign of a city's defeat. Indeed, Pedro de Alvarado attacked and massacred many

*Figure 60. Huitzilopochtli (*Codex Magliabechiano, *fol. 53r, Art Resource)*

Mexica on Toxcatl, Huitzilopochtli's main feast day; this event began their disastrous war with the Spanish.

His ritual and iconographic imagery often indicated his powers of governance and war. Besides his trademark blue-green hummingbird helmet, he also sometimes wore white heron feathers that linked him to Aztlan and royal origins. Like Tezcatlipoca, he could sport a smoking mirror, a cloudy obsidian mirror, and serpent foot, all ancient Mesoamerican signs of rulership. Often he carried instruments of war: a shield, darts, and the terrible xiuhcoatl or fire-serpent. When he destroyed Coyolxauhqui and his brothers on Coatepec Mountain, he appeared as an intense storm or fire; piercing Coyolxauhqui with his lightning-like xiuhcoatl, he completely enveloped his brothers in clouds and finished them off with smoke. The Mexica dressed their dead rulers in his clothing because the governors embodied some of his powers. These powers, which the rulers received upon coronation, assured a forceful success in war and governance. Mexica rulers, furthermore, were closely linked with merchants in rituals in which Huitzilopochtli's substitute Paynal helped assure good success in battle and trade through sacrifice. As the vanguards of the expanding Mexica domain, traders could find themselves engaged in activities more violent than merely buying and selling goods.

Historically, he was probably a very young god, and may even have been a Mexica chief in their early migratory years. One tale first describes him as an image carried in a bundle on the back of the early Mexica ancestors wandering the land. This bundle looked very like the bundle dead rulers were wrapped into before their cremation. Like many Native American medicine bundles, it probably contained Huitzilopochtli's powers embodied by his image and perhaps other potent objects. Yet, at another point, the same story describes him as if he were a real person. This person may have been a chief named for the god, or a great chief who later died and became the god.

A lack of imagery indicates his youth. No great sculptures exist depicting Huitzilopochtli, and he appears in only one codex, which may actually be a picture of a ritual participant wearing his garb. Instead of fine stone, his image was made of perishable materials such as amaranth dough and wood. Moreover, only one object consistently defined Huitzilopochtli, his hummingbird helmet. One of Cortez's captains Bernal Díaz del Castillo reported that the similarity between this and the conquistador helmets convinced the Indians that the Spanish were people like them. All his other garments and decorations, however, changed with the ritual circumstances. Moreover, unlike most other patron deities, he shared the Templo Mayor in the center of Tenochtitlan with another deity, an ancient rain god called Tlaloc. The southern side housed Huitzilopochtli, while the northern side housed Tlaloc; as the year was divided between a rainy agricultural season and a dry warring season, so too the temple. Huitzilopochtli may have been the Mexica's patron, but he shared the limelight.

After the Conquest, however, Spanish commentators and others quickly elevated him to a central spot of importance. He became the principle god responsible for all past Mexica life and success. At the same time, because of his close association with war and sacrifice, the Spanish likened him to the Greco-Roman god Mars or to the Christian Devil, depending on whether the interpreter wished to idealize a lost Indian past or justify its demise. This classic-demonic divide continued into the seventeenth century. But by the early eighteenth century and up through the late twentieth, Quetzalcoatl surpassed him as the quintessential Mexica god—perhaps because, by then, people sought a more benign image of Indian origins, something Huitzilopochtli's bloody history could not provide.

See also Chalchiuhtlicue; Coatlicue; Coyolxauhqui; Devil; Motecuhzoma I, Lord; Quetzalcoatl; Rain and Water Deities; Sky Deities and Beings; Sun; Tezcatlipoca; Tlaloc and the Tlaloques

Suggested reading:

Boone, Elizabeth H. 1989. *Incarnations of the Aztec Supernatural: The Image of Huitzilopochtli in Mexico and Europe.* Philadelphia: American Philosophical Society.

Durán, Fray Diego. 1994. *The History of the Indies of New Spain.* Trans. Doris Heyden. Norman: University of Oklahoma Press.

Sahagún, Fray Bernardino de. 1953–1982. *The Florentine Codex: A General History of the Things of New Spain.* Trans. Arthur J. O. Anderson, and Charles E. Dibble. Monographs of the School of American Research no. 14. Santa Fe: School of American Research; Salt Lake City: University of Utah Press.

HUNAB KU

Time period: Colonial

Cultural group: Yucatec Maya

A mystery surrounds Hunab Ku's (Hoon-ab´ Koo) full character and importance. According to some, because he was the original creator god and father of

Itzamna, Hunab Ku was the most important Postclassic and early colonial era Maya deity. However, many early chronicles, both native and non-native, suggest that Hunab Ku and Itzamna are merely different names for the same divine individual. Different explanations are possible for this discrepancy. If he was truly the creator/father god, then his importance was quickly eclipsed by Itzamna, thus his early significance being masked. Or it could be that Hunab Ku is a colonial Maya name for the Spanish Christian God. In fact one translates Hunab Ku as "Unified God," a concept that fits the Christian God somewhat better than the many diverse deities of pre-Conquest religious traditions. Perhaps Hunab Ku represents an early step in the gradual religious conversion of the Maya, which also would explain why Hunab Ku does not appear in pre-Conquest indigenous literature or art. The colonial Maya considered Hunab Ku, the Christian God, to be the father of all and the Maya universe.

See also Christ; Itzamna; Saints

Suggested reading:

Landa, Diego de. 1978. *Yucatan before and after the Conquest.* Trans. William Gates. New York: Dover.

Morley, Sylvanus G., George W. Brainerd, and Robert J. Sharer. 1983. *The Ancient Maya.* 4th ed. Stanford, CA: Stanford University Press.

ITZAMNA

Time period: Postclassic–Colonial

Cultural group: Yucatec Maya

In some stories Itzamna (Eet-sam-na´) is said to be the son of Hunab Ku (the first god) and the husband of Ix Chel (the primary female deity). Itzamna was the greatest of all the Yucatec Maya deities. Among the Yucatec Maya in the early Colonial period, Itzamna was the god of heaven and sun, and he is described in the codices as the lord of the gods. In keeping with his great importance, he was worshiped under various names and possessed many different attributes.

Itzamna was the Yucatec god of writing and esoteric knowledge, and the god of maize, the sun, and the wind. The Yucatec Maya considered Itzamna the first priest—the one who invented writing and books, gave the names to earthly places, and divided the lands among the people. Itzamna located himself in the heavens; but in the social, earthly world he associated with rulers, scribes, and priests. His terrestrial animal and plant counterparts were the caiman (alligator), a principal bird (maybe the king vulture), the ceiba tree (kapok), and maize. As the one lord god and father of the gods, Itzamna served as the calendar patron of the day called Ahau. The Maya also associated him with sky and earth monsters, the cardinal directions and their four colors (red, white, black, and yellow), and what we call the Pleiades constellation. Later, during the Colonial era, because of Itzamna's prominence and Spanish religious influence, the Maya combined Itzamna with the Spanish Christian God.

Maya texts of the Postclassic and Colonial periods often depicted Itzamna in priestly clothes because of his close association with priests and the priesthood. Maya priests invoked him during New Year rites, and people prayed to him at the beginning of specific years to avert great natural disasters. Early historical reports say that the Maya prayed to Itzamna at the beginning of those years called Ix, in order to avert drought, hot sun, famine, and thefts. The Maya also prayed to Itzamna in other years to fend off other disastrous predictions.

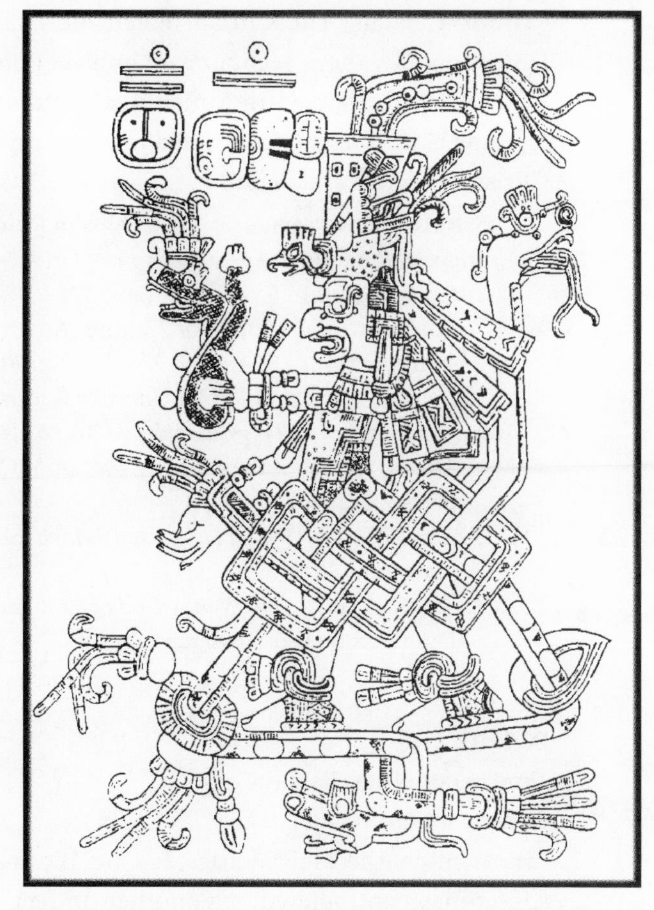

Figure 61. Itzamna, from the Postclassic site of Santa Rita, Corazal, Belize (Bureau of American Ethnology)

In the past, many stories and myths existed concerning Itzamna, the lord of the gods. Unfortunately, today very few such stories remain. What remains are pictures in Maya art, the descriptions of the sixteenth-century Spanish historian Fray Diego de Landa, and the narratives from the Chilam Balams (mythic histories of various Yucatec Maya groups).

No images of Itzamna have been found dating from the late Classic period; but after Spanish contact and during the Colonial period, Itzamna appears as a major deity who in eclipsing all other gods is the equal of, or identical with the Christian God. During the early Colonial and late Prehistoric periods, sculptures of Itzamna were created for ritual purposes of worship, including human sacrifice, new year celebrations, and prophetic divinations.

The Chilam Balam of Chumayel refers to Itzamna only briefly. It states that early in the sixteenth century, Itzamna was provoked by the coming of the Spanish Christian God; later in the same century, a group of Maya called the Itzá visited a place named Itzamna while journeying to a new home. Finally, in the nineteenth century, stories say that Itzamna was one of the lords of the last *katun* calendar cycle (a great cycle of time), which occurred at Coba in northeastern Yucatán. The Chilam Balam of Tizimin similarly mentions Itzamna. Unfortunately, these accounts are probably only excerpts from much longer stories, and few other written historical myths exist concerning Itzamna. Today, Itzamna is no longer encountered in Maya mythology, having been replaced with Christian stories and beliefs.

See also Christ; Hunab Ku; Ix Chel; Sky Deities and Beings; Sun

Suggested reading:

Edmonson, Munro S., ed. and trans. 1982. *The Ancient Future of the Itza: The Book of Chilam Balam of Tizimin.* Austin: University of Texas Press.

Edmonson, Munro S., trans. 1986. *Heaven Born Mérida and Its Destiny: The Book of Chilam Balam of Chumayel.* Austin: University of Texas Press.

Landa, Diego de. 1941. *Relación de las cosas de Yucatán.* Ed. and trans. Alfred M. Tozzer. Papers of the Peabody Museum. Cambridge, MA: Harvard University Press.

Sharer, Robert J. 1994. *The Ancient Maya.* 5th ed. Stanford, CA: Stanford University Press.

Taube, Karl. 1992. *The Major Gods of Ancient Yucatan.* Washington, DC: Dumbarton Oaks Research Library.

IX CHEL

Time period: Late Classic–Colonial

Cultural group: Yucatec Maya

Like many of the Maya deities, Ix Chel (Eesh-chel´) played a variety of roles that sometimes contradicted one another. In fact, much confusion exists as to who she truly was in the late Classic and Postclassic periods; her early Colonial character is clearer. Ix Chel, or "Lady Rainbow," was the female member of the creator couple (with Itzamna). She served as the patron of divination, weaving, medicine, healing, and childbirth. However, she also was associated with floods, destruction, serpents, and sometimes war. And she may have been associated with the moon. The Maya closely linked Ix Chel with the spider, which has connections to weaving, childbirth, divination, and creation. The spider, like Ix Chel, had a dual nature, being associated with childbirth and creation, and with war and destruction. Ix Chel was a complex figure with multiple aspects, varying in accordance with the situation or the time in which she was invoked.

Various reasons exist for her ties with both the creative (healing and childbirth) and the malicious (war and destruction). Among the Maya, rainbows are not harbingers of good and beauty but signs of sickness and disease. However, her name "Lady Rainbow" also indicates the other side of her personality, for sickness and disease are treated through healing and medicine, which are also in her domain. She does not bring sickness but rather serves as the curer, therefore playing a powerful role in Maya society.

*Figure 62. Ix Chel (*Codex Tro-cortesianus, *pl. 30b, Museo de América/Art Resource)*

A few portrayals of Ix Chel exist in late Classic art, largely in the form of small sculptures and painted pottery, which depict her as a powerful old woman, sometimes accompanied by imagery of death. In Postclassic art, her portrayals are more vivid, intertwining a variety of symbols of death and destruction with those of water, life, and weaving. In late Classic and in Postclassic art, Ix Chel often appears with jaguar aspects including fangs, a jaguar eye, clawed hands and feet, and a skirt of crossbones and other death symbols. In the Dresden codex, she is depicted as an aged female, often reddish brown in color.

By the time of Spanish contact, the Yucatec Maya worshiped Ix Chel primarily as a goddess of childbirth, divination, and weaving, as such she may have represented the aged moon. Women from the Maya lands and possibly all of Mesoamerica visited great shrines dedicated to her, which lay off the east coast of Yucatán on the islands of Cozumel and Isla de Mujeres. Ix Chel was an important deity to the Yucatec Maya, and like many Maya gods had very complex aspects as the foreteller and bringer of both life and death. But like the stories of Itzamna and other Yucatec Maya deities, myths of Ix Chel have not withstood the test of time; few, if any, are remembered and retold today.

See also Cihuacoatl; Itzamna; Moon; Rain and Water Deities

Suggested reading:

Coe, Michael D. 1977. "Supernatural Patrons of Maya Scribes and Artists." Pp. 327–347 in *Social Process in Maya Prehistory: Studies in Honour of Sir Eric Thompson,* ed. Norman D. C. Hammond. New York: Academic Press.

Landa, Diego de. 1941. *Relación de las cosas de Yucatán.* Ed. and trans. Alfred M. Tozzer. Papers of the Peabody Museum. Cambridge, MA: Harvard University Press.

Taube, Karl. 1992. *The Major Gods of Ancient Yucatan.* Washington, DC: Dumbarton Oaks Research Library.

JURAKAN

Time period: Postclassic–Contemporary

Cultural group: K'iche' Maya

One of the most important deities among the K'iche' Maya, Jurakan (Hoor-a-kan´) represents fire, water, lightning, thunder, and heavy rain. It remains unclear whether Jurakan was originally a male or female deity, for s/he at times appears as a figure with no ascribed gender. In the Popol Vuh, s/he creates the cosmos, giving reality to the universe. Jurakan also uses the Hero Twins as his/her messengers to, and instruments of change in, the terrestrial and lower worlds. It is by Jurakan's wish that the Hero Twins defeat the three deities 7-Macaw, Zipacna, and Earthquake. S/he also embodies the K'iche' Maya conceptualization of the great unifying force of the universe. The name *Jurakan* is derived from the Carib word *huracan* (hurricane); Jurakan is the hurricane, the terrifyingly unpredictable and destructive forces that bring new life and creation through the water and the wind.

See also Hero Twins; Rain and Water Deities

Suggested reading:

Preuss, Mary H. 1988. *Gods of the Popol Vuh: Xmucane, Kucumatz, Tojil, and Jurakan.* Culver City, CA: Labyrinthos.

Tedlock, Dennis, trans. 1985. *Popol Vuh: The Definitive Edition of the Mayan Book of the Dawn of Life and the Glories of Gods and Kings.* New York: Simon and Schuster.

KINICH AHAU

Time period: Preclassic–Colonial

Cultural group: Yucatec Maya

The name *Kinich Ahau* (Kee-nich´ A-how´), which applies to the Yucatec Maya sun god, translates as "sun-faced lord." At one time many scholars saw this figure as an individual deity, but now most believe him to be the day aspect of Itzamna, although he bears certain traits that are entirely his own. As the sun god, he was considered by some the supernatural patron of warriors and rulers, like Itzamna. Throughout Maya prehistoric art, Kinich Ahau was identified with the jaguar, decapitation, fire, rulership, and dynastic descent.

On Classic and Postclassic Maya sculpture and pottery and in Postclassic codices, one can distinguish Kinich Ahau by an aquiline nose; eyes shaped like crosses; a large square eye in profile; occasionally a beard like the rays of the sun, its curly tendrils sprouting from the corners of his mouth; a spiral protruding from his nose when viewed in profile; and most importantly, the four-petaled Maya glyph *kin* (sun).

Among the Yucatec Maya, Kinich Ahau symbolized the sun's life in its daily travels through the sky. Thus, historically, many Classic Maya rulers assumed the name, powers, and patronage of Kinich Ahau. They did this not only to evoke the protection of a strong, supernatural force; some may have believed and wanted others to believe that they were terrestrial manifestations of the sun god and that through his divine power they kept the sun moving through its natural daily cycle.

See also Itzamna; Pacal; Sky Deities and Beings; Sun

Suggested reading:

Taube, Karl. 1992. *The Major Gods of Ancient Yucatan.* Washington, DC: Dumbarton Oaks Research Library.

Thompson, John Eric Sydney. 1970b. *Maya History and Religion.* Norman: University of Oklahoma Press.

KUKULCAN

Time period: Postclassic–Contemporary

Cultural group: Yucatec Maya

Kukulcan (Koo-kool-kan´) was a mythic/historical figure related to the Mexican feathered serpent deity Quetzalcoatl. However, for the Yucatec Maya, the name refers to two figures: one is the feathered serpent deity, common throughout the Postclassic era; the other is the Yucatec ruler/priest of Chichén Itzá, a mythical/historical figure first appearing around the end of the tenth century.

Like the K'iche' Maya deity Gukumatz, Kukulcan is a feathered serpent god, introduced from highland Mexican peoples. We know little of the pre-Hispanic Kukulcan. However, we find large temples dedicated to this deity at sites throughout northern Yucatán, such as Chichén Itzá, Mayapan, and Uxmal.

According to Fray Diego de Landa, Kukulcan was a great lord of the Maya at Chichén Itzá in northern Yucatán. He is said to have arrived around the end of the tenth century from México, where he was considered a god. Kukulcan established the city of Mayapan as the central capital of the Postclassic Yucatec Maya, and he brought all of the Maya lords to this city, dividing the towns and land among them. After many years he left Mayapan in peace and friendship.

However, the Chilam Balams (mythic histories of various Maya towns) give a different view of the individual known as Kukulcan, who is said to have existed in the fifteenth century at Mayapan, not during the tenth century at Chichén Itzá. These books describe Kukulcan as a priest of the Feathered Serpent who takes over the lordship of the city after the fall of Mayapan and the sacrifice of the Chichén Itzá ruler by the Xiu Maya. Kukulcan then leads the Itzá Maya into a series of skirmishes with the Xiu Maya, in an ill-fated attempt to reestablish Chichén Itzá's control over northern Yucatán. It is unlikely that these two Kukulcans are the same person, assuming that the dates are accurate.

Perhaps after the original Kukulcan's departure, the Quetzalcoatl priests took his name as their own. In addition, scholars have noted that *Can* denotes a prominent lineage among the Itzá Maya. Perhaps *Kukul* was merely a personal name that was given to various scions of this lineage at different times.

Contemporary Yucatec Maya groups continue to tell stories of the feathered serpent. One modern Yucatec Maya story describes Kukulcan as a young boy who was born as a snake. As he grew, it became apparent that he was the feathered serpent. His older sister took care of him and fed him in a cave. However, soon he grew so large that she could no longer feed him, and he flew out of his cave into the ocean, creating an earthquake. To calm his upset sister, who wants to know if he is still alive and well, he now makes the earth shake every July. Another story, by the Lacandon Maya, gives the feathered serpent a minor role among the gods. For the Lacandon, the feathered serpent is a huge, malevolent snake who is merely a pet of the principal sun deity and creator of human beings. Kukulcan, whether the feathered serpent deity, a pet of the creator god, the source of earthquakes, or the great Mexican leader of the Itzá Maya, plays some role in the mythic history of many Maya groups.

See also Feathered Serpents; Gukumatz; Quetzalcoatl

Suggested reading:

Burns, Allan F., trans. 1983. *An Epoch of Miracles: Oral Literature of the Yucatec Maya.* Austin: University of Texas Press.

McGee, R. Jon. 1990. *Life, Ritual, and Religion among the Lacandon Maya.* Belmont, CA: Wadsworth.

Sharer, Robert J. 1994. *The Ancient Maya.* 5th ed. Stanford, CA: Stanford University Press.

Thompson, John Eric Sydney. 1970b. *Maya History and Religion.* Norman: University of Oklahoma Press.

LA LLORONA

Time period: Postclassic–Contemporary

Cultural group: Mesoamerica

Dressed all in white, La Llorona (La Yo-ro´-na) wails in the night, often lurking around water, because her children have drowned. A dangerous woman, in some stories she kills her own offspring or brings misfortune to hapless men. Apparently a relatively new figure, she possibly hides pre-Conquest roots within her mythology, although these roots now lie very deeply buried. Like Malinche, with whom she sometimes fuses, La Llorona expresses more contemporary than ancient images of women; unlike those of Malinche, who remains largely Mexican, La Llorona's tales are spun throughout Latin America.

Women wailing in the night is not a new mythological theme. La Llorona is predated by a number of pre-Conquest Nahua mythic figures who likewise cry out nightly messages. Most of these ancient women either make demands or issue warnings about impending disasters. The female earth monster Tlalteuctli wailed in the night after Quetzalcoatl and Tezcatlipoca twisted her in half to make the earth; she demanded human sacrifice in return for her own sacrificial pain. In 1452, a weeping woman appeared to a saddened Motecuhzoma I during the great drought; he, unlike his heir who bore his name, survived that disaster. Perhaps because of that past warning, Motecuhzoma II told his chieftains to watch out for weeping women, for they could foretell an impending disaster such as conquest. Indeed, the goddess Cihuacoatl cried out in the marketplace that she was going to leave the Mexica, abandoning them to their fate. The post-Conquest La Llorona may carry some of this teary tradition, although she presents a rather different picture, in which deprivation, revenge, or malice is the motive for her wailing. Similar European myths exist that might have provided precedents for the modern Llorona.

As a mother, she wails because of a number of reasons involving her dead children. In some tales, she herself has killed them: (a) out of revenge to get back at their father, who has deserted her; (b) to conceal an illegitimate birth; (c) in order to lead a life free of motherhood's responsibilities; (d) because she wants to develop a new relationship with a man and the children are in the way; (e) because she's either widowed or abandoned, and is suffering from deprivation (in this scenario, she usually kills herself too); or (f) out of some mistake. Sometimes an accident has killed her children, or some other person has murdered them. Usually her children have been drowned, so she wails out her pain by some body of water: a spring, river, lake, or ocean. In the Malinche version of this tale, La Llorona wails because Cortés has abandoned her in favor of a high-bred Spanish wife. One such modern tale interweaves Llorona-Malinche with child sacrifice and Cihuacoatl. In this one, after the ancient gods sacrifice her children in Lake Texcoco, she turns into a female demon and warns Cortés (who admits he has wronged her) that Mexicans will rise someday against the Spaniards. Contemporary ghost tales from Guanajuato say she drowned her children and so now can be heard calling from the river during storms. Other Hispanic tales paint her as a bogeyman who will get you if you are not careful. Young women on sleep-overs challenge each other to say her name three times in front of a mirror, for then she will appear. The normal response to this is: "Not me!," or "I don't think so!" La Llorona even appears in make-your-own-mystery stories for children. A number of feminists have interpreted her figure as that of a passive woman who wails because that is her only recourse in a male-dominated world.

La Llorona also can become an evil temptress bringing great misfortune to hapless men wandering in the woods. No children appear in this story line;

instead, she fuses with a number of other contemporary female demons to lure either young men about to be wed or married men into disaster. One K'iché story tells how she appears to nighttime bathers during Lent, when the moon shines brightly. Dressed in white, she leads them on, crying and singing songs. One might hear people singing at a spring, but when one arrives, no one is there. Her cold iciness can leave a person stiff and unconscious on the road. If that happens, one must pry open his mouth and pour in a bit of kerosene to revive him. She appeared before one young man as his fiancée, telling him to come bathe. But when he had stripped to his underwear, she disappeared. This frightened him so much that he returned home naked, wearing nothing but his shorts. When his real fiancée came calling, she found him lying stiff and dead upon his bed. As with the nasty woman who appears in mirrors, one never knows what might happen if one should meet La Llorona.

See also Cihuacoatl; Cortés, Fernando; Guadalupe; Malinche; Motecuhzoma I, Lord; Motecuhzoma II, Lord; Quetzalcoatl; Rain and Water Deities; Tezcatlipoca

Suggested reading:

Anaya, Rudolfo A. 1984. *The Legend of La Llorona.* Berkeley, CA: Tonatiuh–Quinto Sol International.

Arora, Shirley L. 1997. "La Llorona." Pp. 753–754 in *Encyclopedia of Mexico,* vol. 1, ed. Michael S. Werner. Chicago: Fitzroy Dearborn.

Tedlock, Dennis. 1993. *Breath on the Mirror: Mythic Voices and Visions of the Living Maya.* San Francisco: HarperCollins.

MALINCHE

Time period: Postclassic–Contemporary

Cultural group: Mesoamerican

The historical Malinche (Ma-lin´-chay), also known as Malintzin or Doña Marina (d. 1527), served as the Indian interpreter for Fernando (Hernán) Cortés during the Conquest. Perhaps because her role in that event proved so enormous, at least seven more distinctive mythological strands have developed that reach well beyond and sometimes completely outside her original historical tale, and multiply her personality in some amazing ways.

The few resources documenting Malinche's actual life are far more scarce than the extravagant mythology surrounding her. What little one can learn from early documents suggests that she was born to Nahuatl speaking parents of high lineage, the chiefs of a small town somewhere in the modern states of Jalisco or Veracruz. Bernal Díaz del Castillo, the captain in Cortés's army who documented the Conquest, weaves a romantic tale around her, which he swears is true because he claims to have met her parents. He says that, after her father died, she was given by her mother and stepfather to people from Xicalango because her parents did not want her to succeed to the throne, preferring instead that her half brother become ruler. Díaz claims Malinche's parents faked her death by telling the townspeople that a newly deceased slave's child was Malinche. They then gave her to the Maya of Tabasco. Pre-Conquest women sometimes did become rulers, so it is possible that her stepfather sought to consolidate his political control in this manner.

Cortés received Malinche as part of a package of gifts given him by the Tabasco Maya. The twenty women who came with the package were promptly baptized, given Christian names, and parceled out to various soldiers as concubines. One linguistic theory suggests that Malinche's name might be based on the Nahuatl day-sign *malinalli* (named for a type of grass); but more likely Malinche is a Spanish reworking of Malintzin, which is probably a native Nahuatl reworking of her Spanish baptismal name Marina. Thus even her name embeds the mestizo mix that came to characterize Mexico, a theme appearing in some of her later mythic personalities.

As soon as Cortés realized Malinche could speak both Maya and Nahuatl, the language most widely understood throughout Mesoamerica, she became his translator and lover. Malinche spoke Nahuatl to either a native Nahuatl speaker or someone translating Nahuatl into the local tongue; then she translated that into Maya for Jerónimo de Águilar, a Spanish sailor who had learned to speak Maya while living shipwrecked among the Indians; and finally, Águilar translated the message into Spanish for Cortés. Eventually, Malinche learned Spanish, simplifying this three- and sometimes four-way interpretive process. She bore Cortés a favorite son named Martín; and after the Conquest, Cortés gave her away in a proper Christian marriage to Juan Jaramillo, a Nahuatl gentleman with whom she bore a daughter in 1527. Unfortunately, she died shortly after.

Far more than a translator, Malinche was extremely skilled in the very difficult art of lordly rhetoric used in the presence of notables such as rulers, and she proved a skilled negotiator on many occasions. The only way for her to have learned these skills would have been for her to have trained for court life, which lends some credence to Díaz's story. Given her high birth, it is likely that Malinche saw her loyalty to Cortés as dictated by elite indigenous patterns of marriage alliances. She probably played the role of a primary wife acquired through an alliance deal made between the Maya and Spanish. Thus she was expected to help her husband Cortés; in fact not to do so would be to break the alliance, thereby placing her former Maya stepfamily in jeopardy. Historically then, she was neither a traitor to Mexico nor victim of circumstances, but a highly intelligent woman performing an extremely fine job according to indigenous standards.

Malinche's various mythic strands, however, portray her in a number of quite different ways. Sometimes these strands intertwine with one another, and sometimes they act completely independently. The first appeared during the Conquest while Malinche was still alive; people then often viewed her as a powerful "conquistadora;" and shortly after, they saw her as helping to bring Christianity to a people led astray by pagan beliefs. Indeed, this theme still appears occasionally in contemporary folk dances reenacting the Conquest. But with national independence in the early nineteenth century, a second Malinche emerged who was described in negative terms by Spanish language literature. Mexico then needed a new and more honorable national mythology, so Malinche became the traitor to an ancient noble past. These dark images still appear today. The third and fourth Malinches emerged later in the century, at which time she had taken on Euro-American mythic models of sexuality. In these tales, she became either an insatiable, conniving woman using her sexual wiles for her own gain, or an ideal mother to her mestizo children who becomes the victim of colonization and sexual violation. In the first—like Eve—she despoiled the American paradise; in the second—like the Indians of that paradise and, later, Mother Mary—she faithfully gave Mexico its first true heirs, but was wronged by the very people she served.

Many stories portray these themes, few of which find roots in the original documents describing her life. For example, she never traveled to Spain, her two children were not the first mestizos born (only Martín was mestizo, and he was not New Spain's first), she herself raised her children (they were never stolen from her), and she did not kill herself and her children because Cortés married a noble Spanish woman. This last story line intertwines Malinche with tales of the tragic and often nasty woman La Llorona who cries in the night because her children are dead. Nevertheless, such tales serve a need to portray history in a meaningful way. A fully independent Mexico needed to reject Spain and claim its ancient past, it therefore wanted to explain how its magnificent pre-Conquest civilizations could fall to European hands. To call Malinche a traitor or fallen woman does that, although that story line doesn't give full power to Mexico's mestizo heritage. To paint her as a victim, however, explains her otherwise traitorous actions in the Conquest without rejecting the ancient ways she represents or the new heirs she produced. Recently, a fifth myth has begun to emerge; in this modern tale, Malinche becomes a strong, capable woman caught in male-dominated circumstances beyond her control. This story serves as a feminist counter to the earlier overly negative or idealized Euro-American myths about women.

Oral folk traditions have presented two more themes that have little, if anything, to do with either the historical Malinche or those later tales dominating written literatures. The sixth Malinche must have developed very early. In this tale she takes on many of the characteristics held by ancient and contemporary indigenous goddesses who control the rivers, lakes, and springs and often reside in mountains. As with these deities, frogs, various snakes, and other watery creatures sometimes appear in Malinche's ritual iconography. A volcano in Tlaxcala in the Mexican Highlands bears her name, and people living on its sides see her as the carrier of moist, agricultural fertility. Others align her with Ixtaccihuatl, the great snowcapped female volcano lying just to the west of Mount Malinche; like Ixtaccihuatl, Malinche protects animals needed for food.

The seventh and last mythic strand appears as a hidden theme of indigenous resistance in the same dances that extol the Conquest and its spiritual gifts. The public or officially spoken tales of these dances describe the victory of Cortés and Christianity over Lord Motecuhzoma II and paganism, but the dancers' unspoken actions and costumes portray a more private tale in which Motecuhzoma reappears as a returning ancestor; and Malinche—as his wife, sister, or daughter—helps him reestablish his ancient rule. In La Danza de la Pluma performed annually in Oaxaca, Malinche even becomes two figures: the wife of Motecuhzoma, dressed in resplendent native costume; and Marina the consort of Cortés, dressed in rather plain European garb. In the end, Motecuhzoma defeats Cortés, regains his rule; and Marina abandons Cortés, returning to Motecuhzoma's and Malinche's sides. Thus, her tale comes full circle. Malinche continues to uphold pre-Conquest cultural patterns, but this time patterns bearing a temporal nature and social critique.

See also Cortés, Fernando; La Llorona; Motecuhzoma II, Lord; Rain and Water Deities

Suggested reading:

Anaya, Rudolfo A. 1984. *The Legend of La Llorona.* Berkeley, CA: Tonatiuh–Quinto Sol International.

Díaz del Castillo, Bernal. 1956. *The Discovery and Conquest of Mexico: 1517–1521.* New York: Farrar, Straus and Giroux.

Harris, Max. 1996. "Moctezuma's Daughter: The Role of La Malinche in Mesoamerican Dance." *Journal of American Folklore* 109, 432: 149–177.

Karttunen, Frances. 1997. "Rethinking Malinche." In *Indian Women in Early Mexico,* ed. Susan Schroeder, Stephanie Wood, and Robert Haskett, 291–312. Norman: University of Oklahoma.

MOON

Time period: Preclassic–Contemporary

Cultural group: Mesoamerica

The Moon plays counterpoint to the Sun but also acts independently in Mesoamerican cosmology and mythology. Although the Moon's phases most define its character in mythology, its relationships with the Sun and his alter-ego Venus also shape lunar myths. In Mesoamerican cosmology, the Moon usually moves through the night sky above as the Sun moves through the Underworld;

and when the Sun moves above, the Moon dives below. The Moon frequently acts on it own in determining the timing of rainfall and of childbirth, but at many other mythic times, Moon and Sun have acted in tandem—for example, in creating the world, and in disciplining its inhabitants. The complex interweaving of astronomical, cosmological, and mythic lunar themes presents a good example of how Mesoamerican deities embody particular sets of ideas: a plethora of details assembled under a fairly limited set of related themes, which may appear in groupings or alone depending on the place and time, but which always refer to an overarching idea. In this case, that idea concerns nocturnal, wet fertility in its twin-like essence, combining life with death. The Moon's participation in both creative and destructive deeds makes it fertile. The Moon as an acting, moving being frequently appears as a female creator, sustainer, or destroyer of life; but in almost as many cases, the Moon appears as an equally creative and destructive male. Often these tales describe some sort of relationship between a female moon and a male sun; a male moon and a male sun; or occasionally, a female sun and a male moon.

The Moon's role is not nearly as obvious in the Preclassic era as the Sun's. That doesn't mean it wasn't important; it just means that we still lack good information about it. Moon's mythic Preclassic existence is implied at Izapa by the appearance on a stela of what seem to be the Hero Twins vanquishing the false sun-bird. Since in the later story of the Popol Vuh one twin eventually becomes the Sun and the other the Moon, we can hypothesize that the Moon's mythic role was well developed at this time. This may very well be true, because almost everywhere in the world, lunar calendars preceded solar ones. The earliest known calendar dates appear in the Preclassic era and pertain to the divinatory calendar, which some argue was based on lunar cycles.

The Moon comes into its own in the Classic period, when both male and female moons appear in a variety of mythological situations among the Maya. A young woman sits on a lunar crescent, holding a rabbit, which in Mesoamerica appears on the full moon's surface. In some stories it is an aged goddess; but the Classic Maya seemed to prefer the Moon in her youthful state. The very male, warrior-like, ball-playing Hero Twins also come into their own at this time. The Hero Twins play the roles of Venus, the Sun, and the Moon, thereby marking the close astronomical ties among those celestial objects: Venus travels close to the sun's rising and setting, and the crescent moon often sits near Venus. The twins not only formed the world but also provided the foundations for Maya rulership. One of the major icons of rulers, a woven mat, shows up on the neck of the lunar jaguar Hero Twin; and at Palenque, rulers traced their ancestry to a lunar goddess. Mats, jaguars, and the paired Sun and Moon signified Classic rulers' powers.

During the Postclassic era, lunar veneration flourished in the Yucatán, especially at Tulum. At this coastal center, the aged lunar goddess took precedence—perhaps because there the Moon reached the end of her cycle and disappeared neatly into the Underworld's sea-waters. Some may have called an aged lunar goddess Ix Chel. Elsewhere the youthful and aging Maya goddesses depicted the waxing and waning moons, and the new moon sometimes played the part of a monster who ate the sun (explaining the solar eclipse). In Central Mexico, a male pair resembling the Hero Twins play the role of cosmic creators. In this myth, the gods Nanahuatzin and Tecuiçiztecatl jumped into a fire. As direct results of their sacrificial act, a black eagle and spotted jaguar rose from the fire's ashes, and two suns hovered on the eastern horizon. Another god smashed a rabbit into the second sun, thereby dimming its face; and the sacrifice of all the other gods, along with Quetzalcoatl's gentle puff, got the Fifth Sun's solar and lunar objects moving on their appropriate paths. The Nahua moon goddess, as either a youthful or an aged being, is less obvious than is the Maya moon goddess, although a number of similar traits are shared by various Postclassic moon goddesses in Central Mexican mythology. The youthful, defeated warrior-woman Coyolxauhqui might have been a lunar figure, as in various Maya tradition she was beheaded on the ball court; wore coral snakes and other Underworld signs, and was either the sister or mother of Huitzilopochtli in his hummingbird form, probably linking him also with the Sun. The aged goddess Cihuacoatl shares with Maya lunar figures references to the underworld, weaving, snakes, and jaguars, as well as governance of childbirth and earthly rulership. In both these cases, however, no direct statement in the written sources confirms these goddesses' lunar nature.

With the introduction of Christianity after the Conquest, moon gods and goddesses retained their prominence in mythology, but the Virgin sometimes took over aspects of their roles. The Virgin of Guadalupe, for example, came to stand on a crescent moon, repeating the Biblical tradition that spawned her—a most convenient link between European and Mesoamerican lunar mythologies. Modern Mesoamericans, like their predecessors in pre-Conquest times, sometimes address the lunar goddess as "Our Mother" and venerate her variously as either the wife or mother of God and/or Christ.

For today's Maya, the Moon's astronomical phases have the greatest affect on lunar mythology. The Maya say that the Moon disappears at the time of the new moon for a number of reasons: The Moon is now dead, and evil reigns because her protective light is lacking; or the Moon has gone to the underworld Land of the Dead, the Rain Deities, or a well or sinkhole. The waxing moon often plays the role of a young woman, perhaps one getting ready to bear children. The Tzotzil say people are fertile during the full moon, but the K'iche' say the full moon is masculine, the nocturnal likeness of the sun. For many others, this is the time of aging, a rapprochement with death. Both the K'iche' and Cakchiquel say that rain comes at the new or full moons; indeed, in this region, rain does often fall at these times. Others link the wet and dry seasons to the moon's yearly cycles. Some K'iche' say that the moon stands upright during the dry season so that water can't escape from its crescent, but lies tipped over during the rainy season.

Given the Moon's mythological connections to precipitation, it is not surprising that agricultural cycles were traditionally linked to the moon's phases. The Cakchiquel of Panajachel in the 1930s said that the moon was governed by four phases that also affected life on earth. At the new moon, people and animals were believed to be full of blood, and plants and trees, of sap; all were considered "green," even if they were old, and all were thought particularly vulnerable to death and disease. For this reason during a new moon no one was to spill blood for any purpose, whether gelding a rooster, harvesting grain, or cutting trees. As the moon waxed, people, animals, and plants hardened little by little, making it safe to harvest and cut things during the third stage, when the moon was full. But in the moon's fourth phase, people hurried to finish these activities before the new moon returned. The Yucatec Maya, however, said that maize, beans, and squash should be planted at the full moon in May or June, and everything else during the waning moon. Among the Classic Maya, Yum Kaax was a maize god who sometimes was linked with the moon and perhaps with Venus as the morning star and the rainy season. The Classic Maya God CH was the male counterpart to today's Hunahpu of Hero Twin fame; during their adventures in the underworld, both twins rose and fell with the corn they planted in their mother's courtyard.

The Moon also can govern women's cycles, pregnancy, birth, and motherhood. The Itzá said "her moon lowers" when a woman was menstruating, and the Tzotzil described the new moon itself as menstruating. The Tzotzil also said that women were most fertile at the full moon. Many Mesoamerican women counted the months of pregnancy by lunar phases. The goddess Yohualticitl of the Nahua died in the steam bath, so she now protects new mothers who rest there. And the Chamula say that every day, the Moon feeds maize gruel to her son the Sun.

The Moon often appears in tandem with the Sun, paired as dull and bright, cold and hot, sister and brother, husband and wife (sometimes fooling around with the Sun's rival, Venus), or mother and son. In Panajachel, some said that the Moon was married to the Sun. She came out at night to watch over their children, while her husband watched over their children in the east. Others in Panajachel said that an eclipse happened because the Moon was fighting with her husband. She was angry because the Sun had not been watching his children well and correcting their bad ways. Therefore, an eclipse showed how much closer the earth was to being lost because of all the wicked people. People rushed out to beat pots and pans, making a lot of noise to show that they were helping her, that they didn't want the Sun to strike her any more. They were afraid that if the Sun killed the Moon, she would take with her whomever she could. Moreover, she caused women's periods, and shaped the unborn, so a pregnant woman never came out during an eclipse; the Sun's blows might miss their mark and land on her, deforming or even killing her child. Throughout Mesoamerica, lunar stories are many and varied, but they usually have to do with fertility in its moist, nocturnal forms, both creative–forming babies, animals, and plant—and destructive—smashing ages to create new ones.

See also Christ; Cihuacoatl; Coyolxauhqui; Earth, Agricultural, and Hunting Deities; Fifth Sun; Guadalupe, Virgin of; Hero Twins; Huitzilopochtli; Ix Chel; Quetzalcoatl; Rain Deities; Sky Deities and Beings; Sun; Underworld and Caves, Deities of the; Yum Kaax

Suggested reading:

Aveni, Anthony. 1980. *Skywatchers of Ancient Mexico.* Austin: University of Texas Press.

Milbrath, Susan. 1999. *Star Gods of the Maya: Astronomy in Art, Folklore, and Calendars.* Austin: University of Texas Press.

Sahagún, Fray Bernardino de. 1953–1982. *The Florentine Codex: A General History of the Things of New Spain.* Trans. Arthur J. O. Anderson and Charles E. Dibble. Monographs of the School of American Research no. 14. Santa Fe: School of American Research; Salt Lake City: University of Utah Press.

Tedlock, Dennis, trans. 1985. *Popol Vuh: The Definitive Edition of the Mayan Book of the Dawn of Life and the Glories of Gods and Kings.* New York: Simon and Schuster.

Thompson, John Eric Sydney. 1939. *The Moon Goddess in Middle America.* Carnegie Institution of Washington pub. no. 509, Contributions to American Anthropology and History no. 29. Washington, DC: Carnegie Institution.

MOTECUHZOMA I (ILHUICAMINA), LORD

Time period: Postclassic

Cultural group: Nahua-Mexica

Motecuhzoma Ilhuicamina (Mo-te-koo-zo´-ma Il-wee-ka-mee-na), the fifth Chief Speaker of the Mexica or Aztecs (Nahua, ruled ca. 1440–1469), symbolizes the epitome of good governance. As the first of two Motecuhzomas to rule the Mexica, Motecuhzoma I represents their first real independence and power. Histories portray him as a shrewd and wise warrior and statesman, a noble leader who properly governed his people and created good order for the quickly developing Mexica state.

Motecuhzoma I followed on the heels of Lord Itzcoatl (ruled ca. 1428–1440), who first outlined the basic shape of the Mexica domain. It fell to Motecuhzoma to fill in that outline, thereby establishing the direction of Mexica hegemony for the next four rulers. It took the Spanish, during the reign of Lord Motecuhzoma II (Xocoyotzin) (ruled ca. 1502–1520), to decisively interrupt this thrust toward widespread power.

Motecuhzoma Ilhuicamina's magical birth foretold his great destiny. One night his father, the second Chief Speaker Lord Huitzilihuitl (ruled ca. 1403–1417), dreamed that he should marry the beautiful daughter of Cuernavaca's ruler, a renowned nahualli or magician. This ruler jealously guarded his daughter Miahuaxihuitl from all suitors. All manner of wild beasts—centipede, serpents, bats, and scorpions—surrounded her palace, keeping out intruders. Huitzilihuitl sent an envoy to ask her father for her hand. But he denied the petition because the Mexica were too poor to support Miahuaxihuitl in the manner to which she was accustomed. This left Huitzilihuitl very sad, but a second dream gave him hope. He was to make a beautiful arrow from the best cane, paint it most carefully, and in its center attach a greenstone shining with many brilliant lights. Standing on the borders of Cuernavaca, he shot this arrow high into the air so that it landed in the patio of Miahuaxihuitl's palace. When the princess saw the magical arrow land, she could not help picking it up. Discovering the luminous greenstone, she placed it in her mouth. Instantly she swallowed it, and thus became pregnant with Motecuhzoma I. Later, Lord Huitzilihuitl conquered Cuernavaca and claimed his heir.

Many trials awaited Motecuhzoma Ilhuicamina, including pestilence, floods, frosts, and snow that destroyed their crops, and a four year drought that caused tragic starvation among his people. But he managed them all as well as anyone could. When prosperity finally returned, Motecuhzoma successfully resumed the expansion of his domain through trade, negotiation, and war. He improved living conditions by bringing fresh water to the city, establishing penal and social laws, and setting high standards for civic and social advancement. He also encouraged the development of a sophisticated culture secure in its history and proud of its present accomplishments. Motecuhzoma is famous for reworking the Mexica calendar and recording Mexica history, and he constructed magnificent sculptures, beautiful temples, and rich botanical gardens.

In his quest for knowledge, he sent sixty magicians to their mythical place of origin Aztlan. There the goddess Coatlicue told them that her son Huitzilopochtli, the Mexica patron god, would abandon them; he would lose all the cities he had conquered for them, and return poor to Aztlan. This saddened Motecuhzoma I, causing him to weep. The myth came true when his heir and namesake Lord Motecuhzoma II lost to the Spanish conquerors.

See also Coatlicue; Huitzilopochtli; Motecuhzoma II, Lord

Suggested reading:

Codex Mendoza. 1997. As reproduced in *The Essential Codex Mendoza.* Commentary by Frances Berdan and Patricia Rieff Anawalt. Berkeley: University of California Press.

Durán, Fray Diego. 1994. *The History of the Indies of New Spain.* Trans. Doris Heyden. Norman: University of Oklahoma Press.

Townsend, Richard F. 1992. *The Aztecs.* London: Thames and Hudson.

MOTECUHZOMA II (XOCOYOTZIN), LORD

Time period: Postclassic

Cultural group: Nahua-Mexica

Motecuhzoma Xocoyotzin (Mo-te-koo-zo´-ma Sho-ko-yot´-zin), the ninth Chief Speaker of the Mexica or Aztecs (Nahua, ruled ca. 1502–1520), symbolizes the potential greatness of the Mexica, their demise, and the possible return of indigenous control. On the one hand, he's depicted as a powerful, skillful, and learned ruler who consolidated Mexica power. On the other hand, he lost to the Spanish; so he also appears as a fearful man, who vacillated at inopportune moments. But in the end, his rule and power has not been completely lost; and according to some myths, Motecuhzoma II may even return some day.

Following on the heels of his uncle the great Chief Speaker Ahuitzotl, Motecuhzoma II was the first to rise to power through his military achievements. He conquered some forty-two towns, which served to consolidate Mexica power by quelling rebellions and filling in gaps. Even Tlaxcala, the Mexica's great enemy just to the east, found itself slowly being hedged in by Motecuhzoma II and his allies; if the Spanish had not interrupted these maneuvers, the province might very well have been brought under Mexica control during Motecuhzoma's rule. He was said to be refined and discreet, to carry out his offices with great seriousness, and to be a skilled astrologer and philosopher, a firm judge, and capable in all arts, both civil and military. Moreover, he appears to have imposed a new order on the Mexica, one in which he himself was held with tremendous esteem and fear; an order that apparently was more dictatorial and less consensual than previous forms of governance.

But he also is said to have caved into the Spanish, thereby seriously debilitating the Mexica's chances at victory. At least some of these less flattering stories were probably told after-the-fact of Conquest, mythologically explaining how the Mexica had their world turned upside down. Storytellers relate how many omens predicted Motecuhzoma's downfall. A drought preceded the Conquest; a comet appeared, moving from where the sun set to where it rose; old women dreamed that a great river smashed his palace to smithereens, and old men dreamed that the Huitzilopochtli temple burned to the ground—not a good sign for the only leader able to talk directly with that fierce patron deity. Some say fire really did burn Huitzilopochtli's temple to the ground, and water only made the flames grow higher. Others say the goddess Cihuacoatl wept at night, crying, "My beloved sons, now I am about to leave you!"; and that the support beam of the House of Song, the place where warriors ritually sang and danced, sang out "Woe my evil rump! Dance well, for you will be cast into the water!" Fishermen caught a grey, crane-like bird with a mirror in its head. In the mirror, Motecuhzoma saw a number of men approaching, mounted on deer; but before his astrologers could explain this image, it disappeared. The Chief Speaker became so frightened that he tried to escape to Chapultepec where a cavernous opening led into the Underworld; but he failed at this when a vision of what he was doing warned his ritualist, who then came and talked him out of it.

At several points, Motecuhzoma II even tested Cortés, trying to figure out who he was. Was he really the returning Quetzalcoatl ready to take back his rule from the Mexica, for example? Early on at least, Cortés never comprehended enough about Mexica worldviews to make this claim, which resulted in an encounter of mutual misunderstanding. He accepted Motecuhzoma's gift of the garb of four deities (including Quetzalcoatl's) who empowered rulers; but he refused to eat the gift of food spattered with human sacrificial blood, and the magicians trying to feed him this found they could not magically control him. Finally, as Cortés approached the city, Motecuhzoma's magicians met not him on the road, but the Mexica deity Tezcatlipoca tied in ropes; the god told the Mexica they were already defeated, and he presented them with a vision of Tenochtitlan's neighborhood civic buildings in flames.

Perhaps out of fear, perhaps out of not knowing what to expect, Motecuhzoma welcomed Cortés and his army into Tenochtitlan. The Spanish quickly took him prisoner. Eventually, he died either at the hands of his own people, who had become fed up with his ineffectual rule, or at the hands of the Spanish, who in the last desperate moments of their occupation of Tenochtitlan, killed him along with several Nahua leaders they had imprisoned. The rebellious Mexica already had elected a new ruler and declared war against the conquistadors; sustaining enormous losses, the Spanish narrowly escaped the city. These stories often suggest that Motecuhzoma II failed because he had become overly proud and greedy. Had not the goddess Coatlicue already told his predecessor and namesake Motecuhzoma I that the Mexica would fail for just those reasons? Or, perhaps his new, but rather self-centered dictatorial order could not meet the extraordinary demands placed upon him by the Spanish.

Motecuhzoma II continued to live through the centuries after the Conquest, periodically resurrected in the form of rebellious indigenous leaders such as Can Ek, who claimed to be his spirit. And today he lives on in dances about the Conquest, where his role can be seen in two completely opposite ways. Their official tale is that Cortés battles Motecuhzoma II, wins, and converts the pagans to Christianity. The opposite, unofficial tale is that Motecuhzoma triumphs over Cortés, wins back his rule, all the while poking fun at the Spanish, Euro-Americans, and the Church. The first tale publicly presents the approved story, the second quietly brings to light private indigenous thoughts criticizing Euro-American rule and religion; the first maintains the status quo, the second resists and challenges it. In La Danza de los Matachines performed in New Mexico Indian towns, the public message says the dance is about the conversion of the Indians to Christianity, but the dancers enact a private, more critical message as well. A young girl wearing native dress plays the part of Motecuhzoma's mythical daughter Malinche. She goes to the spirit realm and brings the vanquished Motecuhzoma back to life. In one year that this dance was performed, Motecuhzoma called on his spirit warriors to help fight a great bull. This bull wore a T-shirt emblazoned with the words "The Saints," making an obvious symbolic link between the bull and Euro-American saints. Two native grandfathers then chased the saintly bull down, captured him, and castrated him with a toy laser gun. A sign was even hung on the bull's neck saying "Bull for Sale." The next day, an ancient traditional dance called the "Turtle Dance" was performed. And so the so-called "Conquest" was conquered, and the dance floor cleansed for a far more important event.

See also Acamapichtli, Lord; Ahuitzotl, Lord; Canek; Cihuacoatl; Coatlicue; Cortés, Fernando; Cuauhtemoc, Lord; Huitzilopochtli; Malinche; Motecuhzoma I, Lord; Nahual; Quetzalcoatl; Tezcatlipoca

Suggested reading:

Durán, Fray Diego. 1994. *The History of the Indies of New Spain.* Trans. Doris Heyden. Norman: University of Oklahoma Press.

Harris, Max. 1997. "The Return of Moctezuma: Oaxaca's *Danza de la Pluma* and New Mexico's *Danza de los Matachines.*" *Drama Review* 41, 1 (T153): 106–134.

Sahagún, Fray Bernardino de. 1953–1982. *The Florentine Codex: A General History of the Things of New Spain.* Trans. Arthur J. O. Anderson, and Charles E. Dibble. Monographs of the School of American Research no. 14. Santa Fe: School of American Research; Salt Lake City: University of Utah Press.

Townsend, Richard F. 1992. *The Aztecs.* London: Thames and Hudson.

NAHUAL (NAGUAL)

Time period: Postclassic–Contemporary

Cultural group: Mesoamerica

A nahual (Na´-wal) or nagual, is a spirit being or animistic entity closely associated with a human being. Exactly how, however, varies with time and place.

Among some groups, each person has his/her own nahual acting as a double, a shadow, or protective spirit. Nahuals often are animals such as dogs, horses, opossums, or jaguars, or natural forces such as lightning or meteors. Should one harm another person's nahual, one may harm the person who belongs to that nahual, or at minimum, make him/her very angry. When one is asleep one's nahual can go wandering, something one will see in one's dreams. One can send one's nahual out to perform a task, use it as an advisor, or even turn into it by shifting one's shape from a human to that of the nahual. The pre-Hispanic god Quetzalcoatl's nahual told him how to trick the Lords of the Dead so that he could steal the bones from which people were to be made. And a contemporary Salvadoran story tells about a woman who, on the night of a full moon, would get down on all fours on a particular rock. Turning first three times in one direction, and then three times in another, she turned into a huge pig. She then frightened people bringing their packages home from market because she wanted to steal them. But one night, a neighbor saw her do this, so he hid the rock upon which she had performed her shape shifting turns. When she returned to the spot, finding the rock gone, she turned three times in one direction, and three times in the other anyway, but nothing happened. Unable to turn back into a person, she remained a pig for the rest of her life.

The tradition of nahuals bears great antiquity, reaching from the present far back into pre-Hispanic times. Present day patron saints of towns or "hearts of the people," like their pre-Hispanic forebears, have their own nahuals to help them guard their towns. These nahuallies make nocturnal patrols, giving off evil airs to ward off rival nahuallies. Many today say that each sign of the zodiac has its own nahual; a belief, which is surely related to the ancient idea that each day sign of the divinatory calendar had its personal deity or nahual. Among the K'iche' Maya, the day a child is born determines its nahual. But, one does not tell the child what its nahual is until s/he is old enough to use the knowledge responsibly, otherwise the child might blame the nahual for her/his own bad deeds. Nor do children learn the nahuals of their siblings until they are old enough to act wisely.

In some places, professionals called nahuallies are people adept at prophesy, naming children, and treating illnesses; they sometimes also harm people. Great beings of pre-Hispanic times, such as the Mexica Chief Speaker Motecuhzoma II or the god Tezcatlipoca, often were reputed to be effective nahuallies. Now local curanderos or healers may hold similar reputations. Such individuals are often considered very powerful, even a bit frightening, however helpful or necessary they may be to the community. The linguistic root of the word nahual means to make something clear or audible. In other words, a nahualli's main task is to make things clear to others, and one of his/her main tools for doing so will be speech. Indeed, chants, songs, and poems play a central role in Mesoamerican rituals. It is no accident that a Nahua ruler like Motecuhzoma II was called "Chief Speaker;" like present-day healers, these high-placed governors often controlled events through their words. And it is said that a tiny figure of the Mexica war patron and sorcerer Huitzilopochtli danced in the hand of another sorcerer as a portent of the great ruler Quetzalcoatl's downfall. Like present-day healers, ancient magicians and soothsayers could send their nahuallies out on errands or could shift their shapes into distinctly out-of-the-ordinary forms.

See also Ajitz C'oxol; Calendar Deities; Devil; Dogs; Feathered Serpents; Huitzilopochtli; Motecuhzoma II, Lord; Quetzalcoatl; Saints; Sun; Tezcatlipoca

Suggested reading:

López Austin, Alfredo. 1988. *The Human Body: Concepts of the Ancient Nahuas.* Trans. Thelma Ortiz de Montellano and Bernardo Ortiz de. Montellano, Vol. 2. Salt Lake City: University of Utah Press.

Vogt, Evon Z. 1969. *Zinacantan: A Maya Community in the Highlands of Chiapas.* Cambridge, MA: Belknap Press.

1-DEATH (HUN CAME) AND 7-DEATH (VUCUB CAME)

Time period: Classic–Contemporary

Cultural group: K'iche' Maya

1-Death and 7-Death are the principal lords of Xibalba, the K'iche' Maya underworld. They rule and assign tasks to each of the lords of the underworld, thereby controlling events within their sphere.

Figure 63. 1-Death, Hun Came (Justin Kerr Archives, file no. 7795)

In the Popol Vuh story of the Hero Twins Hunahpu and Xbalanque, the twins' uncle Hun Hunahpu and father Vucub Hunahpu anger the Xibalba lords by making thunderous noises over the lords' heads while playing ball. (In K'iche' mythology, the ball court is the earthly entrance to the underworld.) In retaliation, 1-Death and 7-Death invite these uncle-father twins to play a ballgame so that they might defeat and kill them;

through trickery, the lords of the underworld do indeed defeat and sacrifice the uncle-father twins. Nevertheless, the next generation, the Hero Twins, trick, defeat, and sacrifice 1-Death and 7-Death just as the death lords had done to the twins' uncle and father. They thereby avenge their uncle's and father's deaths.

1-Death is a common figure throughout Mesoamerica as a deity of the Underworld. The Yucatec Maya called him Cizin; the Mexica called him Mictlanteuctli. For the K'iche', 1-Death shared his exploits with 7-Death, his twin counterpart; 1-Death, however, was the dominant one of the pair. Historically, 1-Death has origins early in Maya prehistory, appearing on Maya sculpture and pottery as far back as the Classic period.

See also Cizin; Devil; Hero Twins; Underworld and Caves, Deities of the

Suggested reading:

Taube, Karl. 1993. *Aztec and Maya Myths.* Austin: University of Texas Press.

Tedlock, Dennis, trans. 1985. *Popol Vuh: The Definitive Edition of the Mayan Book of the Dawn of Life and the Glories of Gods and Kings.* New York: Simon and Schuster.

Thompson, John Eric Sydney. 1970. *Maya History and Religion.* Norman: University of Oklahoma Press.

OPOSSUMS

Time period: Preclassic–Contemporary

Cultural group: Mesoamerica

Opossums are archetypal thieves, tricksters, mythic openers of obstructed passages, and mediators between light and night. Their strange physical traits lend themselves to themes of regeneration as well. Odd little holdovers from the Cenozoic era, these nocturnal marsupials appear everywhere in Latin America. Opossums scavenge for a variety of grains, fruit, insects, and carrion. Females have two uteri and two vaginas; their babies are born prematurely and complete their natal growth in their mother's pouch. Males have a bifurcated penis and oddly placed testicles. A Trique myth says this happened when Opossum inappropriately climbed on the back of his daughter-in-law at her wedding to dance; his members have been stuck in that position ever since. Both males and females are endowed with opposable toes, a hairless prehensile tail, and a body so strong that it can withstand many hard blows. They are known to be fierce fighters, defending themselves against enemies like jaguars or rattlesnakes, which may explain why the Chilam Balam of Chumayel says that the years associated with opossums were also associated with abusive rulers. Of course, when feigning death seems the better part of valor, opossums also "play possum." The Maya Dresden Codex linked Grandfather Opossum with the end of a dying year, and the new year with an opossum "coming back to life."

At Tlapacoya, in the Preclassic era (around 1000 B.C.), someone buried a figurine of an opossum in a building dedicated to Quetzalcoatl as Ehecatl (that is, in his wind aspect). Buried with it were twenty female figurines with children in their arms, a bride's trousseau, a wooden cradle, and human bodies curled into the fetal position. Such maternal imagery perhaps prefigures later myths joining opossums with childbirth and nursing. Moreover, throughout time, opossums have shared a great deal with Quetzalcoatl although not always as Ehecatl. Alfredo López Austin points out that both are said to steal fire; discover corn; initiate the dawn, the rain, and open the pathway of the sun; they are associated with the four quarters, the moon, maguey, and dismemberment; enjoy Coyote as a rival; and appear as an old man.

Figure 64. Old fire god. Opossum stole fire from a similar deity. (Museo del Templo Mayor, Mexico City)

Opossum images were so common in the Zapotec region during the Classic period, that some feel the animal must have been a god, although we do not know for sure if he was like Quetzalcoatl. One ceramic figure shows a richly robed opossum; another, a man dressed as the beast. Ears of corn hang around the neck of one, perhaps recalling myths linking Opossum with corn's discovery. Also during the Classic period, a workshop at Teotihuacan produced molds for making small clay opossums. In Postclassic Mixtec codices, opossums were linked with New Year celebrations, the ball game, crossroads, decapitation, the moon, and pulque. This strange creature fascinated King Ferdinand and Queen Isabella of Spain, who had never seen marsupials before. Today, some of these ancient mythological themes survive alongside a number of new ones.

Actual opossums are thieves of the first order, often snitching corn and other goodies from granaries and storerooms. Mythologically, one of the most important things they steal is fire, without which people's lives would be much poorer. A contemporary Huichol myth tells how some people discovered fire; then, because they didn't want others to get it, they guarded it closely. One night Opossum came by and asked to stay a while. They didn't trust her, but she assured them she only wanted to warm herself. Next day she thanked them very much and said she was warm enough to leave. They searched her all over but didn't find the little coal hidden in her pouch. Next night they saw a fire lit on another mesa top, and the night after, several more on other mesas; then they knew it was useless to try to recover it, since now fire was all over the world. In a Cora myth, the sky-dwelling Old One fell asleep by his fire. Opossum took some with his tail, withdrawing it little by little. Old One awoke and accused him of stealing his fire. Opossum replied: "No, No! I'm only blowing on it." Old One fell back to sleep. While he was snoring, Opossum slowly got up, sliding the fire to the cornice of the house. Just then, Old One woke up and saw what he was doing. Leaping, he caught Opossum at the edge, but the fire slid off to earth below. This made Old One so mad that he beat Opossum into little pieces with his cane; the pieces caught on fire and fell over the edge too. When this happened, Old One quit, yelling: "You're not going to steal fire from me, Opossum!" This is how fire fell to earth.

But just as actual opossums can take a great deal of beating without dying, and can come back to life after playing possum, so too can the mythic Opossum regenerate. The Huichol also say that after Opossum stole fire, people pursued her, caught her up, and beat her into many little pieces. They left her for dead. After a bit, she regained consciousness and began thinking about this problem. Beginning to get up, she put all her pieces—skin, hair, sandals, hands, top of her head, brains, everything—back in place. She was all right again and very happy. Then she thought: "Oh dear! Maybe they took that little piece I hid in my pouch." But she looked, and there it was. Taking it, she began to blow it gently into life—*wiwiwiwiwiwi.* Because Opossum brought them fire, the Huichol never eat the animals. The Cora also say that Opossum reconstituted himself after falling to earth.

Other contemporary Mesoamerican tales say Opossum was rewarded with her pouch because she brought fire to warm Mother Mary and the Christ Child. In a less salutary version of this story, the Nahua tell how Opossum wrapped his tail around a burning piece of wood to take it to the shivering Christ Child; but when he noticed that the embers had singed off all the hair on his tail, he cried: "Ah, Jesus! Ah, Jesus!" That is why he has no hair on his tail, and apparently why people invoke Jesus's name when they do something dumb.

As a thief extracts things from difficult places, so Opossum removes the obstacles from blocked passages, opening them up. The ancient Nahua believed an opossum tail made one of the best medicines for extracting splinters or foreign objects from the flesh and even bone, successfully and quickly completing a difficult childbirth, loosening the bowels, and clearing phlegm from the throat. Like all medicines, if misused, it could also produce disastrous results. They said that a dog who one night ate an opossum's tail was found at dawn dragging its intestines behind it.

Perhaps because s/he is such a good extractor, Opossum can bring the dawn, extracting it from the underworld. In the Popol Vuh, Opossum held back the dawn so that Xbalanque had time to carve a new head for his decapitated twin, Hunahpu; and only those who can help the dawn emerge could hold it back. López Austin argues that both Opossum and his frequent mythic challenger Coyote act as intermediaries between light and night. Coyote comes from the day and announces the coming of the night; Opossum comes from the night, announcing the day's coming. He also argues that Opossum travels the underworld's watery pathways, sometimes even standing in for the rain gods, the Bacabs.

Sometimes Opossum's watery pathways are on Earth's Surface. According to a Mazatec myth, at the beginning of time, the animals argued over whether rivers should be straight or curvy. To resolve the conflict, they sought out Opossum, looking in one tavern after another. Finally they found him happily getting drunk, singing, and playing his guitar. "Oh, Grandfather Opossum, should rivers be straight or crooked?" Opossum replied: "You've lost your heads! How can a river be straight? Its current will be too strong. You must make the river curvy with small whirlpools, where one can peacefully fall asleep in one's boat while fishing!" The animals applauded him for his wisdom. Indeed, Opossum is as wise as he is foolish. He brings us fire, only to burn his tail; or as a woman, she hides it in her pouch only to be beaten to pieces. Of course, s/he can put her/himself back together again—and in the end, get warm by the fire, enjoy a good drink, or snooze while fishing.

See also Earth, Agricultural, and Hunting Deities; Hero Twins; Moon; Quetzalcoatl; Sky Deities and Beings; Sun; Underworld and Caves, Deities of the

Suggested reading:

López Austin, Alfredo. 1993. *The Myths of the Opossum: Pathways of Mesoamerican Mythology.* Trans. Bernard Ortiz de Montellano and Thelma Ortiz de Montellano. Albuquerque: University of New Mexico Press.

Sahagún, Fray Bernardino de. 1953–1982. *The Florentine Codex: A General History of the Things of New Spain.* Trans. Arthur J. O. Anderson and Charles E. Dibble. Monographs of the School of American Research no. 14. Santa Fe: School of American Research; Salt Lake City: University of Utah Press.

PACAL

Time period: Classic

Cultural group: Maya

Reputedly the greatest lord to rule the city of Palenque (Chiapas, Mexico), Pacal (Pa-kal´) lived from A.D. 603 to A.D. 683. He was both a historical and a mythic

Figure 65. Pacal's sarcophagus lid, showing him descending into the underworld (drawing by Kay A. Read)

figure, as we know from extensive hieroglyphic writings and images in Palenque sculpture and architecture. His long reign and extensive building program gave him the aura of a great ruler. However, it is how his descendants remembered him after his death that makes him an important mythic figure. In fact, for centuries after Pacal's death, the Palenque rulers and his descendants revered him as an important ancestor with close connections to the cosmos. Lord Pacal's sarcophagus lid portrays him beginning his journey through the afterlife, entering the underworld Xibalba like a setting sun. Some have interpreted this image as symbolic of Pacal's transition from the earthly role of ruler to that of powerful ancestor. Other sculptures and building facades also are dedicated to Pacal and celebrate his divinity and affinity with the cosmos, providing some indication of his close association with a sun deity similar to Kinich Ahau.

See also Hero Twins; Kinich Ahau; Quetzalcoatl; Sky Deities and Beings; Sun; Underworld and Caves, Deities of the

Suggested reading:

Schele, Linda, and David Freidel. 1990. *A Forest of Kings: The Untold Story of the Ancient Maya.* New York: William Morrow.

Sharer, Robert. 1994. *The Ancient Maya.* 5th ed. Stanford, CA: Stanford University Press.

QUETZALCOATL

Time period: Postclassic–Contemporary

Cultural group: Mesoamerica

One of a number of Mesoamerican feathered serpents, Quetzalcoatl (Ket-zal-ko´-wat) was an important—albeit not the most important—deity among the Postclassic Nahua. With the Conquest, he rose to ascendancy, and today he occupies a major spot in Mesoamerica's mythology. Because of his ancient heritage and his many post-Conquest transformations, he has become extraordinarily complex. Quetzalcoatl's personality displays two distinctive, occasionally intertwined sides, each of which has many permutations. The first—his creator side, in which he participated in the creation and destruction of the cosmos and moved the wind—appeared largely in ancient oral traditions. The second—his culture hero side, in which he legitimated emerging states and provided a morally upright governance model—appeared first in oral tradition, but literary traditions quickly picked up these themes and expanded tremendously upon them. Today, Quetzalcoatl's creative side survives only loosely among the many wind deities in folk traditions, whereas his culture hero side deeply permeates literary mythology presenting nationalist symbols and social criticism.

Various Postclassic Nahua stories describe how Quetzalcoatl created the cosmos along with his sometime competitor Tezcatlipoca, or with Tezcatlipoca's counterpart Huitzilopochtli. Quetzalcoatl and Tezcatlipoca are two of four sons born to the creator couple Tonacateuctli and Tonacacihuatl. After waiting 600 years, this old couple tells them to create the world. In one version, Quetzalcoatl and Tezcatlipoca fight violently with each other; first one vanquishes the other, then the other vanquishes the first. With each battle, one of the four ages is destroyed and replaced by another. The fifth and final age is governed by Tezcatlipoca, leaving the door open for Quetzalcoatl's triumphant return; this possibility becomes mythically important sometime around the Conquest, and now underlies much of the literary mythology. In another version, Quetzalcoatl and Tezcatlipoca cooperate, first creating fire, and later, a rather half-baked sun followed by the first man and woman, Oxomoco and Cipactonal, whom they tell to work the earth and weave. They also place the Lord and Lady of Death, Mictlanteuctli and Mictlancihuatl, in the underworld; make the thirteen skies; form the earth from the fish-lizard Cipactli, whom they twist in half; and produce all the rain gods from Tlalteuctli and Chalchiuhtlicue.

But Quetzalcoatl's role was not restricted to the cosmos's creation; many stories describe how he helped create much of the world's basic stuff. He participates in the Fifth Age's formation: first, by sacrificing all the gods; then, by gently blowing on the stalled sun to set it in motion. After the Fifth Age is created, the time comes to create people who will live in that age; so the gods tell Quet-

*Figure 66. Quetzalcoatl (right) and Tezcatlipoca (left) (*Codex Borbonicus, *Museo de América/Art Resource)*

zalcoatl to go to the underworld and retrieve some bones from Mictlanteuctli and Mictlancihuatl. Mictlanteuctli tells Quetzalcoatl he can have the bones only after he blows a conch-shell horn with no holes. Quetzalcoatl tricks the lord by calling some worms to drill holes in the horn, and bees to make it buzz. He tricks the lord a second time with the help of his nahual, who tells him to yell out that he's leaving the bones behind, while actually sneaking off with them. When Mictlanteuctli finds out, he sends his minions to dig a pit in which to catch Quetzalcoatl. Being a trickster, Quetzalcoatl occasionally messes up. He falls into the pit, scatters the two bundles of bones (male and female), thereby mixing them up, and lies there unconscious. When he comes to, his nahual tells him he's ruined them; but oh well, that's the way it goes. So Quetzalcoatl gathers them up and takes them to Cihuacoatl, who grinds the bones like corn, and using some of Quetzalcoatl's blood, fashions the first people.

People have to eat, and Quetzalcoatl helps with that too. He meets a red ant carrying a corn kernel. "Where did you get that?" Quetzalcoatl asks. "Over there!" the ant replies. Quetzalcoatl changes himself into a little black ant and follows him to a great mountain filled with good things. But then Quetzalcoatl doesn't know what to do; the mountain is too big to carry, although he tries. So Oxomoco and Cipactonal cast lots and discover that the god Nanahuatzin should open the mountain. Nanahuatzin (probably lightning) strikes a great blow, and out fly all kinds of corn and seed. But the rain gods instantly snatch it all away. Quetzalcoatl, in fact, is often associated with the rain gods, as the god of wind. He puffed the sun into motion, swept the roads, moved storm clouds, and destroyed the second of the five ages by blowing everything away. Rain ceremonies often celebrated Quetzalcoatl-Ehecatl because this windy god kept the world moving.

Quetzalcoatl's importance as a culture hero appears less clear than his cosmic role, for his many stories present quite a diverse record. As 1-Reed (Ce-Acatl), or Topiltzin-Quetzalcoatl, he probably once was a real ruler who in bearing Quetzalcoatl's name also bore some of the god's powers. Some mythological histories say 1-Reed was conceived when the warrior-god Mixcoatl forcibly lay with Quetzalcoatl's warrior-woman mother; Mixcoatl had been unable to defeat her in battle, so he defeated her this way. Another tale says his mother swallowed a bit of jade, causing his conception. Family rivals killed his father; so when 1-Reed grew up, he sought them out and avenged that death. In so doing, he took control of Tula and the Toltecs. One might understand these myths as tales of internecine warfare and internal political conflict. 1-Reed–Quetzalcoatl wins in the end; for he founds a line of rulers who took his title until the fall of Tula in A.D. 1070 under the reign of Huemac-Quetzalcoatl. They say that Huemac-Quetzalcoatl inaugurated the first human sacrifice; however, archaeological evidence suggests that the practice dates back to the Preclassic Maya.

Other stories say that under Topiltzin-Quetzalcoatl's wise rule, Tula became a center of prosperity, artisanship, and good order. The ears of corn grew as large as a person's arm, the amaranth as tall as a palm tree, and cotton came in many colors; and because all was so plentiful, produce sold at low prices and no one lacked for anything. Moreover, the gold, jade, and feather work were of the highest quality. Tula's chaste Topiltzin-Quetzalcoatl practiced great austerities, did not practice human sacrifice (according to some stories), and maintained good order over a vast area. In these tales, the Toltec heritage models good society, and Topiltzin, good governance. If an upstart group like the Mexica wanted legitimacy, they needed to marry into this line, which they did. Western historians believe that the cult of the feathered serpent emerged around A.D. 900 at Xochicalco in the Mexican highlands and spread from there throughout Mesoamerica, as far south as Guatemala and Chichén Itzá in the Yucatán, where he appeared as Kukulcan. Some scholars think that Topiltzin-Quetzalcoatl traveled to Chichén after he left Tula, but recent archaeological evidence causes others to contest this.

Mythologically, Topiltzin-Quetzalcoatl's rule collapsed because of sorcery and immorality. Tezcatlipoca's magic worked against the Toltecs because Quetzalcoatl had become neglectful of his duties. Many portents led up to their fall; the Toltecs danced and drank too much, they lost in battle, and a local mountain burned. Tezcatlipoca even appeared in the marketplace with a tiny Huitzilopochtli dancing in his hand. The onlookers stoned him to death, but the stench from his body killed many of them, and disposing of the corpse killed many more. In the end, the "dead" Tezcatlipoca made the survivors drunk. In other stories, Tezcatlipoca led Quetzalcoatl astray with pulque and women; ashamed, Quetzalcoatl left Tula and traveled eastward, marking the landscape as he journeyed toward the sea. The Mexica spoke of large rocks as landmarks left by Quetzalcoatl, believing that he sat and rested on them.

Sixteenth-century stories describe him disappearing in many different ways. In one, Quetzalcoatl went eastward and burned himself up. He became the Hero Twins' uncle and father, and his heart rose as the morning star; he vanished into the underworld, and after eight days, reappeared as Venus. In another, he left Cholula for Tlilapan, where he died, his body was cremated, and he became either a star or a comet; and in still another, when he reached the sea, he climbed aboard a raft of serpents and sailed away. Yet another claims that after a series of conquests, Quetzalcoatl simply sickened and died, and his body was burned. Fray Diego Durán (1971) offers at least three more stories, some echoing common folk tales and others the Bible. In the first, as had Nanahuatzin, Quetzalcoatl cracked open a mountain and disappeared into it. In the second, he cast his cape upon the sea, made a sign with his hand, and sailed off. And in the third, just as God parted the waters for Moses, Quetzalcoatl parted the sea with his staff; he and his followers marched through safely but the water engulfed their pursuers. Some believe that such obvious Christian elements suggest that unlike the stories about his role in creation, Quetzalcoatl's culture hero stories had not grown old enough by the Conquest to acquire much consensus. Quetzalcoatl's return in the form of Cortés arose not as a prediction of the Conquest but as an after-the-fact, mythic explanation for it.

Some sources do, however, say that Motecuhzoma II believed Cortés might be the returning Quetzalcoatl, ready to overthrow the rule of Tezcatlipoca-Huitzilopochtli. Upon the first sighting of Cortés's ship off the coast of Veracruz, Motecuhzoma sent out messengers with food for the captain. He told them that if Cortés ate it, it would show that he was the returning god; and if that were true, Motecuhzoma wanted first to die, after which Cortés could take possession. Motecuhzoma also sent the strange Spaniard clothing of four gods—special garments that probably gave his own rulership its power—at least one set of which belonged to Quetzalcoatl. But if the nervous Motecuhzoma believed Cortés to be Quetzalcoatl, others probably did not, for the Mexica themselves may have deposed Motecuhzoma when tensions mounted, and they certainly fought back the invaders most ferociously. Moreover, Cortés's own actions discouraged most post-Conquest mythic remainders; it quickly became painfully clear that Cortés was not the morally upright Quetzalcoatl.

New stories developed that led to Quetzalcoatl's ascendancy as an all-important mythic figure in literary traditions. Durán thought he might have been the wandering apostle Saint Thomas. This explained both where Saint Thomas went after Christ died and why it seemed as though native tradition sometimes echoed Christian teachings. The seventeenth-century Creoles picked up this mythic interpretation and expanded it into a full-blown support of nationalism; because Saint Thomas–Quetzalcoatl predated the Spanish, Mexico could claim its own distinctive moral heritage. Quetzalcoatl becomes an evangelizer, and the noble and chaste foe of human sacrifice (which was encouraged by the Devil); he promoted a belief in a creator god, prophesied the Conquest, and promised to return to restore his own righteous rule. By the eighteenth century, Mexico was able to anchor itself in a noble history separate from Spain and without human sacrifice, enabling it to move toward independence.

After Mexico's achievement of independence, Quetzalcoatl momentarily disappears, although Maximilian briefly represented either a true or a false return in some stories. But revolution in the twentieth century really did bring Quetzalcoatl's return. *Indigenismo* triumphed, and Quetzalcoatl with it. Immortalized by Mexico's top muralists, he represented various noble interpretations of indigenous traditions. José Clemente Orozco made him an emblem of the tragic human condition, comparable to Prometheus. Diego Rivera depicted him as the great moral hero, bringer of freedom and learning, and the source of legitimate Mexican society. Rufino Tamayo painted him as the bright-feathered serpent locked in eternal cosmic battle with the dark jaguar Tezcatlipoca. Quetzalcoatl also fascinated writers and scholars. As a dual lord of sky and earth, Quetzalcoatl became, for D. H. Lawrence, the prototype of the perfect Mexican society founded on a natural, indigenous aristocracy. Writing in a manner mythically like the old friars describing Saint Thomas fighting the Devil, scholar Alfonso Caso described Aztec history as a battle between forces of good and evil, with Quetzalcoatl representing the good. Now this great culture hero has reversed what began at the Conquest; his return represents not the Spanish overcoming the Indians, but the Indians overcoming the Spanish. Although Quetzalcoatl has all but vanished from many folk traditions, his actions, if not his name, survive in cosmic tales about the wind, which still moves rain clouds and blows worlds away. In some places, San Sebastian apparently has taken over Quetzalcoatl's role as the road sweeper; a lightning bolt, not Quetzalcoatl, often meets the ant; and an opossum may steal the corn.

See also Chalchiuhtlicue; Cortés, Fernando; Devil; Dogs; Earth, Agricultural, and Hunting Deities; Feathered Serpents; Hero Twins; Huitzilopochtli; Kukulcan; Motecuhzoma II, Lord; Opossums; Pacal; Tezcatlipoca; Underworld and Caves, Deities of the

Suggested reading:

Codex Chimalpopoca. 1992. As reproduced in *History and Mythology of the Aztecs: The Codex Chimalpopoca.* Trans. John Bierhorst. Tucson: University of Arizona Press.

Durán, Fray Diego. 1971. *Book of the Gods and Rites and the Ancient Calendar.* Trans. Doris Heyden and Fernando Horcasitas. Norman: University of Oklahoma Press.

Lafaye, Jacques. 1976. *Quetzalcoatl and Guadalupe: The Formation of Mexican National Consciousness, 1531–1813.* Chicago: University of Chicago Press.

McVicker, Donald. 1997. "Quetzalcoatl." Pp. 1211–1214 in *Encyclopedia of Mexico: History, Society, and Culture,* vol. 2, ed. Michael S. Werner. Chicago: Fitzroy Dearborn.

Sahagún, Fray Bernardino de. 1953–1982. *The Florentine Codex: A General History of the Things of New Spain.* Trans. Arthur J. O. Anderson and Charles E. Dibble. Monographs of the School of American Research no. 14. Santa Fe: School of American Research; Salt Lake City: University of Utah Press.

RAIN AND WATER DEITIES

Time period: Preclassic–Contemporary

Cultural group: Mesoamerica

Rain and water deities constitute perhaps the largest, one of the oldest, most pervasive and complex group of gods and goddesses in Mesoamerica. This should come as no surprise when one considers the often difficult climatic conditions in the region; for much of Mesoamerica, water comes at a premium for only about one half the year, and it may not come in a desirable form. It can both nourish crops and destroy them with frost or floods. Yet life cannot continue without water. Therefore, these most important deities of moisture cover all aspects of water, including the unexpected, such as the fiery rainfalls and rivers of volcanic eruptions, and drought. The deities of water were created at the beginning of the cosmos, and sometimes cause its destruction. Their products seep, flow, pour, cascade and crash throughout the entire sky and earth; and the deities respon-

Figure 67. *A shell artifact (Museo del Templo Mayor, Mexico City)*

sible for this are male and female, young and old, and interact with both plain folk and royalty. Their age is immense, easily dating back to the Preclassic period, and their variety is almost mind-boggling. Nevertheless, a surprising continuity has existed throughout the ages.

Like a giant terrarium, ancient Mesoamerica had water constantly cycling through its cosmic topography. The salty sea water became sweet as it passed into the land, through the underworld, and up inside the mountains where the water deities stored it. The Mexica claimed that their high mountain basin, Lake Texcoco, actually originated from the sea. They even performed an experiment to prove this. Some men located a point along the seacoast where water was sucked in, and cast a sealed gourd into it. Then people posted around Lake Texcoco watched for it; and lo and behold, it appeared bobbing on the lake's surface a few days later. The Spanish historian Fray Diego Durán thought it likely true that the gourd indeed had traveled underground all the way from the sea, for a large portion of the basin was salty. Emerging from the underworld, water fell back over earth's surface to the sea as rain, hail, frost, snow, springs, creeks, rivers, and river-like lava flows, for volcanoes were said to rain fire upon the earth. Moreover, the sky was even said to consist of water.

An ancient Nahua story tells how the rain and water gods Tlaloc and Chalchiuhtlicue gave birth to all the water deities. They lived in a great lodging in whose patio stood four huge clay pots, one for each of the four cardinal directions. Each pot contained a different type of water: the first with good gentle rains for sprouting crops, a second with nothing but spider webs and blight, a third with frost, and a fourth with drought. The inhabitants on earth's surface received the contents of whichever pot the gods opened. The Mixtec Codex Borgia shows not four, but five rain gods: one is good and controls flowery jade-rain; the second, however, controls nasty fiery-rain; the third, fungus-rain; the fourth, windy-rain; and the fifth, flint blade-rain. It's not clear exactly what each is, but they're surely similar to the kinds of good and bad rains held in the Nahua pots. And like those Nahua pots standing at each of the four directions, the Maya rain gods, the Bacabs, held up the four differently colored corners of the cosmos.

Many say that, when the gods release their waters, they whack the pots with great lightning sticks, thunderously cracking them open and spilling their contents onto earth. The contemporary Yaonáhuac say that the gods crack whip-like lightning bolts to tame the storm clouds. In very ancient times, often these lightning sticks or whips looked like snakes similar to the fire-serpent wielded by Huitzilopochtli when he vanquished his sister Coyolxauhqui on the mountaintop. A Classic Maya ruler's heir inherited the symbol of rulership, a lightning stick mannikin scepter; the Maya rain god Chac also wielded this serpentine stick. Today, gods wielding lightning often are brash, young men like Huitzilopochtli, while thunder gods are aged. This probably has historic roots, for the pre-Conquest Huaxtecs depicted an elderly man leaning on a serpent-shaped cane.

In a sixteenth-century Nahua story, the god Quetzalcoatl discovers that corn and many wonderful grains are locked inside a great mountain, but he is unable to get them out. So, the god Nanahuatzin cracks the mountain open; then the blue, white, yellow, and red rain gods snatch all the seeds away. Likewise, the present-day Yaonáhuac say that the young lightning bolts discovered the corn; but no matter how much they crashed and thundered, they could not open the mountainous granary. Finally they called for Old Thunder-Bolt, or Nanahuatzin, who succeeded. This strenuous activity tired him so, that he asked the lightning bolts to wait while he took a brief nap, but they had no patience. They grabbed all the corn leaving poor Old Thunder-Bolt nothing but debris. Similar tales to this one are told all over Mesoamerica today.

Wind works closely with water gods because it moves clouds and stirs up waves. Quetzalcoatl-Ehecatl controlled the wind among the Nahua and Mixtec, so it is not surprising that he was honored in the same ancient sacrificial ceremonies that honored the rain gods. Some contemporary Nahua say that two kinds of wind exist, one moves rain from the sea, the other from the mountains. Once upon a time, a little cloud had to find out where his wind hid before they could be friends and be puffed through the sky. But like water, wind can be dangerous too. Each of the Mexica five ages perished in ways that sound similar to the bad waters held by the rain gods: the first was eaten by jaguars (rain gods usually sport jaguar fangs); the second by wind; the third by a rain of fire; the fourth by a great flood; and the fifth by drought and earthquakes.

Clearly today's watery gods and their ancient ancestors share a long-lived continuity. A preclassic Olmec-style rock carving at Chalcatzingo, Morelos, depicts a cave shaped like an earth monster's mouth; from its great maw emerges misty clouds raining upon corn, and a ruler sits at its entrance. In Mexica times, rulers bore responsibility for assuring a properly moist world; to accomplish this task, they embodied Tlaloc's powers along with those of other deities. Now Nahua still speak of a watery underground dwelling called Talocan, or the place of Tlaloc, which one enters through a great mawlike cave. One goes to this cave to make offerings to its inhabitants; some even travel in their dreams through this world. And silent sheet lightning courses through a Maya day keeper's blood to call attention to something happening in a dream or on a particular day. These diviners use such electrically spasmodic sensations to explain events or predict the future (see Nahual). They, as did the ancient rulers, also hold responsibility for rituals bringing rains.

If Tlaloc still lives, so does Chac. One Yucatec Maya story tells of the time when Chac wanted a servant, so he stole a young boy and took him to his sky home. But the boy proved quite a problem. He could not obey instructions. One time, in spite of being told not to, he looked in the hole left by a yam he had just dug up for Chac. Below he saw his home. So he got a rope and let himself down through the hole. But the rope reached only part way; and since he could not climb back up, he was left dangling in the wind until Chac found him and hauled him back. Another time, he swept all of Chac's party guests out of the house thinking they were nothing but dirty old frogs. Finally, wishing to play at being Chac, the boy borrowed the god's windbag, gourd, ax, and drum. With these he made a terrible rainstorm, which he could not stop, and the storm mashed the boy. Chac borrowed implements from another Chac to stop the disaster, then he revived the boy by making nine passes over his body. Well, Chac had had it with him, so he sent him home. When the boy arrived he asked his mother if the storm had done a lot of damage. When she said that yes it had, he told her he had caused it and what fun it had been!

In some areas, Saint John (see Saints) and angels have taken the place of the rain gods; and sirens or mermaids have replaced Chalchiuhtlicue and other goddesses. In response to offerings of tobacco, coffee, tamales, and bread, San Juan will send rain, or a siren will release her water from the mountains. In some Nahua towns, San Juan makes the clouds emerge from the ocean, and thunder is the sea's great roar. People celebrate his festival just as the summer rains begin, and they try not to distract him lest he forget his duty. But he can get overly rambunctious too. Once he caused so much rain that many people died; chasing him, the angels threw many clouds at him forcing him down. They tied him to the sea's bottom, so that he couldn't cause anymore damage.

Another Nahua story tells how once a woman could produce many big fat fish simply by washing her hair in the water from the local river. But when her husband found out how she produced these fish he grew upset, telling her that she had been feeding him the filth from her hair. He kicked her out. Sadly—for now she would have no children—she went to bathe in the river with other village women. Diving gracefully into the water, she emerged half fish and half woman, to the fearful amazement of all. Climbing to the top of rock, she played a lovely song on her guitar, and all her children, the fishes, gathered around to listen. Stories say that if you do not respect the siren, taking her children needlessly or not compensating her for her losses, she will retaliate. Many a hapless fisherman has found himself caught in her grips because he was not heedful. If this happens, he may have to give her one of his own children as a return payment for having taken so many of hers. Perhaps this is why the ancient Mexica sacrificed children to the rain gods annually; they needed to repay them in kind. Now all that is required is a soda or a bit of chocolate.

See also Bacabs; Chac and the Chacs; Chalchiuhtlicue; Christ; Coyolxauhqui; Devil; Earth, Agriculture, and Hunting Deities; Feathered Serpents; God L; Huitzilopochtli; Ix Chel; Jurakan; Malinche; Moon; Nahual; Quetzalcoatl; Saints; Sky Deities and Beings; Tezcatlipoca; Tlaloc and the Tlaloques; Underworld and Caves, Deities of the

Suggested reading:

Bierhorst, John, ed. 1986. *The Monkey's Haircut and Other Stories Told by the Maya.* Illustrated by Robert Andrew Parker. New York: William Morrow.

Durán, Fray Diego. 1971. *Book of the Gods and Rites and the Ancient Calendar.* Trans. Doris Heyden and Fernando Horcasitas. Norman: University of Oklahoma Press.

Landa, Diego de. 1978. *Yucatan before and after the Conquest.* Trans. William Gates. New York: Dover.

Sahagún, Fray Bernardino de. 1953–1982. *The Florentine Codex: A General History of the Things of New Spain.* Trans. Arthur J. O. Anderson, and Charles E. Dibble. Monographs of the School of American Research no. 14. Santa Fe: School of American Research; Salt Lake City: University of Utah Press.

Taggart, James M. 1983. *Nahuat Myth and Social Structure.* Austin: University of Texas Press.

SAINTS

Time period: Colonial–Contemporary

Cultural group: Mesoamerica

Mesoamerican saints often carry personalities and powers not borne by their more "official" namesakes or counterparts. Officially, saints in the Roman Catholic Church once were living persons who led exemplary lives. Sometime after their deaths, the Church recognized these individuals by canonizing them, making them Church saints. The Church's faithful invoke the names of saints in prayers, honor their memory by dedicating altars or whole churches to them, celebrate masses and special festival days dedicated to them, and sometimes even preserve their relics as precious remains worthy of particular honor. Saints serve as intermediaries between God and people, pleading on behalf of the prayerful for their special needs. Properly speaking, because of his sacred character, only God can be worshiped; saints should be venerated or offered great respect for their human virtues. They themselves do not perform miracles; only God can do that.

Figure 68. Plaques proclaiming miracles attributed to the deceased Salvadoran Archbishop Oscar Romero, Divine Providence Hospital, San Salvador, El Salvador (Kay A. Read)

The twelve apostles who journeyed with Jesus Christ; his mother Mary; various martyrs who died for Christian causes; and others of high character who present fine role models are among the many who have been canonized.

Unlike the official saints of Roman Catholicism, popular saints in Mesoamerica tend to be linked with local histories and to bear personalities and powers suited to their particular locales. Often these mythic folk are well-known Catholic saints, such as John, Thomas, Michael, Lucia, or the Virgin Mary; in Colonial times, Christ and the Cross became saints. Even today, a town or region might claim its own saint, unknown in Rome. These local saints, whether officially recognized or not, may appear to the faithful in the forms of statues or clouds, and may demand their own churches, much as the old gods required houses. As patrons of particular localities, they establish family and communal landholdings and give a community its identity; their special days therefore are celebrated moments in a group's annual ritual calendar.

Some local saints are associated with ancient Mesoamerican religious themes such as *nahualism* (see Nahual), enabling them to use their powers to help individuals, families and lineages, and towns. In many cases, a saint took over the job of a community's patron deity. In one colonial Nahua town, two elders dreamed that Santiago (St. James) was to replace their former patron deity Quail-Serpent. And so it was. Saints may heal the sick, make the poor prosperous, bring rain, support a farmer's or community's crops, or lead peasants seeking retribution and equality into often violent rebellions. Some local saints incorporate into their personalities classic Catholic taboos such as sexual transgressions that may be shared with pre-Conquest mores.

The historical circumstances surrounding the emergence of Mesoamerica's saints contributed to their uniqueness. The pre-Conquest tradition held that many if not all things of the world held a potentiality for embodying a large variety of powers. The Nahua called these powers *teo,* and everything from gods and mountains to bad little boys could embody them. When the Spanish first brought Catholicism to New Spain, indoctrination in the new religion's subtleties often proved minimal; and because conversion was both rapid and superficial, indigenous converts naturally understood this foreign worldview in their own terms. Saints took on powers not always discernible to the priests: It was sometimes difficult to tell the difference between the powers that made amazing things happen in the ancient Mesoamerican world and the miracles that also caused extraordinary occurrences in the medieval Catholic world. So even in urban areas, where Catholic education was generally more thorough, powerful miracles might be assigned ancient interpretations by indigenous Mesoamericans.

This birth of powerful local saints was encouraged through the centuries that followed by the isolation of the Mesoamerican "Popular" or "People's Church," which tended more and more to embrace popular interests and traditions. The official Church lacked sufficient numbers of clerics to meet the needs of the peasants living in the countryside, so it was common for a priest to visit a parish only once in three or more months and to stay no longer than a day or two at a time. The rest of the time, local folk saw to the day-to-day management of the church and conducted lay worship services, although they could not say mass. As a result, local communities had ample opportunity to incorporate a wide variety of folk traditions that were not historically integral to the official church but that the locals often saw as perfectly "Catholic." In this way, Catholic saints came to move the winds, bring rain, and sometimes even commit transgressions never contemplated by their Roman cousins.

In the town of Ocotlan, just outside Tlaxcala in the Mexican highlands, the Virgin Mary appeared to a peasant named Juan Diego, just as her sister Guadalupe had appeared to a different Juan Diego near Mexico City. It was an early spring evening in 1541, at dusk, when she called sweetly to him to come to where a spring sprang from beneath her feet. The holy water healed people of the smallpox that was ravaging the town. Eventually—so the story goes—the town's skeptical friars followed Juan Diego to an unusually fat tree that bore a statue of the Virgin in its middle. They placed the image in a small side alcove of their small church, but every night she bumped San Lorenzo (St. Lawrence) from his place of prominence, until the friars finally gave up and placed her in his stead, giving San Lorenzo the side chapel.

Like many Mesoamerican saints, the Virgin of Ocotlan, while probably a manifestation of the Spanish Virgin of Balbanera, nevertheless appears today in a concrete statue to help peasants in need, and she acts in very human ways. At present-day Zinacantan, San Miguel (St. Michael) similarly communicates with the faithful, diagnosing illnesses and prescribing cures. People also have found talking saints in caves, in the form of small pictures or statuettes, which they carried home and stored in boxes. San Lorenzo once was a talking saint in Zinacantan. People found him in the woods, dressed in tatters and very hungry. They brought him to the center of town, where they built a church over him. But the elders did not like a saint who talked, so they threw hot water over him to silence him. In the same area, much earlier, San Sebastián, with the help of his brother and sister, survived the deadly spears and arrows of Nahua and Spanish soldiers. His heart, which hung like a target outside his body, could not be pierced. Later the saint and his siblings were transformed into statues. Eventually a book told the villagers that San Sebastián wanted to stay where he was, with a drum that had belonged to his brother, and with his heart-target. So they built a church around him, and this is how he appears today. According to the official Church, San Sebastián was killed by arrows and then brought back to life; his form of death compares well with some pre-Conquest sacrifices in which the offering's heart was pierced by arrows.

Saints often led movements of resistance or popular rebellions against Spanish or Ladino authorities. Between 1708 and 1713, in highland Chiapas, four movements occurred, perhaps in reaction to an earlier attempt to stamp out nahualism. In three, the Virgin descended from heaven, promising to help the Indians; in each case, they built her a chapel on the spot and made offerings to her of food and incense. The fourth occurred in Chenalho. The statue of San Sebastián sweated twice, so the peasants built him a chapel. And then, the town's patron San Pedro (St. Peter) began to emit rays of light, thoroughly frightening everyone into thinking the world was coming to an end. The peasants performed many penances in response. The church officials burned the chapel.

In 1867, the Cuscat rebellion rose up in Chamula, against the harsh economic conditions of the Indians. Local saints and the Mother of God led the revolt. It all began when young Augustina Gomes Checheb saw three stones drop from heaven while tending her sheep; these stones passed to the local official Pedro Diaz Cuscat. Through Augustina and Cuscat, the stones talked to people; then, Augustina miraculously gave birth to several clay figurines, thereby becoming the Mother of God. The figures were installed as saints in a chapel, despite of the local priest's disapproval. On Good Friday, worshipers traveled to the entombed Christ in San Cristobal, where they actually sacrificed a boy between 10 and 11 years old. The sacrifice of the boy symbolically replaced the passion of Christ, allowing the Indians to reject all worship of Ladino and White gods; now they worshiped deities of only local origin. Using the cofradía system, the Indians also assigned saints to each ranch, thereby replicating the ancient social system as well. Eventually the authorities imprisoned Cuscat and Augustina; but a Mexican schoolteacher, Ignacio Fernandez Galindo, took their place, declaring that he was St. Matthew, his wife was St. Mary, and his companion was St. Bartholomew. Tensions led to the outbreak of armed conflict, which petered out around 1871.

More recently, Archbishop Oscar Arnulfo Romero was killed because he supported the peasants' cause during a civil war in El Salvador. Peasant goals often crossed with those of El Salvador's official Church, and Archbishop Romero was the Church's primary representative. At first, he had opposed the rebels, but he was converted to their cause after another priest, along with several peasants and children, was gunned down on the road to town. This opened the archbishop's eyes to the plight of the peasants, and he became a staunch critic of the military's brutality, the wealthy's greed, and the official Church's role in both. On 23 March 1980, Romero told Salvadoran soldiers not to obey military orders to kill; the next day, while saying mass, he was shot by highly trained marksmen, who fled in a shiny black car with opaque windows. On the tenth anniversary of his death, the official Church began motions to canonize him, a move considered moot by some within the Popular Church, who already venerated Romero. Although the canonization process is not yet complete as of this writing, the People's Church has assigned Romero the role of martyr and saint by popular consensus; numerous miracles of healing have already been attributed to him, and he has become the patron of more than one local congregation.

Saints can do many things. Among the Tzotzil, San Miguel can protect you from your enemies; in Oxchuk, Santa Lucia can cure a child of sickness of the eyes; and the water of the Virgin of Ocotlan can cure a variety of illnesses. San Simón or Maximón (Grandfather Simon), who also sometimes goes by the name of Judas, is well known for his ability to help the hopeless. He, however, is not an official saint, although he bears some slight resemblance to various biblical Simons. His primary shrine, at San Andres Itzapa, is maintained by a local cofradía, but many others can be found elsewhere, even in people's homes. Surrounded by written testimonials to the aid he has given people, San Simón's carved wooden statue at San Andres sits upright on a blue ceramic dais. He sports a broad-brimmed Stetson, a faded suit that was once either blue or grey, a crimson tie at his neck, and a shawl around his shoulders. A floral towel covers his lap and legs, and he wears rubber boots. The saint's right hand grasps a silver-tipped cane; his left remains empty so that it can receive the banknotes folded in half that people offer him. People also used to burn candles and copal at his feet, before he was accidentally set on fire; since then, people burn their offerings at a slight distance.

A number of saints have taken over the job of the ancient rain and wind gods. According to some contemporary Nahua, the old thunder-and-lightning people found the baby San Juan (St. John) inside a calabash. They offered him tortillas and coffee, but he didn't want either. Instead, he grew up very large and strong eating nothing but the smoke from copal offerings burned in braziers, and could strike down any enemy. When he grew larger, he went screaming through the fields, so they built him a house at the bottom of the sea.

"Do you like this house?" they asked.

"Yes, I like it. Now I won't leave," he said.

So they told him, "If you don't go, it's all yours, all the water. When God's children make you an offering, throw the clouds up so it rains on earth." The storyteller then tells us that that is why they play music, so that the clouds, which are alive, will come and rain. They also say that because he was forever looking at the sky, San Juan never sees the people celebrating his festival before the rain comes, and they certainly don't want to distract him lest he forget his duty. St. John's feast day falls on 24 June, just three days past the summer solstice, during the rainy season.

Among the Yucatec Maya, San Miguel receives the most bread at rain ceremonies because he is the chief of the Chacs. The Chortí Maya say San Lorenzo is one of the wind gods who carry the rain that makes the corn grow. He also blows the first breath into newborn children and takes it away at death, and he carries away evil winds that curers extract from sick people to make them well. Many of the shrines of San Sebastián were built over those of Quetzalcoatl in his wind form, and it is said that he "sweeps the road," just as the Feathered Serpent did in olden times. Although Fray Diego Durán compared Santiago with the sun, and Cortés and his soldiers used to yell "Santiago y a ellos!" ("[for] St. James and against them!") when they charged into battle, the Totonacs now say that Santiago is the God of Thunder. This may relate to the official St. James, whom Jesus called one of the "sons of thunder" because of his extreme zeal, but it probably doesn't hurt that Santiago's feast day occurs during the rainy season, on 25 July.

But saints' activities are not always completely noble, serious, or even particularly helpful. In the town of Santa Lucia, the story goes that Santa Lucia used to "talk with" San Tomás (St. Thomas) of Oxchuk; in other words, they were having an affair. She loved him so much that she gave him her eyes. This frightened San Tomás a great deal, so he gave them back to her. She never spoke to him again. They say Santa Lucia caused lightning to strike Oxchuk's church because she was so angry. But lightning also struck the church of Santa Lucia so strongly that it had to be rebuilt; that was the fault of San Tomás. They also say that the coupling of the two saintly lovers produced corn, beans, and wheat. Durán thought that Quetzalcoatl was the noble San Tomás; if that is so, then San Tomás apparently had lost his nobility and taken over the philandering side of Quetzalcoatl.

And nor is San Pedro always completely serious. The Nahua tell trickster tales in which San Pedro or his human namesake do some pretty silly things. In one, San Pedro helps a bored shepherd raise the dead, after which the two of them share a chicken for dinner. The shepherd, however, secretly eats the liver himself. Then San Pedro splits the money they received from their amazing feat into three piles.

"Why did you divide it into three when there are just two of us?" asked the shepherd.

"Because the third pile is for the person who would have eaten the liver, but strangely enough, we enjoyed a liverless chicken," the saint replied.

"Oh, well, I ate the liver," said the shepherd, picking up the money. San Pedro then warned him not to try raising any more dead people, and retired to heaven. Of course the foolish shepherd did, and of course he got into trouble with the Devil for trying. In another tale, San Pedro's human namesake fooled a priest by stealing his horse and then selling it back to him after he had white-washed it to disguise it. Unfortunately, he also stupidly told the priest to wash the horse, thereby revealing his lie.

See also Chac and the Chacs; Christ; Cortés, Fernando; Devil; Feathered Serpents; Nahual; Quetzalcoatl; Sun; Underworld and Caves, Deities of the

Suggested reading:

Bricker, Victoria Reifler. 1981. *The Indian Christ, the Indian King.* Austin: University of Texas Press.

Lockhart, James. 1992. *The Nahuas after the Conquest: A Social and Cultural History of the Indians of Central Mexico, Sixteenth through Eighteenth Centuries.* Stanford, CA: Stanford University Press.

Nash, June. 1985. *In the Eyes of the Ancestors: Belief and Behavior in a Mayan Community.* 2d ed. Prospect Heights, IL: Waveland Press.

Tedlock, Dennis. 1993. *Breath on the Mirror: Mythic Voices and Visions of the Living Maya.* San Francisco: HarperCollins.

SKY DEITIES AND BEINGS

Time period: Preclassic–Contemporary

Cultural group: Mesoamerica

The Sky is the opposite of the Underworld, and soars far above earth's surface, which lies sandwiched between the two. In many, many Mesoamerican cosmologies, when day rules the Sky, night governs the Underworld; and when night governs above, day rules below. Both the Sky and the Underworld are watery realms, but the upper forms the liquid walls of a great house, whereas the lower is the damp inside of a great beast; dividing the two, earth's surface serves as both a floor to the first and a roof to the second. Sky and Underworld together encase a dry, airy, inner home in which reside humans and other beings. But unlike the Underworld, the Sky cannot be entered by a living person. Perhaps this is so because humans cannot penetrate the walls of the cosmic house within which they reside; they can only pass through doorways or openings into the world below. Various nonhuman beings can and do pass along pathways coursing through the Sky's watery walls, like swimmers flowing with a river's currents. Depending on the mythic source, deities, saints, and ancestors dwell in the Sky; celestial objects such as the sun, moon, planets, and stars move through its many channels; serpents form Sky's riverways, passing into the Underworld; and birds fly through the warm air-bubble caught inside the celestial walls and earthly floor, occasionally traveling (as do most sky-beings) into the Underworld and out again. In spite of historical and geographical diversity, five related themes appear frequently in numerous celestial myths: (a) the motions of celestial objects; (b) the Sky's role in creation; (c) the cosmic space Sky helps form, and its inhabitants; (d) the role of water and clouds; and (e) the activities of ancestors and the dead, and their relationships to those still living on earth's surface.

Figure 69. The sun and moon from the Primero Memoriales, *fol. 282r (courtesy of Ferdinand Anders)*

The Sky had claimed its important mythical place in cosmic dramas by the Preclassic era. (Significantly, the earliest recorded dates also originated in this era.) Among the Olmec, a celestial plane rose above an earth-dragon floating on the ocean's surface; a fish governed the sea below. The Sky was ruled by a great solar bird-monster who helped grow the plants sprouting from the earth-dragon's back and who created the patterns of time with his motions. The Olmec carved designs commonly called skybands, of alternating suns, moons, stars, and darkness. Atlantean figures held up the sky, one at each of the four corners of the cosmos: The Olmec oriented their buildings and urban plans to celestial motions and the universe's four quarters and cosmic center. In the late Preclassic era, the people of Izapa carved depictions of a long-lipped god, part fish and part human—a probable precursor to the rain god who sent clouds and lightning into the sky's realm. Reminiscent of Olmec carvings, these Izapa artifacts also depict a solar bird-deity, a vulture-precursor to the Postclassic Popol Vuh's 7-Macaw, the false sun whom the Hero Twins defeated before they themselves claimed the celestial realm. Like the twin heroes in that later story, two figures etched on Izapan stones shoot and kill the great solar bird, and one loses his arm in the fight.

By the Classic period, the Sky had become a complex topography through which celestial beings traced their paths. The ancient Mayans likely saw the Popol Vuh's creative events unfold in the Sky's motions; and as did the Olmec, they oriented their urban centers to align with these movements. Likewise, in Oaxaca at Monte Albán and in the Valley of Mexico at Teotihuacan, Mesoamericans coordinated their buildings with the local terrestrial landscape and celestial events. Like many, many others, the Teotihuacanese followed the motions of the Pleiades, noting that it underwent a heliacal rising the same day the sun passed across its zenith. Every fifty-two years, the Pleiades' constant appearance in the night sky prepared the Postclassic Mexica for the sun's nadir, which occurred on a particular autumnal day when the rainy agricultural season was giving way to the dry season of war. At midnight on that date in the year 2-Reed, the Mexica doused all their fires and set a new one in the chest cavity of a human sacrificial offering, feeding the offering's heart to the fire. Every temple and hearth fire in the entire domain was started anew from that one conflagration. It was believed that if this meal was not accomplished, a new sun could not be born because it lacked sufficient nourishment; instead, nocturnal forces would devour all, and the Fifth Sun or Age would end.

With Christianity's introduction in the Colonial period, the cosmos's inhabitants shifted around a bit to accommodate the new deities. Some of the newcomers took over the jobs of some (though certainly not all) of the old patron, wind, or rain gods, and accordingly located themselves on Earth's Surface, in the sea, or in caves. But the celestial nature of Christianity made the sky a favored location. God, Christ, or both at once usually became the Sun, and Saint James or Santiago sometimes took over Venus's job as the Sun's partner and his path the Milky Way. Guadalupe claimed the old pre-Conquest Sun's rays, and the Moon. Of course, the Moon, Venus, and the Milky Way—like many other indigenous beings—continued in clearly pre-Conquest forms right up to the present, in spite of the changes the Conquest brought. And for many today, the inhabitants of both upper and lower realms continue to interact—sometimes pacifically, sometimes not—as they go their often diverse and complicated ways through this cosmic apartment building.

The sky can seem a remote place, beyond the reach of mere humans. As if responding to this sense of distance, the Mesoamerican dead often depart for the Sky's waterways (usually after visiting the Underworld first), and for some, babies come from that faraway place. However, while the Sky and its inhabitants may seem distant (after all, what human can fly or swim there?), its rules are not. Celestial objects move according to highly regularized astronomical laws; their motions structure all existence, and govern all life by diurnal and yearly patterns. The Sun and its companions determine when people will rise from bed, eat, and return again to their nightly slumbers; celestial motions dictate the wet and dry seasons, when people will plant, harvest, hunt, and wage war. Remote though it be, the Sky therefore is not a mysterious place; its rules are clear and theoretically discernable, actually powerful on a daily basis, and even sometimes humanly controllable.

Such powerful, theoretical clarity may help explain the nature of sky mythologies, especially those involving the motions of celestial objects. Astronomical stories generally take one of two forms. The first stresses a strong narrative, telling an often exciting story. But when one looks closer, astronomical information lies embedded in the narration, for the tale's characters act on several levels, at least one of which describes celestial motions, coordinating them with the story's mythic actions. The Hero Twins of the Popol Vuh are not just stupendous siblings who create the cosmos; they also play the roles of actual celestial objects—Venus, the Sun, and the Moon—whose motions really do appear in the sky. Such information may remain hidden to the audience, however, if they are not trained in the complex astronomical system of divinatory knowledge.

The second, more obvious form stresses astronomical knowledge over mythical narrative. The story line may be weak but the tale's structure both strong and theoretically clear. The Mexica myth of the 4-Suns follows a deceptively simple narrative pattern. Each sun or age contains some sort of inhabitants, who live in a particular kind of dwelling and eat a particular food, and each is laid out and then destroyed. The important element throughout is that each age lives for an exact period of mathematically calculable time, whose years coordinate exactly with the solar calendar. This quasi-story is more about astronomical calculation than heroic deeds or events; nevertheless, it was extremely important, for the Mexica Fifth Sun also would live according to that same calendrical pattern. Each previous age had lasted 676 years, or 13 x 52 years; so too would the Mexica Fifth Sun. Such precise knowledge gave people hope that they could control the Sky's effect on terrestrial life through sacrificial rituals; for this reason, every 52 years, the Mexica gave birth to a new sun.

The mathematical dimensions of celestial myths reflect complex astronomical patterns. For example, the Mexica associated the Milky Way with no less than three deities, Citlalicue and Ilamatecuhtli (both goddesses who wore starry skirts), and the god Mixcoatl, whose name meant "Cloud Serpent," and whose black face bore white stars. For many, the Milky Way was a celestial path made either of clouds lit by the night sky, or water flowing like a great celestial river. In one Classic Maya myth carved on bone, the Milky Way in its east-west position became a canoe carrying the Maize God into the Underworld. There he would set up three hearthstones, which would rest at the Place of Creation; these stones were three stars in and near Orion (Alnitak, Saiph, and Rigel). It was here that the first fire would be drilled; the nebula (M42) at the constellation's center was said to be the fire's smoke.

The Classic Maya Lord Pacal (A.D. 615–683) is shown on his sarcophagus lid sliding down the Milky Way (depicted as a great tree) into the earth monster's skeletal mouth. Today's K'iche' say that the black, starless cleft in the Milky Way is the road to Xibalba, the Land of the Dead, and that the Hero Twins' twin fathers were Venus at the end of its morning cycle. At this time, the planet rests near the Milky Way's black cleft, as though ready to descend into the Underworld, where it will disappear before rising as the Evening Star. The twins' twin half brothers, 1-Monkey and 7-Monkey, move through the night sky as Mars in its retrograde motion. And whereas Lord Pacal became a new sun upon death, just as did the Hero Twins, his heir Lord Chan Bahlum lived by the motions of Jupiter, coordinating all his life's major events with that planet's movements. In the 1930s, the Milky Way was Santiago's or Venus's Way, to the Cakchiquel Maya of Panajachel. When Venus appeared in the morning, it was time to grind corn for tortillas; and if the Milky Way appeared very clear at night, the new day surely would dawn cold. They also said that horses must lie down at 3:00 in the morning when Jupiter appeared, otherwise they would be injured; horses already knew this, and this was why they stumbled at that hour if out traveling.

Creation often involves the restructuring of space and its inhabitants after their sacrificial destruction. A great flood collapsed the walls and roof of the Postclassic Mexica Fourth Age. In the "Historia de los Mexicanos por sus pinturas," Tezcatlipoca and Quetzalcoatl traveled to the center of the earth, where the four crossroads met. With the help of four others, they hoisted the celestial roof with all its stars back into place; then the two gods made two great trees to hold it up. Afterward, Quetzalcoatl and Tezcatlipoca created the Milky Way, and Tezcatlipoca turned it into the god Mixcoatl (Garibay, K. 1985, 32–35). Later, the sun and moon were created out of the sacrifices of two gods, Nanahuatzin and Tecuiçiztecatl, who leaped into a fire, as did the Maya Hero Twins in the Popol

Vuh. Today, in a recreation of the cosmos's creation, Chortí diviners ritually hoist the four quarters of the sky into place beginning each 25 April. They do this every night until the rains return. In Panajachel, they said that the Sun or God the Father created everything on earth. But for the Tzeltal, the sun is the youngest of three brothers—God the Father, Jesus his Son, and the Holy Ghost or K'osh—whose mother is Grandmother Moon. K'osh, the brightest in more than one way, eventually tricked his elder siblings, turning them into wild and domestic pigs. After burning the forest to create a cornfield—against the wishes of a great bird who guarded it—he took his brightness into the sky. That is why, every day, darkness follows light.

Maintaining this cosmic space also may require sacrificial destruction either to sustain the living cosmic beings or to create what is necessary for their sustenance. The Mexica said that male warriors who had died in sacrificial rituals captured the sun each day from the Land of the Dead's inhabitants and carried it to its zenith at noon, whereupon dead women warriors captured the sun from the men and carried it down to feed the western-facing earth monster. In Panajachel, they said that the sky met the earth at the horizon, far across the sea. This is where the Lacantunes lived; unfortunately for them, the Sun ate one of them each day as it rose in the east, and another when it set in the west. According to the Cora, Opossum used to live in Old One's house, way up in the sky. Old One was so annoyed at Opossum for trying to steal his fire that he beat him into little pieces, which ignited and fell over the edge onto earth's surface. After landing, however, true to the sacrificial-transformative formula, Opossum pulled himself back together, and now people have fire with which to warm themselves and cook their food.

The Sky's space, like Earth's Surface and the Underworld, is divided into four quarters. Four roads radiate from the center, creating the crossroads at which Quetzalcoatl and Tezcatlipoca met to create the Mexica cosmos. The K'iche' say that the red road moves east; the black, north; the white, west; and the yellow, south. The black road is the cleft in the Milky Way, which leads to the underworld of Xibalba. The ancient Maya said that the roots of the great Milky Way tree lay in the south and its tip arched to the still dark spot near the North Star around which all stars rotated. At creation, the Maya gods made a house divided into eight: four corners, and four sectors. In early Colonial times, the Yucatec Maya said that four trees planted by four skybearers, the Bacabs, held up the sky; in later myths, these four leafy skybearers joined with the four Chacs, or rain gods, to do double duty.

Sometimes the sky is said to contain thirteen levels. The sixteenth-century Mexican *Codex Vaticano Latino* depicts these as vertically arranged, rising to the highest one, in which sits the creator couple. In seventeenth-century Oaxaca, the thirteenth god was called the "God of the Church's Light," and intervened in all aspects of life; the twelfth was a solar god of the hunt. It's unclear, though, whether these two deities sat on celestial levels above all the others in some hierarchy such as that in the *Vaticano Latino,* because the other eleven gods seem associated largely with earthly locations and follow no obvious order, much less a hierarchical one. Moreover, some contemporary myths say that these thirteen celestial layers form the sides of a pyramid with seven steps leading up and six leading down; and in examples of both contemporary and ancient Maya mythic systems, clouds also create thirteen layers with seven rising up and six leading down. The strict vertical depiction in the *Vaticano Latino* may indicate a Colonial re-mythologization of the Mexican myths. The document's annotator draws a clear parallel between this cosmos and a medieval European scheme when he claims that the thirteenth level contained God, or the "first cause" of all. This Spanish scribe probably was attempting to make sense of the strange Mesoamerican cosmos in his own hierarchical terms, just as the Mesoamericans were making sense of his equally strange Spanish cosmos in their own way.

At the first dawn of Mexica time, the sun's rosy rays spread through the half-lit celestial walls like dye spreading in a pool of water. Pools of water also spread in the Panajachel sky. When God made gentle movements, rain fell bit by bit; but when he moved forcefully or suddenly, then it came down in a torrent. Twelve angels did the work of God's rainmaking; each had a gourd that was uncorked during the rainy season, and filled during the dry. If too much fell, they had made a mistake. Clouds heralded rain but also hid the holes in the Panajachel sky through which it fell. Among the Chortí, celestial beings beat the clouds to encourage rain to fall. The rainmakers among the Yucatec Maya are four giants in the sky, and go by the names "Working Angels" or "Owners of the Jar Men." Like the Chacs, their ancient precursors, they stand with the four skybearers at each corner of the universe. These skybearers are subservient to the rainmakers; if lightning strikes the earth, it is because a rainmaker became angry with a skybearer and threw his stone axe at him but missed. Lightning often has been imaged as either a stone axe or a snake. The manikin scepter held by Classic Maya kings was a deified axe with a serpent foot; frequently Chac wielded this weapon as well. The Mexican Postclassic Tlaloc also often wielded lightning imaged as a serpent, and thunder cracked when the Tlalocs broke their water jars.

Others besides rain gods inhabited the ancient, watery skies. Like a rain god wielding lightning, Huitzilopochtli attacked his sister Coyolxauhqui with a fire serpent. Two of these hot celestial serpents bear the sun on their backs, arching along the famous Sun Stone's surface. Some modern-day writers have asserted that Huitzilopochtli is the Sun attacking his sister the Moon, but there is little evidence for this claim, which may be based on nothing more than a contemporary academic myth that assumed the sun must always be male and the moon female. However, feathered serpents do often appear decorated with sky symbols to show the demarcation between sky and that which lies below; their gaping mouths are passages into the Underworld. The words for snake and sky are homophonous in Maya, a linguistic suggestion of this serpentine image.

In addition to the great vulture-macaw false sun, who sat in Preclassic skies and whom the Hero Twins defeated, other birds traveled the Mesoamerican skies. Four birds sat atop the four great trees that held up the pre-Conquest sky, a different one for each tree; and each of the thirteen days of a Mesoamerican "week" claimed its own bird, representing a basic count of the Sun's diurnal travels. During the day, owls hid away in forest and caves; when the night skies rose over earth's surface, they flew out into the air above. The screech owl, or Muan Owl, sometimes is identified with the thirteenth celestial level, clouds, rain, and maize, which makes sense if one accepts the graduated pyramid rather than the hierarchical layers as the pattern of the celestial levels. In the pyramidal model, the Owl would sit on the final and lowest (not the highest) step, at the Underworld's western door. This would link him appropriately, like the maize god, both with the rain gods residing inside mountains and caves and with water's nocturnal fertility. New growth could occur only in close conjunction with the Underworld's watery death.

Yet the underworld Land of the Dead was not the only destination of ancestors and the deceased, who also traveled to the sky to become stars, clouds, birds, and butterflies, all of which could help those living on earth's surface. The Classic Zapotec in Oaxaca depicted the ancestors along with various deities in the upper portions of stone carvings, which corresponded to the sky. Ancient and contemporary Maya have said that rain and celestial clouds, as well as the smoke of incense, contain the stuff of souls—the powerful matter that keeps the universe's beings alive and moving. In Yucatec Maya, *tzak* means to conjure both spirits and clouds. The ancient Maya conjured up their cloud-sitting ancestors by ritually spilling sacrificial blood and burning incense. Today, the Maya of Yalcoba say that the pink clouds of dawn and dusk are the deserving, deceased relatives. And the Totonac dead, after wandering for four years, turn into birds, butterflies, clouds, stars, and planets who help the Sun to rise and move along its westerly path.

Stars were people who had died in Panajachel, and babies came from the skies, where they had been stars, following the sun. People continued on this solar path to the west and death, where they met the sky once again. It was said that the soul stayed on Earth's Surface for three days, visiting all of the places it wished to visit and saying goodbye to everyone. Then it started on its way to Heaven, which was a beautiful path filled with both obstacles and dangers. If one committed some wrongdoings during life, one had to stay awhile in the Underworld to pay off one's debt before rising into the sky. Just about everyone did this; for after all, who is perfect? Heaven was a great city with the best of everything. God the Sun, and all of the apostles, saints, and dead people who had paid for their sins could be found in its center. Saint Peter would let you in if you were worthy; otherwise you might sit outside the great city for years and years until God finally let you in to be judged. Thus, the Mesoamerican Sky is sometimes a living being in its own right and other times a place, a kind of upper story, in which particular beings reside and move around, and from which they influence the quality of life on Earth's surface. In either form, it is always distant, complex, intricate, and absolutely central to both life and death.

See also Bacabs; Calendar Deities; Chac and the Chacs; Earth, Agricultural, and Hunting Deities; Feathered Serpents; Fifth Sun; Guadalupe, Virgin of; Hero Twins; Moon; Opossums; Pacal; Quetzalcoatl; Rain and Water Deities; Saints; Sun; Tezcatlipoca; Underworld and Caves, Deities of the

Suggested reading:

Freidel, David, Linda Schele, and Joy Parker. 1993. *Maya Cosmos: Three Thousand Years on the Shaman's Path.* New York: William Morrow.

Joralemon, Peter David. 1996. "In Search of the Olmec Cosmos: Reconstructing the World View of Mexico's First Civilization." Pp. 51–59 in Elizabeth P. Benson and Beatriz de la Fuente, eds., *Olmec Art of Ancient Mexico.* Washington, DC: National Gallery of Art.

Garibay, K., Angel María, ed. and trans. 1985. *Teogonía e historia de los Mexicanos: Tres opúsculos del siglo XVI.* Mexico City: Editorial Porrúa.

Knab, Timothy J. 1995. *A War of Witches: A Journey in the Underworld of the Contemporary Aztecs.* New York: HarperCollins.

Read, Kay A. 1998. *Time and Sacrifice in the Aztec Cosmos.* Bloomington: Indiana University Press.

Tedlock, Dennis, trans. 1985. *Popol Vuh: The Definitive Edition of the Mayan Book of the Dawn of Life and the Glories of Gods and Kings.* New York: Simon and Schuster.

SUN

Time period: Preclassic–Contemporary

Cultural group: Mesoamerica

The sun god claims a long and complex history. He defines the cosmos and time itself; he often endures a split personality, sometimes even becoming two different beings, and shares his powers with rulers, gods, and saints. Following a westerly path through the sky during the day and an easterly path through the underworld by night (always keeping the north to his right and the south to his left), this powerful being continues to circumscribe the boundaries of Mesoamerican cosmoses in much the same manner as he has for centuries. Time itself springs from his movements; and corn, good health, and drought spring from his heat. It is therefore not surprising that many stories have been and continue to be told about this mythological being, without whom the cosmos could not function.

A celestial bird-monster probably ruled the Preclassic Olmec sky; his solar warmth and energy made things grow, and his path measured time. As early as the Preclassic, the Maya employed a four-petaled glyph called *kin,* which signified at once "sun" and "day." After all, it is the sun's motion that creates both space and time. For many Classic and Postclassic Maya, Kinich Ahau, the sun-faced lord, probably represented the Sun or Itzamna as he moved through the sky during the day. But as he moved into the underworld in the evening, the sun became a jaguar. The pre-Conquest Nahua sun had a similarly split personality. Called *Tonatiuh* (the word also means "age"), he rose like an eagle in the morning sky and descended like a jaguar at night. Central Mexicans created many solar disc images, with the sun's rays emanating outward at the cardinal and intercardinal points, as on the Sun Stone. Such discs often appeared in conjunction with particular Central Mexican rulers, as did the *kin* sign with Maya rulers. Mesoamerican rulers shared the sun's powers, and when they died, they too traveled to the underworld. The same trajectory was followed by the Hero Twins in the Popol Vuh, and by the Classic Maya Lord Pacal of Palenque. Once the Hero Twins had vanquished the Lords of Death, one rose as the heir, and the other, as the moon; when Pacal died, he passed on his power to his son, and rose as the sun. The cycle of death and life reflected in the sun's movements is traced in the architectural structure and the wall friezes in buildings at Palenque and throughout Mesoamerica, and appears also in objects connected with rulership. Given that rulers bore the sun's powers and marked time with their rule, it makes sense that Motecuhzoma II sent Cortés a cape with solar symbols decorating its surface when he first landed on the coast of Veracruz; was the stranger a ruler, perhaps even the new one to come? Fray Diego Durán noted that for the Spanish, Saint James, or Santiago, shone like the sun. After the Conquest, the sun in native mythology became Christ, or God. For some, it was both at once; for others, the solar god had nothing to do with Christ. Today, many mythological beliefs about the sun persist: Every year at the Equinox, thousands gather at the great pyramids in Teotihuacan. In 1999, as the new millennium approached, many of those worshiping at the pyramids voiced their hope that the sun would bring peace, physical fortification, and spiritual energy to earth.

Many peoples tell and have told stories of three or four previous ages or "suns" that preceded the present ones. The Postclassic Nahua said that their age, the Fifth Sun, was born of a great fire from which both an eagle and a jaguar escaped. This

Figure 70. A sun deity on an incense burner from Palenque, Chiapas, Mexico (Kay A. Read)

sun resulted from the gods' sacrifice and it could be kept alive only by similarly divine, sacrificial nourishment: Fray Bernardino de Sahagún reported rituals in which the heart was cut from a live warrior's body and offered to the sun. Just as the gods had sacrificed themselves to make the sun, people too must sacrifice their lives to keep it alive; for if the sun were to die, all would perish.

Both the ancient Nahua gods Huitzilopochtli and Tezcatlipoca also seem to bear some of the sun's powers. The K'iché' say that after they left a mythical place called Tollan to seek their home, the sun rose for the first time at Patohil, Pauilix, and Hacauitz. There the Sun showed himself for the first and last time to be the person he was. His hot, shining countenance dried up the soggy, muddy earth; and then all at once, the gods and the first animals suddenly turned to stone, which is how they remain today. If they had not, all those original voracious beasts—the puma, jaguar, rattlesnake, and yellowbite—might have given nothing but grief to humans, perhaps even preventing them from having their "day" or time. The Zapotec, however, say that the sun was created by a great lightning god named Cocijo, as were the moon, stars, earth, the seasons, days and nights, plants and animals, and rivers and mountains. Cocijo exhaled across the unformed, and everything emerged from his breath.

The Sun brings warmth and prosperity to the earth's surface. He nourishes the good health of both corn and people. When a Postclassic Nahua child was born, the midwife turned its small head toward the hearth fire to capture the sun's heat stored there. She then invoked the names of various deities including Tonatiuh and Tlalteuctli (Sun and Lord of Earth), also called "Our Mother, Our Father the Sun." Since a newborn rapidly loses body heat when first born, this was both a symbolic gesture and a physical necessity. As was true in Colonial times, today Christ often appears in local mythology as the sun. At Easter, the Sun-Christ struggles against the forces of darkness. The Kanhobal Maya say that when Christ died, he ascended a golden ladder, from which he shines down on the earth. The Tzeltal Maya relate that during the third creation or age, Jesus offered to be the sun because Lucibel or Lucifer was not giving enough light. Jesus ascended as the sun, and his mother Mary became the moon.

Other stories describe the sun in less glowing terms. The Chantino of Oaxaca say that the sun and moon were very bad little children who killed their adoptive parents. The Kekchi tell a story of a young hero who courts a beautiful woman. This Sun Lord first tries to fool her with a fake deer, and when this fails, he turns himself into a hummingbird. Entranced, she captures him and makes him her pet; but that night, she wakes to find him lying beside her in bed. She's worried because her magician father will be very angry if he finds out. So after darkening her girl's father's magical vision-giving stone with soot and filling his magic blowgun with chilies, the two escape. When her father discovers them gone, he manages to see where they went by peering through a little spot that Sun Lord unfortunately had left unbesmirched. After choking on the chilies in his blowgun, he loses his temper completely and seeks their death. He demands that a reluctant lightning god Chac create a great storm. But through shape-shifting and other magical acts, the young couple survive. Sun Lord places his beloved on a deer and sends her into the sky as our heavenly mother, the moon. Other stories tell how a young Sun tricks a brother into climbing a tree. There he either turns his sibling into a monkey or a pig. And so this long-lived and powerful being shapes the world both ancient and present, in ways both noble and violent; the Sun's character may be creative, supportive, heroic, hungry, nasty, silly, or gentle. But without him, the world would not exist.

See also Chac and the Chacs; Deer; Hero Twins; Itzamna; Kinich Ahau; Moon; Nahual; Sky Deities and Beings; Underworld and Caves, Deities of the

Suggested reading:

Bierhorst, John, ed. 1986. *The Monkey's Haircut and Other Stories Told by the Maya.* Illustrated by Robert Andrew Parker. New York: William Morrow.

Preston, Julia. 1999. "An Ancient Sun Melts Mexico's Modern Stresses." *New York Times,* 23 March, International section, p. A.4.

Sahagún, Fray Bernardino de. 1953–1982. *The Florentine Codex: A General History of the Things of New Spain.* Trans. Arthur J. O. Anderson and

Charles E. Dibble. Monographs of the School of American Research no. 14. Santa Fe: School of American Research; Salt Lake City: University of Utah Press.

Tedlock, Dennis, trans. 1985. *Popol Vuh: The Definitive Edition of the Mayan Book of the Dawn of Life and the Glories of Gods and Kings.* New York: Simon and Schuster.

TEZCATLIPOCA

Time period: Postclassic–Colonial

Cultural group: Nahua

A Nahua deity of some antiquity, Tezcatlipoca (Tez-kat-lee-po'-ka), or Smoking Mirror, played an extraordinarily important role in Postclassic Mexica life. Fray Bernardino de Sahagún called him a "true god" whose abode was "everywhere—in the land of the dead, on earth, [and] in heaven" (1953–1982, Bk 1:5). As god of the night sun, the night wind, and the cosmos's four quarters (each of which was controlled by one of his four aspects), he played a key role in cosmic creation; oversaw life events both good and bad; educated people and passed judgment on their actions; controlled success in war; legitimated and delegitimated Mexica rulership; and by the end of the Conquest, to some he had become the Devil himself. Tezcatlipoca seemingly has more names than any other Mexica deity, a fact that testifies to the age and depth of his cult. Fray Diego Durán reports that Tezcatlipoca's main festival "excelled even that of Huitzilopochtli", the Mexica patron god who shared some of Tezcatlipoca's powers (1971, 426). With the exception of the rain deities, on whom all life depended, no god was more central to Mexica mythology.

Historically, Tezcatlipoca appears to share a number of traits with God K and the other two gods of the Classic Maya Palenque Triad that legitimated rulership (Schele and Miller 1986, 48–51). Although not exactly alike, Tezcatlipoca shows the clearest affinity with God II (also called "K," or the Manikin Scepter): Both claim a serpent-shaped foot, smoke, and an obsidian mirror as major insignia; both also lay some claim to bloodletting. But Tezcatlipoca shares a few traits with the Triad's other two figures as well. As did God I, Tezcatlipoca wears a shell pendant and earrings; and like God I's namesake of the Popol Vuh, Hunahpu, Tezcatlipoca helped create the cosmos. And like God III in his underworld, jaguar form, Tezcatlipoca claims a close relationship with those felines of the night; in addition, he is the sun as it passes through the underworld, and the patron of war. Although one cannot show direct ancestry between Tezcatlipoca and the Palenque Triad, the links are suggestive.

Of course, Smoking Mirror's insignia also differ from those worn by his possible ancestors. Among the Mexica, he was usually painted black from head to toe, and depending on the circumstances, his attire could include flowery decorations made from popcorn (representing the dry, warring season); a net cape sometimes decorated with skulls and crossbones (for death and the underworld); four arrows in his right hand (used to punish wrongdoers); a deer hoof on his right ankle (for swiftness, agility, and might); a gold headband adorned with an ear and speech glyphs (because he was a good listener); bells on his ankles (he brought music to earth); and other items too numerous to list. Various stories and calendrical or ritual associations also tie him to monkeys, owls, and quail; the first perhaps represent music, and the second and third, the underworld. Indeed, Tezcatlipoca represented a large portion of life's pleasure and pain.

He and Quetzalcoatl created the cosmos together—sometimes in competition, sometimes in cooperation. Like the Palenque Triad gods, both were sons of parents who predated the present era. Those born to Tonacateuctli and Tonacacihuatl included two Tezcatlipocas, the red (called Camaxtli in Tlaxcala) and the black (the eldest and worst); Quetzalcoatl (god of wind); and the Mexica war god Huitzilopochtli (the smallest of all). This same story describes the powerful Tezcatlipoca as knowing all thoughts and hearts, and existing in all places. Another story tells how Tezcatlipoca became upset with Tata and Nene, an old couple who survived the flood that had destroyed the Fourth Age. When the pair came ashore in their cypress log boat, they lit a fire by rapidly twirling a stick in some dry tinder, and cooked some fish. But the fire smoked the skies, which annoyed the star gods so much that Tezcatlipoca cut off the couple's heads and attached them to their rears, thereby creating the first dogs. Tezcatlipoca also was one of several gods who sent Quetzalcoatl to the underworld to retrieve the bones with which people would be made, and he was among the gods who sacrificed themselves to create the Fifth Age.

But not all creation is serious. One storyteller describes how Tezcatlipoca, who sometimes appears as a monkey with a mirror on his back, gave rise to sacred music. One day, Tezcatlipoca created a black god of wind and told him to go get music from the sun. First, the wind went to the sea, where he called Tezcatlipoca's helpers: a turtle, a mermaid, and a whale. These three formed a bridge upon which the wind god crossed the ocean. When the sun saw him coming, he warned his musicians not to answer him, or else they would have to follow the wind back to where he came from. But when the wind arrived, he didn't speak to the musicians; instead, he sang to them. One of them, unable to resist the call, answered. Of course, he had to follow the wind back to earth, and that is how people got music for praying and dancing. The Colonial-era teller of this story adds that this music includes the organ one hears in Christian churches.

In pre-Hispanic times, Tezcatlipoca served as a potent deity leading both the Mexica and their enemies into war. Smoking Mirror also controlled many of life's good and bad things. All Mexica had shrines to him in their houses, and he could bring people whatever they needed. Folks who properly cared for him and behaved in an honorable fashion could receive a successful and prosperous life as their reward. Those who did not or who broke their promises and otherwise behaved dishonorably might be punished with leprosy, pustules, swelling of the knees, cancers, itches, and hemorrhoids. In that case, only praying to Tezcatlipoca and owning up to one's misdeeds helped.

One had to watch out for Smoking Mirror (so named because one could not easily see him), for this skilled *nahualli* or magician (see Nahual) appeared in many places at many times, shape-shifting into many things. Sometimes this was helpful; if a coyote suddenly sprang out at you, Tezcatlipoca was warning you that robbers were nearby and you ought to go home. At other times, it was an ill omen; if a passing skunk left its smell in your house, Tezcatlipoca was saying that the householder would soon die. Or sometimes how one acted affected the outcome. If you heard the sound of an ax splitting wood at night, Tezcatlipoca was lurking nearby and would appear as a headless creature whose split chest made a sucking noise with every breath. Then you should grab him and hang tight until he promised to give you three or four bloodletting thorns before you let him go. If you did, he would reward you with riches and success in war. But if you ran away, then you would suffer disease, slavery, or even death. A child named on Tezcatlipoca's day called 1-Death would be protected, rich, and honored, but only if he or she performed rituals properly and behaved well. A school called the Telpochcalli was housed at Tezcatlipoca's temple in Tenochtitlan; parents, both rich and poor, sent their young boys and girls to serve Tezcatlipoca and receive a good training. It makes sense that a god who judged the worth of people's actions also might bless the children and their education.

Tezcatlipoca's major feast occurred during the fifth month of the Mexica calendar, Toxcatl (3 May–22 May), at the end of the dry, warring season, just before the spring rains fell. They honored him on the first day of this month. A young man, perfect in his physical beauty, played Tezcatlipoca's role for a year before the festival. He was trained to play the flute, to sing, and to speak, joyfully entertaining everyone. This youth lived in luxury for the entire year, and enjoyed the pleasures of four women for twenty days before the festival. Tezcatlipoca's temple, courtyard, and participants were then decorated with many beautiful strands of popcorn strung on strings and dried flowers, symbolizing the fruition of the dry season. On the festival day, the beautiful young Tezcatlipoca willingly mounted the temple's eighty steps, breaking a flute on each. At the top, the priests took out his heart, decapitated him, and rolled his body down the steps; his head was strung on the skull rack to dry; and a new youth was chosen for the next year's ceremony. The Mexica also honored Huitzilopochtli during Toxcatl. Both he and Tezcatlipoca served as patrons of war; shared the same odd foot, ending in a snake or mirror; and wore a netted cape. At this time, Huitzilopochtli's image was taken to the temple and placed upon a serpent bench.

Like Huitzilopochtli, Tezcatlipoca could either lead the Mexica to victory or leave them to their own demise. When Cortés neared Tenochtitlan, Motecuhzoma II sent some nahuallis to cast spells on Cortés before he could do them harm. On the way, the nahuallis met a drunken man bound around the chest with eight ropes; he came from one of Cortés's allied Indian groups, the people of Chalco. The strange gentleman wanted to know why the Mexican nahuallis had bothered to come. Motecuhzoma might be overcome by fear, but there was no help for it, for he had already committed great wrongs and had abandoned his people. The Chalcan told the nahuallis to turn back, and magically showed them a vision of Tenochtitlan's neighborhoods on fire. Thereupon the man simply vanished; that's when they realized they had been speaking to Tezcatlipoca.

After the Colonial period, Smoking Mirror disappears from the scene, perhaps because the Spanish saw him as a great devil and worked hard to eliminate him; Sahagún called Tezcatlipoca Lucifer himself. As the underworld vanquisher of Quetzalcoatl and the Toltecs, Tezcatlipoca played that sinister role well. In one tale, he stole Quetzalcoatl's magical rain mirror, thereby causing drought; in other stories, he led Topiltzin astray. Today, Tezcatlipoca is primarily found in literary mythology, where he appears as a dark figure, recalling his mythic past as the feathered serpent's foe. Some of his magical abilities live on in contemporary folk tales about lightning and the underworld, although these abilities no longer are connected with his name. Little else of this complicated and multifaceted Nahua deity survived the violent watershed of Conquest.

See also Cortés, Fernando; Devil; Earth, Agricultural, and Hunting Deities; Fifth Age; Huitzilopochtli; Motecuhzoma II, Lord; Nahual; Quetzalcoatl; Rain Deities; Sky Deities and Beings; Underworld and Caves, Deities of the

Suggested reading:

Codex Chimalpopoca. 1992. As reproduced in *History and Mythology of the Aztecs: The Codex Chimalpopoca.* Trans. John Bierhorst. Tucson: University of Arizona Press.

Durán, Fray Diego. 1971. *Book of the Gods and Rites and the Ancient Calendar.* Trans. Doris Heyden and Fernando Horcasitas. Norman: University of Oklahoma Press.

Sahagún, Fray Bernardino de. 1953–1982. *The Florentine Codex: A General History of the Things of New Spain.* Trans. Arthur J. O. Anderson and Charles E. Dibble. Monographs of the School of American Research no. 14. Santa Fe: School of American Research; Salt Lake City: University of Utah Press.

Schele, Linda, and Mary Ellen Miller. 1986. *Blood of Kings.* New York: George Braziller; Fort Worth: Kimbell Art Museum.

TIZOC, LORD

Time period: Postclassic

Cultural period: Nahua-Mexica

Lord Tizoc (Tee´-zok), the seventh Chief Speaker of the Mexica or Aztecs (ca. 1481–1486), is more known for what he did not do than what he did. Most histories see him as a weak and ineffectual ruler. Symbolically he is the counterpoint of success, for he failed at his job and reaped the results of that failure—an early death.

Lord Tizoc was the second son of Lord Motecuhzoma I (Ilhuicamina) (ruled ca. 1440–1469) and preceded the great ruler Lord Ahuitzotl (ruled ca. 1486–1502). If Ahuitzotl is the symbol of arrogant success, Tizoc represents insipid failure. It is said that in his first war, he lost 300 warriors. As a last ditch effort, he sent in a troop of young inexperienced boys. Normally such boys would not fight, but simply observe. This time, however, they saved the day by routing the enemy and capturing forty enemy warriors to sacrifice at Tizoc's upcoming coronation ceremony. Since a ruler's first war was a demonstration of his powers, this proved a very inauspicious beginning.

His coronation foretold the nature of his reign. Amidst much gift giving and dancing, Lord Tizoc told the throng that they should enjoy life now, for one's days are numbered and one cannot dance after death. Indeed, he died early. Tizoc ruled for only five years, during which he spent much time in seclusion, failing even to complete the main temple's rebuilding, and his conquests apparently numbered very few. This seems to have frustrated his people so much that someone in his own court used sorcery to poison him. After his death, the Mexica found themselves in such a weakened position that potentially unsympathetic cities could afford to decline invitations to Lord Ahuitzotl's coronation. Some evidence, however, does suggest that he may have accomplished more than most histories let on. Thus for some at least, Tizoc mythically (if not tangibly) represents the depths of poor rulership and the deadly rewards of failure.

See also Ahuitzotl, Lord; Motecuhzoma I, Lord

Suggested reading:

Codex Mendoza. 1997. As reproduced in *The Essential Codex Mendoza*. Commentary and edited by Frances F. Berdan and Patricia Rieff Anawalt. Berkeley: University of California Press.

Durán, Fray Diego. 1994. *The History of the Indies of New Spain*. Trans. Doris Heyden. Norman: University of Oklahoma Press.

Townsend, Richard F. 1992. *The Aztecs*. London: Thames and Hudson.

TLACAELLEL

Time period: Postclassic

Cultural group: Nahua-Mexica

The Tlacaellel (Tla-ka-eh´-lel) was a high ranking official in the Mexica or Aztec government. At times the Tlacaellel seems to have held as much power as the Chief Speaker or ruler, governing alongside him in a dual rulership. This office was also called the Cihuacoatl or Snakewoman, for it took its powers from an extremely effective goddess and woman warrior of the same name. The Tlacaellel largely took care of internal affairs within Tenochtitlan, while the Chief Speaker handled mostly external affairs having to do with lands beyond Tenochtitlan's door. Symbolically the Tlacaellel was the matron or lady of the Mexica house, while the Chief Speaker was its lord.

During Lord Acamapichtli's reign (ca 1369–1403), the Tlacaellel appears to have played a secondary role to the Chief Speaker, but shortly before the reign of Lord Motecuhzoma I (Ilhuicamina) (ca. 1440–1469), the rulership of the Mexica had become a partnership. The Tlacaellel's primary duty was domestic and military counseling par excellence. Other duties included governing the city when the Chief Speaker was at war, receiving prisoners of war and visiting dignitaries in the ruler's absence, grandly welcoming the ruler home from battle, governing the city neighborhood that included the temple of the goddess Cihuacoatl, and judging elite crimes. The Chief Speaker, on the other hand, controlled their farmlands and its work force, expanded the Mexica territory through war and negotiation, harvested sacrificial offerings through war, and safeguarded the royal ancestry and its political ties through shrewdly arranged marriage alliances. Like the lady and lord of a very large household, the Tlacaellel's duties kept him largely at home watching over the house, while the Chief Speaker's duties frequently took him out to the countryside and into foreign lands.

It is said that Motecuhzoma I was born on the same day as his Tlacaellel, the latter having auspiciously arrived just before dawn. Another story relates how once the office of the Chief Speaker was offered to the Tlacaellel, but he declined it declaring that he already had the powers of a king and needed no more. Instead he suggested that the young Ahuitzotl (ruled ca. 1486–1502) become king, and he would personally train him. Ahuitzotl's arrogance did not get the better of him until after his valued counselor died. At times the Tlacaellel was given the same burial rites reserved for rulers, but on one occasion his embalmed body was carried into battle to posthumously apply his superior military powers against their enemies. It worked—they won.

However, by the time of Lord Motecuhzoma II (Xocoyotzin) (ruled ca. 1502–1520), the Tlacaellel's influence had begun to wane; maybe because of a short succession of men holding the office, none staying long enough to consolidate its power. Bit by bit, Motecuhzoma II reduced the Tlacaellel's duties to merely acting as a glorified gofer for the ruler, even executing his sometimes distasteful demands. In the end, the Mexica may have paid dearly for this change in governance, for the lack of a skilled advisor may have hurt their chances of victory over the Spanish. One of the omens prophesying the Mexica's downfall was the Tlacaellel's goddess Cihuacoatl crying in the night: "My dear children, now I am about to leave you." Perhaps she did.

See also Acamapichtli, Lord; Ahuitzotl, Lord; Cihuacoatl; Motecuhzoma I, Lord; Motecuhzoma II, Lord

Suggested reading:

Durán, Fray Diego. 1994. *The History of the Indies of New Spain.* Trans. Doris Heyden. Norman: University of Oklahoma Press.

Read, Kay A. 2000. "More Than Earth: Cihuacoatl as Female Warrior, Male Matron, and Inside Ruler." Pp. 51–67 in *Goddesses and Sovereignty.* Ed. Elisabeth Benard and Beverly Moon. New York: Oxford University Press.

Sahagún, Fray Bernardino de. 1953–1982. *The Florentine Codex: A General History of the Things of New Spain.* Trans. Arthur J. O. Anderson and Charles E. Dibble. 12 books, 13 parts. Monographs of the School of American Research no. 14. Santa Fe: School of American Research; Salt Lake City: University of Utah Press.

TLALOC AND THE TLALOQUES

Time period: Preclassic–Postclassic

Cultural group: Central Mexico

Tlaloc (Tla´-lok) was an ancient Central Mexican god of storms who, along with the goddess Chalchiuhtlicue, controlled all forms of water or lack thereof. Tlaloc, Chalchiuhtlicue, and the Tlaloques (Tla-lo´-kays) lived in Tlalocan. There the Tlaloques guarded the waters of the universe's four quarters. These waters were kept in mountains like great pots; and when it was time to release the water, the Tlaloques broke their pots with sticks, letting the water spill out. Tlaloc's great age and pervasive nature mark him as one of the most important Nahua deities, something understandable in Central Mexico's semiarid environment.

Tlaloc's image appears with lightning bolts on vases as early as 100 B.C. at Tlapacoya in the Valley of Mexico. Of course we do not know if the town's residents called him "Tlaloc," for that is his Nahuatl name and we do not know what language they spoke at Tlapacoya; nor do we know if that Preclassic god served his people in exactly the same way as Tlaloc in the Postclassic period. Nevertheless, Tlaloc's imagery remained remarkably consistent for many centuries, which indicates (if nothing else) his centrality to Central Mexican worldviews. A storm god bearing Tlaloc's goggled eyes and fang-filled mouth appears as one of the most important deities at the great urban center Teotihuacan (ca. 200 B.C.–A.D. 650/750).

According to Esther Pasztory, he even may have served as the city's patron god, sharing his power with a goddess who perhaps was older than he.

At the Nahua Mexica city Tenochtitlan, however, Tlaloc was older than their patron god Huitzilopochtli. Both these deities shared the Templo Mayor, which stood at the ritual center of the huge city. Tlaloc's small house rested atop the northern side of the pyramid, while Huitzilopochtli's rested atop the southern. Their houses marked the sun's travels along the eastern horizon: Tlaloc's marked the summer solstice and wet agricultural season; the gap between their houses marked the fall and spring equinoxes; and Huitzilopochtli's marked the winter solstice and the dry warring season. Symbolically, agriculture and war combine in the caches hidden within the pyramid's bowels. These clearly show the importance of water and nature's fertility over war's activity. Therein one finds buried many of Tlaloc's pots; numerous shells, coral, and other treasures from the sea; and a multitude of water fowl, fish, and other aquatic animals. These are often associated with sacrificial offerings, indicating that war and hunting helped feed this fertile abundance. In fact, in front of Tlaloc's house stood a chacmool, a sculptured man sitting on the ground, his open mouth exposing his teeth, and he is holding an empty bowl probably intended for sacrificial offerings of heart and blood.

The Nahua tell a story of how Tlaloc came to be. The world was created by Huitzilopochtli and Quetzalcoatl. As part of that task, the two gods created Tlaltecuhtli and his wife Chalchiuhtlicue. Tlaltecuhtli was a great toadlike earth monster wearing Tlaloc's face. In fact, Tlaloc's name means something like "inside the earth," a wonderful metaphor for the moist underworld. This story goes on to explain that all the deities of water were born from Chalchiuhtlicue, and that the water gods lived in a great lodging, in whose patio stood four huge clay pots of water. One pot contained very good water, fine gentle rains for sprouting crops. But, the other three were very bad: one contained blight and spider webs; another contained frost; and the last contained drought. The rain gods stood in the four quarters of this house and, depending on which pots they chose to break with their sticks, sent their contents flying to Earth's Surface.

To honor Tlaloc and the Tlaloques, the Mexica celebrated a number of rituals during the driest season until the spring rains good for sprouting were falling. They also celebrated a ritual at the very end of the rainy season, when a thunderstorm or two could still crash through the skies. During the dry season, children were sacrificed on Mount Tlaloc and at the mountain abodes of other rain deities to give them nourishment and strength, for the Tlaloques would need that to break the appropriate pots. Once the rains had started, people sacrificed amaranth cakes and ate a stew made of the flesh of sacrificed slaves, thus sharing their meal with the deities who made all food possible, but who also could send blight, killing frosts, and drought. Tlaloc displayed his dangerous powers by consuming one of the four ages preceding the Mexica Fifth Sun. Volcanic action demolished the Third Sun or Age 4-Rainstorm by raining fire down upon earth's surface from a mountain; Tlaloc's face signifies this age. If the Fifth Age was to continue, people needed to keep these gods well nourished.

If people attended to Tlaloc properly, he could help in wonderful ways. The Mexica defeated the Toltecs, the previous people in power, with Tlaloc's help; the storm god sent drought upon them, while bringing fresh rains to the Mexica. It's not surprising then that one of the four deities from whom Mexica rulers gained their power was Tlaloc, or that Motecuhzoma II made a gift of Tlaloc's garb to Cortés when he first appeared on the coast of Veracruz. After all, life itself depended on this deity. Needless to say, Cortés did not appreciate the significance of this gift.

See also Bacabs; Chac and the Chacs; Chalchiuhtlicue; Christ; Cortés, Fernando; Earth, Agricultural, and Hunting Deities; Feathered Spirits; Fifth Sun; Huitzilopochtli; Jurakan; Motecuhzoma II, Lord; Rain and Water Deities; Sky Deities and Beings; Underworld and Caves, Deities of the

Suggested reading:

Codex Chimalpopoca. 1992b. As reproduced in *History and Mythology of the Aztecs: The Codex Chimalpopoca.* Trans. John Bierhorst. Tucson: University of Arizona Press.

Durán, Fray Diego. 1994. *The History of the Indies of New Spain.* Trans. Doris Heyden. Norman: University of Oklahoma Press.

Pasztory, Esther. 1997. *Teotihuacan: An Experiment in Living.* Norman: University of Oklahoma Press.

Sahagún, Fray Bernardino de. 1953–1982. *The Florentine Codex: A General History of the Things of New Spain.* Trans. Arthur J. O. Anderson and Charles E. Dibble. 12 books, 13 parts. Monographs of the School of American Research no. 14. Santa Fe: School of American Research; Salt Lake City: University of Utah Press.

UNDERWORLD AND CAVES, DEITIES OF THE

Time period: Archaic–Contemporary

Cultural group: Mesoamerica

When one enters the Underworld through one of its cave openings, one passes into a world that is the reverse of the one above. As the bright air rises far above dry Earth's Surface, the dark, wet, subterranean Underworld extends deep below. One world depends on the other; for without both sides of this cosmic coin, the universe would fall out of balance, bringing such disasters as extreme drought or flood. When the two are in balance, the upper world provides the warmth and light of the sun, and the Underworld provides the moisture and nourishment of water, sometimes provided by beings who live in the Underworld or beyond the

Figure 71. The mouth of Loltún Cave, Yucatán, Mexico (Kay A. Read)

bubble covering Earth's Surface. Both the dry air above and the wet realm below are absolutely necessary to the growth and health of those living sandwiched between, on Earth's Surface. But at times the underworld almost seems to take precedence over the upper; for without destruction, creation could not happen, motion would stop, and things would stagnate. The Underworld provides the cosmos with the damaging forces that people may not particularly like but nevertheless know are both necessary and inescapable. Life cannot exist without death, for life rises from the disintegrating, nourishing corruption of the Underworld, like plants springing from dark, rotting loam. The complex, interior realm of Earth houses the forces of night, spawns disease, encases death, and consumes food that is absolutely the opposite of the Upper World's nourishment. At times, Mesoamericans conceive of the Earth as female and the Sky as male; occasionally, the terrestrial realm is viewed as male. More commonly, both the upper and the lower worlds are ungendered, although each harbors its own distinctive male and female beings.

The Underworld is one of the earliest mythic themes in recorded Mesoamerican history. The ritual use of the Loltún Caves in Yucatán suggests the importance of the Underworld even in the Archaic period; the burial of early Preclassic era family members beneath the floors of their houses suggests later cosmologies in which the Underworld houses the dead and the Upper World takes the shape of a human abode. By the time of the Preclassic Olmec, the Underworld begins to appear as a significant part of mythology. A great dragon was said to float on the sea's surface; from this beast's body sprouted all manner of plants. Mountains along its back housed storm clouds, lightning, thunder, and rain; and its mouth formed a cave-like portal to the Underworld. Thus the dragon's back served as the Earth's Surface, on which humans and other beings lived, while the dead dwelt in its guts, and ancestors emerged from its mouth onto its earthy spine. Olmec rulers often appear in the Earth Monster's mouth. In one depiction at Chalcatzingo, the ruler sits on a throne in the terrestrial mouth, from which mist and clouds issue; outside, falling rain produces crops. Then, as today, certain springs and caves served as points of connection between Earth's Surface and the Underworld. In fact, the core of this early Underworld imagery remains remarkably stable throughout centuries of mythic development, although its details vary.

The Classic Maya often depicted the Underworld's entrance as the great mouth of a feathered serpent; like the Olmec dragon, this beast separated the Sky from the Underworld. The K'iche' Popol Vuh offers one of the most comprehensive depictions of the ancient Maya Underworld. Honeycombed and riverlaced like Loltún caves, the Hero Twins traveled down into this dangerous subterranean world in order to eventually defeat and control the gods of death, such as the delightful 1-Death and 7-Death, Pus and Jaundice Masters, Bone and Skull Scepters, and Bloody Teeth and Bloody Claws. In order to defeat them, the Twins sacrificed themselves and returned disguised as fishermen, then musicians; after their final victory, they reemerged into the Upper World as the Sun and the Moon. The Sun traveled the sky above during the day and the Underworld by night, while the Moon traveled above by night and below by day. From this point forward, the Upper World was opposed to the Underworld, yet joined with it by the motions of the Sun and Moon; life now balanced death. The Classic Maya Lord Pacal of seventh-century Palenque also traveled into the underworld to reemerge as the Sun, while his heir stood on the head and strength of the water-lily god, perhaps a Classic throwback to the Preclassic Olmec earthdragon. These Maya rulers, like their Olmec mythological ancestors, claimed a heritage from the Underworld, and like the Hero Twins, they journeyed through it in order to achieve control of its moist forces for the benefit of the living.

Pre-Conquest Nahua sources likewise tell of the great female, aquatic, reptilian monster Cipactli, whom Tezcatlipoca and Quetzalcoatl (after turning into huge snakes) twisted into two parts. One half produced the sky, and the other, the earth. From her hair and hide came trees, flowers, and plants; from her eyes and nostrils came springs and caves, and from her mouth, the valleys and mountains. But this sacrifice now demanded a sacrifice in kind, for she cried for human hearts and could not produce fruits without human blood. The Mexica depicted the Earth Monster as a great toad or crocodile-like being. From its open, toothy mouth hung sacrificial blades; its matted hair sometimes sported insects; snakes often belted its waist, wrists, and ankles; and claw-mouth signs of death and the Underworld adorned its clawed hands and feet. The sun was swallowed each evening into its dark insides, only to be captured each morning by the souls of sacrificed warriors who fought the agents of death. But at noon, the souls of dead women warriors fought the men to recapture the Sun, and then carried him back to the Earth Monster's mouth at dusk. Quetzalcoatl also traveled to the underworld to retrieve the bones of the dead, which Cihuacoatl ground in her metate and used to mold people as though she were patting out tortillas from corn meal. Having been born of the Underworld, the Mexica also said that their dead traveled back to the Underworld and the Land of Death. There they reached a great river, where little yellow dogs carried them across to the other side and they simply disappeared.

Figure 72. Mictlantecuhtli, Lord of the Dead, Codex Magliabechiano, *fol. 79r, (Art Resource)*

When the Spanish arrived, the dark Underworld became the land of the Devil, and the Sky, the land of the new Father God and his solar-inspired son Christ. An imported Spanish depiction of Hell as a monster with a great mouth from which Christ rescued Adam and Eve and other Holy Fathers from the Devil, happened to fit very nicely with the ancient Mesoamerican Earth Monster, although the newly converted understood redemption in their own particular ways. For them, the Christian devils took on many roles of the old gods of death, water, and the Underworld, quickly moving from the European fiery Hell into the dark, dank, and river-laced passages that lay under Mesoamerica's earthly surface. For some at least, the underworld contained four parts: a hell of the damned, a place for unbaptized children, purgatory, and the limbo of the Holy Fathers whom Christ would come and release. These dead fathers became ancestors of the living, whom Christ brought to life according to foreordained, ancient prophecies (Burkhart, 1996, 124, 244). And in seventeenth-century Oaxaca, the several deities governing the underworld, death, and disease all came to be called "gods of hell," "demons," or "Lucifer," whereas their more celestial counterparts remained simply "gods"; nevertheless these terrestrial deities continued to perform their ancient functions of curing disease and caring for the dead (Berlin 1988, 18–24).

In contemporary times, the underworld differs from place to place. Caves serve as openings into its subterranean depths, as may rocks and trees; but those depths are described in varying terms. Most still consider life down below to be in some way the reverse of life above. And, although those reversals can be described in various ways, the Underworld is still wet and houses the dead and ancestors; it still serves as the source of disease and various potent deities, and the place where the Sun goes at night while the Moon travels above. Moreover, as before, its gender sometimes is clearly female, and at other times male; not particularly clear; or clearly unimportant.

Some Nahua of highland Mexico still describe the Underworld as partitioned into four cardinal lands, although these lands are very different from their Colonial-Christian predecessors. The dream traveler enters each through actual caves, streams, sinkholes, pools, or wells. Death and wind govern the northern land; women, the western; heat, the southern; and the ocean, the eastern land. Modern Nahua depict the Underworld as the exact same four-petaled flower that inhabitants of the ancient Classic highland site of Teotihuacan drew, suggesting that these modern mythic landscapes may be ancient indeed. The lords and ladies governing the contemporary Nahua Underworlds can help or hurt people who travel through their depths. They can also send to those living on Earth's Surface rewards or retribution for their past deeds. But only they can choose to do this; the most that humans can do is present these subterranean governors with respectable requests.

The contemporary Totonac also echo an ancient mythology of fate when they say that gods guide souls to a Land of the Dead governed by Linin. If one dies tragically, perhaps by drowning or murder, the god Aksini metes out punishment, making the deceased wander for four years. During this time, they call to unsuspecting people traveling near streams, and try to trap them. When their four years are up, the dead go to help the Sun rise each day, thereby making sure that Linin doesn't get him. Finally, like their Maya counterparts, they turn into stars and planets; or like their ancient Nahua warrior counterparts, into birds and butterflies; or like some southwestern Pueblo peoples, into clouds.

Some modern deities of the Underworld control one's destiny less by ancient standards that recognize fate's importance than by Christian standards based on retribution and redemption. For the Cakchiquel Maya of Panajachel in the 1930s, the Devil became the dark master, the paradigmatic cruel landowner, extracting harsh labor for people's sins. But his interior land, called the Hill, was not always dark and forbidding. People often described the Hill as a lush interior land with a topography like that of earth's surface; it even contained villages, roads, churches, and farms. One entered it through caves, or from behind big rocks and great trees. If one were out in the woods on Earth's Surface and mysteriously heard dogs barking or church bells ringing, it meant that one of these passages had opened. Then one had better leave immediately, or one might soon meet up with the Devil. After all, God best protects people when they are gathered together in their towns, not when they are alone in the forest. Nevertheless, it was in this lush Underworld land that one served time after death, doing harsh labor to pay for one's misdeeds; so even if one avoided the Underworld in life, one probably would not avoid it in death.

If the Panajachel world could be a beautiful land in which the dead did hard labor, it also could be a dark and forbidding place from which the living might nevertheless profit. A story is told of a poor man caught by robbers one day. He had nothing for them to steal, so they made him do some errands for them in a distant town. They told him to take a short-cut through a dark, nasty passage penetrating the innards of a local mountain. On the path, the poor man met a Christ-like figure who stepped down from his cross and told him he could go no further. But he simply knocked the pseudo-Christ to the ground, as the robbers had told him to do, and continued on his way. When he had successfully completed his errands, the thieves released him; and he now had a darn good story to tell his neighbors.

This counter-Christ reminds us that the Underworld is always the opposite of the upper. Some Panajachel said that if a town existed on Earth's surface, its counterpart existed below, only upside-down. So if buildings rose forty stories high in Mexico City, companion buildings extended forty stories below into the Underworld. After working off their debts for the Devil in the Hill, the dead rose to the sky to be with God as stars or planets.

Both the Cakchiquel of Panajachel and the K'iché say that Earth is their mother and sky is their father. Nevertheless, in stories about the Hill, the Panajachel interior landscape's gender is never mentioned; and it is clear that both male and female ancestors and saints live with God the Father in the sky. Among the ancient Nahua, a male and female couple governed the Land of Death, and another couple governed the thirteenth sky; the Devil in his underworld abode was clearly male and shared his home with a number of female inhabitants; and for the contemporary Nahua of the highlands, both helpful and harmful male and female beings of ancient origin inhabit the Underworld, while male and female Christian saints inhabit the upper world. For the Kekchi, however, the Earth is a lord, not a lady, and he bears the most vital importance of all their deities, being sharply separated from the weaker celestial gods Our Lord Sun, Our Mother Moon, and Red Star (Venus). In a somewhat different vein, Hispanic feminist poet Gloria Anzaldúa (1987, 46–51) reinterprets ancient tradition to equate the Mesoamerican Underworld with the Nahua goddess Coatlicue and with Anzaldúa's own idea of a dark earth mother who devours Anzaldúa, thereby dissolving painful oppositions arising from her sexuality and cultural heritage. This dissolution enables her to be reborn.

Cooking fires, food, and comestible sacrifices also reflect oppositions between the lower and upper worlds. In the Underworld they burn bones in their cooking fires, not sticks. Moreover, they don't eat the same things there. The ancient Mexica said that the Lord and Lady of Death ate human hands and feet, stew made of beetles that lived in damp places, tamales smelling of beetle gas, and atole made of pus that they drank from a skull. The K'iche' say in the Popol Vuh, however, that proper sacrifices to the Gods of Death are not to be blood sacrifices, like the hands, feet, and blood that fed the Nahua Earth Monster and her Underworld inhabitants, but only creatures of the night, clotted sap, and the mean and the nasty. Owls and quail (both nocturnal birds) also were common sacrificial meals offered to the Underworld beings by the pre-Conquest Mexica.

A widespread myth says that one must not eat the things of the Underworld, lest one be doomed to stay there forever. The Panajachel constantly reminded hapless Underworld travelers to avoid the food if they wished to escape. And a Lacandon myth tells of a man who, having been drawn into the Underworld by Death Maker's daughter, was hidden by the god's wife under a blanket of chilies grown on Earth's Surface. When Death Maker appeared with the Sun on his shoulder (for he was carrying him through the Underworld), he smelled the chilies and was absolutely revolted; normally he only ate tortillas of bracket fungi, beans of the larvae of green flies, and corn paste made from the decayed flesh of dead human beings. Death Maker's wife warned the man not to eat the food, even if it looked like that on Earth's Surface. Following her advice, he eventually won the upper hand by forcing Death Maker's daughter to eat a tortilla made of real corn, thereby making her his true wife.

The Underworld is also home to the rain gods, and thus not only provides the rotting nourishment required by chilies and corn grown above but also the rain that sustains them. Throughout present-day Mesoamerica, caves are the homes of a variety of dwarves who guard game, crops, and wealth. These dwarves are most likely the relatives of ancient dwarf-like rain gods who lived in caves and mountains and decided what kind of moisture to send: gentle rain, harsh thunderstorms and lightning, damaging frosts and hail, or funguses and rot; or they might decide to simply withhold all moisture, thereby causing drought. Likewise, among the contemporary Kekchi, the earth lord Tzultacaj is the master of the forest and its animals, and controls all rain, and the Lacandon's cave-dwelling rain god Metzabok burns copal to cause rain to fall. In sum, without the creatures of the underworld and its caves, those living on Earth's Surface could not survive. Heaven may be nice for some after death, but the living rely on what goes on beneath them, and it is there that they pay their debts.

See also: Chalchiuhtlicue; Christ; Coatlicue; Devil; Earth, Agricultural, and Hunting Deities; Feathered Serpents; Hero Twins; La Llorona; Moon; Quetzalcoatl; Rain and Water Deities; Sky Deities and Beings; Sun; Tezcatlipoca; Tlaloc and the Tlaloques; Yum Kaax

Suggested reading:

Brady, James E. 1989. "An Investigation of Maya Ritual Cave Use with Special Reference to Naj Tunich, Peten, Guatemala." Ph.D. dissertation, University of California at Los Angeles, Department of Anthropology.

Burkhart, Louise M. 1996. *Holy Wednesday: A Nahua Drama from Early Colonial Mexico.* Philadelphia: University of Pennsylvania Press.

Joralemon, Peter David. 1996. "In Search of the Olmec Cosmos: Reconstructing the World View of Mexico's First Civilization." Pp. 51–59 in Elizabeth P. Benson and Beatriz de la Fuente, eds., *Olmec Art of Ancient Mexico.* Washington, DC: National Gallery of Art.

Knab, Timothy. 1995. *A War of Witches: A Journey in the Underworld of the Contemporary Aztecs.* New York: HarperCollins.

Tedlock, Dennis, trans. 1985. *Popol Vuh: The Definitive Edition of the Mayan Book of the Dawn of Life and the Glories of Gods and Kings.* New York: Simon and Schuster.

YUM KAAX (DIVING GOD)

Time period: Classic–Contemporary

Cultural group: Yucatec Maya

The Diving God, or the pre-Conquest Yucatec Maya god of maize known as Yum Kaax (Yoom Kash´), seems to be closely associated with agriculture and fertility. However, like many Maya deities with multiple sides to their personalities, this god has other associations as well—with death and sacrifice. The Maya codices portray him with maize imagery, but he also appears as a sacrificial offering, eyes closed in death and entrails falling out of his midriff. The association of agriculture and fertility with death makes sense from the standpoint of Maya natural and cosmological orders. Agriculture, and more specifically the growth of maize, takes place through a cycle of life and death. To create a maize plant, one must destroy the life of the land; that is, one must burn the vegetation to clear a new

Figure 73. Yum Kaax, the Diving God, Codex Tro-Cortesianus, *pl. 35a (Museo de América/Art Resource)*

field and must bury the maize seed in the earth. Maize is also the epitome of new life, being both the material of human creation and the basic unit of the Maya diet. Today we can only surmise the gist of the myths behind the pictures of the diving figure on temple ruins, the codical figures with their maize offerings, and the sacrificial figures; no one knows for sure what those myths entailed.

See also Earth, Agricultural, and Hunting Deities; Underworld and Caves, Deities of the

Suggested reading:

Landa, Diego de. 1978. *Yucatan before and after the Conquest.* Trans. William Gates. New York: Dover.

Taube, Karl. 1992. *The Major Gods of Ancient Yucatan.* Washington, DC: Dumbarton Oaks Research Library.

4

ANNOTATED PRINT AND NONPRINT RESOURCES

BOOKS AND ARTICLES

Adams, Richard E. W. ***Prehistoric Mesoamerica.*** Norman: University of Oklahoma Press, 1991.

An introductory textbook to the archaeology and history of ancient Mesoamerica. This book explores the prehistoric cultural and historical development of Mesoamerica before Spanish contact.

Abreu Gomez, Ermilio. ***Canek: History and Legend of a Maya Hero.*** Berkeley: University of California Press, 1979.

A fictional reconstruction of the Yucatec Maya during colonial times and the early days of independence. This short, accessible collection of stories is about a young creole man who is part of an old aristocratic family, and a young Maya boy (Jacinto Canek) who works on the estate (translated from Spanish).

Anaya, Rudolfo A. ***The Legend of La Llorona.*** Berkeley, CA: Tonatiuh–Quinto Sol International, Inc., 1984.

This short, easy to read novel combines one of the many myths about Malinche with the basic myth of La Llorona, thereby creating a new tale. An excellent example of contemporary mythology.

Anzaldúa, Gloria. ***Borderlands/La Frontera: The New Mestiza.*** San Francisco: Aunt Lute Books, 1987.

An intense, beautifully poetic book describing the author's experiences as a Hispanic woman. Offers the reader a skillful re-creation of themes drawn from primarily academically based mythology about women and pre-Conquest deities.

Aveni, Anthony. ***Skywatchers of Ancient Mexico.*** Austin: University of Texas Press, 1980.

Explores the interesting and often complex relationships among worldviews, architectural structures, topography, and celestial motions.

Benson, Elizabeth P., and Beatriz de la Fuente, eds. ***Olmec Art of Ancient Mexico.*** Washington, DC: National Gallery of Art, 1996.

This catalogue for a major exhibition offers a number of excellent short articles exploring various facets of Olmec history, society, and culture, all of which are written by specialists.

Bierhorst, John, ed. ***The Monkey's Haircut and Other Stories Told by the Maya.*** New York: William Morrow, 1986.

An excellent collection of Maya folktales and myths from highland Guatemala.

Boone, Elizabeth H. ***Incarnations of the Aztec Supernatural: The Image of Huitzilopochtli in Mexico and Europe.*** Philadelphia: American Philosophical Society, 1989.

A thorough historical examination of the imagery that depicts the Mexica patron deity Huitzilopochtli from pre-Conquest times to the Colonial period.

Bricker, Victoria Reifler. ***The Indian Christ, the Indian King.*** Austin: University of Texas Press, 1981.

A descriptive study of myths, rituals, and beliefs among some of the Maya people from Chiapas Mexico. This text is best suited for the advanced layperson.

Burkhart, Louise M. ***Holy Wednesday: A Nahua Drama from Early Colonial Mexico.*** Philadelphia: University of Pennsylvania Press, 1996.

A careful, thorough translation and study of a sixteenth-century Christian play written and produced in Nahuatl for indigenous audiences celebrating Holy Week. Includes not only the play, but also good discussions of the historical context in which it was produced, some of its key religious themes, and its blending of indigenous and Christian worldviews.

Carmack, Robert M., Janine Gasco, and Gary H. Gossen. ***The Legacy of Mesoamerica: History and Culture of a Native American Civilization.*** Upper Saddle River, NJ: Prentice Hall, 1996.

An introductory textbook on the modern history and culture of Mesoamerica. This book covers the changes and growth of Mesoamerican indigenous cultures from the time of Spanish contact to the modern day.

Carmichael, Elizabeth, and Cloë Sayers. ***The Skeleton at the Feast: The Day of the Dead in Mexico.*** London: British Museum Press, 1991.

A delightful, solid study of the history of the Day of the Dead and its contemporary practice. Includes many fine pictures.

Codex Chimalpopoca. As reproduced in *History and Mythology of the Aztecs: The Codex Chimalpopoca.* Translated by John Bierhorst. Tucson: University of Arizona Press, 1992.

A sixteenth-century Nahuatl codex containing both the "Annals of Cuauhtitlan (1570), a history of a Mexican Highlands urban center; and a lengthy, at least partly Mexica creation story called "The Legend of the Suns" (1558) (translated from Nahuatl).

Codex Mendoza. As reproduced in *The Essential Codex Mendoza.* Commentary by Frances F. Berdan and Patricia Rieff Anawalt. Berkeley: University of California Press, 1997.

A shortened version of an earlier in-depth, multi-volume study, which includes a reproduction of this important sixteenth-century Central Mexican pictorial document, and a discussion of the codex's history and meaning. The book offers a good introduction to Mexica royal history.

Cortés, Hernán. ***Letters from Mexico.*** Translated and edited by A. R. Pagden. New Haven, CT: Yale University Press, 1986.

The letters of Hernán Cortés, which were sent back to the ruler of Spain Charles V. These report on the conquest of New Spain in fair detail (translated from Spanish).

Cosío Villegas, Daniel; Ignacio Bernal, and Alejandro Moreno Toscano. ***A Compact History of Mexico.*** Translated by Marjory Mattingly Urquidi. Mexico City: El Colegio de México, 1974.

A very short, concise history of Mexico beginning with the Paleo-Indian and ending with Mexico in the 1970s; each chapter is written by an outstanding Mexican scholar. It was originally intended as an introductory textbook for the Colegio's students (translated from Spanish).

Díaz del Castillo, Bernal. ***The Discovery and Conquest of Mexico: 1517–1521.*** Translated by A. P. Maudslay. New York: Farrar, Straus and Giroux, 1956.

A highly readable first-hand account written by one of Hernán Cortés's captains detailing the Conquest of Mexico (translated from Spanish).

Durán, Fray Diego. ***Book of the Gods and Rites and the Ancient Calendar.*** Translated by Doris Heyden and Fernando Horcasitas. Norman: University of Oklahoma Press, 1971.

A rich account describing numerous ritual and calendrical aspects of ancient Mexica religion written by a sixteenth-century friar (translated from Spanish).

———. ***The History of the Indies of New Spain.*** Translated by Doris Heyden. Norman: University of Oklahoma Press, 1994.

The very readable and lengthy retelling of Mexica ancient history, which was produced by a sixteenth-century Dominican cleric (translated from Spanish).

Edmonson, Munro S., Translator. ***Heaven Born Mérida and Its Destiny: The Book of Chilam Balam of Chumayel.*** Austin: University of Texas Press, 1986.

A seventh- through nineteenth-century Maya text containing the history of Yucatán from the perspective of the Maya town Chumayel. It also includes less historical information such as medical, exegetical, astronomical, liturgical, and literary materials (translated from Yucatec Maya).

———. ***The Book of the Year: Middle American Calendrical Systems.*** Salt Lake City: University of Utah Press, 1988.

A somewhat technical, but extremely thorough treatment of just about all of the ancient Mesoamerican calendrical systems. The author takes the position that all are based on a basic count of the days, making it possible to calibrate and coordinate the many, diverse calendars.

Freidel, David, Linda Schele, and Joy Parker. ***Maya Cosmos: Three Thousand Years on the Shaman's Path.*** New York: William Morrow, 1993.

A review and interpretation of Classic Period Maya religion, which uses modern examples to trace Maya religion from early creation myths and the earliest sculptural portrayals of myth to the modern rituals and stories of today's Yucatec Maya.

Furst, Jill Leslie McKeever. ***The Natural History of the Soul in Ancient Mexico.*** New Haven, CT: Yale University Press, 1995.

A delightful book that explores pre-Conquest soul concepts, especially among the Nahua. It does so by drawing comparisons among ancient and current ideas and their relationships to how human bodies function and other physical evidence.

Knab, Timothy J. ***A War of Witches: A Journey in the Underworld of the Contemporary Aztecs.*** New York: HarperCollins, 1995.

A fictionalized novel about a contemporary Nahua community that includes references to mythology about the underworld, ritual practices, and witchcraft. It has been based on actual ethnographic research. Good in the classroom for exploring Mesoamerican cosmology and raising ethical issues.

Lafaye, Jacques. ***Quetzalcoatl and Guadalupe: The Formation of National Consciousness, 1531–1813.*** Chicago: University of Chicago Press, 1976.

One of the classic scholarly historical books on Guadalupe and Mexican history. It explores the formation of national consciousness through the imagery of Guadalupe and Quetzalcoatl.

Landa, Diego de. ***Relación de las cosas de Yucatán.*** Edited and translated by Alfred M. Tozzer. Papers of the Peabody Museum no 18. Cambridge, MA: Harvard University Press, 1941.

A superb source for ancient customs, stories, and descriptions of the Yucatec Maya life during the early years of Spanish Colonialism. Written in 1566, this book describes the Maya culture in extreme detail, both in the text and in the 1941 footnotes.

Lockhart, James. ***The Nahuas after the Conquest: A Social and Cultural History of the Indians of Central Mexico, Sixteenth through Eighteenth Centuries.*** CA: Stanford University Press, 1992.

An extraordinarily well-researched, detailed study of indigenous history in Central Mexico from the Conquest through the 1700s.

López Austin, Alfredo. ***The Human Body: Concepts of the Ancient Nahuas.*** Translated by Thelma Ortiz de Montellano and Bernardo Ortiz de Montellano. Salt Lake City: University of Utah Press, 1988.

An excellent source for the worldview of the ancient Mexica, and how attitudes on the human body interplayed with the cosmos and its other beings (translated from Spanish).

———. ***The Myths of the Opossum: Pathways of Mesoamerican Mythology.*** Albuquerque: University of New Mexico Press, 1993.

Ancient and contemporary mythology surrounding the opossum becomes the device for exploring basic indigenous religious and cosmological concepts. A fine resource for learning about Mesoamerican worldviews (translated from Spanish).

Menchu, Rigoberta. ***I, Rigoberta Menchu: An Indian Woman in Guatemala.*** Edited by Elisabeth Burgos-Debray. New York: Verso, 1984.

The moving biographical account of a living K'iche' woman about her life, worldview, and her trials in the Guatemalan civil war (translated from Spanish).

Milbrath, Susan. ***Star Gods of the Maya: Astronomy in Art, Folklore, and Calendars.*** Austin: University of Texas Press, 1999.

An extremely detailed study of Maya deities and their relationships to the sky, which both builds on and alters the classic work of Eric Thompson and others. While it focuses on a study of ancient star gods, the work contains much about contemporary celestial mythology, often drawing parallels between that and the ancient.

Nash, June. ***In the Eyes of the Ancestors: Belief and Behavior in a Mayan Community.*** Prospect Heights, IL: Waveland Press, 1985.

A highly detailed, thick ethnography of a Maya group in Chiapas, Mexico, which includes a variety of different myths and stories.

Pasztory, Esther. ***Aztec Art.*** New York: Harry N. Abrams, 1983.

A now classic work discussing the art of the Mexica, which also includes a great deal of introductory material, and many fine photos.

Popol Vuh: The Definitive Edition of the Mayan Book of the Dawn of Life and the Glories of Gods and Kings. Translated by Dennis Tedlock. New York: Simon and Schuster, 1985.

An early colonial K'iche' Maya collection of five creation myths of the K'iche' Maya world, starting from the creation of the world to the establishment of the highland Maya tribes and the primacy of the K'iche' (translated from K'iche' Maya).

Read, Kay A. ***Time and Sacrifice in the Aztec Cosmos.*** Bloomington: Indiana University Press, 1998.

An introduction to the pre-Conquest Mexica worldview and its attitudes on time and sacrifice.

Redfield, Robert and Alfonso Villa Rojas. ***Chan Kom: A Maya Village.*** Washington, DC: Carnegie Institution of Washington, 1934.

A classic ethnography of a Yucatec Maya village in the early 1930s containing excellent descriptions of their rituals, stories, and beliefs. This work is accessible to nonprofessionals and professionals alike.

Sahagún, Fray Bernardino de. ***The Florentine Codex: A General History of the Things of New Spain.*** Translated by Arthur J. O. Anderson, and Charles E. Dibble. Monographs of the School of American Research no 14. Santa Fe: School of American Research; Salt Lake City: University of Utah Press, 1953; 12 books, 13 parts.

A vast and important source on religious, social, and environmental aspects of the ancient Mexica. A sixteenth-century Franciscan friar collected and produced this magnificent set (translated from Nahuatl).

Sandstrom, Alan. ***Corn Is Our Blood: Culture and Ethnicity in a Contemporary Aztec Indian Village.*** Norman: University of Oklahoma Press, 1991.

An ethnographic account of a modern town of Nahuatl speakers; it documents, among other things, a number of healing rituals and discusses diverse facets of their religious life.

Sexton, James D. ***Mayan Folktales: Folklore from Lake Atitlán, Guatemala.*** New York: Doubleday, 1992.

An excellent collection of Maya folktales, myths, and stories from highland Guatemala (translated from Tzutuhil Maya).

Sharer, Robert J. ***The Ancient Maya.*** 5th ed. Stanford, CA: Stanford University Press, 1994.

A superb source for the archaeology and history of the Maya world. This book describes the prehistoric cultural and historical development of the Maya before Spanish contact. One of the best introductions available.

Stephens, John Lloyd. ***Incidents of Travel in Central America, Chiapas, and Yucatan.*** Illustrated by Frederick Catherwood. New York: Dover, 1969.

A nineteenth-century traveler's and explorer's guide to archaeological ruins throughout Maya world. This book is an excellent source for beautiful drawings of Maya ruins as they were seen in the 1800s.

Taggart, James M. ***Nahuat Myth and Social Structure.*** Austin: University of Texas Press, 1983.

A scholarly discussion of the relationship between myths and social structure among particular living Nahuatl speakers, includes many translations of myths from their original language.

Tedlock, Barbara. ***Time and the Highland Maya.*** Albuquerque: University of New Mexico Press, 1982.

A revised ethnography of the K'iche' Maya intended for the lay reader, with rich descriptions of K'iche' rituals and cosmology.

VIDEOS

Pre-Conquest Mexican and Mayan

The Fall of the Maya
Films for the Humanities & Sciences, Inc.
Box 2053
Princeton, NJ 08543–2053
1–800–257–5126

When archaeologists first looked at the ruins of the Mayan urban center of Copan, they concluded that the Mayans were a peaceful people devoted to astrology and the arts whose civilization mysteriously disappeared. But as the remaining structures were examined more closely through a complex system of tunnels, and as the codes of the hieroglyphics were finally cracked, scholars began to understand a quite different reality: This often war-like Mayan center revolved around blood sacrifice. Copan eventually was abandoned because of overpopulation and the resultant destruction of its natural resources.

The Five Suns
Patricia Amlin
University of California Extension Center for Media and Independent Learning
2000 Center St.
Berkeley, CA 94704
1–510–642–0460

This animated video, drawn by hand in the style of the sixteenth-century Nahua, traces an origin myth of ancient Mexican peoples of the central highlands. The video begins by describing how the strong sacred forces battled to create the first four, unsuccessful ages, and then how the deities worked together to create the fifth and final age. In addition, *The Five Suns* looks at the position and responsibilities of human beings in the ancient world, and the necessity of sacrifice to keep the natural forces working and maintain life.

Indians of North America: Aztec
Schlessinger Video Productions
P.O. Box 1110
Bala Cynwyd, PA 19004
1-800-843-3620

The Aztecs, who began as wandering hunters and gatherers, eventually settled on an island in the middle of a lake and became one of the largest, most socially complex, and most advanced civilizations of all time. Skilled builders and masons, farmers, engineers, and artists, the Aztecs practiced a religious tradition that revolved around sacrifice to and respect for cosmic forces. Although they were great warriors, they could withstand neither the Spanish conquistadors nor the diseases the Spanish carried; however, traces of this great civilization still exist in Mexico today.

Lost Kingdoms of the Maya
Columbia Tristar Home Video
10202 W. Washington Blvd.
Culver City, CA 90232

This National Geographic video traces the development of Maya civilization from its ancient origins to its eventual downfall, recreating key historical events for the viewer. Archaeologists have found clues in the hieroglyphics and artifacts of Tikal, Copan, and Dos Pilas, which hint at who the Mayans were, how they lived, and how their society was structured. The video also points out that although the great cities of the Maya civilization were abandoned by the end of the Middle Ages in Europe, many Mayans today continue to practice the ancient traditions.

The Popol Vuh
Patricia Amlin
University of California Extension Center for Media and Independent Learning
2000 Center St.
Berkeley, CA 94704
1-510-642-0460

This truly excellent animated video, drawn in the style of pre-Conquest manuscripts, sculptures, and pottery ornamentation, accurately retells a significant portion of a lengthy Maya creation story, parts of which are traceable to the Preclassic era. K'iche' daykeepers still recount the same legend today. The video begins with the creations of the three previous ages and then focuses on the exploits of the Hero Twins as they put the universe in order for the fourth and present age. At once mysterious, exciting, and action-packed, the video will introduce viewers to an important myth of the ancient and modern Maya world.

Teotihuacan: City of the Gods
EVN, Educational Video Network, Inc.
1401 19th Street
Huntsville, TX 77340
1–409–295–5767

Dubbed the "city of gods" by Aztecs who lived almost a thousand years later, Teotihuacan at its height (ca. A.D. 500–600) housed between 150,000 and 200,000 people. The huge Pyramids of the Sun and Moon dominated the city; an Aztec legend said that the gods created these huge structures by sacrificing themselves in order to give birth to the sun. Although much of the city has decayed, many larger structures remain, as does an extensive collection of artifacts including masks, sculptures, pottery, and wall murals and drawings. The remains found here and at other, similar sites in the region give archaeologists clues as to the type of people the Teotihuacanese were and the kind of warfare they waged. In fact, the city was burned in the mid- to late seventh century, perhaps by a rival center that competed with Teotihuacan in sacred warfare focused on the planet Venus

Post-Conquest–Contemporary Mexico

Art and Revolution in Mexico
Films for the Humanities & Sciences, Inc.
Box 2053
Princeton, NJ 08543–2053
1–800–257–5126

Narrated by Octavio Paz, this video explores the major role played by art during the Mexican Revolution of 1910, showing how it propelled the confrontation by educating, inspiring, and motivating people to act. Many types of art from this period, including murals, satirical cartoons, and political posters by artists such as Rivera, Orozco, and Siquieros, are discussed. The viewer will not only become familiar with these artists' creations but will also learn about the effects they had on the people and the revolution.

Celebrating the Day of the Dead
EVN, Educational Video Network, Inc.
1401 19th St.

Huntsville, TX 77340
1–409–295–5767

This video explores the Mexican ritual of the Day of the Dead from the viewpoint of the dead themselves. It also looks at the effect the festival has on the living celebrants—in particular, how it shapes their view of the dead. Lastly, it touches on the mythical origins of the festival, the influence of the Conquest and introduction of Christianity on indigenous ideas about the dead, and the economic and social standing of the festival's participants.

Great Cities of the World: Mexico City
Films for the Humanities & Sciences, Inc.
Box 2053
Princeton, NJ 08543–2053
1–800–257–5126

From the ancient past of Toltec peoples to the Aztecs' erection of the great city of Tenochtitlán; the Spanish conquistadores to the last monarchies; the Revolution of 1910 to the modern day, this video explores the history of one of the largest cities in the world: Mexico City. All aspects of the city's identity are explored, including the environment, people, politics, religions, and cultures. The video explores these facets through each of the city's major historical periods, painting a complete and many-sided picture of this great metropolis.

Contemporary Central America

Romero
Vidmark Entertainment
2901 Ocean Park Blvd., Suite 123
Santa Monica, CA 90405–2906
213–399–8877

Oscar Romero began his career as a quiet, bookish priest, but gradually was transformed into an outspoken activist and champion of the repressed peasants in his native El Salvador. When faced with the brutal deaths and "disappearances" of his friends, parishioners, and people, Archbishop Romero found he could no longer remain apolitical, and he became instead a powerful supporter of popular resistance in this country's twelve-year civil war (1980–1992). This film traces his life from the moment of his transformation to his assassination by government-sponsored extremists, and brings home the fact that even after his death Romero continued to live in the hearts of the people for whom he fought.

Tierra Madre, Terra Sacre
Cinema Guild
1697 Broadway Suite 506
New York, NY 10019
212–246–5522

Although *Tierra Madre, Terra Sacre* (Mother Earth, Sacred Earth) was made before the 1996 signing of a peace agreement that ended a thirty-year civil war in Guatemala, it still captures the plight of today's peasant farmers in that country. The Kekchi Indians, members of the Catholic Popular Church, still recognize the earth as their mother and desperately seek to preserve their ancient heritage and culture, which the government and rich plantation owners have been slowly stripping away. Traditional communal values are extremely important to these farmers, yet the landowners deprive them of their social autonomy and sometimes even of the church that supports and empowers them. The video is in English, Spanish, and Kekchi, and includes English subtitles.

WEB SITES

General Mesoamerica

Ancient Mesoamerican Civilizations: Maya, Mixtec, Zapotec, and Aztec
http://www.angelfire.com/ca/humanorigins/index.html

The brainchild of Kevin L. Callahan (University of Minnesota, Department of Anthropology), this site provides a truly fine introduction to the culture and history of pre-Columbian Mesoamerica, offering an overview and description of Mesoamerican writing systems, government structures, the Maya calendar, and Mesoamerican religious beliefs. It also offers links to related web sites.

Arizona State University Archaeological Research Institute
http://archaeology.la.asu.edu

A virtual museum on ancient cultures links the viewer to the Teotihuacan home page, an exhibit on the Templo Mayor of Tenochtitlán, and a guide to the decorated ceramics of Zacatecas, Mexico. The site offers the general public and experts around the world information about Teotihuacan and the Feathered Serpent Pyramid, the Templo Mayor Project, and Zacatecas ceramic types. Documents available for viewing at the site are suited to a variety of readerships and levels of interest and include basic introductory pages, recent excavation reports, and academic journal articles.

Culture and Society of México
http://www.public.iastate.edu/~rjsalvad/scmfaq/scmfaq.html

Offers information on a range of topics relating to current Mexican society and culture. Also serves as the home page for the Internet discussion group "soc.culture.mexican."

Foundation for the Advancement of Mesoamerican Studies, Inc.
http://www.famsi.org/

This site is the home page for FAMSI, a private research granting institution that provides research grant opportunities and posts the resulting research reports. The site also includes pages for the Schele, Kerr, and the Montgomery archives. The Schele Archive is a database where people can search through 1,000 drawings by Linda Schele, organized by culture, site, time period, architectural feature, artifact, and iconography. The Kerr Archive contains several thousand rollout photographs of Maya vases by Justin Kerr, which are organized by vase type and iconographic content. The Montgomery Archive offers drawings by John Montgomery, indexed by culture, site, time period, and iconography. This site is extremely useful to Mesoamerican scholars and very informative for the enthusiast and layperson.

GB Online's Mesoamerica
http://pages.prodigy.com/GBonline/mesowelc.html

An interested and motivated amateur designed and created this excellent web site. His purpose is to share information with fellow enthusiasts in his quest to learn more by focusing on various aspects of Mesoamerican cultural studies. This site contains a variety of information and links about Mesoamerican writing systems, archaeological sites, contemporary native Mesoamerican issues, pre-Columbian art, and the calendrical system.

Mesoweb
http://www.mesoweb.com/

Mesoweb is an excellent web site devoted to the exploration of Mesoamerican cultures: the Olmecs, Maya, Aztecs, Toltecs, Mixtecs, Zapotecs, and others. Run by three scholars—Merle Greene Robertson, Jorge Pérez de Lara, and Joel Skidmore on behalf of PARI (Pre-Columbian Art Research Institute)—the site focuses on a variety of subjects including renewal ceremonies of the contemporary Tz'utujil; recent discoveries at the site of Palenque in Chiapas, Mexico; a report on the adventures of Teobert Maler, an early-twentieth-century, Austrian-born photographer and explorer; and rubbings of Maya sculptures by Merle Greene Robertson. The site also offers an illustrated encyclopedia of Mesoamerican cultures and a collection of short animations referring to each section of the web site. It also includes links to related sites. Although this particular site is in English, some of the links it provides are in Spanish.

Pre-Columbian Archaeology and Related Links
http://copan.bioz.unibas.ch/mesolinks.html

This site does not contain any information itself but does have an extensive list of other web sites covering all types of resources on Mesoamerican cultures, myth, and history. This includes web sites focusing on regions and archaeological sites; museums, universities, and societies; publishers and bookstores; tourism and field study programs; universities with pre-Columbian programs; language and astronomy; and geography, flora, and fauna.

The Pre-Columbian Graphic Arts Web Site
http://members.aol.com/hasawchan/precolart.html

A great site for schoolchildren and laypersons, this highly interactive web site concentrates on the Maya area but includes information on other topics as well. It uses impressive imagery, animation, and sound effects to provide a brief synopsis of ancient Mesoamerican history and a description of the Maya world. The author has posted a variety of different photographs from around Mesoamerica and many museums and archaeological sites.

Maya

The Hudson Museum, University of Maine
www.umaine.edu/hudsonmuseum/worldvie.htm

This virtual exhibit explains and describes the ancient Maya worldview using pieces from the Palmer Collection of Maya. The site does a very good job of describing and explaining very briefly the pre-Columbian Maya worldview and discussing how the artifact images relate to Mayan stories and myths.

Maya Adventure
http://www.smm.org/sln/ma/index.html

Useful to teachers and students, this site features a variety of online educational activities and an ample collection of images from the anthropological collections at the Science Museum of Minnesota. The site also provides information on the Museum's related programs and exhibits, among them "Cenote of Sacrifice" and "Flowers, Saints, and Toads."

Maya Art and Books: The Foundation for Latin American Anthropological Research
http://www.maya-art-books.org

This site was founded with the goal of facilitating academic access to scholarly information about Mayan daily life 1,000 years ago in Guatemala, Belize, Mexico, and Honduras. It offers extensive photographic records of facts about and artifacts of ancient civilizations of pre-Columbian Mesoamerica.

The Maya Astronomy Page
http://www.astro.uva.nl/michielb/maya/astro.html

This page was designed and created by an astronomy graduate student from the Netherlands. It contains information about Maya astronomical knowledge, as well as the relationships of astronomy with Maya mathematics and calendrical systems. Very useful site for the beginner trying to understand Maya astronomy.

Maya Civilization—Past and Present
http://indy4.fdl.cc.mn.us/~isk/maya/mayastor.html

The focus here is on Maya science and art. The web site offers various teaching materials, including maps, and discussions of numbers and vocabulary, as well as a collection of Maya folktales and art objects. It also includes information about K'iche' Maya Nobel laureate Rigoberta Menchu and the modern Mayan peoples of Mexico and Central America.

Maya Multimedia Project: Interactive Popol Vuh
http://www.stanford.edu/class/anthro98a /Browser/home.html

This interactive web site arose out of an anthropology class taught at Stanford University by James A. Fox. The user can tab through a translation of the Maya Popul Vuh creation myths, and while reading the myth, view various images of Maya art depicting scenes from these myths.

Mayan Folktales
http://www.folkart.com/~latitude/folktale/folktale.htm

This web site is a collection of myths and stories from a Q'anjob'al Maya storyteller from San Miguel Acátan, Huehuetenango, Guatemala. Each month additional folktales are added to the web site, making it a great source for individuals looking for Maya stories.

MayaQuest 98
http://quest.classroom.com/archive/mayaquest1998/default.htm

This phenomenal web site follows an organized team of explorers traveling throughout the Maya area in 1998, visiting modern Maya communities and archaeological sites. Every day during MayaQuest 98, the team of adventurers and experts communicated exciting news, interesting information, and difficult dilemmas from their remote camps in the rain forest to interested viewers in school classrooms and elsewhere. Well worth the visit, especially if you are a kid, a teacher of kids, or simply interested in the topics.

Mundo Maya
http://www.mayadiscovery.com

Provides a brief introduction to the Maya world, describing some of the archaeology of the region, the natural environment, the daily life of the Maya, history, handicrafts, a short collection of Maya legends and stories, and other information. One can view this in either English or Spanish.

La Nave Va: Zapatistas, EXLN, Subcomandante Marcos, Chiapas, and Global Struggles
http://www.utexas.edu/students/nave

The center for information on the Zapatistas, this site gives a description of their movement with news and information, as well as archives of past events. It is a good location for learning more about the Zapatistas from their own point of view, offering an insight into one contemporary movement of resistance.

Rabbit in the Moon: Maya Glyphs and Architecture
http://www.halfmoon.org

A great web site, useful to both amateurs and experts. Learn about ancient Maya hieroglyphic writing, or how to write your own name in Maya glyphs; play Bul, a Maya game of chance; or walk up a Maya pyramid. This interactive site includes tons of information on Maya writing, calendar systems, and culture, as well as useful links to other sites.

Ancient and Contemporary Mexico

Aztec Folktales—Teacher Guide
http://www.sdcoe.k12.ca.us/score/aztec/aztectg.html

Produced by the San Diego County Office of Education, this web site is a great resource for teachers and students. It contains a set of interactive activities for students, involving the reading, analysis, and illustration of Aztec folktales. Students may choose to create Venn diagrams comparing various tales; create a poster using folktales and imagery from the web site; or write poems or a letter from the perspective of an Aztec lord.

Fiestas Mexicanas
http://www.mexicodesconocido.com.mx/fiestas/fiestas.htm

Created by the Mexican Secretary of Tourism, this site describes various contemporary indigenous fiestas found throughout México. It lists the fiestas that take place each month, and the towns and regions where they are celebrated, and provides a description and interpretation of each event. The site is entirely in Spanish.

La Llorona—Teacher Guide
http://www.sdcoe.k12.ca.us/score/rona/ronatg.html

This site, created by the San Diego County Office of Education, is another good teaching resource. It offers a number of interactive activities allowing students to explore a retelling of a popular present-day legend using modern trial proceedings, research techniques, and poetry. This is a great web site for teaching students about contemporary Aztec legends and about modern Mexican cultures north and south of the U.S. border.

Mexico Student Teacher Resource Center
http://northcoast.com/~spdtom/index.html

This somewhat idiosyncratic but interesting and useful site provides introductory background on the history of Mexico. It offers limited information on the Aztecs, the history of Cortés, the French intervention of 1861, the dictatorship of Porfirio Díaz, and the Mexican Revolution from 1910 to 1940. In addition, it offers a collection of graphics with detailed captions, and a guide for research.

Nahuatl Home Page
http://www.umt.edu/history/NAHUATL

Nahuatl, the native language of the ancient Aztecs and of many Mexican highlanders today, is the focus of this web site. Serving as the home page for the

NAHUAT-L discussion list, the site lists many Nahuatl resources and links to related sites. Among the resources available are books on Nahuatl; the table of contents of *Estudios de Cultura Nahuatl* vols. 1–26 (a Mexican professional journal); Aztec calendar programs; an image of the Aztec Sunstone; the Templo Mayor Museum (includes numerous objects in their collection and information on them and related topics on Mexica); pre-Columbian calendars; the *Codex Mendoza;* and other Nahua manuscripts.

Our Lady of Guadalupe Web Site
http://ng.netgate.net/~norberto/materdei.html

This is an excellent and interesting web site for understanding a worshiper's veneration of Guadalupe as well as her iconography. Not a scholarly or research-oriented site, it offers a believer's view of the chronology of Guadalupe's appearances; stories and myths about her; and prayers and consecrations for her. The site can be accessed in English, Spanish, French, and Portuguese.

REFERENCE LIST

Abreu Gomez, Ermilo. 1979. *Canek: History and Legend of a Maya Hero.* Translated by Mario L. Davila and Carter Wilson. Berkeley: University of California Press.

Adams, Richard E. W. 1991. *Prehistoric Mesoamerica.* Norman: University of Oklahoma Press.

Alarcón, Hernando Ruiz de. 1984. *Treatise on the Heathen Superstitions That Today Live among the Indians Natives to This New Spain, 1629.* Translated by J. Richard Andrews and Ross Hassig. Norman: University of Oklahoma Press.

Anaya, Rudolfo A. 1984. *The Legend of La Llorona.* Berkeley, CA: Tonatiuh-Quinto Sol International.

Anzaldúa, Gloria. 1987. *Borderlands/La Frontera: The New Mestiza.* San Francisco: Aunt Lute Books.

Arora, Shirley L. 1997. "La Llorona." In *Encyclopedia of Mexico.* Edited by Michael S. Werner, 1: 753–754. Chicago: Fitzroy Dearborn.

Aveni, Anthony. 1980. *Skywatchers of Ancient Mexico.* Austin: University of Texas Press.

Baldwin, Neil. 1998. *Legends of the Plumed Serpent: Biography of a Mexican God.* New York: Public Affairs.

Bassie-Sweet, Karen. 1991. *From the Mouth of the Dark Cave: Commemorative Sculpture of the Late Classic Maya.* Norman: University of Oklahoma Press.

Benson, Elizabeth P., and Beatriz de la Fuente, editors. 1996. *Olmec Art of Ancient Mexico.* Washington, DC: National Gallery of Art.

Berlin, Heinrich. 1988. *Idolatría y superstición entre los indios de Oaxaca.* Mexico City: Ediciones Toledo.

Berlo, Janet. 1992. *Art, Ideology, and the City of Teotihuacan.* Washington, DC: Dumbarton Oaks Research Library and Collection.

Berrin, Kathleen. 1984. *The Hungry Woman: Myths and Legends of the Aztec.* New York: William Morrow.

———. 1988. *Feathered Serpents and Flowering Trees.* San Francisco: Fine Arts Museum of San Francisco.

Bierhorst, John, editor. 1986. *The Monkey's Haircut and Other Stories Told by the Maya.* Illustrated by Robert Andrew Parker. New York: William Morrow.

Boone, Elizabeth H. 1989. *Incarnations of the Aztec Supernatural: The Image of Huitzilopochtli in Mexico and Europe.* Transactions of the American Philosophical Society. Philadelphia: American Philosophical Society.

Bradomin, Jose Maria. 1994. "The Sacrifice of Cocijo." In *Myth and Magic: Oaxaca Past and Present,* 44–47. Palo Alto: Palo Alto Cultural Center.

Brady, James E. 1989. "An Investigation of Maya Ritual Cave Use with Special Reference to Naj Tunich, Peten, Guatemala." Ph.D. dissertation, Department of Anthropology, University of California at Los Angeles.

Bricker, Victoria Reifler. 1973. *Ritual Humor in Highland Chiapas.* Austin: University of Texas Press.

———. 1981. *The Indian Christ, the Indian King.* Austin: University of Texas Press.

Broda, Johanna. 1969. *The Mexican Calendar as Compared to Other Mesoamerican Systems.* Edited by Josef Haekel and Engelbert Stiglmayr. Series Americana 4, Acta Ethnologica et Linguistica, No. 15, Institut für Völkerkunde der Universitäte Wien. Vienna: Herbert Merta.

———. 1983. "Ciclos agrícolas en el culto: Un problema de la corelación del calendario Mexica." In *Calendars in Mesoamerica: Native Computations of Time.* Edited by Anthony Aven, and Gordon Brotherston, 145–164. Oxford: BAR International Series 174.

Brundage, Burr Cartwright. 1979. *The Fifth Sun: Aztec Gods, Aztec World.* Austin: University of Texas Press.

Burkhart, Louise. 1989. *The Slippery Earth: Nahua Christian Moral Dialogue in Sixteenth Century Mexico.* Tucson: University of Arizona Press.

———. 1996. *Holy Wednesday: A Nahua Drama from Early Colonial Mexico.* Philadelphia: University of Pennsylvania Press.

Burns, Allan F., translator. 1983. *An Epoch of Miracles: Oral Literature of the Yucatec Maya.* Austin: University of Texas Press.

Cantares Mexicanos. 1985. As reproduced in *Cantares Mexicanos: Songs of the Aztecs.* Translated by John Bierhorst. Stanford, CA: Stanford University Press.

———. 1993. As reproduced in *Poesía Náhuatl: Cantares Mexicanos, Manuscrito de la Biblioteca Nacional de México,* 2d ed. Translated by Ángel Ma. Garibay K. Mexico City: Universidad Nacional Autónoma de México.

Carlson, John B. 1976. "Astronomical Investigations and Site Orientation Influences at Palenque." In *The Art, Iconography and Dynastic History of Palenque, Part III.* Edited by Merle Greene Robertson, 107–117. Pebble Beach, CA: Pre-Columbian Art Research, Robert Louis Stevenson School.

Carmack, Robert M., Janine Gasco, and Gary H. Gossen. 1996. *The Legacy of Mesoamerica: History and Culture of a Native American Civilization.* Upper Saddle River, NJ: Prentice Hall.

Carmichael, Elizabeth, and Cloë Sayers. 1991. *The Skeleton at the Feast: The Day of the Dead in Mexico.* London: British Museum Press.

Carrasco, David. 1982. *Quetzalcoatl and the Irony of Empire.* Chicago: University of Chicago Press.

Carrasco, David, Johanna Broda, and Eduardo Matos Moctezuma. 1987. *The Great Temple of Tenochtitlan: Center and Periphery in the Aztec World.* Berkeley: University of California Press.

Carrasco, Pedro. 1971. "Social Organization of Ancient Mexico." In *Handbook of Middle American Indians.* Edited by Robert Wauchope, 10: 349–375. Austin: University of Texas Press.

Caso, Alfonso. 1958. *The Aztecs: The People of the Sun.* Translated by Lowell Dunham. Norman: University of Oklahoma Press.

———. 1971. "Calendrical Systems of Central Mexico." In *Handbook of Middle American Indians,* vol. 10. Edited by Robert Wauchope. Austin: University of Texas Press.

Cervantes, Fernando. 1994. *The Devil in the New World: The Impact of Diabolism in New Spain.* New Haven, CT: Yale University Press.

Chamberlain, Robert S. 1948. *The Conquest and Colonization of Yucatan, 1517–1550.* Washington, DC: Carnegie Institute of Washington Publication 582.

Chase, Diane Z., and Arlen F. Chase, editors. 1992. *Mesoamerican Elite: An Archaeological Assessment.* Norman: University of Oklahoma Press.

Chilam Balam of Chumayel. 1933. Translated by Ralph Loveland Roys. Washington, DC: Carnegie Institution of Washington.

———. 1967. As reproduced in *The Book of Chilam Balam of Chumayel.* Translated by Ralph L. Roys. Original manuscript 1782. Norman: University of Oklahoma Press.

———. 1986. In *Heaven Born Mérida and Its Destiny: The Book of Chilam Balam of Chumayel.* Translator Munro S. Edmonson. Austin: University of Texas Press.

Chilam Balam of Tizimin. 1982. In *The Ancient Future of the Itza: The Book of Chilam Balam of Tizimin.* Editor and translator Munro Edmonson. Austin: University of Texas Press.

———. 1951. In *The Book of the Jaguar Priest: A Translation of the Book of*

Chilam Balam of Tizimin. Translated by Maud Worcester Makemson. New York: Henry Schuman.

Clendinnen, Inga. 1991. *Aztecs: An Interpretation.* Cambridge: Cambridge University Press.

Codex Aubin. 1893. As reproduced in *Histoire de la nation mexicaine.* Paris: Ernest Leroux.

Codex Borbonicus. 1974. Facsimile ed. Commentary by K. A. Nowotny. Graz, Austria: Akademische Druck u. Verlagsanstalt.

Codex Borgia. 1963. Commentary by Eduard Seler. Mexico City: Fondo de Cultura Económica.

Codex Boturini. 1831. As reproduced in *Antiquities of Mexico.* Edited by Edward King, Viscount Kingsborough. 9 vols. London: Robert Havell.

Codex Chimalpahin. 1982. As reproduced in *Relaciones originales de Chalco Amaquemecan: Escritas por Don Francisco de San Antón Muñón Chimalpahin Cuauhtlehuanitzin.* Translated by S. Réndon. Mexico: Fondo de Cultura Económica.

———. 1997. As reproduced in *Codex Chimalpahin: Society and Politics in Mexico Tenochtitlan, Tlatelolco, Texcoco, Culhuacan, and Other Nahua Altepetl in Central Mexico: The Nahuatl and Spanish Annals and Accounts Collected and Recorded by Don Domingo de San Antón Muñón Chimalpahin Quauhtlehuanitzin.* Edited and translated by Arthur J. O. Anderson and Susan Schroeder. Norman: University of Oklahoma Press.

Codex Chimalpopoca. 1992a. As reproduced in *Codex Chimalpopoca: The Text in Nahuatl with a Glossary and Grammatical Notes.* Translated by John Bierhorst. Tucson: University of Arizona Press.

———. 1992b. As reproduced in *History and Mythology of the Aztecs: The Codex Chimalpopoca.* Translated by John Bierhorst. Tucson: University of Arizona Press.

Codex Cospi. 1968. Facsimile ed. Commentary by K. A. Nowotny. Graz, Austria: Akademische Druck u. Verlagsanstalt.

Codex Dresden [*Codex Dresdensis: Die Maya-Handschrift in der Sächsischen Landesbibliothek Dresden*]. 1962 Edited by E. Förstemann. (Reprint of *Die Maya-Handschrift De Königlichen Bibliothek Zu Dresden.* Foreword by E. Lips. Leipzig: Röder, 1880). Berlin: Adademie-Verlag.

Codex Fejérváry-Mayer. 1901. Facsimile ed. Paris: Duc de Loubat.

Codex Magliabechiano. 1983. Facsimile ed. Zelia Nuttal. Berkeley: University of California Press.

Codex Mendoza. 1938. Facsimile ed. Edited by James Cooper Clark. London: Waterlow and Sons.

———. 1992. Commentary and edited by Frances F. Berdan and Patricia Anawalt. 2 vols. Berkeley: University of California Press.

———. 1997. As reproduced in *The Essential Codex Mendoza.* Commentary by Frances F. Berdan and Patricia Rieff Anawalt. Berkeley: University of California Press.

Codex Perez and the Book of Chilam Balam of Mani. 1979. Edited by Eugene R. Craine, and Reginald C. Reindorp. Norman: University of Oklahoma Press.

Codex Telleriano Remensis. As reproduced in *Codex Telleriano Remensis: Ritual, Divination, and History in a Pictorial Aztec Manuscript.* Commentary by Eloise Quiñones Keber. Austin: University of Texas Press.

Codex Tro-Cortesianus. 1967. Facsimile ed. Commentary by Ferdinand Anders. Graz, Austria: Akademische Druck u. Verlagsanstalt.

Códice Tudela. 1980. Facsimile ed. Commentary by José Tudela de la Orden. Madrid: Ediciones Cultura Hispanica.

Códice Vaticano Latino 3738. 1964. In *Antigüedades de México.* With a prologue by Agustín Yánez. 4 vols. (Reprint of Vol. 2 of *Antiquities of Mexico,* Edited by Edward King, Viscount Kingsborough. 9 vols. London: Robert Havell, 1831–1848). Mexico City: Secretaría de Hacienda y Crédito Público.

Códice Xolotl. 1980. Facsimile ed. Edited by Charles E. Dibble. Mexico City: Universidad Nacional Autónoma de México.

Coe, Michael. 1973. *The Maya Scribe and His World.* New York: Grolier Club.

———. 1977. "Supernatural Patrons of Maya Scribes and Artists." In *Social Process in Maya Prehistory: Studies in Honour of Sir Eric Thompson.* Editor Norman D. C. Hammond, 327–347. New York: Academic Press.

———. 1984. *The Maya.* 3d ed. London: Thames and Hudson.

———. 1987. *The Maya.* 4th ed. New York: Thames and Hudson.

Colombres, Adolfo. 1982. *Relatos del mundo indígena.* Mexico: SEP.

Cortés, Hernan. 1986. *Letters from Mexico.* Translated and edited by A. R. Pagden. New Haven, CT: Yale University Press.

Cosío Villegas, Daniel, Ignacio Bernal, and Alejandro Moreno Toscano. 1974. *A Compact History of Mexico.* Translated by Marjory Mattingly Urquidi. Mexico: El Colegio de México.

Cross, F. L., and E. A. Livingstone, editors. 1990. *The Oxford Dictionary of the Christian Church.* New York: Oxford University Press.

Cyphers, Ann. 1996. "Reconstructing Olmec Life at San Lorenzo." In *Olmec Art of Ancient Mexica.* Edited by Elizabeth P. Benson and Beatriz de la Fuente, 61–73. Washington, DC: National Gallery of Art.

Davies, Nigel. 1973. *The Aztecs: A History.* Norman: University of Oklahoma Press.

Díaz del Castillo, Bernal. 1956. *The Discovery and Conquest of Mexico: 1517–1521.* New York: Farrar, Straus, and Giroux.

Diehl, Richard. 1996. "The Olmec World." In *Olmec Art of Ancient Mexico.* Edited by Elizabeth P. Benson and Beatriz de la Fuente, 29–33. Washington, DC: National Gallery of Art.

Durán, Fray Diego. 1971. *Book of the Gods and Rites and the Ancient Calendar.* Translated by Doris Heyden and Fernando Horcasitas. Norman: University of Oklahoma Press.

———. 1994. *The History of the Indies of New Spain.* Translated by Doris Heyden. Norman: University of Oklahoma Press.

Edmonson, Munro S. 1988. *The Book of the Year: Middle American Calendrical Systems.* Salt Lake City: University of Utah Press.

———. 1993. "The Mayan Faith." *South and Meso-American Native Spirituality.* Edited by Gary H. Gossen, 65–85. New York: Crossroads.

Edmonson, Munro S., editor and translator. 1982. *The Ancient Future of the Itza: The Book of Chilam Balam of Tizimin.* Austin: University of Texas Press.

Faust, Betty Bernice. 1998. *Mexican Rural Development and the Plumed Serpent: Technology and Maya Cosmology in the Tropical Forest of Campeche, Mexico.* Westport, CT: Bergin and Garvey.

Florescano, Enrique. 1994. *Memory, Myth, and Time in Mexico: From the Aztecs to Independence.* Austin: University of Texas Press.

Fowler, William J. 1989. *The Cultural Evolution of Ancient Nahua Civilizations: The Pipil-Nicarao of Central America.* Norman: University of Oklahoma Press.

Franch, José Alcina. 1993. *Calendario y religiòn entre los Zapotecos.* Mexico City: Universidad Nacional Autonoma de México.

Freidel, David, and Linda Schele. 1988. "Symbol and Power: A History of the Lowland Maya Cosmogram." In *Maya Iconography.* Edited by Elizabeth P. Benson and Gillett Good Griffin, 44–93. Princeton, NJ: Princeton University Press.

Friedel, David, Linda Schele, and Joy Parker. 1993. *Maya Cosmos: Three Thousand Years on the Shaman's Path.* New York: William Morrow.

Furst, Jill Leslie McKeever. 1995. *The Natural History of the Soul in Ancient Mexico.* New Haven, CT: Yale University Press.

Gann, Thomas. 1900. *Mounds in Northern Honduras.* Nineteenth Annual Report of the Bureau of American Ethnology. Washington, DC: Bureau of American Ethnology.

Garibay K., Angel María, editor and translator. 1978. *Llave de Nahuatl.* 4th ed. Mexico City: Editorial Porrúa.

———. 1985. *Teogonía e historia de los Mexicanos: Tres opusculos del siglo XVI.* 4th ed. Mexico City: Editorial Porrúa.

Gibson, Charles. 1964. *The Aztecs under Spanish Rule: A History of the Indians of the Valley of Mexico, 1519–1810.* Stanford, CA: Stanford University Press.

Gillespie, Susan. 1989. *The Aztec Kings: The Construction of Rulership in Mexica History.* Tucson: University of Arizona Press.

Goldin, Liliana R., and Brenda Rosenbaum. 1993. "Culture and History: Subregional Variation among the Maya." *Comparative Studies in Society and History* 35: 110–132.

Gómara, Francisco López de. 1964. *Cortés: The Life of the Conqueror by his Secretary.* Translated by Leslie Byrd Simpson. Berkeley: University of California Press.

Gonzales Torres, Yolotl. 1991. *Diccionario de mitología y religión de Mesoamerica.* Mexico City: Ediciones Larousse.

Gonzalez-Lauck, Rebecca. 1996. "La Venta: an Olmec Capital." In *Olmec Art of Ancient Mexica.* Edited by Elizabeth P. Benson and Beatriz de la Fuente, 73–81. Washington, DC: National Gallery of Art.

Gossen, Gary. 1986. *Chamulas in the World of the Sun: Time and Space in a Maya Oral Tradition.* 2d ed. Prospect Heights, IL: Waveland Press.

Gossen, Gary, editor. 1986. *Symbol and Meaning beyond the Closed Community: Essays in Mesoamerican Ideas.* Albany: State University of New York Press.

Graulich, Michel. 1997. *Myths of Ancient Mexico.* Norman: University of Oklahoma Press.

Haley, H. B., and F. X. Grollig. 1989. "Death in the Maya Cosmos." In *Perspectives on Death and Dying: Cross-cultural and Multi-disciplinary Views.* Edited by A. Berger, 131–145. Philadelphia: Charles Press.

Hancock, Graham, and Santha Faiia. 1998. *Heaven's Mirror: Quest for the Lost Civilization.* New York: Three Rivers Press.

Harner, Michael. 1977. "The Ecological Basis for Aztec Sacrifice." *American Ethnologist* 4, 1: 117–35.

Harris, Max. 1990. "Indigenismo and Catolicidad: Folk Dramatizations of Evangelism and Conquest in Central Mexico." *Journal of the American Academy of Religion* 58, 1: 55–68.

———. 1992. "Disguised Reconciliations: Indigenous Voices in Early Franciscan Missionary Drama in Mexico." *Radical History Review* 53: 13–25.

———. 1993. *Dialogical Theater: Dramatization of the Conquest of Mexico and the Question of the Other.* New York: St. Martin's Press.

———. 1994. "Reading the Mask: Hidden Transcripts and Human Interaction." *Mind and Human Interaction* 5, 4: 155–164.

———. 1996. "Moctezuma's Daughter: The Role of La Malinche in Mesoamerican Dance." *Journal of American Folklore* 109, 432: 149–177.

———. 1997. "The Return of Moctezuma: Oaxaca's *Danza de la Pluma* and New Mexico's *Danza de los Matachines." Drama Review* 41, 1 (T153): 106–134.

———. 1998. "Sweet Moll and Malinche: Maid Marian Goes to Mexico." In *Playing Robin Hood: The Legend as Performance in Five Centuries.* Edited by Lois Potter, 101–110. Newark: University of Delaware Press.

Henderson, John S. 1997. *The World of the Ancient Maya.* 2d. ed. Ithaca, NY: Cornell University Press.

Henestrosa, Andres. 1994. "The Bat." In *Myth and Magic: Oaxaca Past and Present,* 33–37. Palo Alto, CA: Palo Alto Cultural Center.

Heyden, Doris. 1975. "An Interpretation of the Cave underneath the Pyramid of the Sun at Teotihuacan, Mexico." *American Antiquity* 40, 2: 131–147.

———. 1979. "The Many Faces of the Mother Goddess: Deities of Water and Sustenance." Paper presented at the International Congress of Americanists, Vancouver.

———. 1983. *Mitología y simbolismo de la flora en el México prehispánico.* Mexico City: Universidad Nacional Autónoma de México.

Historia de los Mexicanos por sus pinturas. 1985. In *Teogonía e historia de los Mexicanos: Tres opusculos del siglo XVI.* 4th ed. Edited by Angel María Garibay K., 23–90. Mexico City: Editorial Porrúa.

Histoyre du Mechique. 1905. In *Journal de la Société des Américanistes de Paris.* Edited by Edourd de Jonghe, 1–41.

Hofling, Charles Andrew. 1991. *Itzá Maya Myths: With a Grammatical Overview.* Salt Lake City: University of Utah Press.

Ixtlilxochitl, Don Fernando de Alva. 1985. *Obras históricas.* 4th ed. Edited by Edmundo O'Gorman. Mexico City: Universidad Nacional Autónoma de México.

Jones, Grant Drummond. 1989. *Maya Resistance to Spanish Rule: Time and History on a Colonial Frontier.* Albuquerque: University of New Mexico Press.

Joralemon, Peter David. 1996. "In Search of the Olmec Cosmos: Reconstructing the World View of Mexico's First Civilization." In *Olmec Art of Ancient Mexico.* Edited by Elizabeth P. Benson and Beatriz de la Fuente, 51–59. Washington, DC: National Gallery of Art.

Josserand, J. Kathryn, and Nicholas A. Hopkins. 1997. "Tila, Chiapas: A Modern Maya Pilgrimage Center." In *15th Annual Maya Weekend.*

Karttunen, Frances. 1983. *An Analytical Dictionary of Nahuatl.* Austin: University of Texas Press.

———. 1997a. "La Malinche and *Malinchismo.*" In *Encyclopedia of Mexico.* Edited by Michael S. Werner, 2: 775–778. Chicago: Fitzroy Dearborn.

———. 1997b. "Rethinking Malinche." In *Indian Women in Early Mexico.* Edited by Susan Schroeder, Stephanie Wood, and Robert Haskett, 291–312. Norman: University of Oklahoma Press.

Keen, Benjamin. 1971. *The Aztec Image in Western Thought.* New Brunswick, NJ: Rutgers University Press.

Kelley, David Humiston. 1976. *Deciphering the Maya Script.* Austin: University of Texas Press.

Kidwell, Clara Sue. 1992. "Systems of Knowledge." In *America in 1492: The World of the Indian Peoples before the Arrival of Columbus.* Edited by Alvin M. Josephy, Jr., 369–403. New York: Alfred A. Knopf.

Kircher, John. 1997. *A Neotropical Companion.* Princeton, NJ: Princeton University Press.

Klein, Cecelia. 1988. "Rethinking Cihuacoatl: Aztec Political Imagery of the Conquered Woman." In *Smoke and Mist: Mesoamerican Studies in Memory of Thelma D. Sullivan.* Edited by J. Kathryn Josserand and Karen Dakin, 237–277. London: B.A.R.

Knab, Timothy J. 1995. *A War of Witches: A Journey in the Underworld of the Contemporary Aztecs.* New York: HarperCollins.

Krickeberg, Walter. 1966. *Altmexickanische Kulturen.* Berlin: Safari-Verlag.

Lafaye, Jacques. 1976. *Quetzalcoatl and Guadalupe: The Formation of Mexican National Consciousness, 1531–1813.* Chicago: University of Chicago Press.

Landa, Diego de. 1941. *Relación de las cosas de Yucatán.* Edited and translated by Alfred M. Tozzer. Papers of the Peabody Museum. Cambridge, MA: Harvard University Press.

———. 1975. *The Maya: Diego de Landa's Account of the Affairs of Yucatan.* Translated by Anthony R. Padgen. Chicago: O'Hara.

———. 1978. *Yucatan before and after the Conquest.* Translated by William Gates. New York: Dover.

Laughlin, Robert M., and Carol Karasik. 1988. *The People of the Bat: Mayan Tales and Dreams from Zinacantan.* Washington, DC: Smithsonian Institution Press.

León, Nicolás. 1979. *Los Tarascos: Notas históricas étnicas y antropológicas, colegidas de escritores antiguos y modernos, documentos inéditos y observaciones personales.* Mexico City: Editorial Innovación.

León-Portilla, Miguel. 1992. *Fifteen Poets of the Aztec World.* Norman: University of Oklahoma Press.

Liss, Peggy K. 1975. *Mexico under Spain, 1521–1556: Society and the Origins of Nationality.* Chicago: University of Chicago Press.

Lockhart, James. 1992. *The Nahuas after the Conquest: A Social and Cultural History of the Indians of Central Mexico, Sixteenth through Eighteenth Centuries.* Stanford, CA: Stanford University Press.

Lok, Rosanna. 1987. "The House as a Microcosm." In *The Leiden Tradition in Structural Anthropology.* Edited by R. D. Ridder and J. A. J. Karremans, 211–223. Leiden: E. J. Brill.

López Austin, Alfredo. 1988a. *The Human Body: Concepts of the Ancient Nahuas.* Translated by Thelma Ortiz de Montellano and Bernardo Ortiz de. Montellano, vol. 2. Salt Lake City: University of Utah Press.

———. 1988b. *Una vieja historia de la mierda.* Mexico City: Edicíones Toledo.

———. 1993. *The Myths of the Opossum: Pathways of Mesoamerican Mythology.* Translated by Bernard Ortiz de Montellano and Thelma Ortiz de Montellano. Albuquerque: University of New Mexico Press.

———. 1994. *Tamoanchan y Tlalocan.* Mexico City: Fondo de Cultura Económica.

———. 1996. *The Rabbit on the Face of the Moon.* Salt Lake City: University of Utah Press.

López Austin, Alfredo, Leonardo López Luján, and Saburo Sugiyama. 1991. "The Temple Quetzalcoatl at Teotihuacan: Its Possible Ideological Significance." *Ancient Mesoamerica* 2, 1: 93–105.

López Luján, Leonardo. 1994. *The Offerings of the Templo Mayor of Tenochtitlan.* Translated by Thelma Ortiz de Montellano and Benard Ortiz de Montellano. Niwot: University Press of Colorado.

Love, Bruce. 1994. *The Paris Codex: Handbook for a Maya Priest.* Austin: University of Texas Press.

Markman, Roberta, and Peter Markman. 1992. *The Flayed God: The Mesoamerican Mythological Tradition.* New York: HarperCollins.

Matos Moctezuma, Eduardo. 1990. *Teotihuacan: La metrópoli de los dioses.* Mexico City: Instituto Nacional de Antropología e Historia.

Maxwell, Judith M, and Craig A. Hanson. 1992. *Of the Manner of Speaking That Old Ones Had: The Metaphors of Andrés de Olmos in the Tulul Manuscript: Arte para aprender la lenqua mexicana, 1547.* Salt Lake City: University of Utah Press.

McGee, R. Jon. 1990. *Life, Ritual, and Religion among the Lacandon Maya.* Belmont, CA: Wadsworth.

McVicker, Donald. 1997. "Quetzalcoatl." In *Encyclopedia of Mexico: History, Society, and Culture.* Edited by Michael S. Werner, 2: 1211–1214. Chicago: Fitzroy Dearborn.

Menchu, Rigoberta. 1984. *I, Rigoberta Menchu: An Indian Woman in Guatemala.* Edited by Elisabeth Burgos-Debray. New York: Verso.

Mendelson, Michael E. 1965. *Los Escandolos de Maximón: Un estudio sobre la religión y la visión del mundo en Santiago Atitlan.* Guatemala: Tipografía Nacional.

Mendoza, Arnulfo, and Victor De La Cruz. 1994. "Lorenzo (the Coyote) and Evaristo (the Deer)." In *Myth and Magic: Oaxaca Past and Present*, 71–74. Palo Alto: Palo Alto Cultural Center.

Milbrath, Susan. 1989. "A Seasonal Calendar with Venus Periods in Codex Borgia 29–46." In *The Imagination of Matter: Religion and Ecology in Mesoamerican Traditions*. Edited by David Carrasco, 103–127. Oxford: BAR International Series 515.

———. 1999. *Star Gods of the Maya: Astronomy in Art, Folklore, and Calendars.* Austin: University of Texas Press.

Miller, Mary, and Karl Taube. 1993. *The Gods and Symbols of Ancient Mexico and the Maya: An Illustrated Dictionary of Mesoamerican Religion.* London: Thames and Hudson.

Molina, Fray Alonso de. 1970. *Vocabulario en lengua castellana y mexicana.* Preliminary study by Miguel Leon Portilla. Mexico City: Editorial Porrúa.

Monjarás-Ruiz, Jesús. 1987. *Mitos cosmogónicos de México indígena.* Mexico City Instituto Nacional de Antropología e Historia.

Montolíu Villar, María. 1989. *Cuando los dioses depertaron: Conceptos cosmológicos de los antiquos mayas de Yucatán estudiados en el Chilam Balam de Chumayel.* Mexico City: Universidad Nacional Autónoma de México.

Moreno de los Arcos, Roberto. 1967. "Los cinco soles cosmogónicos." In *Estudios de cultura Nahuatl.*, 7: 183–210. Mexico City: Universidad Nacional Autónoma de México.

Morley, Sylvanus G., George W. Brainerd, and Robert J. Sharer. 1983. *The Ancient Maya.* 4th ed. Stanford, CA: Stanford University Press.

Morris, Earl Halstead, Jean Charlot, and Ann Axtell Morris. 1931. *The Temple of the Warriors at Chichén Itzá, Yucatán.* Publication 406. Washington, DC: Carnegie Institution of Washington.

Motolinía, Fray Toribio de Benevente o. 1971. *Memoriales o libro de las cosas de la Neuva España y de los naturales de ella.* 2d ed. Edited by Edmundo O'Gorman. Mexico City: Universidad Nacional Autónoma de México.

———. 1984. *Historia de los Indios de la Neuva España.* 4th ed. Edited by Edmundo O'Gorman. Mexico City: Editorial Porrúa.

Muñoz Camargo, Diego. 1984. "Descripción de la ciudad y provincia de Tlaxcala: De la Nueva España e Indias del mar océano para el buen gobierno e ennoblecemiento dellas, mandada hacer por la S.C.R.M. del Rey Don Felipe, nuestro Señor." In *Relaciones geográficas del siglo XVI: Tlaxcala.* Edited by René Acuña, 4: 23–285. Mexico City: Universidad Nacional Autónoma de México.

Nash, June. 1985. *In the Eyes of the Ancestors: Belief and Behavior in a Mayan Community.* 2d ed. Prospect Heights, IL: Waveland Press.

Neiderberger, Christine. 1996. "The Basin of Mexico: A Multimillenial Development toward Cultural Complexity." In *Olmec Art of Ancient Mexico.* Edited by Elizabeth P. Benson and Beatriz de la Fuente, 83–93. Washington, DC: National Gallery of Art.

Nelson, Ben A., Andrew Darling, and David A. Kice. 1992. "Mortuary Practices and the Social Order at La Quemada, Zacatecas, Mexico." *Latin American Antiquity* 3, 4: 298–315.

Nicholson, H. B. 1957. "Topiltzin Quetzalcoatl of Tollan: A Problem for Mesoamerican Ethnohistory." Ph.D. dissertation, Harvard University.

———. 1971. "Religion in Pre-Hispanic Central Mexico." In *Handbook of Middle American Indians.* Edited by Gordon F. Ekholm and Ignacio Bernal, 10: 395–446. Austin: University of Texas.

Noguez, Xavier. 1993. *Documentos guadalupanos.* Toluca: El Colegio Mexiquense; Mexico City: Fondo de Cultura Económica.

Orozco, Gilbert. 1946. *Tradiciones y leyendas del Istmo de Tehuantepe.* Mexico: Revista Mucical Mexicana.

Ortiz de Montellano, Bernard R. 1978. "Aztec Cannibalism: An Ecological Necessity?" *Science* 200, 4342: 611–617.

———. 1989. "Mesoamerican Religious Tradition and Medicine." In *Healing and Restoring.* Edited by Lawrence Sullivan, 359–394. New York: Macmillan.

———. 1990. *Aztec Medicine, Health, and Nutrition.* New Brunswick, NJ: Rutgers University Press.

Palomo, Benjamín. 1997. *Hablan los Nahuales.* San Salvador, El Salvador: Talleres Gráficos.

Parson, Elsie Clews. 1936. *Mitla, Town of the Souls: and Other Zapteco-Speaking Pueblos of Oaxaca, Mexico.* Chicago: University of Chicago Press.

Pasztory, Esther. 1983. *Aztec Art.* New York: Harry N. Abrams.

———. 1992. "The Natural World as Civic Metaphor at Teotihuacan." In *Ancient Americas: Art from Sacred Spaces.* Edited by Richard F. Townsend, 135–145, 210. Chicago: Art Institute of Chicago.

———. 1997. *Teotihuacan: An Experiment in Living.* Norman: University of Oklahoma Press.

Paz, Octavio. 1961. *The Labyrinth of Solitude: Life and Solitude in Mexico.* New York: Grove Press.

Peterson, Anna L. 1997. *Martyrdom and the Politics of Religion: Progressive Catholicism in El Salvador's Civil War.* Albany: State University of New York Press.

Peterson, Anna, and Philip Williams. 1996. "Evangelicals and Catholics in El Salvador: Evolving Religious Responses to Social Change." *Journal of Church and State* 38, 4: 873–897.

Phelan, John. 1970. *The Millennial Kingdom of the Franciscans in the New World.* Berkeley: University of California Press.

Pohl, Mary DeLand. 1981. "Ritual Continuity and Transformation in Mesoamerica: Reconstructing the Ancient Maya Cuch Ritual." *American Antiquity* 46: 513–529.

Pomar, Juan Bautista. 1964. "Manuscrito de Jaun Bautista de Pomar, Tezcoco, 1582." In *Poesía Náhuatl.* Edited by Angel María Garibay K. Mexico City: Universidad Nacional Autónoma de México.

Poole, Stafford. 1995. *Our Lady of Guadalupe: The Origins and Sources of a Mexican National Symbol, 1531–1797.* Tucson: University of Arizona Press.

——. 1997. "Virgin of Guadalupe and Guadalupanismo." In *Encyclopedia of Mexico: History, Society, and Culture.* Edited by Michael S. Werner, 2: 1535–1537. Chicago: Fitzroy Dearborn.

Popol Vuh. 1950. In *Popol Vuh, the Sacred Book of the Ancient Quiche Maya.* Translated by Adrián Recinos. Norman: University of Oklahoma Press.

——. 1971. In *The Book of Counsel: The Popol Vuh of the Quiche Maya of Guatemala.* Edited and translated by Munro S. Edmonson. New Orleans: Middle American Research Institute, Tulane University.

——. 1985. In *Popol Vuh: The Definitive Edition of the Mayan Book of the Dawn of Life and the Glories of Gods and Kings.* Translated by Dennis Tedlock. New York: Simon and Schuster.

Preston, Julia. 23 March 1999. "An Ancient Sun Melts Mexico's Modern Stresses." *New York Times,* International section, p. A4.

Preuss, Mary H. 1988. *Gods of the Popol Vuh: Xmucane, Kucumatz, Tojil, and Jurakan.* Culver City, CA: Labyrinthos.

Quiñones Keber, Eloise. 1995. *Codex Telleriano Remensis: Ritual, Divination, and History in a Pictorial Aztec Manuscript.* Austin: University of Texas Press.

——. 1997. "Nahua Rulers, Pre-Hispanic." In *Encyclopedia of Mexico: History, Society, and Culture.* Edited by Michael S. Werner, 2: 999–1003. Chicago: Fitzroy Dearborn.

Read, Kay A. 1987. "Negotiating the Familiar and the Strange in Aztec Ethics." *Journal of Religious Ethics* 15, 1: 2–13.

——. 1994. "Sacred Commoners: The Motion of Cosmic Powers in Mexica Rulership." *History of Religions Journal* 34, 1: 39–69.

——. 1995. "Sun and Earth Rulers: What the Eyes Cannot See in Mesoamerica." *History of Religions Journal* 34, 4: 351–384.

———. 1996. "Sacrifice, Mesoamerica." In *Harper's Dictionary of Religion.* General Editor Jonathan Z. Smith. New York: Harper and Row.

———. 1997a. "Mesoamerica: Calendrics." In *Encyclopedia of Mexico: History, Society, and Culture.* Edited by Michael S. Werner, 2: 821–24. Chicago: Fitzroy Dearborn.

———. 1997b. "Mesoamerican: Religion." In *Encyclopedia of Mexico: History, Society, and Culture.* Edited by Michael S. Werner, 2: 824–829. Chicago: Fitzroy Dearborn.

———. 1998. *Time and Sacrifice in the Aztec Cosmos.* Bloomington: Indiana University Press.

———. 2000. "More than Earth: Cihuacoatl as Female Warrior, Male Matron, and Inside Ruler." Pp. 51–67 in *Goddesses and Sovereignty.* Edited by Elisabeth Benard, and Beverly Moon. New York: Oxford University Press.

Read, Kay A., and Jane Rosenthal. 1988. "Xochiquetzal and the Virgin of Ocotlan." *American Anthropology Association,* photocopied.

Redfield, Robert, and Alfonso Villa Rojas. 1934. *Chan Kom: A Maya Village.* Publication 448. Washington, DC: Carnegie Institution of Washington.

Reents-Budet, Dorie J. 1994. *Painting the Maya Universe: Royal Ceramics of the Classic Period.* Durham and London: Duke University Press.

Rengers, Christopher. 1989. *Mary of Americas: Our Lady of Guadalupe.* New York: Alba House.

Ricard, Robert. 1966. *The Spiritual Conquest of Mexico.* Berkeley: University of California Press.

Riley, G. Michael. 1997. "Cortés, Fernando (Hernán)." In *Encyclopedia of Mexico: History, Society, and Culture.* Edited by Michael S. Werner, 1: 352–55. Chicago: Fitzroy Dearborn.

Robertson, Donald. 1959. *Mexican Manuscript Painting of the Early Colonial Period: The Metropolitan Schools.* New Haven, CT: Yale University Press.

Rodriguez, Jeanette. 1994. *Our Lady of Guadalupe: Faith and Empowerment among Mexican-American Women.* Austin: University of Texas Press.

Roys, Ralph Loveland, translator. 1965. *Ritual of the Bacabs: A Book of Maya Encantations.* Norman: University of Oklahoma Press.

Sáenz, César A. 1976. *El Fuego Nuevo.* Seria Historia 18. Mexico City: Instituto Nacional de Antropología e Historia.

Sahagún, Fray Bernardino de. 1953–1982. *The Florentine Codex: A General History of the Things of New Spain.* Translated by Arthur J. O. Anderson, and Charles E. Dibble. Monographs of the School of American Research no. 14. Santa Fe: School of American Research; Salt Lake City: University of Utah Press.

———. 1979. *Códice Florentino.* Facsimile ed. Manuscrito 218–220 de la Colección Palatina de la Biblioteca Medicea Laurenziana. Mexico City: Archivo General de la Nación.

———. 1982. *Historia general de las coses de Nueva España.* 5th ed. Mexico City: Editorial Porrúa.

———. 1993. *Primero memoriales.* Photos by Ferdinand Anders. Oklahoma: University of Oklahoma Press.

Sandstrom, Alan. 1990. "Nahua Myths: Puyecaco, Ixhuatlan de Madero, Veracruz, Mexico."

———. 1991. *Corn Is Our Blood: Culture and Ethnicity in a Contemporary Aztec Indian Village.* Norman: University of Oklahoma Press.

Sarukhán Kermez, José, et al. 1995. *Dioses de México antiguo.* Mexico City: Antiguo Colegio de San Ildefonso.

Schele, Linda, and David Friedel. 1990. *A Forest of Kings: The Untold Story of the Ancient Maya.* New York: William Morrow.

Schele, Linda, and Mary Ellen Miller. 1986. *Blood of Kings.* New York: George Braziller; Fort Worth: Kimbell Art Museum.

Schellhas, Paul. 1904. *Representations of Deities of the Maya Manuscripts.* Papers of the Peabody Museum 4, 1: 1–47. Cambridge, MA: Peabody Museum of Archaeology and Ethnology, Harvard University.

Séjourné, Laurette. 1989. *El Pensamiento náhuatl cifrado por los calendarios.* Mexico City: Siglo XXI Editores.

Serna, Jacinto de la. 1953. "Manual de ministros de indios para el conocimiento de sus idolatrías y extirpación de ellas." In *Tratado de las idolatrías, supersticiones, dioses, ritos, hechicerías y otras costumbres gentílicas de las razas aborígenes de México.* Commentary by Francisco del Paso y Troncoso, 1: 47–368. Mexico City: Ediciones Fuente Cultural.

Sexton, James D. 1992. *Mayan Folktales: Folklore from Lake Atitlán, Guatemala.* New York: Doubleday.

Sharer, Robert J. 1994. *The Ancient Maya.* 5th ed. Stanford, CA: Stanford University Press.

Siméon, Rémi. 1981. *Diccionario de la lengua Náhuatl o Mexicana.* 2d ed. Mexico City: Siglo Veintiuno Editores.

Starr, Frederick. 1896. "Popular Celebrations in Mexico." *Journal of American Folk-Lore* 9: 161–169.

———. 1908. *In Indian Mexico.* Chicago: Forbes.

Stephens, John Lloyd. 1841. *Incidents of Travel in Central America, Chiapas, and Yucatan.* Illustrated by Frederick Catherwood. New Brunswick, NJ: Rutgers University Press.

———. 1969. *Incidents of Travel in Central America, Chiapas, and Yucatan.* Illustrated by Frederick Catherwood. New York: Dover.

Stracke, Claire T., and Richard J. Stracke. 1997. "Popular Catholicism." In *Encyclopedia of Mexico: History, Society, and Culture.* Edited by Michael S. Werner, 2: 1130–1131. Chicago: Fitzroy Dearborn.

Stuart, L. C. 1964. "Fauna of Middle America." In *Handbook of Middle American Indians: Natural Environment and Early Cultures.* Edited by Robert C. West, 1: 316–383. Austin: University of Texas Press.

Sugiyama, Saburo. 1989. "Burials Dedicated to the Old Temple of Quetzalcoatl at Teotihuacan." *American Antiquity* 54, 1: 85–106.

———. 1993. "Worldview Materialized in Teotihuacan, Mexico." *Latin American Antiquity* 4, 2: 103–129.

Sullivan, Thelma D. 1983. *Compendio de la gramática Náhuatl.* Mexico City: Universidad Nacional Autónoma de México.

———. 1988. *Compendium of Nahuatl Grammar.* Edited by Wick Miller and Karen Dakin. Salt Lake City: University of Utah Press.

Taggart, James M. 1983. *Nahuat Myth and Social Structure.* Austin: University of Texas Press.

Taube, Karl. 1992. *The Major Gods of Ancient Yucatan.* Washington, DC: Dumbarton Oaks Research Library and Collection.

———. 1993. *Aztec and Maya Myths.* Austin: University of Texas Press.

Tax, Sol. n.d. "The World of the Panajachel: As Told by Its Maya People in 1936 and 1937." Unpublished manuscript, Native American Educational Services (Chicago).

Tedlock, Barbara. 1982. *Time and the Highland Maya.* Albuquerque: University of New Mexico Press.

Tedlock, Dennis. 1990. *Days from a Dream Almanac.* Urbana: University of Illinois Press.

———. 1993. *Breath on the Mirror: Mythic Voices and Visions of the Living Maya.* San Francisco: HarperCollins.

Tedlock, Dennis, trans. 1985. *Popol Vuh: The Definitive Edition of the Mayan Book of the Dawn of Life and the Glories of Gods and Kings.* New York: Simon and Schuster.

Tezozomoc, Don Hernando Alvarado. 1980. *Cronica Mexicana.* 3d ed. Mexico City: Editorial Porrúa.

———. 1992. *Crónica Mexicáyotl.* Translated by Adrián León. Mexico City: Universidad Nacional Autónoma de México.

Thompson, John Eric Sydney. 1930. *Ethnology of the Mayas of Southern and Central British Honduras.* Anthropological Series 17 (2). Chicago: Field Museum of Natural History.

———. 1939. *The Moon Goddess in Middle America.* Carnegie Institution of

Washington Publication 509, Contributions to American Anthropology and History no. 29. Washington, DC: Carnegie Institution.

———. 1970a. "The Bacabs: Their Portraits and Glyph." In *Monographs and Papers in Maya Archaeology.* Edited by William Rotch Bullard, Jr., 471–485. Papers of the Peabody Museum 61. Cambridge, MA: Peabody Museum of American Archaeology and Ethnology, Harvard University.

———. 1970b. *Maya History and Religion.* Norman: University of Oklahoma Press.

Torquemada, Fray Juan de. 1969. *Monarquía indiana: De los veinte y un libros rituales y monarquía indian, con el origen y querras de los indios occidentales, de sus poblazones, descrubrimiento, conquista, conversión y otras cosas maravillosas de la mesma tierra.* Introduction by Miguel León Portilla. Mexico City: Editorial Porrúa.

———. 1975–1983. *Monarquía indiana: De los veinte y un libros rituales y monarquía indian, con el origen y querras de los indios occidentales, de sus poblazones, descrubrimiento, conquista, conversión y otras cosas maravillosas de la mesma tierra.* Mexico City: Universidad Nacional Autónoma de México.

Townsend, Richard F. 1979. *State and Cosmos in the Art of Tenochtitlan.* Washington, DC: Dumbarton Oaks Research Library and Collection.

———. 1992. *The Aztecs.* London: Thames and Hudson.

Treviño, Adrian, and Barbara Gilles. 1994. "A History of the Matachines Dance." *New Mexico Historical Review* April: 105–125.

Turner, Victor. 1974. *Dramas, Fields, and Metaphors: Symbolic Action in Human Society.* Ithaca, NY: Cornell University Press.

Umberger, Emily. 1987. "Antiques, Revivals, and References to the Past in Aztec Art." *RES.* 13: 63–105.

Vail, Gabrielle. 1996. "The Gods in the Madrid Codex: An Iconographic and Glyphic Analysis." Ph.D. dissertation, Tulane University, New Orleans; University Microfilms, Ann Arbor.

Vaillant, George C. 1944. *Aztecs of Mexico: Origin, Rise, and Fall of the Aztec Nation.* New York: Doubleday.

van der Loo, Peter. 1987. *Códices, costumbres, continuidad: Un estudio de la religión Mesoamerica.* Indiaanse Studies 2. Leiden: Archaeologisch Centrum R.U.

van Zantwijk, Rudolf. 1985. *The Aztec Arrangement: The Social History of Pre-Spanish Mexico.* Norman: University of Oklahoma Press.

Villagutierre Soto-Mayer, Don Juan de. 1983. *History of the Conquest of the Province of the Itza: Subjugation and Events of the Lacandon and Other Nations of Uncivilized Indians in the Land from the Kingdom of*

Guatemala to the Provinces of Yucatán in North America. Translated by Brother Robert D. Wood, S.M. Culver City, CA: Labyrinthos.

Vivó Escoto, Jorge A. 1964. "Weather and Climate of Mexico and Central America." In *Handbook of Middle America Indians.* Edited by Robert Wauchope, 1: 187–215. Austin: University of Texas Press.

Vogt, Evon Z. 1969. *Zinacantan: A Maya Community in the Highlands of Chiapas.* Cambridge, MA: Belknap Press.

Wauchope, Robert, editor. 1964–1976. *Handbook of Middle American Indians.* 15 vols. Austin: University of Texas Press.

Weaver, Muriel Porter. 1993. *The Aztecs, Maya, and Their Predecessors.* 3d ed. New York: Academic Press.

Wisdom, Charles. 1940. *The Chorti Indians of Guatemala.* Chicago: University of Chicago Press.

Zantwijk, Rudolf van. 1966. "Los seis barrios sirvientes de Huitzilopochtli." In *Estudios de cultura Nahuatl.,* 6: 177–185. Mexico City: Universidad Nacional Autónoma de México.

———. 1985. *The Aztec Arrangement.* Norman: University of Oklahoma Press.

GLOSSARY

Aztecs *See* **Mexica**.

Aztlan The Mexica's mythical place of origin; home to Huitzilopochtli and his mother Coatlicue. It is told how the Mexica used to live on this lush island surrounded by marshes and lagoons. Because they ate humble foods such as corn, illness was unknown among them and people never died; they could even move from youth to age and back again whenever they wanted. But when their patron deity Huitzilopochtli led the Mexica ancestors from Aztlan, everything turned against them. Thick brambles closed over Aztlan, hiding it; stones wounded them; and prickly trees and bushes stung them. They could never return.

During his reign, however, the Mexica ruler Motecuhzoma II sent magicians on a dangerous magical flight to visit Coatlicue in Aztlan. One-third of them perished on the way. Coatlicue told the survivors that soon Huitzilopochtli would return to her, abandoning the Mexica; he would lose all the towns over which he held power, in the order in which he had conquered them. Moreover, the Mexica were doomed because they had grown heavy with their fancy foods and riches.

Ballgame An indigenous Mesoamerican game in which two teams attempted to strike a solid rubber ball through a stone ring or against markers to gain points. Mesoamericans often played this game in an I-shaped ball court made of two long structures—essentially, an alley with two end zones. The scoring rings were set vertically, high up, in the center of each side of the alley. Sometimes decorated markers were placed in the end zones. Points were calculated when a player from either team hit the rubber ball through the rings or onto the markers. The players could not touch the ball with their hands or feet but could only strike it with their wrists, elbows, or hips. Outcomes varied greatly. Sometimes the audience was involved, losing items of wealth to the winning player every time the opposing team scored. Occasionally the winning team sacrificed the losing players, decapitating them or throwing them down temple stairs, trussed up like human balls.

Mythic stories of the ballgame abound throughout Mesoamerica, showing that it was and remains intimately involved in mythology and ritual.

Binding-of-the-Years, New Fire Ceremony A pre-Conquest Nahua ceremony performed every fifty-two years, believed to give birth to a new sun that would travel its celestial and underground path for another fifty-two years. This ceremony occurred when the solar and divinatory calendars both ended on the same day, an event coinciding with the rising of the Pleiades and the beginning of the dry season. Among the Mexica, the ritual took place on top of a small mountain just outside of Tenochtitlán. All of the fires in the entire domain were extinguished, and a new fire was sparked in the chest cavity of a sacrificial offering whose heart had been removed. If the fire priest could not spark the fire, it was feared that the new sun would not be born and all would be eaten by the forces of night. After the new fire was lit, a runner carried the flame to the main temple in the center of Tenochtitlán, to light a new fire there. From there, runners carried fire to all other temples throughout the domain; and from these fires, people sparked their household hearths.

Bloodletting The ritual drawing of blood from the human body to nourish and sustain various beings or to repay a debt incurred by having been nourished and sustained by other beings. Endemic in pre-Conquest traditions, bloodletting continued to play a role in post-Conquest traditions as well: The offering of blood was an integral part of continuing ancient religious patterns, and fit well with Christian notions of sacrifice and communion. In ancient times, bloodletting ranged from sacrificial slaughter of birds and animals, or human sacrifices, to the more common practice of autosacrifice, or the piercing of one's tongue, earlobe, or thigh in order to spatter blood in the direction of the recipient. The recipients of these comestible offerings included celestial and earthly deities as well as patrons of kinship lines. According to mythological tradition, the deities themselves had offered their blood to create humans, and continued to offer their resources, if not their blood, to create food and housing for humans. Hence, humans were in their debt, and had to work to sustain the living forces of the cosmos, if those forces were to continue sustaining them.

Catholicism In Mesoamerica, the faith, worldview, and practices of the Roman Catholic Church introduced by the Spanish conquerors in the early sixteenth century. Officially, the Church is the visible society of baptized Christians professing the same faith under the invisible head of Christ and the visible head of the Pope and Bishops in communion with Christ. Unofficially, the "Popular" or "People's Church" professes a wide range of faith positions and admits to many folk practices not necessarily accepted by the official church. Many of these may have more affinity with widespread ancient worldviews and practices, and at times may even run counter to official Catholic doctrine. Nevertheless, the diverse members of the Popular Church usually consider themselves fully Christian and Catholic, even if they do not always agree with the official Church.

Central Mexicans The peoples of the Mexican highlands, whose main cultural centers are the ancient cities of Teotihuacan and Tenochtitlán (today, the modern city of Mexico City), situated in the Basin of Mexico. This area coincides roughly with the modern Mexican states of the Federal District, Mexico, Morelos, Tlaxcala, and adjacent portions of Pueblo, Hidalgo, Queretaro, Michoacán, and Guerrero.

Cerros An early Preclassic Maya city located in eastern Yucatán, Mexico, and the northern end of the modern country of Belize. Cerros is a comparatively small Maya site, notable because of its beautiful, elaborately decorated, terraced temples. One of these temples has a series of painted stucco-model masks that symbolize a model of the cosmos and represent the ritual and mythic path of the sun and the center's kings.

Chichén Itzá The Postclassic-era Yucatec Maya capital city, located in north-central Yucatán, near the modern Mexican city of Mérida. This urban center, one of the largest in the Maya area, covers an area of at least five square kilometers, and its landscape is relatively densely crowded with buildings and other architectural structures. Today, Chichén Itzá is a protected archaeological site and a favorite destination of tourists from around the world. This city plays an important role in the mythic history and stories of the Yucatec Maya.

Chilam Balams Pre-Conquest and Colonial-era Maya manuscripts that present mythic histories of particular towns and their royal lineages. These manuscripts originated in northern Yucatán and have survived to the modern day. They generally record continuous native histories starting from the tenth century and continuing through the end of the nineteenth. Each draws its name from its town of origin. In Colonial times, the Chilam Balams were translated into phonetic Yucatec Maya and Spanish. The earlier manuscripts or codices, written in hieroglyphs on paper or deer hides, no longer exist.

Codex A pre-Conquest or Colonial-era manuscript that usually contains pictorial elements and that was produced by indigenous artists. Codices vary in subject matter, ranging from local town histories to ritual and calendrical texts. They are most often named after their location, the person who discovered them, former owners, or their places of origin. Pre-Conquest and very early Colonial manuscripts were painted on deer hide or paper made of a particular tree bark, which was coated with a thin layer of plaster. Traditionally, the early codices were rolled or folded accordion- or screen-style. Colonial-era codices usually were painted on European paper and bound in book form.

Cofradías Socioreligious fraternities dating to early Colonial times. Originally, they formed because towns and villages held property communally and performed work cooperatively. After the Conquest, governing groups formed to organize community land use and labor, including duties in the local church. The records of who owned what and did what work were held in a box, or *cofra*—hence the name. At that time, both the land and church often were governed by a particular saint, in much the same way as a patron deity had governed temples and land in ancient times. In the eighteenth century, state governmental and political forces began to usurp much of the cofradías' economic power; therefore, cofradías today are limited primarily to ritual church activities, often centering their worship around the local saint, although these ritual activities still contain a significant social component.

Conquistadors The Spanish warriors and military personnel who traveled in the early sixteenth century with Hernán Cortés and others to conquer the lands and people of New Spain, or Mesoamerica.

Creoles Children of Spanish ethnicity, born in Mesoamerica, often to poor immigrants. Creoles slowly developed into a small middle class. By the nineteenth century, they had become a highly educated group, most of them having been trained by Jesuit priests in humanist philosophy, and generally advocated independence from Spain.

Díaz del Castillo, Bernal A captain in Hernán Cortés's army who witnessed and wrote an invaluable account of the conquest of Mesoamerica, called *The Discovery and Conquest of Mexico: 1517–1521* (see the Annotated Bibliography).

Divination, Divinatory Calendar A cycle of 260 days in the indigenous calendrical system, consisting of 20 thirteen-day "weeks" called *trecenas* in Spanish (20 x 13 = 260 days). Called the *Tonalpohualli* in Nahuatl and the *Tzolkin* in Yucatec Maya, this calendar was and still is often used for divination. The most propitious times for naming a newborn, marrying, taking a trip, closing a business deal, or waging war were identified by reading this calendar. Probably the oldest calendar in Mesoamerica, its origin is unknown; nor are we certain which celestial cycle, if any, it marked. In ancient times among Central Mexicans, the seventy-three divinatory rounds ended on the same day as the fifty-two solar rounds, at which time the Binding-of-the-Years ceremony occurred.

Durán, Fray Diego A sixteenth-century Dominican friar born in Spain and raised in Mexico. Fluent in Nahuatl, he collected stories and information on the Nahua, recording them in two important volumes: *The Gods and Rites of the Ancient Calendar,* and *The History of the Indies in New Spain* (see the Annotated Bibliography). He intended these works to be used for the training of priests unfamiliar with indigenous Mesoamericans.

Encomienda A Colonial system that awarded *encomenderos*—for the most part, Spanish conquerors—rights to the goods and labor of specified groups of indigenous people in return for educating them in Christianity. Unfortunately, the system was much abused, and the Spanish government in the mid-sixteenth century was forced to take steps to alleviate the extremely harsh treatment many of the Indians were receiving.

Epidemics In Colonial Mesoamerica, waves of European diseases, especially smallpox, that decimated the indigenous population. The effect was extraordinarily disastrous because native populations had no natural resistance to these diseases, never having been exposed to them before the arrival of the Spanish. Smallpox contributed significantly to Hernán Cortés's success; in combination with other factors, it reduced the Indian population by 90 percent by the end of the sixteenth century.

Farabundo Martí National Liberation Front (FMLN) The revolutionary army of guerrillas who waged civil war in El Salvador (ca. 1980–1992). Named for the esteemed revolutionary Farabundo Martí, who was executed in a rebellion in the 1930s, the FMLN consisted of five separate but allied organizations with somewhat differing political ideologies, all of which sought to change the political and economic situation responsible for the extreme hardship suffered by peasant populations. Today the FMLN is a political party in the new, democratic system.

Four or Five Ages A widespread and very ancient genre of creation myth that conceives of the present world as the fourth or fifth created in a series. The previous worlds or ages all failed or were destroyed, each in its turn. In some versions of this story, especially very early ones, the present age is also foredoomed. In contemporary versions of this myth, often God, Christ, Joseph, or the Devil participate in the creation and destruction of the ages.

Hidalgo y Costillo, Father Miguel A Jesuit priest from Dolores, Mexico, who on 16 September 1810 freed the prisoners in his village and locked up the Spanish authorities in their stead. Calling to parishioners from the doorway of his church, he summoned them to join him in overthrowing the oppressive Spanish government, and garnered tremendous support. This cry, or *grito de Hidalgo,* began the Mexican war of independence from Spain, which was won on 27 September 1821.

Kaminaljuyu A late Preclassic-era Maya city located in the southern Guatemalan highlands, in the Valley of Guatemala. Having both a dense population and extensive cultural offerings, this large and powerful city also supported long-distance trade links with other areas of Mesoamerica, especially Teotihuacan and Central Mexico. The site of Kaminaljuyu lies under today's Guatemala City, and most of the ancient city's remains have been destroyed by urban expansion and modern settlement.

K'iche' Maya A large and historically important Maya group that live today in the Guatemala highlands. The K'iche' were the largest group of Maya that the Spanish encountered during their conquest of Guatemala, and they controlled a huge portion of the highlands. Through myth and history, they trace their origins to the legendary Toltecs. They continue to maintain a rich tradition of native myth and storytelling.

La Venta An early Preclassic Olmec city, inhabited from 1400 to 600 B.C. Located in the Gulf coast Mexican state of Veracruz, on an island in a large wetland area, La Venta is famous for its pyramid shaped like a volcano and its large stone representations of the heads of Olmec kings. The site is and was considered a cultural center early in Mesoamerican history and myth.

Ladino A Spanish-speaking Indian who adapted to the new culture during Colonial times. Today, however, this term usually means someone who is either a mestizo—a person of mixed European and Indian heritage—or a non-Indian.

Landa, Fray Diego de The first Catholic bishop of Yucatán, appointed in the sixteenth century. He collected stories and information on the early Colonial Yucatec Maya, recording them in the important book *Relación de las cosas de Yucatán.* He wrote the book in response to charges concerning his strict methods of governance, which included burning both thousands of native texts, and Maya natives at the stake (see the Annotated Bibliography).

Loltún Cave A cave located in northern Yucatán that has had historical and mythic importance throughout Mesoamerican history. This cave contains sculptures and representations of people probably dating back to archaic times and up to the modern day, suggesting that it has been a center of ritual and mythic importance for millennia.

Maize, Corn The staple food of Mesoamerica. Cosmologically and mythologically it plays an enormous role. Maize is the paradigmatic food, symbolic of all food crops, and often is equated with various deities, the sun, rulers, people, and a healthy cosmos. As corn lives, so too does the cosmos and its beings.

Maya People living largely in the Yucatán peninsula, from the semiarid northern end down to southern tropical rainforests, along the Pacific coast, and across the forested mountains of Guatemala. All Maya people speak a Mayan language, of which there are approximately thirty, not all of which are mutually intelligible. Thus, among the Maya, many different groups exist, including the Yucatec, the K'iche', the Kekchi, the Lacandon, the Cakchiquel, the Tzotzil, the Tzetzal, the Tzutuhil, the Mam, the Mopan, and others. Throughout the Postclassic and Colonial periods and up to the present day, Maya groups have migrated around the Maya region. Nevertheless, in general, today's groups live in the same areas where they lived in pre-Conquest times.

Mexica, Aztecs The Nahuatl-speaking group based in Central Mexico that dominated a significant portion of Mesoamerica from about 1350 until 1521, when the Spaniards defeated them. Their urban center Tenochtitlán now lies under Mexico City. The name *Aztecs* is a somewhat imprecise label popularized by nineteenth-century scholars, and *Mexica* is probably closer to what they called themselves.

Mexico, Basin or Valley of In pre-Conquest times, the large, extraordinarily rich wetland area lying at ca. 8,000 feet in the middle of the central Mexican highlands. Bounded by mountain ranges on all sides, the ancient city of Teotihuacan rose along its eastern side, and Tenochtitlán rose on an island toward its western side. In the centuries following the Conquest, the basin has gradually been drained and mostly filled in. Today, Mexico City sprawls at its center.

Mestizo Today, a person of mixed white, Indian, and in many cases, African descent; although, in the Colonial-era *casta* or caste system, mestizos would not have included persons of African descent. *Mestizaje* is a process whereby cultural and biological blending create a mestizo population—a process that has been endowed with mythological overtones of strength and creativity by some modern Mesoamericans.

Mictlan The pre-Conquest Nahuatl name for the Land of the Dead, located in the underworld. A damp place of rotting, corruption, and illness, it was populated by numerous deities, animals and birds of the night, and the dead. The sun traveled through Mictlan when it was night above Earth's surface. Today, Mictlan still exists in similar forms among the Nahua.

Mixtec People living in what is now the Mexican states of Oaxaca, Guerrero, and Puebla, beginning ca. 1300 B.C. They overlapped with the Zapotec in the area, and they are most known for their codices, eight of which offer genealogical histories of the royal families. the Mixteca style of painting influenced some Mexica styles.

Monte Albán The largest and most prominent ancient city in the Valley of Oaxaca, Mexico. Monte Albán is located atop a large, central ridge that overlooks the three major arms of the valley. There formal public architecture was arranged around several central courtyards, and the dwellings spilled down the terraced hillsides. This densely populated city, home to approximately 5,000 Zapotec, was founded early in the Preclassic period and occupied almost until the Spanish Conquest.

Nahua People living largely in central Mexico, whose language is Nahuatl. In pre-Conquest times, the Mexica of Tenochtitlán and the inhabitants of many neighboring urban centers were Nahua. Because of Nahua migrations in the late Classic and early post-Classic periods and the prevalent influence of the Mexica, Nahuatl loanwords are common in other Mesoamerican languages, and towns called by Nahuatl names can be found as far away as El Salvador. Today, Nahuatl speakers live throughout central Mexico; and there are even a few who still speak Pipil (a Nahua dialect) living in El Salvador.

Oaxaca A cultural region that coincides approximately with the modern state of Oaxaca, located in southwestern Mexico along the Pacific coast. The Oaxaca culture area is largely defined by and dominated by the Valley of Oaxaca, where most of the population lives. The population is ethnically mixed and includes Mixtecs and Zapotecs.

Olmec A group of people and an ancient culture that existed in southern Mexico on the Gulf coast from 2,250 to 300 B.C. The so-called Olmec heartland was situated along the Gulf of Mexico in the modern Mexican states of Veracruz and Tabasco. In the past, scholars saw the Olmec as a "mother-culture," because it was one of the earliest expressions of Mesoamerican civilization. The Olmec built several large cities with temples, sculptures, and art, but are best known for their sculptures of large stone heads weighing between two and three tons each, representing Olmec kings or mythical ancestors. Today the native people of this region speak Olmec languages but are no longer identified as Olmec.

Palenque A late Classic Maya city located at the foot of the mountains overlooking the Gulf coastal plains in the Mexican state of Chiapas. This site is famous for its beautiful architecture and sculpture with buildings distributed across the landscape. It is best known for the hieroglyphic texts on the buildings and sculpture telling about its royal and mythic history. Even today, this city is an important part of the mythic history and stories of many modern Lacandon Maya people. Today, ancient Palenque is a protected archaeological site near the modern town of Palenque, Chiapas, and a favorite tourist attraction.

Popol Vuh An important ancient text of the K'iche' people of highland Guatemala. The Popol Vuh is a collection of five connected myths that describe the creation of humans, the exploits of the Hero Twins, and the forming of the various Maya tribes of the Guatemala highlands.

Popular or People's Church (Iglesia Popular) See Catholicism

Protestantism Christian groups that separated from the Roman Catholic Church during the Reformation (in the sixteenth century). In Mesoamerica, mainline and evangelical Protestants began missionary efforts in the late nineteenth century. Evangelical Protestant groups underwent particularly rapid growth in the 1960s and 1970s, mostly in the Central America. Hence, today, Protestantism in Mesoamerica often is identified with evangelical Protestantism. Evangelical Protestantism stresses Biblical scripture over the authority of the institutional church, and personal experience over theological doctrine, and teaches that salvation in the afterlife depends on individual conversion to and continued practice of the faith.

Rebellions Native revolts against harsh Spanish or governmental rule and social and economic abuses began in the sixteenth century and continue at present. Between 1531 and 1801, rebellions against Spanish rule were particularly frequent. After independence, they continued primarily in the areas of ancient Maya settlement, which correspond roughly to today's southern Mexico and Central America. One could argue that the Central American civil wars of the twentieth century were continuations of peasant rebellions that began almost 500 years before, and that the most recent Zapatista rebellion in Chiapas, Mexico, is a modern form of these revolts.

Sahagún, Fray Bernardino de A sixteenth-century Franciscan friar who produced a twelve-volume, medieval-style encyclopedia on the Nahua called *The Florentine Codex: A General History of the Things of New Spain.* One of the more sympathetic and intelligent collectors of data on the Mexica, Sahagún employed indigenous students in administering a questionnaire to town elders as part of his strategy. This incredibly vast, absolutely invaluable collection was reproduced in three languages: Nahuatl, Spanish, and Latin (see the Annotated Bibliography).

San Lorenzo An early Preclassic Olmec city located near the Gulf coast of Mexico. San Lorenzo is the earliest known Olmec center, inhabited from 1700 to 900 B.C. The site is located on the edge of a river, atop a large ridge that overlooks open country, with mountains in view to the west. It is particularly famous for its great number of stone sculptures.

Sandinistas Rebel guerrillas who won the Nicaraguan civil war in the late 1970s and ran the government until the early 1980s. They had named themselves for the assassinated Augusto César Sandino, who led rebel troops in the late 1920s and early 1930s. In the 1980s, social tensions led to renewed conflict, which continued until 1990, when an anti-Sandinista president was elected. The Sandinistas continued to influence politics into the late 1990s.

Solar Calendar A cycle of 365 days in the indigenous calendrical system consisting of 18 twenty-day "months," called *metztin* in Nahuatl, plus five extra days, called *nemontemi* (18 x 20 = 360 + 5 =365). Called the *Xiuhmolpilli* in Nahuatl and *Haab* in Yucatec Maya, and governed by the sun's motions, this calendar structured the yearly agricultural and seasonal ceremonies. Because these rituals often were celebrated and controlled by the state, the calendrical round all but disappeared after the Conquest. Prior to Spanish rule in central Mexico, a Binding-of-the-Years ceremony was held when 52 solar years ended at the same time as 73 rounds of the divinatory calendar.

Tenochtitlán The late highland Mexican, Postclassic capital city of the Mexica, located on an island in the Basin of Mexico. This city of 150,000–200,000 served as the nexus of a vast domain. It had four administrative sectors, and the great Templo Mayor arose from its center. Highly efficient, raised-mound agricultural fields called *chinampas* ringed the island. Hernán Cortés and his army, amazed at the city's vastness and splendor, centered their conquest efforts on Tenochtitlán. Mexico City now stands atop its remains.

Teotihuacan The highland Mexican, early Classic capital city of the greatest domain ever in Mesoamerica. This city of 150,000–200,000 probably set the patterns for urban structures and relations all over Mesoamerica, trading with people as far away as modern Honduras. Its original name is unknown, for the Mexica gave the city its present name, Teotihuacan, which means "The Place Where the Gods Were Created." Mythologically, the Mexica Fifth Sun was born in this city, as were the age's people, and Mexica ancestors traveled there before coming to Tenochtitlán.

Toltecs, Tula *Tollan* or *Toltecs* can refer to one of two things: either the residents of the highland Mexican, Postclassic city of Tula and Tollan the home of Topiltzin Quetzalcoatl; or the residents of any number of urban centers that lived and died before the Conquest. Residents of Teotihuacan, for example, were sometimes considered Toltecs. In this sense, *Toltecs* carries the nuance of "revered ancestors," and Tula (or Teotihuacan), of the venerated ancestral home.

Venus The deified planet who closely follows the sun as both the morning and evening stars. Venus is one of the most significant celestial objects in Mesoamerica. In ancient Nahua mythology, Quetzalcoatl was the morning star and the dog-like Xolotl the evening star; but Venus has an extraordinarily long history in Mesoamerica, and its glyph appears everywhere.

Xibalba The K'iche' Maya underworld and land of the dead. Xibalba was a dreadful, frightening place where those who did not die a violent death went. It is not the same as the Christian hell, for it did not matter whether one had sinned or not; this was where all the souls of the dead went. Xibalba was a location of supernatural geography, where the dead may have to go through trials of fortitude. It was also where the deities of the Underworld and caves lived. The Hero Twins of the Popol Vuh traveled through this land on their quest to conquer the Lords of Death. Having accomplished their goal, they arose as the Sun and the Moon, which then made their daily travels through both Xibalba and the celestial world.

Zapatistas A rebel group in Chiapas, Mexico, that protests against unfair economic and social conditions. Named for the famed Mexican revolutionary leader Emiliano Zapata. The Zapatistas revolted on 1 January 1994. The revolt, far less violent and shorter than previous rebellions, has used computer technologies to its advantage, and continues to negotiate with the Mexican government for improved conditions. Its mysterious poet-leader Subcommander Marcos and his partner Ramona have become folk heroes in Mexico.

Zapotec People living in the Valley of Oaxaca, whose language is Zapotec. The Zapotecs established and lived in the great city of Monte Albán. By the end of the Postclassic period the Zapotecs had abandoned Monte Albán and were living in separate communities throughout the Valley of Oaxaca, just as the Mixtec started to migrate into the Valley of Oaxaca. Today, Zapotec speakers still live in the Valley of Oaxaca, continuing their long, rich tradition of myth and folklore.

INDEX

About the Authors

Kay Almere Read is an associate professor of comparative religion at DePaul University in Chicago. She is the author of *Time and Sacrifice in the Aztec Cosmos* (Indiana University Press, 1998) and numerous articles.

Jason J. González is a graduate student in anthropology, specializing in Maya archaeology, at Southern Illinois University at Carbondale. He has extensive fieldwork experience and is the author of several articles and conference papers.